THE PRIME MINISTERS

THE PRIME MINISTERS

VOLUME THE FIRST
SIR ROBERT WALPOLE TO SIR ROBERT PEEL

EDITED BY HERBERT VAN THAL
WITH AN INTRODUCTION BY G. W. JONES

LONDON
GEORGE ALLEN & UNWIN LTD
RUSKIN HOUSE   MUSEUM STREET

Printed in Great Britain
in 12 pt Barbou type
by W & J Mackay Limited
Chatham

CONTENTS

CONTENTS

ILLUSTRATIONS

All portraits, except Nos. 5, 7, 12 and 13, are from the National Portrait Gallery, with whose permission they are published in this volume. Nos. 5 and 7 are from the Mansell Collection, and No. 13 from the Radio Times Picture Library.

INTRODUCTION

THE OFFICE OF PRIME MINISTER

G. W. JONES

THE OFFICE OF PRIME MINISTER

There is really in law no office of prime minister. No statute grants him powers. Only in 1905 did the prime minister even become known to the law, when by royal warrant he was declared as having precedence next after the Archbishop of York. Statutes occasionally mention him, as in 1937 when the Ministers of the Crown Act referred to the salary to be paid to the 'Prime Minister and First Lord of the Treasury'. Even the name came into official use only from 1878 when, in the Treaty of Berlin, the Earl of Beaconsfield was called 'First Lord of the Treasury and Prime Minister of Her Britannic Majesty'. The office of prime minister has been based on convention, and has been shaped by personal and political factors. It is often noted that the office is what the holder makes of it, and that is why a sensible way to study the development of the office is by biographies of its holders.

Some prime ministers have been assertive, keen to stamp their ideas on the whole government and frequently interfering in the departments of their ministers, taking initiatives and revelling in the shaping of specific policies, above all in foreign affairs, the area most susceptible to prime ministerial involvement. Others have been passive, content to preside over a team of prima donnas and to arbitrate in disputes between them. The office of prime minister is sufficiently unstructured for different men with different personalities to make entirely different use of it, and in this respect there has been little change over the years, certainly no progression from the passive to the assertive. The indolent Melbourne merely presided, while Peel engaged himself in the work of every department. Lloyd George was the most powerful prime minister of any, but he was followed by Bonar Law, the unknown prime minister, and the even more retiring Baldwin, who was in turn succeeded by the dynamic Chamberlain. To arrive at the top, and to stay, demands assertion and ambition, but the drive to become prime minister does not necessarily manifest itself later in a desire to dominate what cabinet colleagues are doing. Further, those who have been responsible for choosing prime ministers have not always picked the most assertive. At times the conciliator and healer of party wounds has been selected, at other times a harsher character. The fussy Eden was followed by the subtle Macmillan; and the bland Sir Alec Douglas-Home was replaced by the abrasive Edward Heath.

In addition to the temperaments of prime ministers and the way they have conceived their role, the office has been much affected by the political circumstances of the time and by the cabinet colleagues prime ministers have faced. Some prime ministers reach office in a very strong position, often after winning an election, and can select their ministers and shape policies with little challenge. Later, however, troubles mount up, public support is eroded, criticism from the party grows and rivals manoeuvre to unseat them. Much of a prime minister's time, his most precious resource, may have to be expended simply on retaining his position. Others may take over in difficult circumstances, surmount the problems, win public applause and then decline, battered by events over which they have little control, like foreign affairs, the performance of the economy or personal scandals. It might be expected that war raises up prime ministers, like Lloyd George and Churchill, but it has destroyed the careers of as many as it has elevated, like Asquith and Chamberlain. A prime minister faces not only a changing situation but also a group of colleagues between whom the balance of power is constantly shifting. They are far from being his subordinates, and their ambitions and fortunes rise and fall, at times to support and at others to undermine his authority.

Despite all these variables certain general political forces and developments have contributed to shape the office of prime minister from Walpole's time onwards: the waning of the influence of the Crown, for example, the extension of the franchise, the rise of political parties, the decline of the House of Lords and the growth in the functions of government and its full-time officials. Changes in the Constitution emerged by fits and starts; the development was not even. With hindsight it is all too easy to see certain isolated incidents as establishing some new convention, whereas they were really the result of temporary personal and political factors. One has to be wary of dating certain practices before the basic political forces had begun to operate. For example, it is sometimes suggested that the doctrine of collective responsibility can be identified from 1746, when the King forced out the Pelhams and replaced them with Granville and Bath. Forty-five of the Pelham administration resigned too and the King, finding that he could not secure a stable administration with a firm majority in the Commons, dismissed Granville and took back the Pelhams. This episode, however, was unique at the time and marked no major change in the Constitution. In 1782, although North and most of his ministers resigned, the King's favourite, Thurlow, remained as Lord Chancellor, and a year later George III was able to dismiss the Fox–North Coalition and by royal favour alone sustain Pitt in office, despite a number of Commons defeats, until his eventual triumph at the general election. Governments of the eighteenth century rarely came and went as a body: collective responsibility was slow to develop.

The office of prime minister was itself slow to develop before the eighteenth century, because kings were their own prime ministers. The monarch directed his Government, initiating and formulating its policies and watching over their implementation. He selected and dismissed his ministers, who were truly royal servants dependent on his favour. His closest advisers were those who possessed particular talents he valued, such as military prowess, diplomatic skill, administrative capacity and political acumen. They were a loose group of individuals, bound together only by a common allegiance to the Crown. He consulted them individually whenever he felt the need of their advice or else met them together in sessions of his Privy Council and its committees. Occasionally one minister might come to exercise a preponderant influence, and the King would for a time follow his suggestions on a wide range of issues. Opponents of the minister and his policies would depict him as an overmighty subject holding the King in thrall. As long as he retained the confidence of the King, however, he was secure. But once the King withdrew his support, the minister faced exclusion from the court, disgrace, exile and sometimes the block. Precursors of the prime minister might be found in Henry VII's Morton, Henry VIII's Wolsey or Cromwell, Elizabeth's Burghley, James I's Cecil and Charles I's Buckingham and Strafford. Most came to a sorry end, although some were more circumspect and survived and indeed prospered.

During Elizabeth's reign, Parliament was at times very critical of her Government's measures, and a major task of some of her ministers, therefore, became the management of Parliament, especially the Commons. On its front bench sat a few of her Privy Councillors to argue the Queen's cause. James I and especially Charles I, finding that words were not enough to persuade Parliament, tried to rule without it, but the Civil War established Parliament as a permanent part of the Constitution. Charles II, determined never again to endure exile, tried

to produce an amenable Parliament, remodelling the borough corporations which sent representatives to the Commons. In his reign his chief
ministers, Clarendon and later Danby, began the first systematic
attempts to build a block of loyal government adherents in the Commons through a careful distribution of patronage, pensions and preferment. Their attempts failed and Charles II sought to dispense with
Parliament. His brother James II also found Parliament impossible to
control, and his efforts to tamper with the justices of the peace, who
played a major part in electing country representatives to the Commons, helped provoke the Glorious Revolution. From 1689 annual
sessions of Parliament were necessary to provide the King with the
money he needed, especially for his wars.

Now that the King could no longer ignore Parliament one skill became increasingly necessary for his ministers: the ability to win its
support. A figure like Sunderland, who could take over and elaborate
the methods of Clarendon and Danby, soon became a leading minister.
Between 1689 and 1714 such a broker would undertake to act as an
intermediary between the Crown and the parties in Parliament, forming alliances amongst selected peers who were prominent in the Lords
and controlled some nominations in the Commons. Patronage was
dispensed to create ties of loyalty, and to the aristocratic dependants in
the Commons would be added those MPs from constituencies controlled by the Crown. But because the latter group was so small and party
loyalties were so strong, the Crown could never be certain of Parliamentary support which could be eroded by incompetence, disasters or
demands for heavy taxes. William III relied heavily on his parliamentary manager, but he never allowed one man to engross his ear on the
policies of his Government. Anne, however, because of her poor health
and inferior abilities, let her parliamentary managers, notably Godolphin
and Harley, supervise the Government generally, although she was no
figurehead. So great was the influence of Godolphin and Harley that
they were called 'prime ministers', a term first used for the chief
ministers of the King of France.

In 1721 Walpole emerged as the single most important minister. His
pre-eminence was to last for twenty-one years and to earn him in
popular estimation the title of Britain's first prime minister. Before
Walpole, the King's chief ministers had invariably been members of the
House of Lords and had exercised their influence from a variety of the
great offices of state: as Lord Chancellor, Secretary of State or, most

commonly, Lord Treasurer. Walpole was the first chief minister to operate from the Commons, and he began the association of the King's first minister with the position of First Lord of the Treasury. In this department, the centre for the distribution of patronage, especially government jobs, Walpole was able to form his alliances, win elections and build a block of supporters in Parliament. In this department, too, he was strategically placed to shape and then pilot through the Commons the Government's annual money bills, its main legislation. For this reason, also, Walpole held the office of Chancellor of the Exchequer.

Walpole's dominance depended above all on royal favour. The King was still the major force in government decision-making. His closet was where the main decisions were taken and where Walpole courted him, even using the Queen to further his policies. Walpole also depended on the House of Commons, which could obstruct the King's legislative proposals and bring down his ministers, for patronage could tie many to the Government but was never enough to bind a sure majority. Walpole wooed the Commons, paying attention to its moods, deploying his debating skill to allay its anxieties, and winning its support by argument and by adopting policies of which it approved. The independent country gentry who could not be bought were especially cultivated by Walpole, who loved to display himself as at heart really one of them. Management of the Commons was Walpole's *forte*. The King's support alone could not sustain Walpole when he lost his majority in the Commons due to mismanagement of the war. The confidence of both the Court and the Commons was essential to keep him in office.

There was strictly no office of prime minister. Indeed the term was used as one of opprobrium against Walpole who in fact denied that he was prime minister. Later in the century both George Grenville and Lord North disavowed the expression as applied to them. The King was the head of his Government and dealt with each minister individually about departmental matters without the interposition of a chief minister, or a Cabinet. The Commons, too, opposed the development of the office of prime minister, since it wanted to hold each minister responsible to it, and any sole or prime minister would blur that line of direct responsibility. Walpole was prime minister because of his personal sway, not because he held a particular office.

The Hanoverians only rarely attended Cabinet, thus leaving the chairman, the prime minister, the most important member except for the rare occasions when he was overshadowed by more powerful colleagues as happened to the Earl of Wilmington, 1742-3, or the Duke of Portland, 1783. But kings were still decisive. They selected all the ministers, each one of whom enjoyed direct access to the Crown. The King expected the Cabinet to discuss only matters he had referred to it and to give advice only when he asked it to. He kept control over major policy, and at times had to intervene in detail more than he desired, like George III coping with the indecisiveness of Lord North. The withdrawal of the King from the Cabinet did help it attain some sense of unity from regularly working together, and this was strengthened by bonds of patronage, family connection and a broad adherence to party principles. But because the discipline and ideology of the modern mass party were as yet absent, faction leaders were ready to break away, hoping for royal favour and advancement. This prevented the prime minister from heading a united team, and he still needed the assistance of the Crown to help him win elections. An eighteenth-century prime minister was not prime minister because he won an election; he won the election because the King had made him prime minister.

The decline in the influence of the Crown was the most important factor shaping the rise of prime ministerial power. Pitt, installed in office by royal injunction alone, was the prime minister who did most to weaken the Crown. Although Rockingham's economical reforms had eradicated some of the positions with which the Crown might reward its supporters, Pitt's administrative reforms, which sought to make government cheaper and more efficient, eliminated still more. Pitt also reduced the crown's power by insisting that his Cabinet consist only of men loyal to him – he forced the ejection of Thurlow in 1792 – and also that it should discuss any matter it liked and give advice to the King unasked. The King, however, had confidence in Pitt, and would never have tolerated his main rival, Fox, as chief minister. Pitt's longevity in office, 1783-1801 and 1804-6, further enhanced his personal authority, as did the King's insanity, beginning in 1788, which left more and more business in the hands of his ministers, especially the prime minister. The war, too, raised Pitt's stature, since he appeared as the national leader against revolution and the French. Yet Pitt was not prepared to press Catholic emancipation against the King's wishes: on some policies the King was still decisive. Although Pitt disclaimed the title of prime minister, he admitted that a principal minister was needed. In the first decade of the nineteenth century the title became acceptable, and Perceval used the term quite comfortably.

The incompetence of George IV and William IV, and the political immaturity of Victoria in her early years, further diminished the power of the Crown, while Liverpool's fifteen-years term as prime minister, even serving George IV who disliked him, strengthened the hold of the King's ministers. The rise of new political issues, the growing public interest and participation in politics, stimulated by the expansion of literacy and the provincial press, and the emergence of a variety of pressure groups, lobbying for numerous causes, all helped to focus more authority on the Cabinet and its chairman, and less on the monarch who seemed increasingly out of touch with the new popular politics.

The Parliamentary Reform Act of 1832, sweeping away rotten and nomination boroughs, finally shattered the capacity of the Crown to win elections. In 1834-5 the King's weakness was starkly revealed. William IV dismissed Melbourne and appointed Peel. At the ensuing general election royal influence was not enough to secure Peel a majority. In six weeks he was defeated six times by the new Commons. The King recognised that he had to return to Melbourne. In 1839 Melbourne's Government met a number of defeats in the Commons, and Victoria reluctantly asked Peel to try to form an administration. He refused when she rejected his request to dismiss some Whig ladies from her bedchamber as a gesture of her good faith, and so Melbourne continued with his minority Government. Peel had thought that a sign of royal confidence was necessary for him to serve as prime minister. In 1841 Victoria's support of Melbourne at the general election failed to bring him a majority in the Commons, where his Government was defeated. He then resigned and the Queen sent for Peel. He formed an administration and insisted on the removal of the Whigs from the Queen's bedchamber. The Commons had imposed a prime minister on the Queen and he had imposed on her his views as to who should be her intimate advisers. The precedent had been established that the Commons not the Crown determined the fate of governments.

Between 1832 and 1867 the power of Parliament to make and unmake prime ministers was at its peak. Royal and aristocratic 'influence' had not yet been replaced by 'party' as the device to bind followers and leaders. Elections in these years produced Parliaments made up of loose groupings with unstable attachments. Governments rarely had a clear majority, and suffered frequent defeats, but only resigned when the votes indicated a clear discrediting of the administration. This fluidity enabled the Crown to play a role as an intermediary in the negotiations that led to the choice of a prime minister. It had to select one who was able to win the support of enough leaders of the shifting groups to ensure a majority, or at least enough votes to carry on. The individual preference of the monarch could be important in this situation. A prime minister in the mid-years of the century emerged from a mixture of royal favour, support from the leaders of the groups in the Commons, backing from the peers, and popular acclaim – in varying proportions at different times. Once in office the main task of the prime minister was not so much retaining the support of the Crown as retaining the support of his colleagues and leaders of groups in the Commons.

The widening of the franchise in 1867 and 1884, the rough equalisation of electoral divisions in 1885, the secret ballot of 1872 and the limitations on election expenses in 1883 finally put paid to the exercise of patronage or influence as the means by which monarchs and peers could manipulate elections to the Commons. The verdict of the electorate was now decisive in the choice of a prime minister. After Disraeli's defeat at the general election of 1868 he resigned before meeting the Commons, as did Gladstone in 1874. A clear majority for one party and its leader precluded any independent judgement by the Crown, or by the Commons. The Crown's personal preference could be influential only if no party had a clear majority or if a party with a clear majority had no obvious leader, as when a prime minister died in office. Victoria had, reluctantly, to appoint Gladstone in 1892, but she was able to select Rosebery in 1894 after Gladstone's resignation left a void in the leadership. And in the twentieth century the Crown's influence on the choice of prime minister was significant only in 1923 and 1931, and possibly in 1957 and 1963. Now that both parties have laid down clearly that their parliamentary parties will elect their leaders, the freedom of the Crown has been so circumscribed that it can be decisive only when no one party has a clear majority in the Commons.

Nor is the choice of a prime minister limited by the title Deputy Prime Minister, which has been used informally and infrequently since 1942 to describe the minister who performs prime ministerial functions in Cabinet and Parliament if the prime minister is absent or indisposed. However, there is strictly no such position, since it would seem to limit the Crown and the parliamentary party by putting into the hands of the existing prime minister the power to choose his successor. The title

First Secretary of State has sometimes been used since 1962 for the minister to whom the prime minister deputes his duties when absent.

To win the newly enfranchised voters after 1867 the parliamentary parties began to create highly organised central machines linked to local parties. And outside Parliament emerged the Labour Party with a disciplined organisation, seeking to win elections, achieve power and carry out a distinctive programme. The rise of new political issues which polarised opinions, and the more passionate intensity with which politics was conducted, strengthened attachments to the party organisations. Members of the Commons were now elected because of the party label they bore and the leader they championed. In the House they were obliged to support him, unless some exceptional issue justified rebellion and the bringing down of their own government. The influence of the prime minister was thus enhanced now that he was sustained by the votes of the electorate, the party organisation and a normally reliable majority in the Commons.

With these resources he could by the 1870s select whom he wanted for his ministers. The Queen might try to influence his choice, objecting to some, urging the claims of others and suggesting reallocations of responsibilities, but her views amounted to advice only. The Crown's influence over the Cabinet was limited to advising, encouraging and warning. The Queen had the right to be consulted but could not pre-vail against a united Cabinet with a firm majority in the Commons. The prime minister was the only channel of communication between the Cabinet and the monarch; at his discretion he might inform her of the different views expressed, but rarely who held them so that she could not intrigue behind the scenes to shape Cabinet policy. Besides some little scope in the choice of prime minister, the only important power left to the Crown was to grant or refuse a prime minister's request for a dissolution of Parliament. But this power seems very limited, and there is no British precedent for refusing a request to dissolve. Thus by the twentieth century the powers of the Crown had been narrowly con-fined. In 1936 the prime minister and Cabinet were able even to compel the abdication of the King.

The prime minister's power over his colleagues increased too. His ability to dismiss them emerged later than his ability to appoint them. Even at the end of the nineteenth century Salisbury felt that he could remove a minister from office only for some clear and palpable failure. Asquith, however, claimed that a prime minister had to be a good butcher, and Lloyd George wielded the axe with dexterity. In the latter part of the nineteenth century it became established that only the prime minister could call cabinet meetings, and since 1918 the decision to request a dissolution is no longer made by the Cabinet, but by the prime minister alone, although most prime ministers usually discuss possible dates with their leading colleagues.

As the franchise was widened the prime minister needed to appeal increasingly to the mass electorate. Although Chatham and Grey had earlier been the darlings of the mob, and although Peel's Tamworth Manifesto might be seen as an early popular appeal, Gladstone's demagogic pilgrimages, typified by his Midlothian campaign of 1879–80, inaugurated the new era. Previously, the public's participation in politics was limited to sporadic bouts of rioting in protest against some enormity. Now they selected the Government and prime minister; they may not have appreciated the significance of the issues being debated but at least they understood the clash of the gladiatorial party leaders. This personalisation of politics, accelerated by Gladstone and Disraeli, increased the stature of the prime minister, and influenced the qualities that were regarded as necessary in the model prime minister. The new mass media of communications of the twentieth century, especially television, made it even more vital for a prime minister to be adept at projecting an attractive public image.

The extension of the franchise and the growing public involvement in politics raised the importance of the House of Commons at the expense of the House of Lords. Of the 22 men who were prime ministers between 1721 and 1834, 14 were in the Lords and 8 in the Commons. Of the 11 between 1834 and 1902, 8 were in the Lords and 5 in the Commons (Russell and Disraeli are counted twice because they headed administrations as commoners and as peers). Since 1902 all 15 have been from the Commons. It was clear that the Commons was the main arena of politics: here the life of the Government was at stake, and its measures, especially financial Bills, could succeed or fail; and here too, in the twentieth century, was the Opposition. When Lord Curzon was not made prime minister in 1923 one reason advanced was that a prime minister should sit in the Commons to be able to reply to the attacks of the Opposition. In the nineteenth century when prime ministers had been peers difficulties had frequently arisen between themselves and the Leaders in the House of Commons. The answer was to have a prime minister in the more important chamber. In 1963 when Lord Home was asked to try to form a government he renounced his peerage and sought election to the Commons.

The reduction of aristocratic participation in Cabinets to around two or three has had the effect, it is sometimes argued, of strengthening the control of the prime minister over his Cabinet. Members of the Commons are said to be more ambitious for office than peers, and to be more likely to defer to prime ministerial views in the hope of promotion or to avoid dismissal. However, the eighteenth and nineteenth centuries show scant evidence that political and personal ambitions, and desire for office, were absent from the aristocratic temperament.

In their allocation of duties all prime ministers since Walpole have held the office of First Lord of the Treasury, except Salisbury during most of his premierships. Until the time of Peel all prime ministers in the Commons were also Chancellors of the Exchequer. After Peel the position of Chancellor of the Exchequer was usually held by another minister, save when Gladstone and Baldwin held it for brief periods. Occasionally a prime minister held some other office in which he was especially concerned, like Wellington, Salisbury and MacDonald, who were also Foreign Secretaries, or Churchill, who was also Minister of Defence. Some have for a short time held non-departmental posts like Lord Privy Seal or Lord President of the Council. But in the twentieth century prime ministers have generally regarded holding offices other than that of prime minister and First Lord of the Treasury as too great a burden. Before 1942 prime ministers in the Commons had acted as Leaders of the House of Commons, but Churchill felt the task too onerous with his other duties and so a separate responsibility was created. A prime minister, however, is normally close to his Leader of the Commons and above all to the Chief Whip, since he wants to keep his finger on the pulse of the Commons. Indeed when Parliament is sitting he normally has daily chats with his Chief Whip about the state of the party in Parliament. Thus some of the functions, especially the details, once performed by the prime minister have been transferred to other ministers in order to reduce his workload.

The great increase in the scope and complexity of government activities in the twentieth century has considerably altered the position of the prime minister, adding to his resources in some ways but constraining him in others. Peel broke his health with the strain of trying to oversee the work of all departments, and in this century no one man can control all that government does. Public expenditure has soared, the number of civil servants grown and the departments of state have become huge administrative empires. At the head of these departments are ministers with statutory powers, and they are the main components of the Cabinet. If the prime minister wants to achieve anything in government, he must work with and through them. They have at their disposal their departments to back and brief them, while the prime minister lacks comparable administrative support and the time to master issues with equal thoroughness. He may have chosen his ministers, and could dismiss them, but usually some of them command so much political support within the party and among the public that he could not exclude them without seriously undermining his Government. His Cabinet ministers are his colleagues, not his subordinates; with them he is engaged in constant negotiations and consultation. He is the most important member of the Cabinet, responsible for drawing up its agenda, for guiding its discussions and for summing up its decisions, and therefore his backing is eagerly sought by ministers for their proposals. But he could not impose his own view on a reluctant Cabinet: he is only as strong as the Cabinet lets him be.

His personal staff is small: now half a dozen civil servants in his private office, separated from a few cronies and political assistants at No. 10 Downing Street, like Harold Wilson's Marcia Williams or Edward Heath's Douglas Hurd. His staff, and its size, is not very different from what was available at the start of the nineteenth century, except that the private office contains about three more people and consists wholly of civil servants. Only in wartime have prime ministers established something akin to a prime minister's department. Lloyd George formed a secretariat, the 'garden suburb', under Professor Adams, and Winston Churchill set up a statistical section under Professor Lindemann. Both units provided their prime ministers with a stream of advice about proposals coming up from the departments. Such prime ministerial personal staff aroused the enmity of other ministers and their civil servants and seemed to undermine Cabinet government. After the wars they were disbanded, and prime ministers have subsequently been punctilious about not having their own department to oversee the work of their colleagues and have stressed that Britain has a Cabinet and not a presidential form of government.

Prime ministers have been able to find some of the administrative assistance they require, while staying within the constraints of the British Constitution, by using the Cabinet Office. First set up in 1916 to serve the War Cabinet, it helps the prime minister to draw up the Cabinet agenda, processes departmental submissions, records Cabinet decisions, circulates them to departments and tries to ensure they are obeyed. It is a general co-ordinator of government, servicing the vast network of Cabinet committees. It provides briefs on topics relating to more than one department. It is the home for a number of special agencies like the Central Statistical Office, the Chief Scientific Adviser and his staff and the Central Policy Review Staff set up in 1970 for strategic policy analysis. During the 1960s the Cabinet Office greatly increased in size and in its range of interests, and its official head, the Cabinet Secretary, is a key adviser of the prime minister. But this important nerve centre of government is not simply at the disposal of the prime minister. It serves the Cabinet as a whole, although the prime minister as chairman of the Cabinet and co-ordinator-in-chief of governmental activities makes most use of it, and directs it.

The prime minister has been depicted as at the apex of the civil service. Since 1920 his approval has been necessary for the leading permanent positions in the departments: permanent secretary, deputy secretary and principal finance and establishment officers. The official head of the home civil service has been a particularly close adviser of the prime minister, and since 1968 the prime minister has been Minister for the Civil Service. However, he does not spend much time on the internal problems of the civil service. He leaves the running of the department to other ministers, and ratifies choices for the top official appointments which come from the consensus of the foremost civil servants themselves. The prime minister does not control the civil service: it largely controls itself.

It is also often said that the prime minister is in a position of impregnable power. At the apex of his party he is depicted as commanding the loyalty of its members both inside and outside Parliament. His Government is never toppled, it is argued, since his majority, however small, will always hold because of party discipline and loyalty. But Asquith in 1916 and Lloyd George in 1922 showed that prime ministers of coalitions are particularly vulnerable to a loss of support from their partners, while MacDonald in 1931 and Chamberlain in 1940 showed that prime ministers can lose enough of their own party's support to make continuing in office an impossibility. In any case all prime ministers have constantly battled against plots and rumours of plots to unseat them. Their office has never been secure.

Although the prime minister is the single most important member of the Cabinet, power has not yet become concentrated in him. He is constrained by two principles of the British Constitution, which still operate. The doctrine of 'individual ministerial responsibility' puts authority into the hands of his ministers, who in addition are buttressed by the administrative resources of their departments and the political resources of their supporters in the party. The doctrine of 'collective Cabinet responsibility' ensures that the Cabinet is still the place where the politically controversial and most important decisions are taken. Britain's executive is genuinely collective. And responsibility to Parliament is still meaningful. Politicians become prime ministers chiefly because they have impressed their parliamentary colleagues by their performances in the Commons, and they retain their positions by demonstrating their continuing parliamentary versatility. Once their hold over the House, in debate or at question time, falters, criticism rises and speculation is rife about the need to change the leader. Prime ministers take great pains to prevent the occurrence that could pull them down – the conjunction of backbench disaffection with the emergence of a single rival around whom the disaffected and the most weighty Cabinet colleagues could coalesce. The resources of the prime minister are great, but so are the constraints on his use of the resources. The Cabinet, his ministers and his party in Parliament cannot be overruled.

FURTHER READING

Carter, Byrum E., *The Office of Prime Minister* (London, 1956)
Crossman, R. H. S., Introduction to Walter Bagehot, *The English Constitution* (London, 1963)
Jennings, Sir Ivor, *Cabinet Government* (Cambridge, 3rd edition, 1959)
King, Anthony (ed.) *The British Prime Minister* (London, 1969)
Mackintosh, John P., *The British Cabinet* (London, 2nd edition, 1968)
Walker, Patrick Gordon, *The Cabinet* (London, 2nd edition, 1972)

1

SIR ROBERT WALPOLE

BY

GEOFFREY HOLMES

*Robert Walpole, born 26 August 1671, third but first surviving son
of Robert Walpole, MP, of Houghton, Norfolk, and Mary, daughter
of Sir Jeffrey Burwell. Educated at Eton and King's College,
Cambridge. Married (1) 1700 Catherine, daughter of John Shorter,
Baltic merchant, three sons (Robert, later Lord Walpole, Edward
and Horace) and two daughters. (2) 1737 Maria, daughter of
Thomas Skerrett, two illegitimate daughters. Whig MP for Castle
Rising 1701–2, King's Lynn 1702–Jan. 1712 (expelled from the
House for alleged corruption), Feb.–Mar. 1712 (election void) and
1713–42. Member of Prince George's Admiralty Council 1705–8;
Secretary-at-War 1708–10 (Acting Secretary Jan.–Sept. 1710);
Treasurer of the Navy 1710–11 (dismissed); Paymaster of the
Forces 1714–15; Chancellor of the Exchequer and First Lord of the
Treasury 1715–17 (resigned); Paymaster of the Forces 1720–1;
Chancellor of the Exchequer and First Lord of the Treasury 1721–42
(resigned). KB 1725; KG 1726; created Earl of Orford 1742.
Died 1745.*

SIR ROBERT WALPOLE

Sir Robert Walpole[1] is traditionally considered the first British prime minister; and traditions, however capriciously and illogically their seeds are planted, are notoriously difficult to uproot. In this case tradition will serve as usefully as anything else to mark one of the major watersheds in Britain's political and constitutional development. For how does one define a 'prime minister' in an age when no such office was legally recognised and the term itself, more often than not, was used pejoratively? The criteria are so variable that we would do well to recognise that a cast-iron definition of the indefinable is impossible.

There were many respects in which even Walpole cannot be compared with a modern prime minister. He was not carried to power on the tide of a party electoral victory: that was not how the political system worked in the eighteenth century. What is more, for twenty years Walpole led a government which was never certain, in the twentieth-century sense, of commanding a majority in the House of Commons. He was never asked by either of the two kings he served, George I and George II, 'to form a ministry'; and in the early years of his supremacy he had to share office with some very uncomfortable bedfellows. There were many of his party, the Whigs, to whom he became anathema, who rejected his primacy and who opposed him venomously.

On the other hand he was by no means the first English politician to be labelled 'prime minister' by his contemporaries. A macabre opposition pamphlet of 1733, entitled *A Short History of Prime Ministers in Great Britain*, found abundance of historical material for its cautionary tales. More reputably, there were several seventeenth-century precedents, especially Danby in the 1670s; and two far stronger ones in the early eighteenth century, Lord Godolphin and Robert Harley, Earl of Oxford, who presided over the Treasury in succession from 1702 to 1714. It was after the Revolution of 1688, when Parliament finally came to stay, with automatic yearly sessions of four to six months' duration, that the Treasury took on a new political dimension. Since 'govern-

[1] The name is often spelt 'Walpool' in contemporary correspondence, which suggests that this is how it was pronounced.

ment business' and 'financial business' were largely synonymous, and the Treasury was the most obvious channel of official patronage, it was always easier after the Revolution for the effective head of the Treasury to undertake with more success than any other minister the maintenance of a regular working partnership between the executive and the legislature. And the long wars against Louis XIV's France made this new task crucial.

Under William III royal control remained too firm to allow a 'prime minister' to emerge. But under the invalid and far less able Anne both Godolphin and Harley wielded a good deal of the power, and enjoyed much of the status, that Walpole made his own as First Lord of the Treasury from 1721[2] to 1742. They also experienced – as Walpole did – some of the limitations attendant on any minister's authority at a time when the royal prerogative still carried meaning and when possessing the sovereign's full confidence was an essential ingredient in political mastery. There were, however, important differences. Walpole, for instance, was every inch a party man, serving the national interest as he saw it but wearing his Whiggery as proudly as he wore his Garter ribbon and star. Godolphin and Harley, under whom the young Walpole had served, were birds of a different feather. Though forced to work within the existing two-party framework, each was fundamentally anti-party, concerned as the Queen's 'Manager' or 'Undertaker' with harnessing the power of the dominant party to the working needs of government, while keeping at bay as far as possible its most violent partisans.

This led to two further differences of significance between their primacy and Walpole's. The Cabinets over which they effectively presided, under the Queen, were generally less homogeneous than those of the later era and invariably more difficult for the chief minister to dominate (though the solidarity even of Walpole's Cabinets can be exaggerated); while the discipline which Walpole at his peak was able to impose on *all* office-holders was far more rigorous than anything Godolphin or Harley could achieve. In this respect, perhaps more than any other, Sir Robert's long ministry saw the emergence of a prime ministerial authority without precedent and, as it seemed to many contemporaries, unconstitutional.

[2] Space does not permit discussion of the controversial question of how far Walpole was, in effect, prime minister in his first year at the Treasury, and whether he could have triumphed over his chief rival, Sunderland, had not the latter been prematurely removed from contention by death in April 1722.

Finally, although Godolphin was a competent parliamentarian and Harley a skilful one, their position rested more on the trust of the monarch than on the approbation of Parliament. Walpole's rested equally on both; and his personal dominance over Parliament was certainly more complete. A basic factor here was his realisation that in order to be in the best position to control Parliament the King's leading minister must sit, and continue to sit, in the Commons. It cannot be overstressed how much Walpole was an innovator in this respect; how far he defied convention when in 1723 he accepted a peerage for his son, Robert, instead of for himself; and how important in the long term his innovation was – even if not all his successors followed his pattern. And for Walpole mere presence in the Commons, and periodic participation in key debates, was not enough. Until 1733 he was the only Commoner in the Cabinet; and both before and after that he acted as the day-to-day leader of the House, piloting it through its business with the aid of a handful of loyal subalterns and, from 1727 onwards, of his invaluable 'Governor', Speaker Onslow. Considering also the 'incredible . . . variety and quantity of business he dispatched',[3] one can fairly say that in terms of sheer burden of work he could comfortably stand comparison with any modern peacetime prime minister.

Rarely, if ever, have two decades of British history seemed to historians so overshadowed by the figure of one man – other than a king or queen – as the 1720s and 1730s seem to be by Walpole. This is altogether natural. To contemporaries the presence of 'the great man' (George II's *gros homme*) was just as engulfing. Not since Burghley had there been such an epic period of continuous high office. And in length there has been no equal since 1742. It has a mesmeric quality which can easily tempt the unwary into assuming that all these twenty-one years, save the last two or three, saw Walpole's power at much the same pitch of unquestioned supremacy. This was not so. A graph of his authority in the ministry and at Court, for instance, would start relatively low; would begin to rise quite steeply in April 1722, when the Earl of Sunderland died, and sharply again after the defeat of a younger rival, Lord Carteret, in 1724; but would only reach the highest plateau in 1730, when Townshend resigned. And from 1737, the year Walpole's position was damaged by the Prince of Wales's quarrel with his parents and by the death of Queen Caroline, the year too that loyal Cabinet colleagues

[3] John, Lord Hervey, *Some Materials Towards Memoirs of the Reign of King George II*, ed. Romney Sedgwick (London, 1931), i, 17.

such as Newcastle and Hardwicke first began to kick over the traces, the line would fall progressively. Even in Parliament, throughout his career from 1721 to the election of 1741 there were peaks and troughs. The Excise crisis is well known. But there were other near-disasters. Only through the abstention of forty Tories did Walpole escape defeat over the emotive issue of the Prince's allowance in February 1737. Twelve months later an Opposition motion to reduce the Army only failed by fifteen votes in a crowded House of 518. The Walpole 'machine' was no automaton.

In certain respects Walpole left his stamp on eighteenth-century England less by what he did than by how he did it. His methods, for good or ill, provided the blueprint for the next two generations of Whigs. This is not to say the positive achievements of his regime were negligible. In some fields they were very far from that. But (in spite of his massive personal authority) it is not easy in every case to assess just how far Walpole himself was responsible for them.

This is true even of the most conspicuous legacy of the 1720s and 1730s, the legacy of political stability. For close on a century prior to the Revolution of 1688 the Constitution had been in a state of acute imbalance. The natural governing class of the country, the aristocracy and landed gentry, had been for much of this time divided in interest and loyalty. Religion and politics had been mutually embroiled. After 1689 the more serious constitutional problems were slowly resolved, but the division of both the political and the religious nations into two contesting parties, ideologically at odds, persisted. Relatively little of the social order remained untouched by the violence of Whig–Tory conflict, and in particular great bitterness was engendered between the landed interest of the country, the overtaxed, economically struggling 'mere gentry', and the rising power of High Finance, which as Henry St John wrote in 1709 was 'a new interest . . . a sort of property which was not known twenty years ago'.[4] An uncertain or insecure succession to the throne and two unpopular foreign rulers stimulated Jacobite intrigue; and although the 1715 rebellion did much to discredit the Tory party and open the way to an unchallengeable Whig supremacy, fear of conspiracy persisted. Also the Whigs in their hour of victory fell prey to fratricidal struggles; and in 1720 – the year Walpole returned to office for the third time as Paymaster-General – the whole political

4 Bodleian Library MS Eng. Misc. e.180, f. 4: to Lord Orrery, 9 July 1709 (copy).

world was convulsed by a major scandal, the South Sea Bubble. By 1721 nine Englishmen in every ten must have seriously doubted whether even under their 'Revolution Constitution' a strong, stable government, commanding widespread support in the country and based on a tranquil social order, would ever be attainable.

The next twenty years were to prove that it was attainable. And clearly it would be absurd to minimise Walpole's personal contribution to a political edifice whose strength and durability long outlived him.[5] The pursuit of tranquillity and stability, social as well as political, had been an overriding concern of his administration. He saw them both as ends eminently desirable in themselves and as prerequisites for the preservation of security; and this – the security of the Hanoverian dynasty and the security of the new United Kingdom of Great Britain from Jacobite activity and foreign threats – was with Walpole a persistent, almost obsessive, preoccupation. By the late 1730s Walpole could point to twenty-five years without major war, to substantial though not universal economic prosperity, low taxation, the repair of the social fabric by the reconciliation of the landed and moneyed interests, and a marked lowering of the political temperature – all part of the climate that made stability possible and all traceable, to a greater or lesser degree, to his specific policies.

And yet the achievement of political calm under the first two Hanoverians was far from being a one-man miracle. Even in the turbulent atmosphere of Anne's reign important lessons had been learnt, especially about the manipulation of patronage and the techniques of imposing effective executive control on the legislature. Between 1714 and 1721, too, there were strong favourable currents running which Walpole was later able to channel, and without which the most outstanding political talent must have been powerless. One such current was steadily bearing away much of the ideological debris of Stuart England, in particular its more violent religious emotions: one has only to compare the electoral issues and propaganda of, say, 1710 with those of 1722 to appreciate this. Another current was carrying along the electorate itself, so volatile and unmanageable since the late 1670s, towards certain captivation. The crucial event here was the Septennial Act of 1716.

By establishing the convention that Parliaments should last for their

5 See J. H. Plumb, *The Growth of Political Stability in England 1675–1725* (London, 1967), especially the masterly final chapter.

statutory maximum of seven years, except when interrupted (as in 1727) by the death of a monarch, this Act exposed Walpole to only three general elections in nineteen years after 1722. Had he been forced to fight ten elections in just over twenty years, as his predecessors had under the Triennial Act between 1695 and 1715, it is hard to imagine that either he or the stable political system he created could have survived as long as they did. While it is true that large sums of money had been staked on the roulette wheel of electoral fortunes during the fierce Whig–Tory conflict of 1690–1715, the obviously enhanced value of parliamentary seats after the passing of the Septennial Act encouraged still heavier investment in the constituencies, by the great landed magnates and also by the Treasury. As these investments became more secure, so contests became fewer. In the process the contribution to Walpole's remarkably successful electoral organisation of the 'government boroughs', which could return thirty to forty members, of the big local overlords, such as Edgecumbe and Newcastle, and of such large-scale borough owners as Bubb Dodington, was made possible.[6]

Walpole reaped a further harvest from the Septennial Act. The patronage of the Crown appreciated in value no less than the parliamentary seat. When the recipient of an office early in the lifetime of a Parliament could look forward – provided he behaved with reasonable discretion – to at least a six- or seven-year tenancy, the Government's purchasing power could hardly fail to benefit. The contribution of Walpole's patronage system both to political stability and to the solidity of his own regime is now a historical commonplace. The truth is, however, that the total fund of patronage was not as great as it had been under Anne (there had of necessity been some contraction of the inflated wartime administration, and Walpole was apt to complain that there was 'not enough grass for the beasts to feed on'); but the scope of the patronage directly at Walpole's disposal as First Lord, together with the patronage of other departments which he voraciously engrossed, was certainly wider than any previous minister had enjoyed. The key to his position at the heart of the web is a factor often overlooked. The position was one which the great party chieftains of 1689–1714 would have dearly prized; but it was always denied them by the prejudices of the the Crown and the interposition of the Crown's 'Managers'. It was only when the post-Revolution generation of

[6] cf. the situation from 1701 to 1715 in W. A. Speck, *Tory and Whig: The Struggle in the Constituencies* (London, 1970).

Managers finally died out in 1714, with the fall of Oxford and the resignation of Shrewsbury, England's last Lord High Treasurer, that for the first time since the Revolution a political party found itself in direct control of the administration. And for almost seven years before Walpole became prime minister his party used this control to eliminate its opponents from all positions of influence, great and small. The way was thus prepared for him not merely to concentrate this power, uniquely, in one pair of hands, but to turn it in time as ruthlessly against rival or dissident Whigs as against Tories.

In one other respect Walpole found himself rowing with a powerful tide after 1721. He belonged to a generation which from youth to mature manhood had experienced the two most ambitious and costly wars that Englishmen had ever known. The Utrecht peace settlement of 1713 was born of mutual exhaustion. Although war had yielded Britain rich dividends, it had bled the gentry white by its financial demands, had seriously burdened other sections of the community, had added new ferocity to party conflict and had imposed heavy strains on society. Even the Whigs who had supported the struggle against France and the Bourbons most eagerly had been satiated by 1713; and Walpole himself shared in this universal reaction and repugnance scarcely less than the most xenophobic Tory squire. Peace alone did something to repair the damage to the body politic in the eight years after Utrecht. But the Fifteen rebellion, and the South Sea crisis five years later, followed inside two more years by the uncovering of the Atterbury plot, all seemed to emphasise how sick the patient still was; and they made it the more receptive thereafter to the tranquillising medicine that Walpole prescribed.

Most directly the post-war reaction ensured a strong body of support at almost all times until the late thirties for the foreign policy of the Walpole administration. This had a constant aim – to secure the dynasty and the Protestant succession and to maintain the European balance of power by diplomatic negotiation and combination – but varying emphases, resulting in the main from Walpole's own profound ignorance of Europe in 1721. He had no linguistic ability and at 44 had never set foot on continental soil. To earn and keep the confidence of a German monarch, as well as to make a respectable showing in the House of Commons, he had perforce to improve his grasp of European issues and take a stronger interest in them. But as long as his brother-in-law Lord Townshend, Secretary of State for the North, conducted foreign policy in broad accord with the prime minister's priorities, the First Lord interfered as little as possible. After the eruption of a major European crisis in 1725-6, however, Townshend began to develop in Walpole's eyes a rather alarming capacity for brinkmanship, not to mention a disturbing disregard both for the traditional Whig friendship with the Habsburg Emperor[7] and for the financial implications of an over-ambitious policy. This is why from 1728 onwards Britain's foreign policy began increasingly to bear the Prime Minister's own more con-ciliatory, conservative and pacific stamp. And from 1730, when Towns-hend resigned in disgust, until 1738, Walpole dominated the country's European relations, through two compliant Secretaries of State,[8] just as thoroughly as he dominated every other field.

In the early years of his activity he claimed two important diplomatic *coups*, the Treaty of Seville with Spain (1729) and the second Treaty of Vienna with the Emperor Charles VI (1731), which seemed at first blush to have settled the outstanding problems of these two powers not merely with Britain but with each other. Of both treaties Walpole was inordinately proud, and they gave him a quite misplaced confidence in his own talent and far-sightedness as a diplomat, a confidence he un-wisely backed to the hilt in the Polish Succession crisis of 1733-5. In this crisis he used his now titanic authority to overbear the judgement of George II, Queen Caroline and most of his colleagues in order to preserve Britain's neutrality.

Walpole always remained unrepentant about this crucial decision. But in the light of subsequent events his foreign policy after 1733 is hard to defend with conviction. By 1735 Britain was more isolated than she had been for almost twenty years. Her *entente* with her old enemy, France,[9] which had been the cornerstone of both Townshend's and Walpole's diplomacy, was in ruins, though Walpole perversely refused to recognise the fact. Charles VI was alienated; and Spain, which had commercial and colonial differences with Britain, was encouraged to pursue them in the assurance that Walpole would never resort to force. Nor would he have done so even in 1739, when he reluctantly em-barked on the so-called 'War of Jenkins's Ear', if his parliamentary sup-port, his hold over the King and above all his authority over his long-docile fellow ministers had not threatened to crumble as a result of his attitude. 'It is your war,' he acidly told the Duke of Newcastle, 'and I wish you joy of it.'

[7] Since 1711, Charles VI.   [8] Newcastle and Harrington.   [9] Dating from 1716.

The peace Walpole had kept in the 1730s had not been peace with honour. But neither had it been peace at any price. He always maintained, and reiterated in a great speech to the Commons in 1739, that in both Britain's economic interests – 'the interests of a trading nation' – and those of her Protestant dynasty, a policy of neutrality and negotiation was profitable and right. His opponents sneered at his argument that war would provide the Jacobites with an opportunity they could never hope for in peacetime; the Jacobite bogy, they insisted, was just a convenient screen for Walpole to hide behind; but in the end the Forty-five rebellion was to prove him right. The economic argument was more controversial. So far as we can tell from statistics of somewhat questionable validity, some important branches of trade and many industries did make mildly accelerated progress during the years of 'business as usual' in the thirties; and the merchant shipping fleet, notoriously vulnerable in wartime, unquestionably expanded. On the other hand the aggressive mercantilist war against Spain which more and more of the Government's Whig opponents were demanding in the late 1730s, and even such a war undertaken as early as 1733 against France and Spain combined, might *if vigorously and efficiently conducted* (and this was both the crux of the matter and the great imponderable) have paid off more handsomely in terms of colonial gains and valuable future markets.

Walpole, for his part, could justifiably claim that his pacifism had at least been in the interests of the landed classes, that it had kept the Land Tax low and helped to cement the social harmony he had consciously sought since the start of his ministry. But to argue, as he did in his 1739 speech, that it had also preserved 'the balance of Europe' was self-delusion. On the contrary, the scales had been decisively tilted in favour of the Bourbon powers, by then in close alliance; Britain's international prestige was probably at its lowest ebb since the 1680s; and the pathetic failure of Walpole as a war minister in the years 1739–42 reflected in some measure the deflation of national morale as well as his own patent lack of stomach for the job in hand. If France had not been deterred from entering the colonial war by the death of Charles VI, Walpole's political career might have ended not merely in disappointment but in humiliating defeat.

It would be unjust, however, to assess him as a prime minister on his record in foreign policy. Walpole, after all, was First Lord of the Treasury. It was his reputation as the leading Whig financial expert which enabled him to lay claim to this office in the first place. It is primarily on his record as a finance minister, and on the success of his superintending interest over the whole field of the economy, that history must judge him.

It is significant that three of the most important and imaginative of Walpole's financial achievements predated his premiership: they were the fruits of earlier spells of office. His financial blueprint for untangling the ravelled affairs of the South Sea Company in the winter of 1720-1 helped to restore public confidence and government credit, so badly shaken by the Bubble crisis. The decisive first step in his plan to reduce the interest payable on most segments of the long-term National Debt had been taken earlier still, in 1717;[10] and in that same year one of his few genuine innovations, the 'Sinking Fund', devised as a mechanism for progressively paying off the capital of the £40 million War Debt (which then seemed a ruinous burden) had been launched by Stanhope soon after Walpole's resignation from the ministry.[11] These two measures, dating from the first and more adventurous half of a parliamentary career of forty-four years, proved the twin keys to the effectiveness of much of his financial policy as prime minister, and were primarily responsible for his remarkable success in keeping peacetime taxation so low. For by persisting with the Sinking Fund to the very end of his ministry, long after anxiety about the size of the National Debt had become a thing of the past, he was able to cream off into the ordinary revenue the Fund's handsome surplus, accruing from successive interest reductions.

Thanks to the success (as he saw it) of his foreign policy, Walpole was never faced with the necessity of raising the huge sums that had annually confronted Godolphin and Harley. With a modest annual budget varying between 2 and 3½ millions, the need for loans was limited, and when it did arise Walpole had at his disposal the techniques of loan management perfected by Montagu and Godolphin. He was the fortunate heir of the 'Financial Revolution'; though he could thank his own fostering of credit and assiduous cultivation of the City and

[10] His scheme to consolidate the whole Debt in the first instance at 5 per cent, despite being truncated after he left office in 1717, was of great importance. It was later taken further, with a three-stage conversion to 4 per cent in the years 1727-30.
[11] The Fund was fed mainly from the appropriated taxes 'released' by the reduction of interest payments. The best treatment of Walpole and the National Debt is in P. G. M. Dickson, *The Financial Revolution in England* (London, 1967).

financial corporations for the fact that he was able to raise a £1 million loan in 1727 at an astonishing 3 per cent. Such circumstances, it might be thought, offered a glorious opportunity for a minister of Walpole's ability and authority, particularly one with his enviable faculty for making financial complexities intelligible to the most doltish back-bencher, to effect the basic reforms in the fiscal system which his hard-pressed predecessors had not had time to conceive or carry through.

Walpole's *forte*, however, lay not in striking originality but in making the existing system work more efficiently and in rationalising it – as with his radical simplification of Customs duties in 1722[12] – where rationalisation did not reduce the amount of 'grass' available for 'the beasts'. By demanding higher standards from revenue officials and extending the authority of the Customs Commissioners to Scotland, that home-from-home for smugglers, he did what he could – though it was for the most part a losing battle – to reduce the staggering amount of duty evasion. But his celebrated Excise scheme of 1733 was the nearest Walpole came to a truly courageous fiscal reform. This scheme, which involved the relief of imported colonial tobacco, and later of imported wine, from all but nominal customs, and their subjection instead to a bonded ware-house system and an internal excise duty, was far more than an anti-smuggling device to save £500,000 a year. It was the culmination of a long-term strategy for shifting the incidence of taxation away from land and property and on to consumable commodities: ultimately, Walpole seems to have hoped, there would be no direct taxation at all except in time of emergency and war. A pilot scheme in 1724 had proved a striking minor success,[13] and by 1731 the Land Tax had been reduced to one shilling in the pound. The 1733 Excise scheme would have brought this process to its logical conclusion. The case for it on financial grounds was unanswerable. But it was abandoned in the face of an exceptional display of popular hostility, incited by opposition charges that the Government was planning a General Excise and a massive invasion of personal liberty by its inquisitorial officials.

The abortive Excise project does demonstrate, however, that Walpole's policies at the Treasury had social and political as well as financial ends. In addition to a sound and efficient revenue system, he also sought

[12] See below.
[13] Applying the excise to tea, coffee and cocoa, it had increased revenue on these goods by about £120,000 a year.

an *acceptable* system – one that would be sufficiently fair to conciliate all the important social interests in the country, as well as weaning the squirarchy from its natural Tory allegiance.

Whether Walpole's fiscal measures were part of an overall economic strategy as well is a question on which not all modern historians are agreed.[14] Some would argue that not until the Younger Pitt, at the earliest, did Britain have a prime minister or a Treasury minister who envisaged an organic connection between the raising of money and the regulation of the national economy, or who even recognised a responsibility to pursue a coherent 'economic policy'. It has certainly been shown beyond much doubt[15] that the so-called 'system' of protective tariffs, so marked a feature of Hanoverian England until the 1780s, developed fortuitously as a result of the desperate revenue problems of the governments of the war years 1689–1712, not of a planned ministerial initiative or as a response to contemporary economic dogma. So that Walpole's highly important tariff reforms of the early 1720s, with their emphasis on the deterring of foreign manufactures and the encouragement of domestic industry, should be seen largely as an attempt to impose some order on a haphazard and irrational state of affairs, with a particular eye to satisfying those struggling native industries, such as linen, silk and paper-making, which had benefited from their adventitious tariff cocoon in the previous thirty years. In addition, one can point to measures later in the ministry's life which clearly reflect the lobbying of politically influential pressure groups, the West India interest and others, rather than the implementation of any national policy for the good of the economy at large;[16] while parliamentary historians have revealed that several notable economic measures commonly attributed to Walpole, for example the South Carolina Bill of 1730, were in fact the result of backbench initiatives of which the Prime Minister did not always approve.

These examples of pragmatism dent the traditional picture of Walpole as the watchful economic overlord with a master-plan. But they do not necessarily destroy it. Walpole's rueful reference to the Carolina Act – 'that he was always against repealing old laws, made for the

[14] Argument is inhibited by the fact that much economic groundwork for a close analysis of Walpole's administration still remains to be done.
[15] By Professor Ralph Davis. See 'The Rise of Protection in England', *Economic History Review*, xix (1966).
[16] Of these measures the Molasses Act of 1733 is but the best-known instance.

benefit of trade, and *breaking into the Navigation Act*[17] – illustrates one element of underlying consistency. And there can be no question that his Government remained faithful to the pledge given in the Speech from the Throne of October 1721: '. . . to make the exportation of our own commodities and the importation of the commodities used in the manufacturing of them as practicable and as easy as may be; by this means, the balance of trade may be preserved in our favour, [and] our navigation greatly increased. . . .' The cosseting of the re-export trade in colonial goods (its encouragement was to have been a major bonus of the Tobacco Excise Bill of 1733), and the crucial link in Walpole's mind between a pacific policy and economic progress, confirm an impression of overall coherence.

What is less certain, because of the different interpretation that can be put on the available statistics, is how far the effects of Walpole's policies answered their intentions. Historical orthodoxy long identified his regime with prosperity and economic growth. It is now apparent that there were important limits to what Walpole's or indeed any eighteenth-century government could achieve in the face of adverse circumstances of market fluctuation, or the natural rise and fall of certain branches of trade, or the discrimination of foreign governments against British goods. Thus Walpole could not possibly have sustained the extraordinary rate of progress the woollen cloth industry had achieved in the seventeenth century; nor could he prevent the relative decline of the sugar trade in the face of increasing French competition after 1720. Yet he still presided over the most prosperous economy in Europe. He had certainly by 1738 achieved his aim of a substantially healthier balance of trade; he had seen English shipping steadily though not spectacularly increase since 1723;[18] and he could point to the slow if painful advance of most of the heavily protected industries. Perhaps, as with so much else, he could have done more had he not been so preoccupied for much of the thirties with his political position and become less and less susceptible to new ideas or bold initiatives.

It is odd that two decades as important as the years 1720–40 in the evolution of the prime minister's office and power should have been in some ways retrogressive in the development of the Constitution. There

---

[17] Historical Manuscripts Commission, *Egmont Diary*, i, 173. Author's italics.
[18] See Ralph Davis, *The Rise of the English Shipping Industry* (London, 1962), especially pp. 27–8.

was one highly important exception. After 1733, when for the first time his administration had to fight for its life in both Houses, Walpole established the principle that *everyone* who held office or commission under the Crown, however petty, was expected politically to dance to the tune of the First Lord of the Treasury, or risk dismissal. Admittedly this principle had been foreshadowed under some of Walpole's immediate predecessors; but minor placemen had rarely been subject to more than occasional, limited purges, and Harley had held in 1706 that as long as an office-holder supported the ministry on votes of supply he should be allowed considerable latitude on other matters.[19] So the change in the 1730s was of great moment.

But what was an advance in terms of the growth of party discipline and executive control over the legislature was a setback in the development of what has been called 'the non-political civil service'. The Managers of the post-Revolution period had done much to ensure that in certain government departments[20] a solid core of experienced 'professionals' would be permitted continuity of office, regardless of the party seesaw. Walpole did not abandon this policy entirely. But even in the case of offices from which MPs were barred (and there were thousands, especially in the revenue field), he showed more political discrimination and paid less regard to professional competence or reputation. In Cabinet government, too, the newly established conventions of the post-Revolution period – regular, minuted meetings of a Cabinet of about a dozen leading ministers at which major policy issues were debated in the royal presence – were rudely disturbed by Walpole's preference for working behind the scenes with a smaller inner group of four or five. The change made for smoother policy-making; but it created suspicion and added to the reputation of the Walpole regime for autocracy and highhandedness.

In this, as in so much else, however, Walpole was a realist and not a theorist. In all his years in office there was never a time when he hankered after perfection, or let preconceived notions or ideal considerations disturb his clear-headed sense of what was attainable, or of what in political terms was necessary, merely desirable or frankly irrelevant. Much of his (in many ways misleading) reputation for 'letting sleeping dogs lie' is simply a reflection of this realism.

[19] Historical Manuscripts Commission, *Bath MSS*, i, 110–11.
[20] Most notably the Treasury, the Navy Office, the Post Office and most of the revenue departments.

In view of the host of abuses and institutions crying out for remedy in early Hanoverian England – social injustices by our standards appalling, religious discrimination, a demoralised state Church, a scandalous penal system, an administrative structure still plagued in many parts with sinecurists and enmeshed in antiquated procedures – Walpole's record of positive legislation over two decades may seem pitifully meagre.[21] But it is significant that in the 1720s and 1730s Walpole, freely slandered for so much else, was rarely criticised for this. He was observing the conventions of his day: that the prime business of government was to *govern* rather than to legislate or reform. And he could make the confession, 'I am no saint, no Spartan, no reformer' without a qualm; for he was at one with the bulk of his contemporaries in believing that government intervention to remedy most social abuses was either irrelevant or unwise at a period when society at large seemed to have rediscovered stability.

Even the historian must concede that since the years of Walpole's premiership were also years of relatively static population and prices, of a lull in the industrial advance made during the war years, and of urbanisation (outside London) at a gentle pace, the need for active paternalism was not urgent. In so far as Walpole had a 'social policy' it might appear to have been a largely oppressive one: he certainly believed in low wages on economic grounds, promoted laws against workers' 'combinations' (nascent unions), and had no hesitation in endorsing increased severity in dealing with crimes against property (it was in 1726 that the notorious 'Waltham Black Act' passed into law). And yet occasional stirrings of a social conscience can be detected. Relief of the poor was sometimes recommended to Parliament's attention (for instance in the King's Speech of 1730); though Walpole usually thought it proper to let the legislature decide how best it should be achieved, and firmly believed that, except in emergencies, the proper initiatives in such matters should be local, private or institutional. Where the Poor Law machinery or the private philanthropy of landlords and businessmen fell short there was the contribution of the Churches – the new Charity Schools, for instance, and the many

[21] Almost half the 600 government-sponsored Bills introduced into the Commons between 1715 and 1754 were regular supply Bills or annual mutiny Bills; and only a very small proportion of the remainder could be considered, in any meaningful sense, 'reform legislation'. See R. Sedgwick, *History of Parliament: The House of Commons 1715-54* (London, 1970), i, 5.

Societies for Reformation of Manners which had sprung up after 1688.

Walpole's attitude towards both the Church of England and Dissent was likewise pragmatic. In his apprentice years from 1701–14 he absorbed something of the anti-clericalism of the Augustan Whigs, exposed as they were to the electoral hostility of the High Churchmen, among them 80 per cent of the parish clergy; and his Commons speeches of this period also reflect his party's sympathy with Protestant nonconformity. But the Sacheverell affair of 1710, in which he was a leading prosecutor, taught him a lesson he was never to forget;[22] so too did the vital support given by the Low Church bishops to the Whig Opposition in the House of Lords in its darkest days from 1711–14. By 1721, although the Tory Occasional Conformity and Schism Acts had been repealed, the Test and Corporation Acts of Charles II's reign still remained on the Statute Book, subjecting the dissenters to continuing civil disabilities. Stanhope's attempt to neutralise these Acts in 1719 had failed, no small thanks to Walpole, who then and ever after was adamant that full civil rights for dissenters, as re-urged in the 1730s, could not be granted without offending the bishops and risking a flare-up of the ugly High Church passions of 1710. The farthest he would go in the cause of further toleration was an Annual Indemnity Bill, first passed in 1727. And since this was not always annual, and the indemnification it gave seems to have been uncertain, it left the Whigs' dissenting allies unsatisfied.

The state Church itself had little to thank Walpole for, except the retention of the Test. Politically the Church leadership gave his regime invaluable support; for the celebrated partnership of the years 1723–36 between the Prime Minister and Bishop Gibson of London, made possible by the monastic habits and infirmities of Archbishop Wake, ensured that all but a handful of bishoprics, deaneries and Crown livings in that period were filled by sound Whigs and pro-Walpoleans. Yet in return for this political support, much of it vastly time-consuming, Walpole gave Gibson no official backing for the latter's ambitious and far-reaching reform programme, including a radical administrative reorganisation; and without such encouragement the Bishop's plans withered on the vine. Walpole and his colleagues could not, of course, be entirely blamed for the Church's palpable decline in the twenties and thirties. But their cynicism assuredly did nothing to arrest it.

[22] See Geoffrey Holmes, *The Trial of Doctor Sacheverell* (London, 1973).

Britain, therefore, had some cause to rue, as well as good cause to bless, the long supremacy of Sir Robert Walpole. As well as the criticisms that can be made of specific fields of policy, it is also undeniable that the tone of politics declined between 1721 and 1742. By contrast with some of his recent predecessors Walpole's personal example was hardly edifying. Corruption and a blatantly materialistic view of politics manifestly increased during his period of office. And yet if we judge Walpole's premiership as an exhibition of the political art, in the widest sense, it would be grudging not to bestow on it the accolade.

Although he had been trained in a very different arena, he proved superbly adaptable to a new ambience in which the electrifying issues of Queen Anne's day had been defused and in which politics had become more intimate and personal than at any time since the sixteenth century. Walpole stood head and shoulders above all his contemporaries on such a scene, partly because he was so adept at balancing the major interests within the victorious party oligarchy, and partly because he was himself such a consummate master of personal relationships.[23] Above all he was one of the greatest parliamentarians who have ever lived. Patronage and discipline combined may have held together 'the Court and Treasury party', the core of his majorities in each Parliament, 1722-7, 1727-34, 1734-41. But his true calibre was shown in his peerless handling of the Independents, the 150-200 backbenchers, mostly country gentlemen, who were tied by interest neither to the Court nor to the power politicians of the Opposition. These men could in the last resort make or break any ministry. Indeed, in the end Walpole fell essentially because his foreign policy and his ineffectual war policy disenchanted too many of the country members whom he had successfully wooed for so long. For at least seventeen years, however, he had commanded their confidence and for the most part their support; commanded it by his highly effective debating skills, trenchant and direct; by his techniques of communication, to which he devoted enormous pains; by the genuine respect he showed for the House of Commons, whose 'approbation' he once declared[24] was 'preferable to all that

[23] Though as a matter of sober fact, because of the unfortunate gaps in his surviving correspondence, we know a good deal less about this aspect of his primacy than we should like to do – except as regards his relations with a number of fellow ministers, like Newcastle, and of course as regards the Court, where he hardly put a foot wrong until 1737.
[24] In the House of Commons, February 1739.

power, or even Majesty itself, can bestow'; and not least by his success in cultivating the image of himself, despite his vast fortune and princely style of living,[25] as just such another homespun, earthy, hearty, fox-hunting squire as the average backbencher.

In short, what set Robert Walpole apart from any other prime minister of the eighteenth century, save the Younger Pitt, was his capacity to achieve the maximum conceivable measure of influence and dominance *within the existing political system*. He accepted, and trimmed his sails to meet, all the rough weather which challenged the ambitious politician in early Hanoverian England: the fragmentation of the ruling one-party oligarchy; the uncertain favour of kings and courtiers; above all the crucial fact that because of the power of the independent member, the prime minister and his government never controlled an absolute majority of the Commons. Playing to perfection the dual role of 'minister with the King in the House of Commons' and 'minister for the House of Commons in the closet', Walpole mastered all the inherent difficulties of the political world in which he lived; and not only that, he turned them into positive and long-term assets. No politician can do more.

BIBLIOGRAPHY

The character of both Walpole and his age have been unforgettably captured in the first two volumes of J. H. Plumb's trilogy *Sir Robert Walpole* (London, 1956, 1960). The third volume, which will take the story from 1734 to 1745 is in active preparation. Meanwhile Archdeacon W. Coxe, *Memoirs of the Life and Administration of Sir Robert Walpole*, vol. i (London, 1798) remains a valuable storehouse of information. A brief single-volume study of outstanding merit is H. T. Dickinson, *Robert Walpole and the Whig Supremacy* (Teach Yourself History series, London, 1973). Through the author's kindness I was able to read the book in typescript while preparing this essay, to my great profit.

On particular aspects of Walpole's premiership the following works can be strongly recommended: C. B. Realey, *The Early Opposition to Sir Robert Walpole, 1720–1727* (Philadelphia, 1931); P. G. M. Dickson, *The Financial Revolution in England* (London, 1967); J. B. Owen, *The Rise of the Pelhams* (London, 1957).

[25] See J. H. Plumb, *Sir Robert Walpole: The King's Minister* (London, 1960), pp. 81–91 and *passim*.

2

THE EARL OF WILMINGTON
and the Carteret Administration
under Wilmington

BY

HERBERT VAN THAL

Spencer Compton, born 1673; third son of the second wife of the 3rd Earl of Northampton. Educated at St Paul's School and Trinity College, Oxford. Unmarried. Chairman of the Committee of Privileges 1705; Treasurer to Prince George of Denmark 1707; with Walpole in the committee for Sacheverell's impeachment 1709; elected member for the Borough of East Grinstead 1713; MP for the County of Sussex 1714; Privy Councillor 1716; Speaker of the House of Commons 1721; Paymaster-General 1722; KB 1725; Lord Privy Seal and Lord President of the Council 1733; First Lord of the Treasury 1742. Died 1743.

THE EARL OF WILMINGTON

Spencer Compton was born in 1673, the youngest of the three sons of Mary Noel, the second wife of James, third Earl of Northampton. The Comptons had long been supporters of the Crown, one of Spencer's uncles having been made Bishop of London by Charles II. Spencer was educated at St Paul's and then took his degree at Trinity College, Oxford. For a while he practised at the bar in the Middle Temple. In 1698 he travelled abroad, and was elected Tory Member for Eye in Suffolk, but shortly afterwards changed his allegiance to the Whigs, a not uncommon procedure in eighteenth-century politics. He applied himself assiduously to detail work in Parliament, and by 1705 was Chairman of the Committee of Privileges; two years later he became Treasurer to Queen Anne's consort, Prince George of Denmark.

During these years he had kept up a friendship with Walpole, and in 1709 he was nominated with him to draw up the articles of impeachment against Dr Sacheverell.[1]

In 1710 Compton lost his seat in Parliament, and it was not until the new Parliament of 1713 that he was re-elected for the borough of East Grinstead. On the accession of George I in 1714, with the new election, he was nominated for both the borough of East Grinstead and the county of Sussex. He chose to represent the county, and when the new Parliament assembled he was chosen Speaker, though he declared that he had 'neither memory to retain, judgement to collect nor skill to guide their debates'. The King, however, declared he was perfectly well satisfied, and confirmed the choice of the House. When the Prince of Wales came over from Hanover and set up his own household, Compton was appointed Treasurer; his tact in this post would have served him well later if he had had the ability to use his political powers. On 6 July 1716 he became a Privy Counsellor.

When George I died in Hanover in 1727 on his way to Osnabrück, it was natural that speculation was rife as to the future, and the fact that there had been little love lost between the late King and his son boded

[1] *Journals of the House of Commons,* xvii, 241.

ill for members of Walpole's administration. Sir Robert immediately set out to see the new King, George II, at Richmond. When he arrived, Hervey relates,

'. . . the Prince was laid to sleep (as his custom had been for many years after dinner), and the Princess was in the bedchamber with him, when the Duchess of Dorset, the lady-in-waiting, went in to let them know Sir Robert was there, who was immediately brought in. All he [Walpole] said was, 'I am come to acquaint Your Majesty with the death of your father.'

The King seemed extremely surprised, but not enough to forget his resentment to Sir Robert one moment; neither his confusion, nor his joy at this great change, nor the benevolence so naturally felt by almost everybody towards the messenger of such good news, softened his voice or his countenance in one word or look. Whatever questions Sir Robert asked him with regard to the council being summoned, his being proclaimed, or other things necessary immediately to be provided, the King gave him no other answer than 'Go to Chiswick and take your directions from Sir Spencer Compton.'[2]

So Sir Robert made his way to Chiswick, while the King and Queen prepared for their journey to London. At Chiswick, Walpole told Spencer Compton:

'The King, Sir, has sent me to you in such a manner as he declares he intends you for his minister, and has commanded me to receive all my instructions from your mouth. It is what I as well as the rest of the world expected would be whenever this accident happened. You have been the Prince's Treasurer ever since he came to England; it is a natural promotion to continue you upon his being King: your services entitle you to that mark of his favour, and your abilities and experience in business will both enable you to support the employment and justify him in bestowing it. Everything is in your hands; I neither could shake your power if I would, nor would I if I could. My time has been, yours is beginning; but as we all must depend in some degree upon our successors, and that it is always prudent for these successors by way of example to have some regard for their predecessors, that with the measure they mete it may be measured to them again, for this reason I put myself

[2] John, Lord Hervey, *Memoirs*, ed. Sedgwick, i, 22.

[50]

under your protection, and for this reason I expect you will give it. I desire no share of power or business; one of your white sticks, or any employment of that sort, is all I ask as a mark from the Crown that I am not abandoned to the enmity of those whose envy is the only source of their hate, and who consequently will wish you no better than they have done me the moment you are vested with those honours and that authority, the possession of which they will always covet, and the possessor of which, of course, they will always hate.'[3]

Naturally, the 'plodding' Compton was highly gratified at Walpole's address to him, and promised him 'his protection, and asked in return the assistance of Sir Robert'.

Together they went to see the Lord President of the Council, the Duke of Devonshire, who was laid up with gout. At a meeting of the Privy Council, only the Lord Chancellor, Lord Trevor, the Privy Seal and Sir Paul Methuen were present. It was after the meeting that Compton told Walpole that he was unable to draft the King's speech and prevailed upon him to do so. Walpole at first, only too naturally, refused, but Compton 'insisted' and 'Walpole took up the employment immediately retiring to another room, and naturally slipped in a charming and appreciative tribute to the ability of the late ministry'.[4]

When Compton made his way to Leicester Fields he found it jammed with the multitudes, while the King's house was thronged, and he had to force his way to the King's closet, where his appointment was confirmed. On returning to Devonshire House, Compton found his speech written by Walpole, which he assiduously copied, and returned to Leicester Fields with Walpole. The King carefully read the speech, though he asked for a passage in the Declaration to be altered. This matter greatly embarrassed Compton, who went to Walpole to ask him if he would not persuade the King to allow it to remain as it was, in which Walpole succeeded.

How was Compton going to form his administration? Of the principal ministers of state, it was known that the King had little regard for them. He thought Walpole's brother Horace, Ambassador to France, 'a scoundrel and fool', while he detested the Duke of Newcastle. As to his other minister of state, Lord Townshend, 'the King looked upon him as

3 Hervey, op. cit., i, 23.
4 J. Plumb, *Walpole*, ii, 165.

no more than an able minister, and "scanty genius"'.[5] Even Walpole's son-in-law was dismissed his post as Master of the Robes. However, the first matter that would come up to Parliament would be the Civil List, and already the King had had a long talk with Walpole on 15 June which considerably raised that minister's hopes. Some shrewd moves immediately took place. Thus Horace Walpole went forthwith to Versailles to see Cardinal Fleury and secured a letter of full assurance from the Cardinal of France's fidelity to George II, whereupon he immediately set forth for England and arrived at Kensington, where the Court now was, on 19 June. At first the King was angry at seeing him, but he was appreciative of his splendid activities, while his ministers became very active over the Civil List at the public's expense. Pulteney, who, strangely enough, had never wanted the responsibility of First Lord, offered the King over £800,000 a year. It was pretty obvious that Compton was not going to stand up to this intrigue. Hervey, who has detailed the whole story for us, now took it upon himself to tell Walpole that he really need not worry. Queen Caroline had not forgotten her old friend. She had at once discerned that Compton's capabilities were quite unequal to the task that the King had thought he could do. It was the Queen who was to be his Court influence, and she had no intention of allowing her husband to appoint anyone other than Walpole.

Walpole had in 1721 and 1725 carried votes for the discharge of the debts of the Civil List amounting in the aggregate to over £1,000,000, but in 1727 there was again a debt of £600,000, as well as the jointure to be provided for, and when Compton suggested £50,000 for the Queen, Walpole simply undertook to double it.[6] Any hesitations the King may have had over Walpole were now overcome. Thus ended Compton's first hope of the Premiership. As compensation Walpole recommended the King to make Compton a baron, with the result that he became Lord Wilmington. On this occasion, said Hervey,

'I think he might have said, like Agrippina, the mother of Nero, in Racine's *Britannicus*,

> "*Tous ces présents, hélas! irritent mon dépit,*
> *Je vois mes honneurs croître, et tomber mon crédit.*"

But Wilmington did not seem to feel the ridicule or the contemptible-

[5] Hervey, op. cit., p. 29.
[6] I. S. Leadman, *Political History of England*, xi, 334.

ness of his situation. That snowball level of his, which had opened and that gathered so fast, melted away at as quick a pace; his visionary prospects of authority and grandeur vanished into air, and yet he seemed to be just as well satisfied to be bowing and grinning in the antechamber, possessed of a lucrative employment without credit, and dishonoured by a title which was the mark of his disgrace, as if he had been dictating in the closet, sole fountain of Court favour at home, and regulator of all national transactions abroad.'[7]

When the new Parliament was opened by George II on 23 January 1728, Wilmington held the lucrative post of Paymaster-General of the Forces, and in May 1730 he succeeded Lord Trevor as Lord Privy Seal. In December of that year he was created Viscount Pevensey, and Earl of Wilmington. Three years later he was installed a Knight of the Garter.

In 1739 the Cabinet was divided on the question of the war with Spain. The mob was being fanned for war over 'Jenkins's ear', and Walpole, the great peace minister, was having to deal with a King who too was urging war; and far worse for Walpole, Queen Caroline had died on 20 November 1737. The intrigues against Walpole were considerable. Despite the past, despite Wilmington's own assertions of his own limited capabilities, together with the help he had received from Walpole, new ambitions now began to stir within him, urging him into seeking high office again. Walpole had not the control in the Lords that he had in his own House. Although the Duke of Newcastle was a member of Walpole's Cabinet, he had joined the war party. Likewise Carteret had made a most powerful speech attacking the Spanish right to search British ships for contraband goods. The Opposition opinion was consolidated in the belief that it would be entirely to our advantage to have a maritime war with Spain. However, it was not until 1742 that Walpole fell. The final onslaughts began on 21 January, when Pulteney delivered his attack by moving to refer to a secret committee papers relating to the war. Walpole was not defeated upon this issue, but over a comparatively minor question on the 28th, relating to the Chippenham election, when the Government was in a minority of one. On 2 February the petition was decided against the Government by 241 to 225. Walpole decided to resign. 'All cry out,' wrote Horace Walpole, 'that he is

[7] op. cit., i, 39ff.

still minister behind the curtain.'[8] He was created Earl of Orford, and recommended that the King should send for Pulteney, and a place be found for Carteret. Newcastle had little chance in view of the King's hatred of him, while the Tories were 'political pariahs'.[9] Pulteney explained that his answer must be guided by the rest of the party, adding dramatically that the 'heads of parties are like the heads of snakes, carried on by their tails'.[10] Years before, Pulteney had sworn in a moment of pique with Walpole never to take office again. Now, with his nerve about to desert him, he conveniently recollected this rash vow and replied that consideration for his own reputation would not allow him to go back on his word.[11] Pulteney told the King that he would prefer to go to the Lords. He was created Earl of Bath. Walpole welcomed him saying, 'You and I are now two as insignificant men in England.' The King sent for his old crony Wilmington who was the true King's man. He and his friend, the Duke of Dorset, along with Dodington, were then a small clique. But their abilities were not great enough – the true head of the administration was Carteret.

THE CARTERET ADMINISTRATION UNDER WILMINGTON

Save to historians and those who have studied the political history of the period, Carteret's qualities are not extensively remembered.

Born of a good family, which in the eighteenth century was of essential value, 'he left no diary, no intimate journal, scarcely a private letter, nor for all his immense erudition, any writings beyond his official correspondence'. Of his contemporaries, Smollett said, 'There was no minister in this nation worth the meal that whitened his periwig.' Lord Chesterfield, who, on the contrary, bore him no love, declared, 'When he dies, the ablest head in England dies too.' While Horace Walpole, who admired none but himself, confessed that of the five great men whom he had known during his lifetime, Carteret was 'most a genius of the five'.[12]

Carteret was born at Hawnes, his father's seat in Bedfordshire, on 22

[8] Turberville, *The House of Lords in the Eighteenth Century*, p. 247.
[9] Pemberton, *Carteret*, p. 184.
[10] ibid., p. 184.
[11] ibid., p. 185.
[12] Baring Pemberton, *Carteret*, p. 4.

April 1690. He went to Westminster and at the age of fifteen to Christ Church, Oxford, where he matriculated in January 1706. The only degree he took was that of Doctor of Civil Law. He was successfully married to Frances, daughter of Sir Robert Worsley, Bt, and had four daughters but no heir. All his daughters made brilliant matches. Carteret's career began in the reign of Queen Anne.

Although he was born of a Tory family, and his friends at Oxford were of the same party, after the death of Queen Anne Carteret joined the Whigs, and was a confirmed supporter of the Hanoverian Succession. His learning and knowledge of languages were to serve him well, since he was able to converse freely with both George I and George II in German. Yet at the accession of George I he received no better appointment than that of a Lord of the Bedchamber, with which he seemed satisfied. During the time of the great Whig schism, Carteret's benefactor was Stanhope, and he soon made a very considerable mark in European diplomacy. Especially brilliant was his success at the Court of Sweden, to which he was accredited in his twenty-ninth year, in persuading that country to agree to terms with her adversaries. But the years of Carteret's diplomatic triumphs do not concern us here, save to emphasise that he was far more successful abroad than at home, except during his short appointment as Lord Lieutenant of Ireland when he so adroitly handled the issue that was caused over 'Woods's Copper Coinage'. Yet this urbane man, whose love of Homer and wine, whose brilliance and learning would take him far, never ruled this country as was thought he would. Whilst it is probably true that Carteret possessed a greater degree of genius than any of his contemporaries, it must be admitted that genius was not what England required in the third and fourth decades of the eighteenth century so much as matter-of-fact business acumen.

Carteret, after he left office as Lord Lieutenant of Ireland, found himself in the wilderness, and in 1731 joined the Opposition. But the whole position within the parties was to be altered with the tragic death of Queen Caroline. It was the signal for the decline of Walpole himself. Two years later the great minister was to give way to the clamour of war with Spain. Carteret was now to see events moving quickly in Europe. The death of the Emperor Charles VI was to bring the Pragmatic Sanction into force, whereby his daughter the Empress Maria Theresa succeeded to his dominions, and at the same time a flute-loving King ascended the throne of Prussia, who was quickly to play the bully to the young Queen of Hungary, and in December 1740 to seize Silesia. It came to Carteret to advise her to accept the terms of the Treaty of Breslau and cede Silesia to the King. Twenty years later, when Frederick was writing the history of his times, he recognised the skill of Carteret, and wrote, '*Le Lord Carteret fut le principal promoteur de cet ouvrage.*'

The only Act of Parliament that was passed under Wilmington was the Place Bill,[13] limiting the number of offices tenable by Members of Parliament. The new administration consisted of two distinct strands – of Carteret's small personal following and of Walpole's old henchmen, Newcastle and Hardwicke with the Duke of Devonshire.[14] Carteret did not even bother to cultivate his two most powerful followers, Chesterfield and Argyll, and this was to limit his administration painfully.

In the year 1743 England entered the War of Austrian Succession, and the French were defeated at Dettingen, when the King himself bravely led his troops, and where he narrowly escaped death. Carteret was there too. He sat in a coach and six well out of cannon shot, wearing an anxious expression on his face and immersed throughout the action in the solution of a new problem, raised by events of the preceding four weeks. But the French had to withdraw from Germany.

The following month Wilmington died, and on his death Henry Pelham, brother of the Duke of Newcastle, became Prime Minister, while Carteret was out in the wilderness again. He was created Earl of Granville.

Of Wilmington, Hervey composed a ballad:

> The Countess of Wilmington, excellent muse,
> I'll trust with the Treasury, not with the purse,
> For nothing by her I've resolved shall be done:
> She shall sit at that board as you sit on the throne.[15]

Hanbury Williams was even less complimentary:

> See you dull important lord
> Who at the longed for money board

[13] The Place Bill had been formerly introduced in 1740 and defeated.
[14] Turbeville, *History of the House of Lords in the Eighteenth Century*, p. 250.
[15] Bingham, *Prime Ministers*, 'Wilmington'.

Sits first but does not lead,
His younger brethren all things make,
So that the Treasury's like a snake,
And the tail moves the head.[16]

Of all our First Lords of the Treasury, Wilmington was the most shadowy figure. He was a stop-gap. Yet, as Mersey has observed, 'he filled for nearly thirty years the four highest places in the State to which laymen can aspire.'[17] He was, in short, an uninspired, slogging Parliamentarian, not without occasional wit. He spoke slowly and with clarity, and he was able to control the House of Commons when he was Speaker. He died a wealthy man. He never married and his wealth passed to his nephew, the fifth Earl of Northampton, and eventually to the Cavendishes.

As to Granville, he had great parts, and a most uncommon share of learning. He was one of the best speakers in the House of Lords, in both the declamatory and the argumentative way. He had a wonderful quickness and precision in seizing the stress of a question, which no art, no sophistry, could disguise from him.

BIBLIOGRAPHY

Baring, Pemberton, *Carteret* (1936)
Bingham, Clive, *Prime Ministers of England* (1922)
Compton, William, 6th Marquis of Northampton, *History of the Comptons of Compton Tyngates* (1930)
Feiling, Keith, *History of the Tory Party 1714–1832* (1938)
Ilchester, Earl of, *Lord Hervey and his Friends 1726–38* (1950)
Leadham, I. S., *Political History of England 1702–60* (1909)
Lucas, R. L., *George II and His Ministers* (1910)
Plumb, J., *Sir Robert Walpole* (2 vols, 1956)
Sedgwick, Romney (ed.), *Some Materials Towards Memoirs of the Reign of King George II* by John, Lord Hervey (3 vols, 1931)
Torrens, William, *History of Cabinets* (2 vols, 1894)
Turberville, A. S., *The House of Lords in the Eighteenth Century* (1927)
Williams, Basil, *The Whig Supremacy 1714–16* (1939)
Williams, Sir Charles Hanbury, *Works* (3 vols, 1822)

[16] ibid.
[17] ibid.

3

HENRY PELHAM

BY

AUBREY NEWMAN

Henry Pelham, born c. January 1696, second son of Thomas, 1st Baron Pelham, and Lady Grace Holles, daughter of Gilbert, 3rd Earl of Clare. Educated at Westminster School and Hart Hall, Oxford. Married 1726, Lady Katherine Manners, daughter of John, 2nd Duke of Rutland. Two sons (Thomas and Henry) died 1739; six daughters, of whom Catherine married Henry, 9th Earl of Lincoln, and Grace married Lewis Watson, later 1st Baron Sondes. MP for Seaford 1717–22 and Sussex 1722–54; Treasurer of the Chamber 1720–22; Lord of the Treasury 1721–4; Secretary-at-War 1724–30; Paymaster-General 1730–43; First Lord of the Treasury, August 1743–54; Chancellor of the Exchequer December 1743–54. Died 6 March 1754.

HENRY PELHAM

Henry Pelham's career illustrates the basic principles making for equilibrium in eighteenth-century politics. The career of Sir Robert Walpole had, to some extent, clouded these principles, for his success had been seen in terms of his own personality rather than in the political compromises that he personified. It took time for contemporaries to realise that political stability was secured not through formal office but through the gaining of confidence in the holder of office among two different sources of political authority, the King and the leading 'party' in the House of Commons, and that it would inevitably take time for each of these factors in the political equation to recognise the emergence of a new dominant personality, the prime minister. Accordingly it was not immediately evident to contemporaries that Walpole's true successor was neither Wilmington nor Carteret but rather a comparatively insignificant scion of one of the great Whig families, dependent on his brother not merely for an income but also for his very seat in the House of Commons.

Henry Pelham was the second son of a Sussex landowner who had risen in the social and political scale as a result of several fortunate marriages. His elder brother, Thomas, Duke of Newcastle, inherited most of the family wealth and power, so that Henry's political future depended in the first instance on the support that his brother could give him. There was little direct competition between them; both went to Westminster, but while Thomas went to Cambridge Henry went to Oxford, and a contemporary poetaster in a lampoon against the two commented:

> Harry, meanwhile consider'd that
>   His means were slender, small his 'State;
> And therefore to make good the Ballance,
>   Resolves he will improve his Tallents.
>
> Closely to Study he applies,
>   In hopes by this in time to rise,

By dint of merit to a station,
To be the wonder of the Nation.[1]

In the 1715 rising he served as a volunteer and was present in that capacity at the Battle of Preston. Very soon after he came of age his brother had a vacancy in Parliament created for him in his quasi-family constituency of Seaford, and in the following general election secured his return for the county of Sussex. Election by a county was normally considered to be the most prestigious of the ways of entering the House of Commons, but usually was a great handicap to a rising politician. The progression from one office to another, normally regarded as the regular pattern of a career, involved at each stage a fresh election to the House, and a county was usually an expensive and bothersome constituency in this respect. Speaker Onslow, for example, was warned by Sir Robert Walpole of the inconveniences that ensued from sitting for a county: 'What! Will you take a county upon you? Consider what that is with regard to re-election; and should any accident happen to prevent your being chosen Speaker, you will, I suppose, be not unwilling to come into other offices and trusts, perhaps frequent elections may not be so practicable in a county as in a borough.'[2]

Pelham therefore was almost unique among eighteenth-century politicians in sitting for a county seat and yet being able to rely on a re-election at need. In fact the county of Sussex was virtually a pocket borough of the Duke of Newcastle, who prided himself on retaining control over it and on ensuring that his brother was elected. So far indeed did he control the county that in 1722 he was able to breach a long-standing convention of a division in the representation between the east and west of the county, foisting two 'easterners' on the electorate, one of them being his yet unknown and politically inexperienced younger brother. Newcastle's regard for the career of his younger brother and heir presumptive was further illustrated at the time of Pelham's marriage. Half of the Pelham estates were granted to him and he was then assured of an independent and substantial income.

Provided with a secure political base, Henry's political career depended however upon his own talents as a political leader and as a manager in the House of Commons. His first political appointment had

[1] Quoted in S. H. Nulle, *Thomas Pelham-Holles* . . ., pp. 172 and 174.
[2] Onslow MSS, Historical Manuscripts Commission, 14th Report, app. part ix (1895), p. 517.

been to a place in the gift of his brother as Lord Chamberlain, and his first recorded speech on a motion on the Civil List debts which he himself, as Treasurer of the Chamber, proposed, and which Robert Walpole seconded. But when Walpole moved to the Treasury Henry Pelham moved with him, and gradually showed his mastery not merely of financial matters and procedures but, more importantly, of the relationships between government finance and the procedures of the House of Commons. His successive appointments as Secretary-at-War and Paymaster-General involved him in considerable activity in the Commons, so that Walpole seems increasingly to have relied upon him for the proper execution of the albeit limited range of government business there. As Carteret later angrily commented: 'He was only a chief clerk to Sir Robert Walpole, and why he should expect to be more under me I can't imagine. He did his drudgery and he shall do mine.'[3] A different picture is however presented by Lord Hervey in his *Memoirs*:

'Mr Pelham . . . was strongly attached to Sir Robert Walpole, and more personally beloved by him than any man in England. He was a gentleman-like sort of man, of very good character, with moderate parts, in the secret of every transaction, which, added to long practice, made him at last, though not a bright speaker, often a useful one; and by the means of a general affability he had fewer enemies than commonly falls to the share of one so high a rank.'[4]

After Walpole's fall, Pelham was his obvious heir as leader of the 'Old Whigs' in the House of Commons; his close connection with Sir Robert and his abilities as a 'man of business' which earlier had made him Walpole's virtual deputy pointed him out as the successor. There were however three obstacles – rivalry among the other ministers, suspicions among the 'party' in the Commons that he could not adequately defend its interests, and the need to gain the fullest confidence of the King – and until these could be overcome his position could hardly be held as assured. In the meantime he continued as Paymaster-General, and after the elevation of Walpole's main rival, William Pulteney, to the House of Lords became the effective 'leader' of the Commons. As

[3] *Diary of the First Earl of Egmont*, Historical Manuscripts Commission (1923 ff.) iii, 187.
[4] John, Lord Hervey, *Some Materials Towards Memoirs of the Reign of King George II*, ed. Romney Sedgwick (London, 1931), 120.

such Pelham was responsible during the session of 1742-3 for the conduct of essential governmental business, including presiding over the regular meeting of government supporters before the opening of the parliamentary session, and the allocation of House of Commons business among various supporters or potential supporters of the administration. His activities were so successful, and his abilities were so marked, that after the end of that session it was generally agreed that 'at the beginning of the next sessions . . . Lord Wilmington . . . was to have changed his employment. For it was well understood that Mr Pelham was not to go into the House of Commons any more but as head of the Treasury.'5 Before that date however Wilmington died, and although there was an attempt among the other ministers to have Pulteney appointed as First Lord of the Treasury, Pelham's interest, in alliance with that of Walpole and a substantial part of the coalition, was sufficient to secure his appointment as First Lord of the Treasury and then to add to that the post of Chancellor of the Exchequer.

This was however merely the first step in establishing his ascendancy over his fellow ministers, while his authority among the 'Old Whigs' was as yet far from clear. Moreover, the true lead in the closet was still in the hands of his principal ministerial rival, John, Lord Carteret. The process by which Pelham demonstrated his superiority took a further three years, and was eased as much by Carteret's own neglect of elementary rules of parliamentary tactics and his inability to court and conciliate possible followers in the Commons as by Pelham's skill in emphasising to George II his own indispensability for the smooth running of the King's business in the Commons and for the maintenance of a Whig majority. A letter from Walpole to Pelham in 1743 not only gave sound advice but showed how clearly Walpole himself had understood the process by which he had retained power for so many years.

'The King must, with tenderness and management, be shewn, what he may with reason depend upon, and what, he will be deceived and lost, if he places any confidence and reliance in. The King saw last year, what part the Whigs acted; and, I should hope, he may be convinced, that the Whig party will stand by him, as they have done, through his whole reign, if his majesty does not surrender himself into hands, that mean and wish nothing but his destruction, and want to be armed with his

5 Henry Fox to the Duke of Marlborough, 26 April 1743. J. B. Owen, *The Rise of the Pelhams*, pp. 159–60.

authority and power only to nail up his cannon, and turn it against himself. . . .

Address and management are the weapons you must fight and defend with: plain truths will not be relished at first; in opposition to prejudices, conceived and infused in favour of his own partialities; and you must dress up all you offer, with the appearance of no other view or tendency, but to promote his service in his own way, to the utmost of your power. And the more you can make any thing appear to be his own, and agreeable to his declaration and orders, given to you before he went, the better you will be heard: as, the power to treat with such persons, as should be necessary to carry on his service in your hands; the encouragement and hopes to be given to the Whigs, by you, as arising from himself. Hint, at first, the danger he will run, in deviating from his own rule; shew him the unavoidable necessity there will be, of dissolving this parliament, if he departs from the body of the Whigs; and let him see the consequences of going to a new election, in the height of the war, which will certainly end in a rank Tory Parliament, that will at once put a stop to all the measures that are now in practice, and for ever defeat all his views and desires, which are made the pretences to him, of hazarding the change.'[6]

The process by which Pelham managed to gain the confidence of both Commons and King extended over the period from 1743 till 1746; it was marked firstly by Carteret's dismissal from office in 1744, much against the King's will, and then, more significantly still, by the removal of Carteret and his associates from any private influence over the King in the spring of 1746. The first step had to be the achievement of some degree of ascendancy in the Commons, if only to persuade the King that Pelham alone was capable of 'doing the King's business'. A judicious combination of bargaining with various opposition groups that might be brought over to support the administration and firmly defending the essential interests of individual members of the 'Old Whigs' went far towards convincing the latter that Pelham could be relied on and thus establishing his general position in the House of Commons. It took time, and there was a considerable period of suspicion of him. But by early 1745 the opposition elements in the House had been for practical purposes reduced to groups of individual backbenchers with little or no organisation or leadership; virtually all the ablest speakers

[6] 20 Oct. 1743. Owen, op. cit., pp. 188–9.

had been added to the ministry in some way or other, and without leaders what was left was politically negligible. Even so the King was reluctant to give the Pelhams his fullest support, preferring to consult in private the erstwhile ministers whom he could not see in public; the danger remained that Carteret might be able to gain back former supporters who had earlier deserted him but who could now see in him a surer channel to royal favour than the Pelhams. For his part Pelham could not be sure that his own position was secure until he knew that he possessed the absolute confidence of the King and an assurance of royal consultation with him on all major issues and appointments. The relationship was therefore unstable. Horace Walpole wrote: 'It is not easy to say where power resides at present: it is plain that it resides not in the King; and yet he has enough to hinder anybody else from having it. His new governors have no interest with him – scarce any converse with him.'[7]

The King's dilemma was that he was unwilling to lose Carteret as his principal adviser, but if Carteret were unsuitable he did not really mind having the Pelhams instead. What he did strongly object to was giving an impression of having driven out Carteret for the sake of the Pelhams. Thus he continued to consult Carteret unofficially and to make himself as disagreeable as he could to the Pelhams without openly breaking with them. Various minutes of conversation between the King and one or other of the Pelham group show this clearly. On 9 April 1745, for instance, Newcastle wrote to Lord Hardwicke, his close friend and Lord Chancellor: 'My brother goes to Court on Thursday with the seals in his pocket to give, as he finds things. I shall do the same.'[8] And on the eve of the King's visit to Hanover that year Newcastle wrote to the King's second son, the Duke of Cumberland: 'We . . . here, my Lord Chancellor, my brother, and myself, represented, in the most dutiful manner, the impossibility of *our* opening another session of Parliament, if His Majesty, at his return, should not have a more favourable opinion of us, and our endeavour for his service, than he has, at present.'[9]

Only the strains of the military situation abroad and at home – this was the year of the 1745 rebellion – prevented the Pelhams from offering their resignations. The beginning of 1746 seemed to offer to the King an opportunity to reshape his ministry and drive out the Pelhams,

[7] Letter to Horace Mann, 24 Dec. 1744, *Correspondence*, ed. W. S. Lewis, xviii, 552.
[8] British Museum Additional MS 35870, f. 95.
[9] 3 May 1745. BM Add. MS 32704, f. 194.

while they for their part determined on making a stand, using their desire to appoint William Pitt to office as the main issue. On 10 and 11 February 1746 the leading ministers resigned. Their surrender of office lasted for two days, for within that time it became clear that Carteret and his connections had no chance of controlling the Commons, while even the City financiers demonstrated their opinion of the King's alternative ministers by withdrawing from arrangements already made for financing the war: 'No Pelhams, no money.' It was not however that the Pelhams were the only possible ministers, or that these particular Whigs had 'the King in chains'. Rather it was that the Commons had declared quite clearly their opinion of Carteret. Had the King been prepared to turn to any other of the Whig leaders, the Commons – and even for the moment the Pelhams themselves – would have acquiesced. But if George could not have Carteret he was prepared to turn back again to the Pelhams, even though they went so far as to make 'conditions':

'Out of duty to the King, and regard to the public it is apprehended that His Majesty's late servants cannot return into his service, without being honoured, with that degree of authority, confidence, and credit from His Majesty, which the ministers of the Crown have usually enjoy'd in this country, and which is absolutely necessary for carrying on his service. That His Majesty will be pleased entirely to withdraw his confidence and countenance from those persons, who of late have, behind the curtain, suggested private councills, with the view of creating difficulties to his servants, who are responsible for everything, whilst those persons are responsible for nothing.'[10]

A year later Pelham consolidated his position by a snap election; this caught a new opposition group completely unprepared. Thereafter his authority was virtually unshaken. New opposition groups emerged, as had occurred under Walpole, and inevitably they attracted the malcontents. The leader of these was the Prince of Wales, Frederick Louis. Pelham always recognised the difficulties that a Prince could make for any administration: 'The House of Commons is a great unwieldy body, which requires great Art and some Cordials to keep it loyal; we have not many of the latter in our power; the Opposition is headed by the Prince, who has much to give in present as we have, and more in

10 BM Add. MS 35870, f. 117.

Reversion. This makes my task an hard one, and if it were not for that I should sleep in quiet.'[11]

Despite any anxieties that might have come from this quarter, however, the threat was ended in 1751 with Frederick's death and the speed with which nearly all of the Prince's group, the Leicester House faction, precipitated themselves into the Pelham circle. Pelham had still to be careful in his management of the Commons and its various elements, and he had still to be careful in his management of the King's whims and fancies, but he had no serious political rival to contend with. This indeed is the principal feature of Pelham's ministry. No great issues emerged after 1747, such as had bedevilled Walpole, while there were no other leading politicians to compete with him. All who had any ability had been bought off, and Pelham had achieved in effect that great ambition of eighteenth-century ministries, a 'broad-bottom'. To manage to include in office both Pitt and Henry Fox, and not merely to secure their nominal services but to use their debating talents as well, was an achievement no other minister could parallel, and illustrates clearly Pelham's gift of political conciliation, particularly important when he came to concentrate on those changes of policy that he wished to implement.

Pelham's interests were largely domestic. Walpole had tried to insinuate his influences into every aspect of policy, but Pelham, sensing the strength perhaps of Newcastle and Hardwicke, the other members of the 'triumvirate', gave the impression of being uninterested in matters of foreign policy. Those he left largely to his elder brother, Newcastle, save when they impinged on domestic and particularly financial issues. An example of his assiduity in financial matters is illustrated by his record at the Treasury. Between 1743 and 1754 there were over 500 meetings of the Board of the Treasury of which Pelham missed only four. He had a clear policy for the finances. As early as 1748 he wrote to Newcastle:

'You know, I have had very little comfort in the great scene of business, I have long been engaged in. I have no court ambition, and very little interested views; but I was in hopes, by a peace being soon made, and by a proper economy in the administration of the government, afterwards, to have been the author of such a plan, as might, in time to come, have relieved this nation from the vast load of debt, it now labours

[11] Pelham to Newcastle, 18 May 1750. BM Add. MS 32720, f. 348.

[68]

under; and, even in my own time, had the satisfaction of demonstrating to the knowing part of the world, that the thing was not impossible. Here, I own, lay my ambition.'[12]

His ambition was to lower the rates of interest on government debts and reduce strictly government expenditure. Walpole had made an attempt at the former but had failed, fearing to lose support in the City of London. Pelham however had a broader base of support in the City, and indeed the events of 1746 had shown the confidence reposed in him by the City brokers. Above all, he had earlier secured the influential support of Sir John Barnard who had been the spokesman in 1737 of the City opposition. Pelham was therefore able in 1749 to propose that interest rates be reduced almost immediately from 4 per cent to $3\frac{1}{2}$ per cent and later to 3 per cent. It was this reduction of interest rates and consolidation of debt into two major categories that was to make possible the large-scale floating of loans and raising of taxes which marked the financing of the Seven Years War.

Pelham's management of the ordinary finances of the Crown was equally striking, even though in this he was often brought into conflict with Newcastle and the King. Their foreign policy involved large payments to various foreign princes, and although Pelham was prepared to acquiesce in its main lines he objected strongly to a continual paying out of subsidies, not only because it involved raising large sums of money but also because it offered opportunities for charges in Parliament that the ministers were following 'Hanoverian' measures. When Newcastle pressed him hard in 1750 on subsidy treaties with Bavaria and Saxony Pelham replied:

'The Civil List, you know, is much in debt . . . I have endeavoured to lessen the expenses at home as much as possible, and have succeeded as far as relates to my own Office, but a long series of uninterrupted extravagance to call it by no worse name, having got into all the great offices of the Kingdom, makes it very difficult, if not impracticable for the best intentioned to get the better of habit and custom.'[13]

Although he was prepared to spend money when it was needed – he never for example cut the Navy and Army expenditures to the low

[12] 4 Aug. 1748. BM Add. MS 32716, f. 13.
[13] 13 July 1750. BM Add. MS 32720, f. 355.

levels that Walpole permitted – Pelham insisted none the less on economy and reforms of procedures. His prudence, and his mastery of the Commons, were welcomed by George II, who in conversation with Newcastle compared Pelham's management of the finances very favourably with that of Sir Robert Walpole, who had 'managed the money matters very ill: he did not indeed give money abroad, but he gave it away liberally at home . . . with regard to money matters . . . your brother does that, understands that, much better.'[14]

Pelham's major difficulties came largely from the jealousies felt by his brother; Newcastle was reluctant to cede to him the premier place in the King's affairs, and particularly reluctant to leave entirely to Pelham detailed domestic affairs or election arrangements. Newcastle wrote to Hardwicke: 'He will do everything himself – he consults none of his friends – he neither has time or patience to give it all the attention, *alone*, that such a great undertaking does require, and things arise which he did not expect.'[15] There were indeed many differences between the two and not only on political issues. In 1744, for instance, Newcastle wrote angrily to Hardwicke of his brother's 'cruel behaviour' and threatened that he would 'break off all correspondence with my brother and his family'; this was at a time when the two were trying to oust Carteret from office. There were occasions when the only communication between the two was through Hardwicke, whose son later commented, 'I have heard him say – he was tired with carrying water between the br[other]s.'[16] On the other hand, despite all their differences, they realised the essential need to retain a unity of purpose and there was obviously very great affection between them. Any illness in one precipitated very anxious inquiries from the other, and Newcastle took tremendous pride in his brother's family. His substantial endowment of them has already been mentioned, and later he had his title recreated for the benefit of Pelham's eldest son-in-law.

Pelham's death came on the eve of the general election of 1754. His health had not been good during the previous winter, and he had gone to Scarborough to recuperate, but even so his death on 6 March 1754 came as a surprise to all and as a severe shock to Newcastle, who was sunk for several days in violent grief, unable and unwilling to attend to

[14] Newcastle to Pelham, 1 July 1752. Owen, *The Rise of the Pelhams*, pp. 319–20.
[15] 17 Oct. 1753. BM Add. MS 32733, f. 81.
[16] 14 Oct. 1744. Quoted in Philip C. Yorke, *The Life and Correspondence of Philip Yorke, Earl of Hardwicke* (Cambridge, 1913), i, 362–3.

any business at all. There were many comments on Pelham by contemporaries, almost all of whom pointed to his integrity in both public and private life. Horace Walpole, in words that have often been quoted, wrote that 'he lived without abusing his power, and died poor',[17] while Lord Chesterfield commented:

'Mr Pelham had good sense, without either shining parts or any degree of literature. He had by no means an elevated or enterprizing genius, but had a more manly and steady resolution than his brother the Duke of Newcastle. . . .

He was a very inelegant speaker in Parliament, but spoke with a certain candour and openness that made him well heard, and generally believed.

He wished well to the public, and managed the finances with great care and personal purity. He . . . had many domestic Virtues and no Vices. If his place, and the power that accompanies it, made him some public enemies, his behaviour in both secured him from personal and rancorous ones. Those who wished him worst, only wished themselves in his place.'[18]

But the most heartfelt comment came from the one man who had originally shown himself opposed to him. George II, who had gone to great lengths to keep Carteret instead of Pelham, lamented, 'Now I shall have no more peace.'[19] The truth of that was to become evident in his relations with Pelham's successors.

BIBLIOGRAPHY

Coxe, William, *Memoirs of the Administration of the Right Honourable Henry Pelham* (2 vols, London, 1829)
Nulle, S. H., *Thomas Pelham-Holles, Duke of Newcastle: His Early Political Career, 1693–1724* (Philadelphia, 1931)
Owen, J. B., *The Rise of the Pelhams* (London, 1957)
Walpole, Horace, *Memoirs of the Last Ten Years of the Reign of George II*, ed. Henry Fox, 3rd Lord Holland (2 vols, London, 1822; 2nd edn, 3 vols, London, 1847)
Wilkes, J. W., *A Whig in Power: The Political Career of Henry Pelham* (Northwestern University Press, 1964)

[17] Horace Walpole, *Memoirs of the Reign of George II*, i, 371.
[18] *Characters by Lord Chesterfield* . . . (London, 1778), pp. 39–40.
[19] H. Walpole, op. cit., i, 378.

4

THE DUKE OF NEWCASTLE

BY

H. T. DICKINSON

Thomas Pelham-Holles, born 21 July 1693, elder son of Thomas, 1st Baron Pelham, and Lady Grace Holles, sister of John Holles, Duke of Newcastle. Educated at Westminster School and Cambridge University. In 1711 added the name of Holles to that of Pelham on succeeding to the bulk of the estates of his uncle, the Duke of Newcastle. Created Earl of Clare on the accession of George I, and Duke of Newcastle in 1715 after raising a troop for service against the Pretender. Lord Chamberlain in the Stanhope–Sunderland administration 1717; Secretary of State 1724–54 under Walpole and Pelham; succeeded his younger brother as First Lord of the Treasury 1754–6 and also 1757–62; returned to office as Lord Privy Seal July 1765–August 1766. Died 17 November 1768. Married Lady Henrietta Godolphin. No issue.

THE DUKE OF NEWCASTLE

No eighteenth-century politician has left behind him such a wealth of detail about his career as the Duke of Newcastle and yet surprisingly little has so far been written about him. The sheer mass of his correspondence in the Newcastle and Hardwicke papers in the British Museum has no doubt daunted many would-be biographers, but it is also likely that many historians have been reluctant to spend years of their lives wading through the voluminous correspondence of a man who has become notorious for his fussiness and fretfulness, for his petty jealousy and his unwillingness to assume responsibility for any policy, and for his inability to pursue any political objective to his own satisfaction or to the nation's profit. Indeed, many of his contemporaries and most historians describe Newcastle as the epitome of unredeemed mediocrity, as a veritable buffoon in office. Horace Walpole, for example, condemned him for his excessive love of power when he lacked the ability to put such power to any constructive use: 'He was a Secretary of State without intelligence, a Duke without money, a man of infinite intrigue, without secrecy or policy, and a Minister despised and hated by his master, by all parties and Ministers, without being turned out by any!'[1] Lord Hervey was equally contemptuous of Newcastle's irresolution and dismissive of his weak understanding,[2] while Lord Waldegrave concluded: 'Talk with him concerning public or private business, of a nice or delicate nature, he will be found confused, irresolute, continually rambling from the subject, contradicting himself almost every instant.'[3]

The memoirs of Horace Walpole, Lord Hervey and Lord Waldegrave are among the most valuable and stimulating sources we have for the political events and characters of Newcastle's day. Their opinions have certainly influenced all later historians writing about this period.

[1] Horace Walpole, *Memoirs of the Reign of King George II*, ed. Lord Holland (1846), i, 166.
[2] John, Lord Hervey, *Some Materials Towards Memoirs of the Reign of King George II*, ed. Romney Sedgwick (1931), i, 209; ii, 344-5, 518; iii, 654-5, 949-50.
[3] James, Earl Waldegrave, *Memoirs from 1754 to 1758* (1821), p. 12.

The popular view of Newcastle is, in fact, largely based on the contemptuous opinions of him expressed by these three writers. There are, however, two important reasons why these sources should be handled with some caution. In the first place, all three of these writers were motivated by strong personal prejudice against Newcastle. And secondly, if their opinions are accepted without reservation, it becomes impossible to understand how Newcastle ever achieved high office let alone stayed in power for nearly forty years.

Horace Walpole bore a grudge against Newcastle because he was convinced that, when Secretary of State, he had betrayed his father, Sir Robert Walpole, and had helped to push him out of office. Lord Hervey hated Newcastle because he knew that in the 1730s he had opposed his own promotion to the office of Lord Privy Seal. Lord Waldegrave's political career had also been blighted by Newcastle. In 1757 Waldegrave was all set to rescue George II from the Devonshire-Pitt administration by agreeing to accept appointment as First Lord of the Treasury, but this scheme collapsed when Newcastle agreed to co-operate with William Pitt in a new administration and to fill this office himself. While these three political commentators were certainly motivated by personal antipathy towards Newcastle, it was probably not prejudice alone that blinded them to Newcastle's merits. He certainly betrayed many of the characteristics they lampooned so effectively, but they were not perceptive enough to see that Newcastle's irresolution, his hypochondria, his nervous twittering, and his inability to express himself with either clarity or conviction, obscured mundane, but genuine, talents.

Without such talents Newcastle would not have held office for so long. He was clearly not just an incompetent neurotic or simply a figure of fun. High offices were not given to him merely because he was a duke with a huge rent roll or because he was the patron of innumerable pocket boroughs. Wealth he certainly possessed, and he spent lavishly to further his political career, but money alone could not have bought him office and his personal electoral influence has usually been grossly exaggerated. Sir Lewis Namier has calculated that he could only nominate members for about twelve seats and even some of these had to be carefully nursed.[4] Much more important than Newcastle's personal electoral influence was his willingness to act as patronage manager

[4] Sir Lewis Namier, *The Structure of Politics at the Accession of George III*, 2nd edn. (1957), p. 9.

THE DUKE OF NEWCASTLE

for the whole government interest. His untiring and single-minded devotion to tedious and even dirty electoral business made him unique among important ministers of state. Newcastle was prepared to spend his time, his nervous energy, and his own fortune on the kind of work that other magnates and other ministers shirked. Sir Robert Walpole and Henry Pelham both relied upon him to put the Government's patronage to its best use in producing Parliaments amenable to their policies.

This steady application, rather than his persistent political intrigue at Court, is the most important explanation of Newcastle's success. His voluminous correspondence provides ample, though hardly eloquent, testimony to his sleepless, indefatigable attempts to make friends and influence people. Not content with the myriad tasks of a government election manager, he sought to engross other forms of patronage. As Secretary of State for twenty years and later as First Lord of the Treasury he controlled many appointments to minor offices. From the late 1730s he was also the most influential voice in ecclesiastical promotions and, in 1748, he secured his own election as Chancellor of Cambridge University so that he would have a few other rewards at his disposal. Most of the patronage Newcastle dispensed was, of course, the Crown's. His sovereign never gave him an entirely free hand, but, in the 1740s and 1750s, Newcastle was the chief link in the patronage system and the main channel through which preferments flowed. Anyone anxious to secure political or ecclesiastical preferment for himself, his relations or his dependants, knew that he must address his appeals to Newcastle.[5]

In part, Newcastle undertook such herculean drudgery because he hated to offend a possible supporter and because he constantly needed to be reassured that he was important and influential. But his labours also repaid handsome political dividends. He made himself indispensable

[5] For Newcastle's patronage system, see S. H. Nulle, 'The Duke of Newcastle and the Election of 1727', *Journal of Modern History*, ix (1937), 1–22; Basil Williams, 'The Duke of Newcastle and the Election of 1734', *English Historical Review*, xii (1897), 448–88; Mary Bateson, 'Clerical Preferment under the Duke of Newcastle,' ibid., vii (1892), 685–96; Norman Sykes, 'The Duke of Newcastle as Ecclesiastical Minister', ibid., lvii (1942), 59–84; Norman Sykes, *Church and State in England in the Eighteenth Century* (Cambridge, 1934); D. A. Winstanley, *The University of Cambridge in the Eighteenth Century* (Cambridge, 1922); Philip Haffenden, 'Colonial Appointments and Patronage under the Duke of Newcastle, 1724–39', *English Historical Review*, lxxviii (1963), 417–35.

[77]

to any ministry that desired a stable majority in Parliament. Robert Walpole, Henry Pelham and William Pitt all had greater talents and pursued more constructive policies, but they all came to recognise the value of Newcastle's assistance. Newcastle's critics, with their greater intelligence and superior wit, easily underrated him. They laughed at the fuss and bustle, and nicknamed him 'hubble bubble', but they overlooked the patient hours of labour that he devoted to politics. Lord Chesterfield was one of the few men of fashion who appreciated the key to Newcastle's success. He said of him: 'The public put him below his level: for though he had no superior parts, or eminent talents, he had a most indefatigable industry, a perseverance, a Court craft, and a servile compliance with the will of his sovereign for the time being.'[6]

Newcastle's main claim to fame was as a hardworking electioneer and manipulator of personal and political allegiances, but he was also a competent, if undistinguished, Secretary of State for thirty years. Though held in contempt by some men of wit and fashion, he was honest, generous and shrewd. His capacity for work and his ample store of sound common sense enabled him to bear his heavy official burdens with greater success than his harsh critics would allow. He was not only conscientious in the performance of his official duties; his grasp of what was essential to Britain's interests was quite sound. He fully realised that Britain's most important rival was France and that Britain needed a European ally to engage the larger French armies. This acceptance of a continental role for Britain was not just to safeguard Hanover and so win favour at Court, though Newcastle recognised that this was politically advisable. He was also aware that France could not exert her full power in a contest with Britain for naval and colonial supremacy if a considerable proportion of her forces were engaged in a European war. It must be admitted that, in seeking a counter-weight to France in Europe, Newcastle may have been too ready to spend lavishly to secure the dubious support of petty German princes and he may have adopted the wrong measures to re-establish friendly relations with Austria, but his basic objective was far from foolish. Indeed, it could be argued that Newcastle was a better Secretary of State than any of the politicians who held the other secretaryship in the 1730s and 1740s. Carteret's foreign policy was more brilliant, but it was also widely regarded in Parliament as being more dangerous and

[6] Cited by Sir Lewis Namier, *England in the Age of the American Revolution*, 2nd edn (1961), p. 67.

expensive. Newcastle's chief mistake, in fact, was to concentrate too exclusively on protecting British interests. He therefore failed to appreciate how the other major powers viewed the European situation. Nevertheless, William Pitt, the greatest critic of his foreign policy, eventually admitted the wisdom of fighting France in Europe in order to distract her from the war in the colonies. The two men shared the same objective, but Newcastle lacked Pitt's consummate ability in pursuing it.[7]

While seeking to defend Newcastle from some of the indiscriminate criticisms that have been levelled against him, and while recognising that Newcastle's long tenure as Secretary of State was not undeserved, it must be acknowledged that Newcastle lacked the essential requirements of an able Prime Minister. He was an able subordinate to a first minister with the abilities of Robert Walpole, Henry Pelham or William Pitt, but he was incapable of leading a ministry himself, particularly in times of stress and war. His talents were essentially second-rate. He was prepared to devote his life to trifling details, but he could rarely devise or implement a coherent political strategy. Throughout his political career he relied on the strength and advice of abler men. After more than forty years in office he still sought the advice of his great friend and confidant, the Earl of Hardwicke, on how to reply to the Town Clerk of Bristol when the freedom of that city was bestowed on him in 1760.[8] It was this kind of constant demand for help, advice and reassurance that made him appear a fool to many of his contemporaries. It led Lord Waldegrave, this time fairly, to observe: 'Upon the whole, he seems tolerably well qualified to act a second part, but wants both spirit and capacity to be first in command: neither has he the smallest particle of that elevation of mind, or of that dignity of behaviour, which command respect, and characterise the great statesman.'[9] Thus, by a lifetime of hard work and intrigue, Newcastle eventually rose to a post, that of Prime Minister, for which he was eminently unsuited by temperament or ability. Nor was he happy in the role until he had handed over

[7] For a defence of Newcastle's foreign policy, see Reed Browning, 'The Duke of Newcastle and the Imperial Election Plan, 1749–54', *Journal of British Studies*, vii (1967), 28–47, and the introduction to *British Diplomatic Instructions*, vol. vii, 'France', part iv, '1745–89', ed. L. G. Wickham Legg (Camden Society, 1934), vol. xlix.
[8] Namier, op. cit., p. 71.
[9] James, Earl Waldegrave, *Memoirs*, p. 14.

real responsibility to his masterful Secretary of State, William Pitt.

For some thirty years, from 1724 to 1754, Newcastle held high office without having to assume responsibility for the ministry's policies and without having to map out a coherent political strategy. During these years Robert Walpole and Henry Pelham strove, not with complete success since Newcastle was jealous of power and was not above conspiring against his mentor or his brother, to restrict Newcastle to his vital but subordinate role in the Government. It was not until after Henry Pelham's death, on 6 March 1754, that Newcastle was in a position to lead the ministry. His conduct on the death of his brother was a mixture of pathetic, even comical, grief[10] and a ruthless determination to outmanoeuvre his rivals in the scramble to fill the vacant post of First Lord of the Treasury. After the long careers of Walpole and Pelham, who had made it appear essential for the Prime Minister to sit in the Commons in order to manage votes of supply and win general approval for the Government's policies, many commentators expected that the post of First Lord of the Treasury would be filled by one of the three leading men in the lower house – Henry Fox, the Secretary at War, William Pitt, the Paymaster-General, or William Murray, the Solicitor-General. All three candidates, however, laboured under serious handicaps. Henry Fox was hated by Lord Chancellor Hardwicke, because of his earlier hostility to the latter's famous Marriage Act, and disliked by the Scottish members and the Leicester House faction because of his connection with the Duke of Cumberland. An able debater and an experienced politician, Fox was, nevertheless, widely distrusted by the independent backbenchers because of his lack of political principles and his unconcealed desire to line his own pockets. William Pitt was an even greater orator and had a greater capacity for carrying through a difficult undertaking. He was also more honest and more popular on the back benches, but he suffered from bad health which frequently kept him away from the Commons, he lacked the backing of a major Whig connection and, worst of all, he was hated by George II for his frequent disparaging remarks about Hanover, which he had once described as 'that despicable little Electorate'. William Murray, the third candidate, was an able debater and a first-class lawyer, but he was a Scotsman, suspected by some of harbouring Jacobite sympathies, and he lacked the determination and political cou-

[10] See *The Letters of Horace Walpole*, ed. Mrs Paget Toynbee (Oxford, 1903), iii, 220: to Richard Bentley, 17 Mar. 1754.

rage to bear the heat of constant parliamentary battles. Since none of these three candidates had an overwhelming claim to succeed Henry Pelham and each of them was ready to oppose the advancement of one of the others, Newcastle hoped to secure the support of all three while keeping them all in subordinate positions within the ministry.[11]

Within a week of his brother's death Newcastle had outmanoeuvred his rivals within the ministry. He and Hardwicke were able to persuade the King to appoint him to the vacant post of First Lord of the Treasury, the most important office in the Government. While his appointment shows that George II preferred him to any of the other candidates for this office, it did not mean that Newcastle enjoyed the full confidence of the King. George II was used to Newcastle and feared him less than he did Pitt or Fox, but he did not hold him in high esteem. Newcastle's position at Court was not as secure as Walpole's and Pelham's had been. In the Commons, it was much weaker. He was sufficiently well versed in the realities of eighteenth-century politics, however, to realise that it would not be easy to lead the ministry from the Lords. He recognised that, unlike Walpole or Pelham before him, he would need not only a Chancellor of the Exchequer to steer his financial measures through the Commons, but a 'Leader of the House' to manage both the Court and Treasury party and the independent backbenchers. Since various colonial disputes with France were threatening to erupt into a full-scale war, the task of managing the Commons could only be performed by a consummate politician. It was to prove impossible to find a man of such outstanding gifts, who was prepared to play second fiddle to the Duke of Newcastle.

The task of explaining to the Commons the technical details of Treasury affairs was entrusted to Henry Bilson Legge, a competent, if uninspired, Chancellor of the Exchequer, but Newcastle could not find an able, yet docile, Leader of the House. He first approached Henry Fox with the offer of the post of Secretary of State and the responsibility of managing the Commons. Despite making these concessions, he insisted on reserving to himself the sole dispensation of secret service money, which was already being lavishly spent on the forthcoming general election. Fox was at first willing to accept this arrangement, but

[11] ibid., iii, 216–17: to Horace Mann, 7 Mar. 1754; H. Walpole, *Memoirs of the Reign of King George II*, i, 381–7; and P. C. Yorke, *The Life and Correspondence of Philip Yorke, Earl of Hardwicke* (Cambridge, 1913), ii, 206–8: Hardwicke to the Archbishop of Canterbury, 11 Mar. 1754.

he soon broke off negotiations when he discovered that Newcastle intended to manage the general election himself and to control all nominations to places in the reconstructed administration.[12] If Newcastle retained full control of all this Crown patronage and refused to let Fox have some say in how it should be dispensed, then the latter would appear to be the Leader of the Commons in name only. Fox would bear the most important responsibility within the ministry without controlling the means to gratify those he might need to win over to the ministry's side by the judicious award of a place, pension or favour. Newcastle evidently wanted his services without being ready to pay the market price for them.

Fox was naturally dissatisfied with Newcastle's behaviour, but he remained Secretary at War. Pitt, on the other hand, was furious at the way in which he had been passed over in the promotion stakes in favour of men of inferior ability. After Fox had refused the post of Secretary of State, Newcastle turned to Sir Thomas Robinson, a diplomat of little talent and a politician of negligible importance. Newcastle took refuge in the not unreasonable excuse that the King refused to countenance the appointment of Pitt to a position that would bring him into constant attendance at Court, but Pitt complained that Newcastle had not tried hard enough to remove George II's prejudice against him. Thus Newcastle found himself opposed in the Commons by its two most able members, Pitt and Fox, though they both continued to hold minor offices in the administration. Within days of assuming the office of Prime Minister, Newcastle found himself unable to impose his authority on his ministerial colleagues and saw his decisions challenged by his own subordinates. To answer their criticisms, particularly of his foreign policy, Newcastle had to rely on Legge, Robinson and William Murray, who was promoted to Attorney-General. Even when acting in concert these three were not a match for the combined talents of Pitt and Fox. While Newcastle monopolised Crown patronage and yet failed to pursue a clear policy, his subordinates, bereft of power and direction, gradually lost control of the Commons.

In exceptionally favourable circumstances Newcastle's ministry might have limped along for some time without coming to grief, especially as the general election of 1754 returned a Parliament to Newcastle's satisfaction. It was, after all, never easy, even for politicians with the talents of Pitt and Fox, to persuade the independent back-

12 *The Letters of Horace Walpole*, iii, 219–20: to Richard Bentley, 17 Mar. 1754.

benchers to defeat a ministry that enjoyed the confidence of the King. In 1754, however, it was clear to all that Britain was drifting close to war with France, both in India and North America, while all the major powers of Europe were desperately seeking reliable allies in case of a general conflagration. News of the French victory over Washington on the Ohio, in July 1754, forced the Government to consider sending reinforcements to the American colonies. Newcastle feared to take strong retaliatory action because he dreaded assuming responsibility for provoking France, but he was not strong enough to resist the demands at home that he should respond to the French threat. His half-hearted measures failed to deter France or to satisfy opinion at home. He failed to urge the fleet under Admiral Boscawen to make every effort to destroy the French reinforcements ordered to Canada, and he supplied General Braddock with an inadequate expeditionary force to push back the French forces on the Ohio. As a result, Admiral Boscawen only managed to intercept two French frigates, while the impetuous General Braddock was defeated and killed by the French in April 1755.[13]

There is some justification for Newcastle's hesitant and ambiguous orders to Boscawen, and later to Hawke, for he feared being irrevocably committed to a war with France until he had built up a powerful network of alliances in Europe. His basic aim was sound. He wanted to deter France from attacking Hanover and to persuade her to fight a colonial war, where she would be at some disadvantage because of Britain's naval superiority, or, if France waged a continental war, to have enough support in Europe to tie down a great part of the French army. Newcastle proved incapable, however, of building up a strong system of continental alliances. The Dutch were anxious to avoid war at all costs, while the Austrians were hoping to effect a *rapprochement* with France in order to concentrate their attentions on Prussia. Newcastle was able to negotiate expensive subsidy treaties with Bavaria, Saxony and Hesse, but he needed the support of a more powerful ally. In September 1755 he arranged a treaty with Russia, whereby 55,000 Russian troops were to be held in readiness in case Hanover was attacked. Then, quite illogically, he began to negotiate with Prussia for the neutralisation of Germany, which would have prevented the Russians marching to the aid of Hanover if she were in fact attacked. Thus, by trying to hold too many cards at once, Newcastle helped to

[13] T. W. Riker, 'The Politics behind Braddock's Expedition', *American Historical Review*, xiii (1907–8), 742–52.

set in train the diplomatic revolution by which Austria and France were driven together and Britain was eventually forced to accept the offer of Prussian support.[14]

Newcastle's fear of provoking France and his failure to build up a continental alliance system which would deter her, drew increasing criticism upon his administration and exposed the weakness of its leadership in the Commons. He was soon forced to admit that he could not afford to continue without the full support of either Pitt or Fox. As early as January 1755 Fox had been partially accommodated by the offer of a seat on the Cabinet council, but Newcastle was well aware that Pitt was the more dangerous critic of his policies and that he had greater influence with the independent backbenchers. His renewed negotiations with Pitt broke down, however, when it became clear that the King was still opposed to his promotion to Cabinet office and Pitt refused to support policies that he had no hand in shaping. Newcastle could only have made terms with Pitt if he had risked his influence at Court by bullying the King into submission, and had also agreed to give up some of his power so that Pitt could influence the ministry's policies and act as its leader in the Commons. He was not prepared to do either until worsening circumstances really did force his hand.

It was only when Legge, the Chancellor of the Exchequer, embarrassed his ministerial colleagues by opposing the Hessian subsidy as wasteful, and Pitt attacked the Government's whole system of subsidy treaties, that Newcastle conceded that he must strengthen the ministry in the Commons. Since Fox was now prepared to be satisfied with Cabinet office and a degree of influence over the dispensation of Crown patronage, whereas Pitt wanted to dictate the Government's policies, Newcastle at last came to terms with the former. In November 1755 he agreed to make Fox both Secretary of State, in place of Sir Thomas Robinson, and Leader of the Commons. On 20 November both Pitt and Legge were dismissed from office. This decision freed Pitt from any inhibition about attacking the ministry's policies. He lashed the subsidy treaties as designed entirely for the preservation of Hanover and as an impracticable and desperate project which would ruin the country. The

---

[14] For Newcastle's foreign policy in these years, see Basil Williams, *Carteret and Newcastle* (Cambridge, 1943), chap. 10; and D. B. Horn, 'The Diplomatic Revolution', in *Cambridge Modern History* (Cambridge, 1957), vii, 440–64, and 'The Duke of Newcastle and the Origins of the Diplomatic Revolution', in *The Diversity of History*, ed. J. H. Elliott and H. G. Koenigsberger (1970), pp. 247–68.

fierceness of this attack alarmed and intimidated most of the ministerial spokesmen in the Commons. Fox had the courage to stand up to him, but he could not frame a policy that would answer Pitt's criticisms.[15]

Newcastle had not conceded enough power to Fox for the latter to control the Government's policy and he himself still failed to give a clear lead to his subordinates. Far from heeding Pitt's advice to concentrate his attention solely on the developing colonial conflict with France, he continued to worry about the safety of Hanover. In January 1756 he negotiated an agreement with Prussia to keep all foreign troops out of Germany. Newcastle believed that this would secure Hanover against French aggression and free Britain from the need to fight on the Continent, but this piece of improvisation soon recoiled on his head. The Russians believed that it ran counter to the aims of the subsidy treaty negotiated in 1755, while the Austrians and French were encouraged to sink their long-standing differences in the face of Anglo-Prussian friendship. Newcastle's plan for a vast system of continental allies against France completely collapsed and he was left only with the chance of forging a more effective treaty with Frederick II of Prussia.

A major colonial confrontation with France had meanwhile become ever more likely, but Newcastle still feared to take the responsibility for declaring war, despite Fox's suggestion that Britain should strike the first telling blow. When Newcastle did finally agree to declare war, in May 1756, he had still not ensured that adequate preparations were made for the conflict. Instead, fearing that France might launch a sudden invasion, Newcastle humiliated the nation by hurrying over Hessian and Hanoverian troops because the country was not in a position to defend itself. France was then given the opportunity to take advantage of Britain's preoccupation with the threat of invasion to send an expedition against Minorca. When Admiral Byng, sent out rather belatedly to relieve Minorca, failed to save the island, an angry and alarmed public rallied to Pitt and condemned the Newcastle administration. The loss of Oswego in North America, the alliance signed by the

---

[15] For the failure to win over Pitt and Pitt's criticisms of Newcastle's foreign policy, see Yorke, *The Life and Correspondence of Philip Yorke, Earl of Hardwicke*, ii, 230-2, 237-42: Hardwicke to Newcastle, 9 Aug. 1755 and Newcastle to Hardwicke, 3 Sept. 1755; and *The Letters of Horace Walpole*, ed. Mrs Paget Toynbee, iii, 365-67: to Henry Seymour Conway, 15 Nov. 1755.

French and Austrians, and the Prussian invasion of Saxony which precipitated a vast continental war, threw the Government into a mood of despair and confusion.

Newcastle sought to escape responsibility for these disasters. When a deputation from the City of London made representations to him about Admiral Byng's failure to save Minorca, the Prime Minister apparently blurted out: 'Oh! indeed he shall be tried immediately – he shall be hanged directly.'[16] Byng was, in fact, subsequently executed for dereliction of duty, but the public as much as Newcastle desired to see him sacrificed. Nevertheless, Newcastle's attempts to avoid, or at least to share, the blame for recent disasters only encouraged his subordinate ministers to push the responsibility back onto his shoulders. With some justification, they believed that Newcastle should take the blame for these failures since, for the last two years, he had sought to avoid sharing power with his ministerial colleagues. Ministers who had been unable to shape government policy were not now prepared to face the violent public reaction to recent events and a House of Commons which was demanding searching inquiries into the whole conduct of the war. In October 1756 William Murray, seeing his chance to escape the savage criticisms of Pitt, insisted on being promoted to the vacant post of Lord Chief Justice, thus removing himself to the Lords as Earl of Mansfield. At the same time Fox deserted the ministry altogether and resigned as Secretary of State. Without able defenders in the Commons and now fully exposed to public and parliamentary censure, Newcastle's nerve cracked. On 26 October 1756 he too resigned. His fall was not due to the loss of his majority in the Commons, but to the absence of able supporters to answer the criticisms of Pitt and to deflect the wrath of the public.

Newcastle's two years as Prime Minister showed that he lacked the capacity to devise and implement effective policies to meet a crisis situation or to delegate power and responsibility to ministerial colleagues who might have been able to perform such tasks. The very office of prime minister suffered from Newcastle's brief tenure of supreme power. Not only was he himself unable to take over the role and mantle of Robert Walpole and Henry Pelham, but he made sure that no other politician could assume such power. Pitt at last became Secretary of State when Newcastle resigned in 1756, under the nominal

16 H. Walpole, *Memoirs of the Reign of King George II*, ii, 231.

leadership of the Duke of Devonshire, but he was unable to construct a stable ministry capable of winning the war. It was widely recognised that the King would prefer the return of a Newcastle administration. Without favour at Court and with most ambitious politicians and placemen still looking to Newcastle as the chief source of Crown patronage, Pitt therefore could not count upon the backing of the Court and Treasury party. Since the war was still going badly, Pitt was not in a position to rally enough independent backbenchers to him either. Only after Pitt reluctantly agreed to join forces with Newcastle, in June 1757, did he find acceptance at Court and a secure majority in Parliament.

In this new administration Newcastle was once more First Lord of the Treasury and so, perhaps, nominally Prime Minister. In reality, however, he did not wield such power. There can be no doubt that William Pitt was the guiding force in the Government. He alone relished responsibility, had a clear idea of how he wished to conduct the war against France, and had the energy and capacity to push through his plans. Nevertheless, it would be unfair to regard Newcastle as a mere cypher in this great war administration which led Britain to victory over France. His task was not merely to manage elections and to dispense Crown patronage, as his critics have too often asserted. The Seven Years War was, after all, the most expensive conflict Britain had yet experienced. As First Lord of the Treasury Newcastle, with the assistance of Henry Legge, who served once more as his Chancellor of the Exchequer, had to provide the vast sums needed to finance Pitt's world-wide campaigns. In 1757 the Government had only to raise about £8½ million, but by 1759 this had increased to £12¾ million and, two years later, to a staggering £19½ million. Such huge sums could not be raised by taxation alone, although the major sources of supply – the Land Tax, the Malt Tax, and a variety of customs and excise duties – were all increased. Newcastle feared the political reaction to more radical proposals to increase taxation and so he resorted to large-scale borrowing instead. As a result, the National Debt more than doubled during the war. To borrow such huge sums the Treasury had to be on excellent terms with the financial interest in the City of London. It was in this sphere that Newcastle showed his great value to the Government. He had always followed his brother's practice of forging a close association with the moneyed interest without alienating the important commercial interest. Without Newcastle, Pitt might have had considerable difficulty in finding the money to finance his military and naval operations.[17]

Newcastle could have exploited his political power as First Lord of the Treasury more effectively, especially as he still retained greater influence with George II than Pitt, but he allowed himself to be over-ruled by Pitt in most conflicts of opinion. Even then, it would be an over-simplification to regard Pitt as the sole mind and voice of the administration. His was certainly the most influential voice in all deliberations upon strategy, but the Government was guided by an inner Cabinet composed of Newcastle, Hardwicke and Holderness, besides Pitt himself. Pitt did manage to reduce Holderness, the other Secretary of State, to a subordinate position, but he could not control his other Cabinet colleagues or dictate to the various heads of departments. Hardwicke still drafted the King's Speech for the opening of each session[18] and he and other lawyers helped to defeat Pitt's projected Habeas Corpus Bill. Pitt certainly bullied the timorous Newcastle and, on occasion, interfered with his running of Treasury business,[19] but most of the time he was content to let Newcastle run his own department in his own way. It has also been shown that Pitt was never able to dictate to the Admiralty and overrule Admiral Anson, the First Lord.[20] It therefore seems that there was no real prime minister in these years and little in the way of Cabinet government. Each department was directly responsible to the King and there was relatively little inter-ference by any ministers, even Pitt, in the day-to-day running of other departments. At times, in fact, there was no effective liaison between ministers and many messages had to be carried by Count de Viry, the Sardinian minister at the Court of St James.[21] It must be admitted, how-ever, that Pitt drew up the magnificent war plans and did most to put

[17] For Newcastle's financial policy, see Reed Browning, 'The Duke of Newcastle and the Financial Management of the Seven Years War in Germany', *Journal of the Society of Army Historical Research*, xlix (1971), 20–35; and Lucy Sutherland, 'The City of London and the Devonshire-Pitt Administration, 1756–7', *Proceedings of the British Academy*, xlvi (1960), 164 and 171–3.

[18] *Correspondence of William Pitt, Earl of Chatham*, ed. W. S. Taylor and J. H. Pringle (1838), i, 448: Newcastle to Pitt, 3 Nov. 1759.

[19] ibid., i, 305–8: Pitt to Newcastle, 4 April 1758, and Newcastle's reply, 5 April 1758.

[20] Richard Middleton, 'Pitt, Anson and the Admiralty, 1756–61', *History*, lv (1970), 199–206.

[21] Namier, *England in the Age of the American Revolution*, p. 81.

them into effect. Nevertheless, he depended more on his ministerial colleagues, particularly Newcastle, than has generally been recognised. Newcastle was once more at his best, playing a vital subordinate role to a great minister.

Thus, whether he liked it or not, Newcastle had to be content to play second fiddle to Pitt in the last years of George II's reign. On the accession of George III, in 1760, he found that his political influence was curtailed even further. George III had been convinced for some years that Newcastle was nothing but a knave and he was anxious to remove him and most of the 'Old Whigs' from office as soon as possible. He had no desire to be bullied by Pitt either, and so he planned to replace him as the leading voice in the ministry by his favourite, the Earl of Bute, as soon as a suitable opportunity should present itself. His plan to purge his ministry of his grandfather's advisers had to hang fire, however, until the war had been clearly won. It would be difficult to remove such a successful team of ministers until it was clear that they had become dispensable. In the meantime, George III took Crown patronage out of Newcastle's hands and appointed Bute as Pitt's fellow Secretary of State. Both he and Bute also skilfully played upon the petty jealousies and disputes of Newcastle and Pitt so that they would not unite in opposition to their plans for the piecemeal reconstruction of the administration. This policy worked only too well, particularly as Newcastle and Pitt began to disagree about the future conduct of the war. Pitt was anxious to expand the war in order to attack Spain before she could ally with France, whereas Newcastle, alarmed at the enormous and spiralling cost of the war, was anxious to negotiate peace as soon as possible. When Pitt resigned on this issue, in October 1761, Bute replaced him with the Earl of Egremont and chose George Grenville as Leader of the Commons. Newcastle was now virtually isolated in the Cabinet and was treated with scant respect by both the King and his ministerial colleagues. Bute was now the real head of the ministry, though Newcastle remained First Lord of the Treasury with the unenviable task of continuing to raise huge sums of money. He could not even count upon the support of his own subordinates at the Treasury. These men recognised that Newcastle could no longer further their careers and so they deserted him to worship the rising sun at Court. Newcastle still clung pathetically to office until he at last discovered this treachery and acknowledged that he had lost all influence at Court and in the Cabinet. When he failed to persuade the Cabinet to continue paying the annual subsidy to Prussia, he finally resigned, on 26 May 1762.[22]

Newcastle had enjoyed a political career of unprecedented length and, in recent years, he had experienced many weary battles with his ministerial colleagues, but he was still reluctant to retire from active politics. He continued to entertain hopes of returning to power, either in alliance with Pitt or with the support of the younger Whigs who resented the ascendancy of Bute. His only weapon against Bute's Court influence, however, was the dubious support of his former political allies who were still in office. When, in November 1762, he asked them to resign so that he could demonstrate his power to the Government, he found that half of those he approached would not desert the Court in order to follow him into the political wilderness. Just in case Newcastle did not now appreciate his lack of power and influence, the ministry decided, in December 1762, to dismiss from office all those friends and dependants of Newcastle who could not be trusted to support the Government's peace negotiations. Newcastle was now to learn that the patronage he had dispensed for decades was not his to control. The real source of patronage was the Crown and yet Newcastle had expected men still in office and place to look to him for direction and not to the Court. Now he discovered that the Court was prepared to dismiss even minor office holders in the revenue service simply because they owed their first appointment to Newcastle's influence. This 'Massacre of the Pelhamite Innocents' finally convinced the political world that Newcastle's day was over and that a new power reigned at Court. Newcastle had witnessed, and, in part, had assisted in, the destruction of the prime minister's office as it had existed in the days of Robert Walpole and Henry Pelham. Now his opponents were dismantling the patronage system he had created with such loving care.

BIBLIOGRAPHY

(The place of publication is London unless otherwise stated.)

The nearest approach to a biography is Basil Williams, *Carteret and Newcastle* (Cambridge 1943). Newcastle's early life is covered by Stebelton H. Nulle, *Thomas Pelham-Holles, Duke of Newcastle: His Early Political Career, 1693–1724* (Philadelphia 1931). There are a number of articles covering certain aspects of Newcastle's career, including Philip Haffenden, 'Colonial Appointments and Patronage

[22] For a study of Newcastle's relations with Bute, 1760–2, see Namier, op. cit., chapters 2 and 5.

under the Duke of Newcastle, 1724–39', *English Historical Review* (1963); S. H. Nulle, 'The Duke of Newcastle and the Election of 1727', *Journal of Modern History* (1937); Basil Williams, 'The Duke of Newcastle and the Election of 1734', *English Historical Review* (1897); Mary Bateson, 'Clerical Preferment under the Duke of Newcastle', EHR (1892); Norman Sykes, 'The Duke of Newcastle as Ecclesiastical Minister', EHR (1942); Reed Browning, 'The Duke of Newcastle and the Imperial Election Plan, 1749–54', *Journal of British Studies* (1967); D. B. Horn, 'The Duke of Newcastle and the Origins of the Diplomatic Revolution', in *The Diversity of History*, ed. J. H. Elliott and H. G. Koenigsberger (1970); T. W. Riker, 'The Politics behind Braddock's Expedition', *American Historical Review* (1907–8); Reed Browning, 'The Duke of Newcastle and the Financial Management of the Seven Years War in Germany', *Journal of the Society of Army Historical Research* (1971); and Reed Browning, 'The Duke of Newcastle and the Financing of the Seven Years War', *Journal of Economic History* (1971). There is a detailed study of one aspect of Newcastle's career in James Henretta, *Salutary Neglect: Colonial Administration under the Duke of Newcastle* (Princeton 1972) and of the Duke's personal finances in Ray A. Kelch, *Newcastle: A Duke without money* (1974).

The hundreds of volumes of Newcastle letters among the Newcastle and Hardwicke papers in the British Museum have never been exhaustively quarried by any student of the Duke. These letters have been extensively used and much quoted, however, in William Coxe, *Memoirs of the Life and Administration of Sir Robert Walpole* (3 vols, 1798); William Coxe, *Memoirs of the Administration of Henry Pelham* (2 vols, 1829); John B. Owen, *The Rise of the Pelhams* (1957); Philip C. Yorke, *The Life and Correspondence of Philip Yorke, Earl of Hardwicke* (3 vols, Cambridge 1913); and in Sir Lewis Namier's two brilliant studies, *The Structure of Politics at the Accession of George III* (2nd edn, 1957), and *England in the Age of the American Revolution* (2nd edn, 1961).

There are a number of biographies of Newcastle's major contemporaries, including J. H. Plumb, *Sir Robert Walpole* (2 vols, 1956, 1960); H. T. Dickinson, *Walpole and the Whig Supremacy* (1973); John W. Wilkes, *A Whig in Power*, a biography of Henry Pelham (Northwestern University Press 1964); Basil Williams, *The Life of William Pitt, Earl of Chatham* (2 vols, 1913); Brian Tunstall, *William Pitt, Earl of Chatham* (1938); and T. W. Riker, *Henry Fox, First Lord Holland* (2 vols, Oxford 1911).

There is a great deal about Newcastle in the major printed primary sources for this period. Particularly worth mentioning are *Some Materials Towards Memoirs of the Reign of King George II*, by John, Lord Hervey, ed. Romney Sedgwick (3 vols, 1931); *Memoirs of the Reign of King George II*, by Horace Walpole, ed. Lord Holland (3 vols, 1846); Horace Walpole, *Memoirs of the Reign of King George III*, ed. Sir Denis Le Marchant (4 vols, 1845); *The Letters of Horace Walpole*, ed. Mrs Paget Toynbee (16 vols, Oxford 1903); *Memoirs from 1754 to 1758*, by James, Earl Waldegrave (1821); *The Political Journal of George Bubb Dodington*, ed. John Carswell and L. A. Dralle (Oxford 1965); *Letters from George III to Lord Bute, 1756–66*, ed. Romney Sedgwick (1939); *Correspondence of William Pitt, Earl of Chatham*, ed. W. S. Taylor and J. H. Pringle (4 vols, 1838); *Correspondence of John, Fourth Duke of Bedford*, ed. Lord John Russell (3 vols, 1842–6); and *The Grenville Papers*, ed. W. J. Smith (4 vols, 1852–3).

5

THE DUKE
OF DEVONSHIRE

BY

G. M. D. HOWAT

William Cavendish, born 1720, eldest son of William Cavendish, 3rd Duke of Devonshire, and Catherine Hoskins, daughter of John Hoskins. Known as the Marquis of Hartington until his father's death in 1755. Married 1748 Charlotte Boyle, Baroness Clifford (died 1754). Four children, the eldest of whom, William (1748–1811) became the 5th Duke. Whig MP for Derbyshire 1741–51; summoned to the House of Lords in his father's barony of Cavendish June 1751; PC; Lord Lieutenant of Ireland 1755–Oct. 1756; First Lord of the Treasury, Nov. 1756–July 1757; Lord Chamberlain 1757–62; Lord High Treasurer of Ireland until his death on 3 October 1764. KG 1756.

THE DUKE OF DEVONSHIRE

Devonshire was a man whose personal character won universal approval from his contemporaries, and whose political qualities secured modest approval from most of them. To Horace Walpole he was a fashionable model of goodness, to Lord Hardwicke a worthy man, to the Duke of Newcastle an honest gentleman, to George II a very good man. Lord Waldegrave, after suggesting he was better qualified for a court than politics, saw him as possessing the virtues of punctuality and diligence. The only stinging criticism came from Horace Walpole, who went on to say he had 'an impatience to do everything, a fear to do anything, always in a hurry to do nothing'.[1] Walpole had his own reasons for being less than fair to a supporter of the Duke of Newcastle, and Devonshire's career scarcely justifies the jibe. Historians, pausing for a moment to comment on Devonshire, have found him of 'stainless private character',[2] 'an honest neutral',[3] 'the honest broker'[4] and 'distinguished by unsullied uprighteousness and honour'.[5] These were nineteenth-century judgements. Modern historians have seen no reason to depart from them: 'an amiable, straightforward man of no particular parts'[6] and 'notable for common sense rather than statesmanship'.[7]

By background and connection William Cavendish could have been expected to make his career in politics. His family were constantly reminding the Hanoverians that they had conferred the Crown upon their ancestors – in common with other great eighteenth-century households. Cavendish's entry into the House of Commons, as Lord Harting-ton, on attaining his majority, was in accordance with the customs of the age. That entry coincided with the closing months of Sir Robert Walpole's tenure of office. The young man gave his support to the elder

[1] H. Walpole, *Memoirs of the Reign of King George II*, i, 170.
[2] See Lord Macaulay, *Essays*, v, 401 (1865 edn).
[3] F. Harrison, *Chatham*, p. 80.
[4] Lord Rosebery, *Chatham: His Early Life and Connections*, p. 343.
[5] See Sir Denis Le Marchant's editorial comment in H. Walpole, *Memoirs of the Reign of King George III*, ii, 21.
[6] Brian Tunstall, *William Pitt, Earl of Chatham*, p. 262.
[7] G. A. Sherrard, *Lord Chatham: Pitt and the Seven Years War*, p. 143.

statesman, canvassing for him in his last administration, and rebuking those 'shabby fellows' who were absent from the House when they might have been lending support.[8] Once Walpole had fallen, Hartington transferred his loyalties to the men who dominated politics in the last twenty years of George II's reign. Henry Pelham confided to the third Duke of Devonshire that his son was 'our mainstay among the young ones, of themselves liable to wander'.[9]

During the ten years in which he represented the 4,000 voters of Derbyshire, Hartington remained extremely loyal to the Pelhams, becoming a 'bigot to their faction',[10] and sharing with them the view that 'party' mattered in politics, an opinion that made relations with the rising William Pitt difficult. Hartington's opposition to Pitt in 1751 on the issue of whether or not to reduce the number of seamen was designed to indicate that Pitt could not expect Hartington's support if he deserted Pelham.

Just before Hartington left the Commons to enter the House of Lords in his father's barony of Cavendish, he had been offered – but declined – the post of tutor to the future George III. He took his seat in the Lords in June 1751, having already enhanced his political importance by the estates in Yorkshire, Derbyshire and Ireland which his marriage had brought him. The Irish connection, and his friendship with the Duke of Newcastle whom he strongly supported for the office of First Lord of the Treasury on the death of Henry Pelham in March 1754, led to his appointment to the lord-lieutenancy of Ireland in 1755. There his personal qualities made him popular at a time when the administration of his predecessor, the Duke of Dorset, had brought about a period of violence and dissension largely due to the claims of the Irish Parliament to dispose of its surplus money as it wished.

In Ireland, he was a good administrator. At the same time, he kept in touch with affairs in England through his correspondence with Henry Fox[11] and Newcastle.[12] It was the crisis in those affairs that brought him back to England in October 1756 to a nation hostile at Newcastle's conduct of the Seven Years War. He came as head of a great Whig

[8] W. Coxe, *Walpole*, i, 590.
[9] Quoted in Romney Sedgwick, *History of Parliament: the Commons, 1715–54*, p. 538.
[10] H. Walpole, *Memoirs of the Reign of King George II*, i, 160.
[11] Lord Waldegrave, *Memoirs*, p. 146ff.
[12] See Sir Lewis Namier, *England in the Age of the American Revolution*, p. 113.

family: his father had died on 5 December 1755. He found the Government shaken by events abroad and at home. Abroad, Frederick the Great had been successful in Saxony, and Minorca had been lost. On the colonial front Montcalm had captured Fort Oswego, and the French threatened the whole North American interest. From India had come news of the loss of Calcutta. At home, ministerial dissension was acute, and Newcastle himself came in for major criticism. Since he had been reluctant to confide in his colleagues in the opening months of the war, they abandoned him to the wrath of the House of Commons and, in particular, that of Pitt. Pitt, excluded from senior office in 1754, and dismissed from the paymastership in 1755, flayed the minister who had paid little attention to his views.

This, coupled with Fox's resignation from the secretaryship and public hostility, brought about Newcastle's resignation on 26 October 1756. Within two days George II had approached Fox, who was unable to form a ministry without Pitt's co-operation. On 28 October, the King saw Devonshire, while keeping the options open by seeing Pitt the same day. Five days later Devonshire commented that the King's manner grew softer, which only made 'the matter harder'.[13] Pitt's own ineligibility stemmed from several factors: his lack of influence, his opposition to Newcastle and the distaste in which he was held by George II. For the King, the problem lay in giving office to a politician of comparative experience, yet with the backing of a great family, in the face of strong men of ability who found it difficult to accept each other. In this perplexity he 'ordered the Duke of Devonshire to try to compose some ministry for him'.[14] Pitt himself commended the Duke for office,[15] and agreed to serve as Secretary of State. Devonshire, informing George that he felt at liberty to resign if he 'disliked the employment',[16] set about constructing a government. In practice, it was Pitt's word that counted: those who were advanced, advanced on his nomination. Thus, the appointment of Henry Legge as Chancellor of the Exchequer – when Devonshire preferred Fox – indicated Pitt's authority.

Nevertheless, Devonshire was now First Lord of the Treasury, the politician appointed to this office who was, at that moment, most likely

[13] W. S. Taylor and J. H. Pringle (eds), *Correspondence of William Pitt, Earl of Chatham*, i, 181.
[14] H. Walpole, *Memoirs of the Reign of King George II*, ii, 154.
[15] Lord Hardwicke, *Correspondence*, ii, 376.   [16] Waldegrave, op. cit., p. 86.

to be able to form an administration. Rosebery quaintly calls him 'prime minister under Pitt'.[17] He was in three senses 'prime minister': he was closest to the closet in November 1756, he commanded support from prospective members of the Government, he could manage Parliament.[18] This was the theory. In practice, Pitt, as everyone knew, would dictate policies. Yet Devonshire was no bad choice. Absence in Ireland absolved him from identification with the disasters of recent months, and he was ready to see himself as an intermediary with no grand ambitions for extended office. He was prepared to work with Pitt and make Pitt's ultimate accession to power the more possible. If only on grounds of age, Devonshire was to be reckoned with. He was thirty-six – the youngest man in the Government. Pitt was twelve years his senior. Men like Newcastle and Hardwicke, temporarily in the wilderness, were more than thirty years older.

Within three weeks the new Government had declared its policy in the war. Pitt's speech in the Commons thanked the King for his Hanoverian troops, a matter of concern and surprise to some of his colleagues. Devonshire's speech in the Lords echoed similar sentiments. Government policy over the war was vigorous. Increased Supply was obtained, troops sent to America and a Militia Bill passed.[19] Pitt and Devonshire were frequently in consultation, yet it would be absurd to doubt the realities of the situation. It was Pitt who summoned a Cabinet on 16 December to discuss the sending of troops to America. It was Pitt who wrote over eighty letters of importance on government affairs.[20] When Louisburg was captured by Amherst in July 1758, it was the culmination of plans laid by Pitt in the spring of 1757.

With one *cause célèbre* the Devonshire ministry was closely involved. Admiral Byng's failure to save Minorca had been contributory to Newcastle's fall. Byng was court-martialled in February 1757 and, under a recent change in the Articles of War, sentenced to death. It was a sordid affair involving too closely politics and the armed forces. Pitt sought in vain to save Byng's life. Devonshire, the nominal head of the ministry, was content to let events take their course.[21] It was Pitt's advocacy of

[17] Lord Rosebery, *Chatham: His Early Life and Connections*, p. 289.
[18] See J. P. Mackintosh, *The British Cabinet*, p. 54.
[19] For general comments on these events, see B. Williams, *Life of William Pitt*, i, 283ff.; Tunstall, *William Pitt*, pp. 161ff.
[20] Williams, op. cit., i, 314.
[21] H. Walpole, *Memoirs of the Reign of King George II*, ii, 179.

Byng's cause that contributed to his own resignation in April 1757. It had not improved his relations with George II and he was content to go – knowing he would soon be back. It left Devonshire leading 'a mutilated, enfeebled, half-formed system'.[22] He realised the time had come to leave office himself, acting in the handsomest manner in a disagreeable situation. He recognised that Pitt was the hero of the hour, on whom eighteen towns conferred their freedom. In May Devonshire helped Newcastle towards securing permission from George II to negotiate the forming of a new ministry. In June he was urging Lord Hardwicke, in letters on two consecutive days, to assist in setting up an administration 'to prevent king and country being undone' in the confusion.[23] In July, he resigned. The Pitt-Newcastle administration was reluctantly formed, charged with the business of winning the war.

There can be little doubt that Devonshire's tenure of the Treasury was a makeshift device. Great things had never been expected of him.[24] The ministry was handicapped by George II's relations with Pitt, then by Pitt's departure and, marginally, by Pitt's ill health before he left. To Walpole, the very cement seemed disjunctive: Devonshire was bound to offend one of two great men, Fox or Pitt. Devonshire lacked the influential patronage of Newcastle, if only by comparison with that wielded by the elder duke.[25] This affected the confidence he could command in the City.[26] He was far more than the 'baby politician' that Walpole labelled him in April 1757. But he was far less than the circumstances of the nation's policies demanded. He had been assiduous in attendance at the Lords while in office, and a busy committee man. They were insufficient qualifications.

Devonshire became Lord Chamberlain and so remained until 1762. The office itself cast him as a political supernumerary. Henceforth his political influence lay in his family standing and in his relations with Newcastle, which remained close for the rest of his life. With the death of George II in October 1760 both men moved into the category of the proud dukes of whom the new King was suspicious. Devonshire

[22] Hardwicke, *Correspondence*, ii, 407.   [23] Ibid., ii, 401.
[24] Waldegrave, *Memoirs*, p. 141.
[25] See Namier, *England in the Age of the American Revolution, passim* for comments on the political patronage of the period.
[26] See Lucy Sutherland, 'The City of London and the Devonshire-Pitt Administration', in *Proceedings of the British Academy*, xlvi (1960).

persuaded Newcastle not to resign despite the growing influence of the Earl of Bute who, by March 1761, had become Secretary of State. When political relations between Newcastle and Pitt were threatened later in the summer Devonshire did his best to act as intermediary.[27] By now he desperately wanted the war to end, hoping, as he wrote to Newcastle, some expedient might be found to prevent its continuance. His views changed somewhat when Pitt resigned in October 1761. He was disturbed at the failure of Bute and Newcastle to get on with each another, and he had doubts about the peace terms being considered by Bute in whose abilities he had little confidence. While he had concurred in the need for Pitt's resignation – over Spain – he was not optimistic about the alternatives.

But gradually Devonshire was to become a more isolated figure. When Newcastle at last left office, on 26 May 1762, on the issue of the Prussian subsidy, Devonshire (with Hardwicke) alone supported him. Five months later he himself ceased to be Lord Chamberlain and a Privy Councillor.

The circumstances of his dismissal were these: Devonshire had indicated after Newcastle's resignation that he would seldom or never attend Bute's Councils. In October George III wished him to attend a Cabinet Council to discuss the final terms of the peace, and Devonshire refused on the grounds that he was insufficiently informed on the subject. Shortly afterwards the King's coach overtook Devonshire's on the way to London. George assumed the Duke was coming 'to cabal against' him[28] and to resign office as a protest against the Government. Thus when Devonshire came to Court to take leave before going north to Chatsworth, George refused to see him, and dismissed him. A few days later, on 3 November, he himself erased Devonshire's name from the list of Privy Councillors.

The affair was blown up by George's critics. Newcastle told Hardwicke it was an affront upon one of rank,[29] and told the Marquis of Rockingham it was 'the most extraordinary thing' that had happened in any court in Europe.[30] In the King's defence it may be said that Devonshire was in a false position by retaining office and yet withdrawing from Councils. The King, always suspicious of faction, had a right to his advice. But the manner of Devonshire's dismissal indicated George III's sensitivity where the Whigs were concerned. The King's latest

[27] Hardwicke, op. cit., iii, 274.   [28] ibid., iii, 429.   [29] ibid., iii, 428.
[30] Lord Rockingham, *Memoirs*, i, 135.

biographer considers that no incident in his reign showed George in such a poor light.[31]

Subsequently Devonshire relinquished his lord-lieutenancy of Derbyshire in sympathy with Newcastle and Rockingham whom the King dismissed from theirs. He made one last major political gesture when his house in London was the scene of a dinner-party to plan the opposition to the Government's Cider Tax. This brought Devonshire and Pitt together, and contributed to Bute's resignation in April 1763. Thereafter, Devonshire withdrew from active politics, becoming the recipient of long letters from Newcastle. His last months were spent at Spa in Germany, in indifferent health. He died in October 1764, aged only forty-four.

Devonshire had been a moderate among men of great political passion. If scarcely a spectator in the play of events, he had never bestrode the stage. His death, coming just after those of Hardwicke and Legge, deprived the Whigs of three material men.[32] Given health, he might have returned to office in the Crown's restless pursuit of ministers up to 1770. He had been a man with a concern for king and country. He died the acknowledged leader of the Whigs.[33]

BIBLIOGRAPHY

The Duke of Devonshire is frequently mentioned in the printed primary sources for the eighteenth century. These include:

Correspondence of the 4th Duke of Bedford ed. Lord John Russell (3 vols, London, 1842–6)
Letters from George III to Lord Bute, ed. R. Sedgwick (London, 1939)
The Life and Correspondence of Philip Yorke, Earl of Hardwicke, ed. P. C. Yorke (3 vols, Cambridge, 1913)
Correspondence of William Pitt, Earl of Chatham, ed. W. S. Taylor and J. H. Pringle (4 vols, London, 1838)
Marquis of Rockingham's Memoirs, ed. Lord Albemarle (2 vols, London, 1852)
Memoirs of Earl Waldegrave, 1754–8 (London, 1821)
Memoirs of the Reign of King George II by Horace Walpole, ed. Lord Holland (3 vols, London, 1846)
Memoirs of the Reign of King George III by Horace Walpole, ed. Sir Denis Le Marchant (4 vols, London, 1845).

[31] John Brooke, *King George III*, p. 97.
[32] H. Walpole, *Memoirs of the Reign of King George III*, ii, 21.
[33] H. Walpole, op. cit., ii, 21; Rockingham, op. cit., i, 176.

Devonshire has been the subject of no biography but these biographies on William Pitt are useful in understanding his career:

Ruville, A. Von, *William Pitt, Earl of Chatham* (3 vols, London, 1907)
Sherrard, O. A., *Pitt and the Seven Years War* (London, 1955)
Tunstall, Brian, *William Pitt, Earl of Chatham* (London, 1938)
Williams, Basil, *The Life of William Pitt, Earl of Chatham* (2 vols, London, 1913)

The constitutional and political aspects of the period may be pursued in:

Christie, I. R., *Myth and Reality in Late Eighteenth-Century Politics* (London, 1970)
Foord A. S., *His Majesty's Opposition, 1714–1830* (Oxford, 1964)
Namier, Sir Lewis, *The Structure of Politics at the Accession of George III* (London, 1957 edn)
Namier, Sir Lewis, *England in the Age of the American Revolution*, 2nd edn (London, 1961 edn)
Pares, Richard, *King George III and the Politicians* (Oxford, 1953)

There is a brief summary of Devonshire's House of Commons career in:

Sedgwick, Romney, *History of Parliament: The Commons, 1715–54* (London, 1970)

The manuscript diary of the 4th Duke of Devonshire and his correspondence are in the Chatsworth collection.

6

THE EARL OF BUTE

BY

JOHN BREWER

John Stuart, 3rd Earl of Bute, born 25 May 1713, elder son of 2nd Earl of Bute and Lady Anne Campbell, daughter of 1st Duke of Argyll. Educated at Eton. Married Mary, daughter of the Hon. Edward Montague. Elected representative peer for Scotland 1737; admitted to the Privy Council 1760; Secretary of State 1761; First Lord of the Treasury 1762; KG 1762. Resigned office 1763. Died 10 March 1792.

THE EARL OF BUTE

John Stuart, third Earl of Bute (1713–92), held the post of First Lord of the Treasury for a mere eleven months. From 26 May 1762 until 8 April 1763 he was Prime Minister both in form and substance. Yet before as well as after his tenure of the highest political office, he could justly claim to have been the effective leader of the Government. The significance, therefore, of Bute's contribution to eighteenth-century political and constitutional development cannot be discerned simply by an examination of his brief and troubled administration. Rather the few months in which he officially led the nation have to be placed in the context of his entire political career.

Bute can best be described as a well-connected Scottish aristocrat. His family with its sound pedigree had long been allied both by marriage and in politics to the Whig overlords of Scotland, the Dukes of Argyll. Indeed with the death of the third Duke in April 1761, he inherited the Scottish patronage of the Argylls. Temperamentally Bute was not gifted with the qualities that make a successful politician. His early ally and subsequent opponent, Lord Shelburne, remarked of him:

'His bottom was that of any Scotch nobleman, proud, aristocratical, pompous, imposing. . . . He was insolent and cowardly, at least the greatest political coward I ever knew. He was rash and timid, accustom'd to take advice of different persons, but had not sense and sagacity to distinguish and digest, with a perpetual apprehension of being govern'd. . . . He was always on stilts. . . . He felt all the pleasure of power to consist either in punishing or astonishing.'[1]

This uncharitable description bears a semblance of truth. Bute, as Allan Ramsay's portrait of him so tellingly reveals, was both vain and aloof. Yet these qualities stemmed not from arrogance, but from the shyness of a man who had lived as a recluse, and who considered himself (with some justice) to be a scholar and an intellectual. Bute was

[1] Quoted in Sir Lewis Namier, *England in the Age of the American Revolution*, 2nd edn (London, 1961), p. 131.

always far happier classifying his botanical collection, patronising Scottish *literati*, or corresponding with antiquarians about the flora, fauna and economic development of his native Isle of Bute, than he was when he paced the corridors of power. (Throughout his political career he suffered from a gastric malady that was much more intimately connected with the workings of politics than with the workings of his own physiology.) The subtleties of political intrigue, the process of distributing 'loaves and fishes', and the rigours of attending to the 'eternal round of clashing business',[2] were all regarded with equal distaste by this stiff and mannered man. He was born to be a courtier, not a politician. The *bon mot* of his first patron, Frederick, Prince of Wales, captures Bute perfectly: 'Bute, you would make an excellent ambassador in some proud little Court where there is nothing to do.'[3]

Granted the personal indisposition of Bute towards high political office (an indisposition that he frequently admitted),[4] the question arises of how he came to assume such an exalted political station. His road to power was to some extent an unusual one. He rose not because of his political experience, his ability to command a personal following, nor because of his connection with the great Whig families, much less because of his skill in parliamentary debate. He achieved political honour through the Court and through personal favour. In this respect few careers better emphasise the potency of personal considerations in eighteenth-century politics.

In 1747, during a shower at Egham races, the fortuitous absence of a fourth player at cards drew Bute into the orbit of Frederick, Prince of Wales. For the next thirteen years Bute's career focused on the Court of the heir to the throne. After Frederick's untimely death in 1751, he became the confidant of the royal widow, Princess Augusta. This friendship (an intimacy that was subsequently elevated by Bute's enemies into a *mésalliance d'amour*) led in turn to Bute's unofficial appointment as the moral and intellectual preceptor of the young Prince of Wales, the future George III.

Bute very rapidly became much more than George's teacher: he became, to use the young Prince's own words, his 'dearest friend'. To a

[2] Bute to Campbell (16 June 1762 ?), Bute MSS, Mount Stuart. I wish to acknowledge the gracious permission of the Marquess of Bute to cite from these manuscripts.
[3] Horace Walpole, *Memoirs of the Reign of King George III*, ed. Sir Denis Le Marchant (4 vols, London, 1845), i, pp. 299-300.
[4] See, for instance, Bute to Campbell, 30 January 1763, Bute MSS.

quite remarkable degree Bute established a hold over the impressionable George. The Prince corresponded almost daily with his mentor, he was constantly in Bute's company, and imbibed his personal ideals and political principles from the Scottish Earl. Indeed, so great was Bute's influence in shaping the young man's mind that from about 1757 to 1763 it is almost (though not completely) impossible to distinguish the political views of George and his favourite.[5]

The political attitudes that Bute nourished in the young King can best be seen as an amalgam of the political views and analyses of Leicester House (the opposition Court of George II's reign) and the precepts of 'country party ideology'. In the field of foreign policy this composite political creed was to some degree isolationist and pusillanimous. Bute opposed Britain's involvement with continental connections during the Seven Years War, and condemned the influence of George II's beloved Hanover on the formulation of foreign policy. Bute aspired to end European conflict with a just and equitable peace, and to sever all alliances with the major political powers of Europe. He also sought (with complete success) to convince the future King that Hanover should play little or no part in the making of foreign policy.

As far as domestic politics were concerned, Bute was strongly opposed to those who had established Whig hegemony under George II. He reprobated the establishment by Walpole, Newcastle and Pelham of a political system based on the use of patronage, the retention of party distinctions, and the constraint of the *personal* powers of the monarch. His own formulation of politics envisaged a regime of strict economy in which places and pensions were reduced, and political corruption cut to a minimum. He had no truck with party which he saw as a means of maintaining oligarchical control of government, and of constraining the 'independency' of the Crown. In sum he desired a ruler who would rescue 'Monarchy from the inveterate Usurpation of Oligarchy',[6] and act the role of the Patriot King as envisaged by Bolingbroke.

[5] The development of this relationship can be followed in Romney Sedgwick (ed.), *Letters from George III to Bute 1756–66* (London, 1939), *passim*.

[6] Dodington to Bute, 22 December 1760, Bute MSS 1760/206, printed in John Carswell and L. A. Dralle (eds), *The Political Journal of George Bubb Dodington* (Oxford, 1965), p. 407. For a summary of Bute's political views see John Brewer, 'The Misfortunes of Lord Bute: A Case Study in Eighteenth-Century Political Argument and Public Opinion', *Historical Journal* xvi, i (1973).

These attitudes were customarily held by country gentlemen and backbench Members of Parliament. Rarely were they the creed of a courtier, let alone that of a royal favourite. As opposition ideology they were commonplace, but employed by those who held or were to hold power they represented a major political *volte-face*. Moreover they threatened the position as well as the attitudes of the nation's traditional political leaders. It was obvious to the likes of the Duke of Newcastle and the Elder Pitt that once the Prince of Wales ascended the throne Bute's political influence would become paramount and that they, as supporters of the war and continental alliances, as well as those who were *de facto* responsible for constraining the Crown, would become expendable.

Their fears were not unfounded. From the first days of George's reign it was apparent that Bute was effectively the King's chief adviser. Access to the monarch could only be procured via the favourite. As George told Newcastle: *'My Lord Bute is your good Friend, He will tell you my Thoughts at large.'*[7] Not even Devonshire, who as Lord Chamberlain ought to have had ready access to the King, could establish direct contact with George. No measure was concerted without Bute's consultation, and on the occasions when the King appeared in public, the favourite was almost always at his side.

Both Bute and the King were eager to give institutional recognition to the favourite's *de facto* power. Only Pitt's opposition (and a certain amount of chickenheartedness) prevented Bute's appointment as First Lord of the Treasury on the first day of the reign. As it was, he received immediate nomination to the Privy Council. During March of 1761 he was squeezed into the ministry as Secretary of State, and in May 1762 he finally laid hold of the office for which he was predestined, becoming First Lord of the Treasury.[8]

His rise can only be described as meteoric. At George III's accession Bute was not even a member of the legislature, much less the holder of a public office. (He was simply the Groom of the Stole in the Prince of Wales's Household.) His only parliamentary experience had been acquired in the years 1737–41 when he had sat in the House of Lords as a

[7] Newcastle to Hardwicke, 26 October 1760, British Museum Add. MSS 32, 999 f.106, printed in George Harris, *The Life of Lord Chancellor Hardwicke* (3 vols, London, 1847), III, p. 215.

[8] These events may be followed in detail in Namier, *England in the Age of the American Revolution*, pp. 120–70, 283–326.

Scottish representative peer. Yet, within the space of two years, he had become the nation's political leader by virtue of being the personal favourite of the King.

Bute's rapid elevation and assumption of office displeased many. Indeed there can rarely have been a prime minister who was more publicly abused, maligned and manhandled. He was attacked by the mob, threatened with assassination, burnt in effigy on both sides of the Atlantic, and vilified in pamphlets, prints, newspapers, songs, plays and handbills. In order to escape public insult he frequently travelled in disguise, or at least incognito. His rapid rise made him vulnerable to the accusation that he was simply a favourite or 'overmighty subject' who, because of his ideas on monarchy and the end of (Whig) single-party rule, could be seen as 'Tory' and even despotic. Indeed, as the exemplar of the philosophy of royal personal rule, he was readily portrayed as denying the notion of 'responsible government'. His nationality, his paternal name of Stuart, and his putative affair with Augusta, the Princess Dowager, were all added to the indictment against him. At every level of society, from the drawing-rooms of St James's to the gutters of Billingsgate, Bute's name was anathema. Despite his employment of coffee-house spies and newspaper propagandists, the royal favourite was unable to win popular support.[9]

Nevertheless, with the power and favour of the Crown behind him, Bute's parliamentary position was strong. And, once in office, he set about realising his chief political aspirations. The first and most important of these was the successful termination of the Seven Years War and the pursuit of a policy of diplomatic disengagement in Europe. This process of withdrawal had begun before Bute's premiership. Negotiations to end the war had been opened with France in 1761, though these had proved unsuccessful. More significantly, in April 1762 a Cabinet dominated by Bute's supporters had determined not to renew the subsidy that Britain had been paying to Frederick the Great of Prussia. They had also ensured, in a manoeuvre which had been responsible for Newcastle's resignation, that no more money could be invested in a continental war.[10] At the head of the Government Bute accelerated this policy of disengagement. Using the Sardinian ambassadors in London and Paris as a means of exchanging views, he reopened peace

[9] For a detailed substantiation of this paragraph see Brewer, 'The Misfortunes of Lord Bute', *Historical Journal* (1973).
[10] Namier, op. cit., pp. 302–26.

negotiations with France. These negotiations were tortuous and fraught with difficulty. On three important issues – the fate of the island of St Lucia, the negotiation of a peace that did not include Spain, and the question of compensation for Havana – Bute faced a revolt amongst his Cabinet colleagues. In the autumn of 1762, however, the Duke of Bedford was dispatched to Paris as special plenipotentiary, Cabinet difficulties were overcome, and the preliminaries of peace were signed in November. The Peace of Paris finally completed in February 1763 was undoubtedly the greatest achievement of Bute's administration. Although attacked in the press, unpopular in London, and condemned by some sections of the merchant community, it produced an honourable settlement at the end of (to use George III's own words) 'a bloody and expensive war'. Britain held or made substantial gains in Canada, the West Indies – notably St Vincent, Dominica, Tobago – and in India, whilst conceding comparatively little imperial ground to France. The final treaty also saw the triumph of Bute's policy of disengagement from Europe.[11]

Parallel with his diplomatic achievements were Bute's activities on the domestic front. He and the King had always been averse to the political hegemony of the so-called 'Old Corps' of Whigs – a loose-knit coalition of the great Whig factions that had dominated governmental politics since the fall of Walpole. The opposition mounted against Bute's peace by those sections of the Old Corps loyal to Newcastle provided the favourite with the opportunity to destroy the power of the old coalition. Even at the very beginning of the reign Bute and George had begun to undermine Old Corps hegemony, notably by the appointment of a number of Tories to offices in the royal bedchamber.[12] But the confrontation over the peace enabled Bute to make far more sweeping changes. Urged on by Henry Fox, whom Bute had had appointed as the new leader of the majority in the House of Commons, the favourite implemented a thorough removal of the office-holders who had voted in Parliament against the peace preliminaries, together with their allies and dependants. Even the most insignificant local office-holders were dismissed. This 'Massacre of the Pelhamite Innocents' not only undermined the patronage system that Newcastle had so skilfully cultivated,

[11] There is a useful summary of the negotiations and the final terms of the treaty in Lawrence Henry Gipson, *The Great War for Empire, the Culmination, 1760-3* (New York, 1954), pp. 299-311.
[12] Walpole, *Memoirs of . . . George III*, i, pp. 29-30.

it also struck a considerable psychological blow. The end of the dominance of the Old Corps was there for all to see.[13]

By early 1763, therefore, it seemed as if Bute had gone some way towards achieving his chief political aspirations. The nation was at peace, the direction of its foreign policy had changed, and it appeared as if the old political machine had been destroyed, guaranteeing the monarch fuller political powers. But these achievements had cost Bute much. In attacking Newcastle and the Old Corps, the favourite had perforce to use the instruments of patronage, the very gravy-train that he condemned. Bute may have undermined one system of 'corruption', but he had also, as he himself lamented,[14] failed to create a purer politics. Moreover, as a *parvenu* and favourite who had in some sense sought to alter the direction of politics, he had successfully alienated many of the nation's politicians. In this respect he made the politicians more determined than they ever had been to constrain the Crown, for it was only by constraining the King that they could remove the influence of Bute. Bute's transitory success, therefore, was the harbinger of the political conflict between the King and the politicians that was to continue for the next generation. He helped create the spirit of mutual distrust that continued to mar politics until the French Revolution, and which was in part responsible for the political instability of the period.[15] Yet the greatest cost Bute paid for his success was personal: he hated the vituperation that he suffered at the hands of the mob and in the newspapers, the distrust that his friends and colleagues showed towards him, and the sordid jobbery of day-to-day politics. He was scarcely in office than he wanted to resign, and as soon as it was clear that peace would be concluded he made preparations for his retirement. His departure was only delayed by the problem of forming a new administration.

Appropriately enough it was just at the moment when he was determined to resign that his opponents united most strongly against him. His Chancellor of the Exchequer, Sir Francis Dashwood, had proposed a tax on cider, the collection and enforcement of which might have necessitated the entry of excise officers into private dwellings. This measure was seized upon by Bute's opponents and portrayed as part of a scheme to introduce a 'general excise' on the lines that Walpole was

[13] Namier, op. cit., pp. 403–15.
[14] Bute to Campbell, 27 November 1763, Bute MSS.
[15] The best discussion of this problem is in Richard Pares, *George III and the Politicians* (Oxford, 1953), pp. 100–9.

said to have proposed in 1733. When Bute left office, therefore, on 8 April 1763, he resigned in the wake of yet another wave of popular hostility which many felt was responsible for his retirement.

Yet if Bute could do without politics, the King could not do without Bute. George continued to consult the favourite fairly regularly for the next two years, as well as on the specific occasions of the Stamp Act crisis and the negotiation with the Opposition in 1767.[16] Naturally this did not endear the favourite to the incumbent ministers, and after September 1763 every administration insisted that the King cease to consult Bute. By 1766, however, the King's infatuation with his dearest friend had waned, and thereafter Bute's influence declined rapidly. He was abroad for much of 1768–9, and by 1770 his power over the King was negligible.

But Bute continued to be attacked although effectively in political retirement. The activities of his former allies, now the 'King's Friends', and the persistent failure of the politicians to establish an understanding with the King, were both taken as signs of Bute's continued activity as 'minister behind the curtain'. In this respect he served after his retirement as a scapegoat for the errors and misunderstandings of others. Throughout the 1770s his prime political concern seems to have been to avoid the calumny and controversy that dominated his earlier career.[17]

As a Prime Minister Bute was not a success. His sole substantial achievement lay in the treaty of the Peace of Paris. He was unable to reform domestic politics in the way that he wished. Indeed, he succeeded in strengthening rather than weakening party feeling, and increasing rather than dissipating hostility between the Crown and the politicians. The failure of his political career is at once indicative of the naivety of his political aspirations, and of the barriers that existed even in the 1760s to obstruct the success of a premier who held office solely by virtue of personal favour. According to one interpretation of the British Constitution George III was legitimately entitled to appoint Bute to the highest office, but in the light of the political circumstances of the second half of the eighteenth century such a move can only be

[16] This claim is less contentious than it sounds. (See 'Journal of a Late Conference', August 1767, National Library of Scotland, Minto MSS M II/56; 'To the King from Ld Egmont relating what passed with Mr Norton upon his Commission', 11 February 1766, British Museum Add. MSS 47012, f. 22.)
[17] Brewer, 'The Faces of Lord Bute: A Visual Contribution to Anglo-American Political Ideology', *Perspectives in American History*, vi (1972), pp. 113–14.

1. Robert Walpole, 1st Earl of Orford. Studio of J. B. van Loo

2. The Earl of Wilmington, by Sir Godfrey Kneller

The Right Honble Henry Pelham,
Chancellor of the Exchequer, &c &c 1751

3. Henry Pelham, by William Hoare

4. Thomas Pelham Holles, 1st Duke of Newcastle (right, with the Earl of Lincoln), by Sir Godfrey Knelle

5. William Cavendish, 4th Duke of Devonshire, by Sir Joshua Reynolds

6. John Stuart, 3rd Earl of Bute, by Sir Joshua Reynolds

7. George Grenville, by William Hoare

8. Charles Watson-Wentworth, 2nd Marquis of Rockingham. Studio of Reynolds

described as politically injudicious. Perhaps if Bute had been psychologically more predisposed to governing, he would have proved a greater success. But it is doubtful if he would therefore have been the progenitor of less political conflict.

BIBLIOGRAPHY

There is no satisfactory modern biography of Bute. Less than adequate, although it serves as a lightweight introduction, is J. Lovat-Fraser, *John Stuart, Earl of Bute* (London, 1912). There is also a fair amount of information on family matters in Hon. Mrs E. Stuart Wortley (ed.), *A Prime Minister and his Son. From the Correspondence of the 3rd Earl of Bute and of Lt-General the Hon. Sir Charles Stuart, KB* (London, 1925). Much the best book on Bute is Romney Sedgwick's edition of *Letters from George III to Lord Bute 1756–66* (London, 1939), the introduction of which discusses the relationship between the King and his favourite. Scholars should be warned, however, that Sedgwick's edition of the letters is not definitive. There are 400 items of communication between George and Bute in the Bute manuscripts at the Cardiff City Library which were undiscovered when Sedgwick wrote. Sedgwick's analysis is best supplemented by the discussion of Bute in Sir Lewis Namier, *England in the Age of the American Revolution* (2nd edn, London, 1961), and Richard Pares, *George III and the Politicians* (Oxford, 1953). Two articles that touch on the issues that Bute's career raised are: John Brewer, 'The Faces of Lord Bute: A Visual Contribution to Anglo-American Political Ideology', *Perspectives in American History*, vi (1972), and John Brewer, 'The Misfortunes of Lord Bute: a Case Study of Eighteenth-Century Political Argument and Public Opinion', *Historical Journal*, xvi, 1 (1973). For want of a better reference work, the entry on Bute in the *Dictionary of National Biography* is thorough, though it does not include recent interpretation. Bute's manuscripts are to be found in three locations: the bulk of his surviving papers are at Mount Stuart, Isle of Bute, the family seat; there is a substantial collection of papers in the City Library at Cardiff; and there are a few items in the British Museum, including a letter book that duplicates much of the material at Mount Stuart.

7

GEORGE GRENVILLE

BY

PETER D. G. THOMAS

George Grenville, born 14 October 1712, second son of Richard Grenville, MP, of Wotton, Bucks., and Hester, daughter of Sir Richard Temple, 3rd Bt., MP, of Stowe, Bucks. Educated at Eton and Christ Church, Oxford. Inner Temple 1729; called 1735; bencher 1763; Lincoln's Inn 1734. Married 1749 Elizabeth, daughter of Sir William Wyndham, 3rd Bt., MP, and sister of Charles, 2nd Earl of Egremont; four sons (of whom the third, William, was Prime Minister 1806-7 as Lord Grenville, q.v.); five daughters. MP for Buckingham Borough 1741-70; Admiralty Board 1744-7; Treasury Board 1747-54; PC 1754; Treasurer of Navy 1754-55, 1756-57, 1757-62; Leader of the House of Commons 1761-2; Secretary of State May-October 1762; First Lord of Admiralty 1762-3; First Lord of the Treasury and Chancellor of Exchequer 1763-5. Died 13 November 1770. His sister Hester married William Pitt, later 1st Earl of Chatham, q.v., in 1754, and his brother became 2nd Earl Temple in 1752.

GEORGE GRENVILLE

In the earlier eighteenth century the Grenvilles were the leading Whig family in Buckinghamshire, untitled squires but predestined to be Parliament men. George's father made the family fortune by marrying the favourite sister of Lord Cobham of Stowe, who settled his vast estate on the eldest Grenville boy, Richard. After Richard inherited Stowe and became Lord Temple in 1752 he allowed George to have the old family home at Wotton. George must have been glad of the house, for in 1749 he had married Elizabeth, daughter of the former Tory leader Sir William Wyndham: he was then thirty-six and she was twenty-nine but, according to Lady Bolingbroke, looked more like forty-nine, for smallpox had marred her looks. This was a fortunate marriage to a devoted wife, who bore him nine children and took such a keen interest in her husband's career that she kept a political diary long attributed to him. 'She was the first prize in the marriage lottery of our century,' wrote one of Grenville's friends to another in 1765.[1]

This background of what seems to have been a happy family life contrasts with Grenville's historical reputation as a cold public figure. He had the misfortune, in this respect, to incur the enmity of the famous contemporary observer Horace Walpole. Apart from putting the worst possible construction on Grenville's political actions, Walpole made this sort of remark: 'Scarce any man ever wore in his face such outward and visible marks of the hollow, cruel and rotten heart within.'[2] Even if such bias is discounted, it is clear that in public life Grenville was tactless, obstinate, and ungenerous. Here is a comment on him by his cousin and friend Thomas Pitt: 'He had nothing seducing in his manners. His countenance had rather the expression of peevishness and auster-ity. . . . He was to a proverb tedious. . . . He was diffuse and argu-mentative, and never had done with a subject after he had convinced your judgement till he had wearied your attention. The foreign ministers complained of his prolixity, which they called amongst each

[1] *Historical Manuscripts Commission Reports, Lothian MSS* (1907), p. 259.
[2] Horace Walpole, *Memoirs of the Reign of King George III*, ed. G. F. Russell Barker (4 vols, London, 1894), i, 215.

other, the being *Grenvilisé.*[3] Yet through all the calumny and candour of contemporary comment there emerges the impression of an upright man, devoted to duty and endowed with an admirable sense of public responsibility.

George Grenville practised law until he became MP for the family pocket borough in 1741. Throughout his life he was dependent on his eldest brother for both his parliamentary seat and his house, held on an annual lease, and much of his quest for family sinecures and his parsimonious attitude to national finance may be explained in terms of this personal insecurity; until he became Prime Minister he saved his annual salary from each office to increase his capital. Grenville entered Parliament as a member of Lord Cobham's band of 'Boy Patriots', seeking office after the fall of Sir Robert Walpole in 1742. For his first twenty years at Westminster he played a subordinate role to William Pitt and brother Richard: and although he held minor posts from 1744 onwards these two self-centred and arrogant men evidently made unscrupulous use of a supporter able enough to win a reputation for himself. Within a decade or so of entering the Commons Grenville was reckoned to be one of the leading members there. He was a professional politician in a sense that few men of his day were: Thomas Pitt recalled that Grenville was 'a man born to public business, which was his luxury and amusement. An Act of Parliament was in itself entertaining to him, as was proved when he stole a turnpike Bill out of somebody's pocket at a concert and read it in a corner in despite of all the efforts of the finest singers to attract his attention.' Grenville came to feel resentment that he was being deprived of a reward proper to his talents. Even in the later 1750s, when Pitt was winning the Seven Years War as Secretary of State and Temple was also in the Cabinet as Lord Privy Seal, they failed to exert their influence on George's behalf, despite many promises and a hint that he would become Chancellor of the Exchequer. Grenville did much of the ministry's parliamentary chores, being reckoned 'the second of Pitt's party' in the House of Commons; and he ran the Navy Office with notable efficiency. But his reaction to his lack of progress was to opt out of the political battle. By 1760 arrangements were in hand for him to become Speaker of the House of Commons, a post that would have well suited a man so concerned with both the procedure

[3] For Thomas Pitt's pen portrait of Grenville see Sir Lewis Namier and John Brooke (eds), *The House of Commons 1754–90. The History of Parliament* (3 vols, London, 1964), ii, 539.

and the prestige of the House. Then Grenville's prospects and career were transformed by the accession that year of George III.

The new King and his favourite Lord Bute had a high opinion of Grenville; and when Pitt resigned as Secretary of State in October 1761 Grenville accepted an invitation to become Leader of the House in his place. His decision to desert his family and political connections must be seen against the long background of disappointment arising out of his political tutelage to Pitt and Temple. Six months later Grenville helped to force the resignation of the Duke of Newcastle from the Treasury by opposing his war finance, and became Secretary of State when Bute succeeded Newcastle. Grenville's career then suffered a setback. Handicapped by Bute's hold on patronage, he had not been a success as Leader of the Commons: and during the summer of 1762 he attacked in Cabinet the peace terms negotiated by Bute. In October he was replaced as Leader of the House by Henry Fox, and demoted from Secretary of State to First Lord of the Admiralty. He had apparently reached his political ceiling. 'Grenville has thrown away the game he had two years ago,' George III commented to Bute when discussing in March 1763 who could succeed his favourite at the Treasury:[4] but the King had to fall back on Grenville as the only man to keep out the opposition leaders Newcastle and Pitt when Fox declined to do so.

Few ministers can have taken office in such humiliating circumstances. Grenville had to accept an administration chosen for him by Bute, even his own Treasury Board; and when he saw George III on 5 April, only the day before the change became public knowledge, the King made it quite clear that he was a poor substitute for Bute and owed his post entirely to the favourite's nomination. News of the ministry was greeted with scepticism about Grenville's ability to stand alone – for although fifty years of age he had hitherto always played a subordinate role – and with derision, the widespread conviction being, as the Duke of Devonshire told Newcastle, that 'Lord Bute undoubtedly means to be the Minister behind the Curtain'.[5] Contemporary opinion was wrong. Bute's intention to retire from the centre of politics, decision-making, was quite genuine: but George III would not let him go. The King insisted on consulting Bute on public business after his resignation. Grenville and his colleagues found themselves with

[4] *Letters from George III to Lord Bute 1756–66*, ed. R. Sedgwick (London, 1939), pp. 200–1.
[5] British Museum Additional MS 32948, folios 86–7.

ministerial responsibility but without the effective power that could only come from complete royal confidence. A Bute problem existed, but not the one depicted by contemporaries and some historians.

Grenville and his two Secretaries of State, his brother-in-law Egremont and the experienced Halifax, formed the inner core of the administration, being known as the 'Triumvirate': they shared responsibility for patronage as well as policy, an arrangement Sir Lewis Namier described as 'the premiership in commission'. After several months of unease they presented the King with an ultimatum. At the beginning of August all three in turn told George III that he had to choose between supporting his existing ministry and forming another one. There followed a political crisis, prolonged by the sudden death of Egremont on 21 August. In negotiations chiefly conducted by Bute, George III found out that any alternative ministry would be even more unacceptable to him than the one he had, and Grenville was able to make the condition that he would continue in office only if the King would 'arm him with such powers as were necessary, and suffer no secret influence whatever to prevail against the advice of those to whom he trusted the management of his affairs'.[6] Bute had created a minister he could neither control nor remove.

The crisis of August 1763 was a triumph of minister over King: but the events also threw the two men closer together. If George III could no longer consult Bute, Grenville had lost Egremont and feared isolation in a Cabinet composed not of his friends but of men chosen to strengthen the King's Government, like the Duke of Bedford and the Earl of Sandwich. On 8 September he told George III that 'these might prove too strong for him; his only reliance was upon his Majesty's truth and honour, and on that he trusted he might depend. The King assured him he might.'[7] When other ministers began to put forward pretensions George III told Grenville that 'he meant to put his government solely into his hands', and refused to consider applications for favours until he had privately consulted Grenville.[8]

Grenville was now Prime Minister in reality, having established his position against both the royal favourite and his Cabinet colleagues.

[6] *The Grenville Papers: Being the Correspondence of Richard Grenville, Earl Temple, KG, and the Right Hon. George Grenville, their Friends and Contemporaries*, ed. W. J. Smith (4 vols, London, 1852–3), iii, 197–201 (Mrs Grenville's diary).
[7] *Grenville Papers*, iii, 205 (Mrs Grenville's diary).
[8] *Grenville Papers*, iii, 207–12 (Mrs Grenville's diary).

His claim to control of patronage was based on his role as Leader of the House of Commons, the unofficial but universally acknowledged position of manager of 'His Majesty's affairs in the House of Commons' which as invariably fell to the First Lord of the Treasury if a commoner as the post of Chancellor of the Exchequer. Grenville's previous failure as Leader caused many to think the task beyond him; but circumstances were now different. Grenville had the power of patronage, the prestige of being the King's first minister – always a great advantage in handling the Commons, and a new self-confidence that was to be reflected in his parliamentary performance. He was to be a notable success even though he at once faced a political crisis that was to blow up into one of the great parliamentary battles of the century. It began with the arrest of MP John Wilkes under a general warrant for a libel in a weekly political paper, *The North Briton*. The decision was made by Secretaries of State Halifax and Egremont, but the whole administration had to face the political consequences.

The ministry at first saw the question as simply being whether or not Wilkes should have been immune from arrest by virtue of parliamentary privilege: and Grenville's strategy was to pass resolutions in the Commons declaring that the offending paper had been a seditious libel and that privilege did not cover such an offence. He proposed to make the subject a vote of confidence and resign if defeated. When the parliamentary session opened in November events showed that there was no danger of that. Grenville won by 300 votes to 111 on the first trial of strength, and carried his resolutions by similar majorities. But after the Christmas recess there came an opposition attack on the procedural issue of the general warrant, an authority to arrest unnamed persons. The use of this had aroused widespread uneasiness, and in February 1764 the administration carried two divisions on the point by narrow margins of ten and fourteen votes. Opposition hopes of overthrowing the ministry were illusory, for many of the hundred or so members who deserted the Government on this subject did not intend to force such a change, and it was not the matter Grenville had deemed a question of confidence; but the parliamentary victory nevertheless represented a personal success for him. Before the crucial debates Grenville briefed meetings of supporters on the line to take, the contention that the matter should be left to the law courts; he made a politic concession over a grievance felt by many MPs, a Cider Tax imposed the previous year; and he himself took the leading part when the parliamentary

battle appeared to swing against him, as even Horace Walpole acknowledged. 'Grenville, not losing courage on this turn of fortune, replied
ably and freely.'[9]

After February 1764 Grenville's hold on the Commons was never
again threatened while he was minister. He had, indeed, already been
well on the way towards winning the confidence of the House. Although no orator, he possessed many qualities that served him well
there, as Thomas Pitt recalled despite the qualification that his

'prolixity rendered him an unpleasant speaker in the House of Commons.
Yet though his eloquence charmed nobody, his argument converted
. . . The abundance of his matter, his experience of the forms and
practice of the House . . . his skill upon all matters of finance, of commerce, of foreign treaties, and above all the purity of his character gave
him weight. . . . He never took notes; he never quitted his seat for
refreshment in the longest debates, and generally spoke the last when
his strength and his memory served him to recollect every argument
that had been used, and to suffer scarce a word of any consequence to
escape his notice.'

Grenville's knowledge of parliamentary lore was invaluable in an age
whose political thinking was typified by his own legalistic cast of mind.
He was reckoned the foremost man in the House for grasp and exposition of national finance, and his economy commended itself to tax-
burdened country gentlemen. He had immediately thrown himself into
the work of the Treasury, and his two Budget Days were personal
triumphs. But his greatest asset was his honest character. Before, during
and after his ministry, on such matters as war and peace, Wilkes and
America, Grenville said and did what he thought was right, without
trimming to the winds of political expediency: and he won respect even
from those who disagreed with him.

Within a year of taking office Grenville enjoyed royal favour to the
exclusion of his ministerial colleagues, and was paramount in the House
of Commons. His is commonly regarded as the strongest ministry of the
troubled first decade of George III's reign. Entrenched in both Court
and Parliament, he bid fair in 1764 to become a Prime Minister in the
mould of Walpole and Pelham. Yet a year later he was dismissed without any prospect of ever returning to office. He had contrived to give
[9] H. Walpole, *Memoirs . . . George III*, i, 291.

such personal offence to the King that George III said afterwards, 'I would rather see the devil in my closet than Mr Grenville.'[10]

Part of the explanation was his verbosity. 'When he has wearied me for two hours,' complained George III, 'he looks at his watch, to see if he may not tire me for an hour more.' This fault was compounded by what Grenville said. Many of these harangues were constitutional lectures, based on the ministerial need for patronage and his suspicion of Bute's interference in that field. Grenville insisted on appointing to every office, and whenever his suggestions met with royal objections he blamed Bute and gave little credence to George III's denials, conveying the impression that he thought his sovereign a dishonest man. This incessant pressure gradually alienated the King. George III later recalled his anger when in October 1764 Grenville 'had the insolence' to tell a Court official 'that if people presumed to speak to me on business without his previous consent he would not serve an hour'.[11] Matters grew worse during the next six months: as Grenville failed to have his way in a series of patronage matters his behaviour became ever more outrageous in the King's eyes. George III had already decided to get rid of him before the Regency Bill crisis of April 1765 which is often said to have precipitated his fall. Grenville, ungracious and uncompromising, survived as minister until July only because the King could not find any alternative administration before then: and George III was so determined to dismiss him that he then called on the young and inexperienced Marquis of Rockingham.

No part of this quarrel concerned policy. George III left that to his Cabinet, and indeed he approved of what the Grenville ministry did with respect to Wilkes, America and Europe. By this time the Cabinet was a small, efficient body, consisting of nine members during the Grenville administration; and decisions were forwarded to the King in the form of minutes embodying recommendations. They were taken after genuine discussion, with particular weight being given to the opinion of the departmental head concerned. Grenville, although Prime Minister, could expect to have his way only over Treasury matters: on other subjects he had to deploy the two weapons of financial costs and his responsibility for government measures in the Commons, arguments

10 *Memoirs of the Marquis of Rockingham and his Contemporaries*, ed. Earl of Albemarle (2 vols, London, 1852), ii, 50.
11 *The Correspondence of King George the Third from 1760 to December 1783*, ed. Sir John Fortescue (6 vols, London, 1927-8), i, 168.

not always applicable to the matter under consideration. He often failed to carry his point of view on foreign policy, the province of the two Secretaries of State; for he favoured a firmer line with France over the implementation of the peace terms than that adopted by his colleagues. America fell within the department of the Secretary of State for the South; and on 16 September 1763 Grenville objected in vain to Secretary Halifax's policy of leaving the Mississippi valley without a settled form of government and reserving it for the Indians, which was embodied in the royal Proclamation of the next month. The Prime Minister could thus be overruled in Cabinet on important matters of policy: but Grenville's characteristic application and determination soon enabled him to dominate his colleagues. The Cabinet minutes came to bear the imprint of his dictation; and Horace Walpole later recalled that 'there sprung up out of great weakness a strong and cemented ministry, who all acquiesced in the predominant power of Grenville'.[12]

Contrary to general expectation Grenville had proved big enough for the post of Prime Minister. Here is the comment of one supporter, Lord Buckinghamshire, three months after Grenville's dismissal: 'Reflection but the more convinces me of the calamity England has sustained by his being compelled to quit an office which he is not only the best but the only man in these times duly qualified to fill.'[13] This judgement was implicitly confirmed by men who disliked Grenville. In June William Pitt, when declining to form a ministry himself, had advised George III to continue Grenville at the Treasury: '. . . as things now stood without him he saw nothing in that department either solid or substantial. In opposition too he might give great trouble, his knowlege in revenue matters was considerable and perhaps bitterness and rancour were not the smallest ingredients which went to the composition of his character.'[14] And Horace Walpole made this reflection on Grenville's death: 'Mr Grenville was, confessedly, the ablest man of business in the House of Commons, and, though not popular, of great authority there from his spirit, knowledge, and gravity of character.'[15]

Office had given Grenville stature and a party of his own: and respect

[12] H. Walpole, *Memoirs . . . George III*, i, 234.
[13] *HMC Reports, Lothian MSS*, p. 258.
[14] *The Jenkinson Papers 1760–6*, ed. N. S. Jucker (London, 1949), p. 377. Memorandum by Gilbert Elliot, MP.
[15] H. Walpole, *Memoirs . . . George III*, iv, 125.

for his personal and political qualities enabled him to retain the loyalty of most of his friends even when it became evident that he was doomed by the antipathy of the King to spend the rest of his life in opposition. During his last years Grenville, resigned to the role of elder statesman, was always heard with respect in the Commons, and in 1770 he achieved the remarkable feat of carrying an important Bill against the Government: the so-called Grenville Act established a fairer method of deciding disputed parliamentary election cases. This was a fitting end to the career of a man rooted in the House of Commons, and a more appropriate legacy than the ill-fated Stamp Act of 1765 imposing taxation on the American colonies for which he is best known – a measure no one in office and few in opposition questioned at the time of its passage.

BIBLIOGRAPHY

There is no full biography of Grenville. His career until 1763 has been described in Lewis M. Wiggin, *The Faction of Cousins: A Political Account of the Grenvilles 1733–63* (New Haven, 1958). For an unpublished account of the Grenville ministry see John R. G. Tomlinson, 'The Grenville Papers 1763–5' (University of Manchester MA Thesis, 1956). Grenville's relationship with the King is examined in John Brooke, *King George III* (London, 1972), pp. 102–22; foreign policy in the introduction by Frank Spencer to his *The Fourth Earl of Sandwich: Diplomatic Correspondence 1763–5* (Manchester, 1961); and American policy in my forthcoming book *British Politics and the Stamp Act Crisis*. Papers of especial relevance are Dora M. Clark, 'George Grenville as First Lord of the Treasury and Chancellor of the Exchequer, 1763–5', *Huntingdon Library Quarterly*, xiii (1949–50), 383–97; Ian R. Christie, 'The Cabinet During the Grenville Administration', *English Historical Review*, lxxiii (1958), 86–92; and Sir Lewis Namier's biography of Grenville in Sir Lewis Namier and John Brooke, eds, *The House of Commons 1754–90. The History of Parliament* (3 vols, London, 1964), ii, pp. 537–44.

8

THE MARQUIS
OF ROCKINGHAM

BY

PAUL LANGFORD

Charles Watson Wentworth, 2nd Marquis of Rockingham, born
13 May 1730, son of the 1st Marquis. Educated at Westminster
School and St John's, Cambridge. Styled Viscount Higham 1739–46
and Earl of Malton 1746–50; created Irish peer (Earl Malton)
1750 and succeeded as 2nd Marquis of Rockingham 1750. Married
Mary Bright, daughter of Thomas Bright of Badsworth. Took his
seat in the Lords May 1751; Lord Lieutenant of North and West
Ridings of Yorkshire 1751–62; Lord of the Bedchamber to George
II and George III 1751–62; FRS 1751; FSA 1752; Vice-
Admiral of Yorkshire 1755–63; KG 1760; PC 1765; First Lord
of the Treasury 1765–6 and from 27 March 1782 till his death on
1 July of the same year. Reappointed Lord Lieutenant 1765 and
Vice-Admiral 1776; High Steward of Hull 1766.

THE MARQUIS OF ROCKINGHAM

It is a minor irony of eighteenth-century history that the Marquis of Rockingham, in many ways one of the least impressive of Georgian prime ministers, should have figured so prominently in the mythology constructed by a succeeding age. To Whiggish Victorians Rockingham's career seemed flawless. As the successor in the Whig leadership to the Duke of Newcastle he apparently cleansed and purified a party soiled by the corruption of the Walpole and Pelham regimes, and by opposing tyranny both at home and in the colonies, he preserved the cause of liberal reform which was to be inherited by the party of Charles James Fox, Lord Grey and Lord John Russell. Moreover as the patron of Edmund Burke he brought into the Whig tradition the man who did more than any other to influence the way in which later generations saw the political history of the late eighteenth century. It is scarcely surprising then that Rockingham came to be seen as such an important figure. He took his place in history as one of those, in Macaulay's words, 'worthy to have charged by the side of Hampden at Chalgrove, or to have exchanged the last embrace with Russell on the scaffold in Lincoln's Inn Fields'.[1]

Yet Rockingham's ministerial career, at least, was extremely insubstantial. He was First Lord of the Treasury for only fifteen months, from July 1765 to July 1766 and again from March 1782 until his death in the following July. Strictly speaking he was Prime Minister for an even shorter period. In the early months of his first administration, it was the King's uncle, the Duke of Cumberland, who was truly Prime Minister. Though he held no official position, Cumberland had been personally commissioned by George III to form a ministry from the opposition Whigs, and took the lead in the direction of policy and patronage. Lord Shelburne's description of the new regime as 'the Duke's Administration, with Lord Rockingham at the Treasury', was extremely apt.[2] In fact Rockingham accepted the Treasury with extreme reluctance and for two reasons only. In the first place he was

[1] Lord Macaulay, *Essay on the Earl of Chatham* (London, 1887), p. 151.
[2] Lord E. Fitzmaurice, *Life of William, Earl of Shelburne* (London, 1875–6), i, 335.

very much a personal friend of Cumberland's, and expected to act only as his lieutenant. In the second the obvious alternatives for the office were either unco-operative, like William Pitt, or unacceptable, like the Duke of Newcastle. In any event Rockingham began his tenure of the Treasury without effective power; he became the King's minister quite fortuitously when Cumberland died barely three months after the formation of the new ministry, on 31 October 1765. Even his second period in office after sixteen years in opposition barely entitled him to the status of Prime Minister. He was given the Treasury by George III in March 1782 with extremely bad grace and only because no alternative could be found. To all intents and purposes one of his Secretaries of State, Shelburne, was treated by the King as joint Prime Minister.[3] Such authority as Rockingham retained was shattered by his own illness and the bitter conflict which broke out in his Cabinet between Shelburne and the other Secretary of State, Charles James Fox. In short, only in the winter and spring of 1765–6, in the period between Cumberland's death and his own dismissal, can Rockingham be seen very plausibly as effective premier.

If Rockingham's tenure as Prime Minister was limited, so were his talents. When he was first placed in office in 1765 his political experience was absurdly slight. He had been an independent-minded Court magnate under the Pelhams, and had followed Newcastle and Devonshire into opposition to the Bute and Grenville ministries. He had held no office or position of consequence and outside Yorkshire had played little part in politics. As Horace Walpole remarked he was 'only known to the public by his passion for horse races'.[4] Moreover he was personally ill suited to either ministerial business or political in-fighting. He was ever a valetudinarian, and throughout his life suffered from mysterious and debilitating ailments. In addition his principal characteristic was 'indolence of temper',[5] that is to say, idleness. At the Treasury he depended entirely on his Chancellor of the Exchequer, William Dowdeswell; in the Cabinet he was hopelessly unbusinesslike, on one occasion actually forgetting to attend one of his own Cabinet meetings.[6]

[3] See J. A. Cannon, *The Fox-North Coalition* (London, 1969), p. 5.
[4] Horace Walpole's *Memoirs of the Reign of King George III*, ed. G. F. R. Barker (London, 1894), ii, 140.
[5] British Museum Additional MS 32977, Newcastle Papers, f.39: J. White to Newcastle, 6 Sept. 1766.
[6] Add. MS 32972, f.94: Rockingham to Newcastle, 1 Dec. 1765.

He was also a notoriously poor parliamentary performer. During his first administration he spoke only twice, and on each occasion merely because the taunts and jeers of his opponents compelled him to rise to his feet.[7] In matters of policy he was irresolute, procrastinating and apparently incapable of initiative. George III remarked that Rockingham 'never appeared to him to have a decided opinion about things', and the Duke of Richmond's verdict was similar: 'Lord Rockingham's disposition is always to defer, and by too fine-spun schemes to bring about what he wishes. He loses many opportunities by being always too late and while he is talking and schemeing [sic] perhaps to prevent a thing, it is done.'[8] Though the legislative achievements of his first ministry were not inconsiderable, most of them were either essentially negative, like the repeal of the Stamp Act, the repeal of the cider excise, and the general warrants resolutions, or carried out largely by way of concession to the commercial interests, like the Free Port and American Duties Acts. Grenville's charge in the spring of 1766 that the ministry was little more than the tool of the mercantile pressure groups was not altogether wide of the mark.[9] Finally his political strategy was disastrous. His first administration was short-lived not, as generations of Whig apologists claimed, because the King conspired against it from its inception, but because it proved so inefficient. George III came to see his ministry, as Newcastle remarked, as 'an administration of boys',[10] and certainly Rockingham's political decisions seemed to justify such a description. His ludicrous courtship of the Elder Pitt, his needless alienation of the King and many of his friends at Court, his abysmal complacency and inactivity in the closing stages of the administration, all bore testimony to Rockingham's apparent naivety and incompetence. Junius' comment on the collapse of the first Rockingham administration, that it 'dissolved in its own weakness', was by no means unjustified.[11]

Despite Rockingham's limitations, perhaps because of them, there

---

[7] The two occasions were 20 January 1766 and 28 May 1766.

[8] Fitzmaurice, *Life of Shelburne*, i, 373; 'The Duke of Richmond's Memorandum, 1–7 July 1766', ed. A. G. Olson, *English Historical Review*, lxxv (1960), 479.

[9] Add. MS 32975, f.58: West to Newcastle, 30 April 1766, quoted in L. S. Sutherland, 'Edmund Burke and the First Rockingham Ministry', *Eng. Hist. Rev.*, xlvii (1932), 66.

[10] Add. MS 32976, f.325: Newcastle to C. Yorke, 29 July 1766.

[11] *The Letters of Junius*, ed. C. W. Everitt (London, 1927), p. 105.

were some features of his tenure as Prime Minister that were both unusual and significant. Particularly intriguing was the curious way in which he treated the King. Since in the eighteenth century prime ministers were nominees of the Crown above all else, those who neglected the arts of the courtier did so at their peril. Rockingham's immediate predecessor at the Treasury, George Grenville, had proved, despite his mastery of the Commons, an abominably bad courtier and paid for it with the loss of his ministerial career. It was therefore all the more incumbent upon Rockingham to secure George III's favour. Yet he perversely declined to make a point of cultivating the closet and indeed at times seemed intent on treating the King as a mere cypher. During the administration of 1765–6 George III was slighted repeatedly. His views on the Stamp Act crisis were neglected, his recommendations of an alliance with Lord Bute's friends ignored, his objections to the appointment of Richmond as Secretary of State in May 1766 overridden, and his indignation at Rockingham's treatment of the princes of the blood in the matter of financial provision in June brushed aside. In the succeeding years attitudes naturally hardened and it was not to be expected that during Rockingham's brief second administration relations between King and minister would be anything but frosty. However, in 1765–6 Rockingham had every opportunity to establish himself in the closet; that he failed to do so was very much his own fault. No doubt his treatment of the Crown looked forward to the views of Charles James Fox and the practice of the nineteenth century, when the monarchy's role in politics gradually diminished. But it also did much to cut short Rockingham's ministerial career and return his party to the political wilderness.

A further respect in which Rockingham arguably broke new ground was in his attitude to party. Unlike most politicians of his day, he saw his party not as a means to power but rather as an end in itself. Indeed it is scarcely too much to claim that in terms of personal ambition he valued the leadership of his party far above the premiership. To many contemporaries this seemed the ultimate proof of his folly, yet it undeniably gave to his political career a peculiar emphasis. Precisely what kind of party Rockingham led is a matter for dispute. It is possible to see the Rockingham Whigs either as one of the characteristic aristocratic factions thrown up in the maelstrom of the 1760s, or as a great country party comparable to the Tories of the previous reigns; the truth doubtless lies somewhere between these two extremes. What is

certain is that Rockingham's extraordinary worship of his party radic-
ally affected his tenure as Prime Minister. 'Lord Rockingham,' Newcastle remarked in May 1766, 'thinks *he* shall keep *the Whig* party together, and I suppose be himself at the head of it.'[12] The results of
Rockingham's obsession were seen both in relation to men and to
measures.

So far as personnel was concerned it is no coincidence that the
Rockingham administrations saw two of the greatest upheavals among
office-holders of the century. In 1765 and 1782 old scores were paid off,
old enemies ejected from office and a great corps of loyal 'Whigs' restored to place and profit. Still more significant was the firmness with
which Rockingham and his friends adopted what amounted to a party
programme. 'Then for the first time were men seen attached in office to
every principle they had maintained in opposition,' Burke boasted on
behalf of Rockingham's first ministry.[13] On all three issues that had
principally occupied the opposition to the Bute and Grenville administrations, Rockingham and his colleagues took action when in office. A
serious, if largely unsuccessful, attempt to revive the Anglo-Prussian
alliance and adopt a tougher line with the Bourbon courts was made,
resolutions against general warrants were carried through the House of
Commons, and the objectionable elements in Bute's cider excise were
repealed.[14] The same concern with consistency dominated Rockingham's thinking during the years of opposition and emerged especially
clearly in the discussions that preceded his second administration. The
negotiations of 1780, for example, broke down because Rockingham
refused to accept the King's stipulation 'that those who come into office
must give assurance that they do not mean to be hampered by the tenets

---

[12] *Newcastle's Narrative of the Changes in the Ministry, 1765–7*, ed. M. Bateson
(London, 1898), p. 56.
[13] *Burke's Works* (ed. Bohn), i, 330.
[14] Contrary to popular belief, however, the Rockingham Ministry's most important
legislative measure, the repeal of the Stamp Act, was not the result of promises
made in opposition. Rockingham and his colleagues had done little to oppose Grenville's American measures when they were passed and showed no disposition to
repeal them when they entered office. On the contrary the initial response of the
Rockingham ministry to the news of the Stamp Act riots in the summer and autumn
of 1765 was to threaten enforcement of the Act and repression of resistance by force.
Only under the pressure of the business interests in Britain did Rockingham discover
a desire to reverse Grenville's colonial policies.

they have held during their opposition'.[15] When George III was eventually compelled to accept Rockingham's terms in 1782 they were carried out to the letter. Not merely the termination of the American war, which was clearly unavoidable anyway, but a detailed programme of 'economical reform' embodied in Burke's Bill, Crewe's Bill and Clerke's Bill, all passed in 1782, bore testimony to the consistency and good faith of the Rockinghams. Contemporaries were struck by the novelty of Rockingham's practice in this respect. As William Knox pointed out in 1789, opposition leaders did not normally adhere in office to the principles that they had espoused out of it: 'When an opposition gets into office and the King trusts them with the exercise of his power, the farce is at an end, and, after a few awkward apologies, and a few ineffectual votes with old connections, by way of consistency, the business of Government is expected to be taken up, and carried on in the usual way. Such however, was not the conduct of the Old Whigs.'[16] Rockingham's behaviour both in 1765–6 and 1782 contrasted markedly, for example, with that of Carteret and Pulteney in 1742 and that of Pitt in 1757.

Rockingham's preoccupation with what today would be described as a party platform was only part of a wider and characteristic concern with public opinion. Again the novelty lay largely in the fact that Rockingham seemed to take seriously principles to which most politicians merely paid lip-service. Whether in office or in opposition his chief consideration was 'the publick in general', 'the general disposition of the publick', 'the general predominant opinion of the nation'.[17] During his first ministry both his greatest blunder and his greatest achievement derived largely from this concern. His failure to establish his ministry on a firm basis was fundamentally a result of his repeated refusals to contemplate an alliance with Bute's friends, a strategy that would have earned him the loathing of the metropolis and the press while making his position at Court and in Parliament unassailable. At the same time his solution to the imperial crisis, the repeal of the Stamp Act, was the

[15] *The Correspondence of George III from 1760 to December 1783*, ed. Sir J. Fortescue (London, 1927), v, 3099. See also I. R. Christie, 'The Marquis of Rockingham and Lord North's Offer of Coalition June–July 1782', in *Myth and Reality in Late Eighteenth-Century British Politics and Other Papers* (London, 1970).
[16] W. Knox, *Extra Official State Papers* (London, 1789), pp. 2–3.
[17] *The Correspondence of Edmund Burke*, ed. T. W. Copeland (Cambridge, 1958–), ii, 498; ii, 191; iv, 163.

result not of any great concern for American liberty, but rather of his ready response to the pressure of British merchants and manufacturers. Nothing pleased Rockingham more than to excel even Pitt, the acknowledged master of politics out of doors, in obtaining the applause of the City of London and business communities up and down the country. As the second Earl of Hardwicke told him, in August 1766, 'You are really beating the late Great Commoner at his own weapons and receiving those eulogiums which his *puffs* have hitherto supposed, that nobody was *entitled* to but himself.'[18] Whatever his other faults, Rockingham was not neglectful of opinion outside the restricted world of Whitehall and Westminster.

Together these features of Rockingham's conduct as Prime Minister add up to one straightforward fact: he behaved in power very much as if he were in opposition. His neglect of Court and closet, his preoccupation with his party, his unceasing cultivation of extra-parliamentary support all smacked more of the 'outs' than the 'ins'. George III was puzzled by this – he remarked to Bute on the curious way in which Rockingham and his colleagues were 'still imbibing those strange ideas in government, that they addopted [*sic*] whilst in opposition'.[19] In part this bizarre phenomenon, so much at variance with the attitudes of old corps Whiggism under Walpole and the Pelhams, was the product of the circumstances that had beset the 'Old Whigs' since the death of Henry Pelham in 1754. They had seen the Elder Pitt achieve the heights of power and prestige apparently supported by little but the force of public opinion. They had as they believed been gratuitously humiliated and spurned by the young George III and the upstart Bute. They had had to learn, most of them for the first time in their lives, the arts of systematic opposition, and had witnessed the spectacular embarrassments that John Wilkes had inflicted on the Court. Against this background it need not be altogether surprising that Rockingham and his friends took up rather eccentric positions when they were restored to office themselves. Their animus against the Court and its more loyal adherents, their excessive concern with opinion outside Parliament, their anxiety to establish their new administration on a rigidly partisan

18 Sheffield City Library, Wentworth Woodhouse Muniments, R1–679: 24 Aug. 1766. I am indebted to the Earl Fitzwilliam and his trustees for permission to consult and quote from these manuscripts.
19 *Letters from George III to Lord Bute, 1756-65*, ed. R. Sedgwick (London, 1939), p. 242.

basis, all had much to do with their experience of the decade before
1765. But equally important was the mentality that Rockingham personally brought to his party and his administration. Though Rockingham
himself had been a courtier in the 1750s he retained in his political make-
up an authentic streak of the old country Whiggism which had always
been strong in the north. In Yorkshire he was very much at home
among the country gentlemen and businessmen to whom the Court
mentality was wholly alien.[20] His friends were men like Sir George
Savile and David Hartley, themselves thoroughly impractical 'country'
politicians steeped in the political traditions of 'independence'. Once
Rockingham was released from the Court orbit by the breakdown of
relations between George III and the 'Old Whigs' he began to exploit
this heritage on the national scene, and with his elevation to the
Treasury in 1765 it became a critical factor in the direction he and his
party took. Edmund Burke was to weave the party's political experience in the mid-sixties into a sophisticated theory of party and opposition. But at base the traditions and principles that Burke employed to
such effect were those of his patron.

In retrospect it is clear that Rockingham's political attitudes did
nothing but damage to his own ministerial career. After resigning from
the Court of George III in 1762 he spent all but fifteen months of the
remainder of his career in opposition. His two brief periods as Prime
Minister he owed not in the least to his own tactics or activities. In 1765
it was the accident of Grenville's folly at Court that put him in office and
in 1782 it was the accident of military disaster in North America that did
so. In each case the failure of the existing regime, not the strength of
the Rockingham party, was the decisive factor. Yet the whole story
could so easily have been different if in his crucial year of power from
1765 to 1766 Rockingham had adopted a totally different strategy. By
resolving to establish himself in the favour of the King, by rebuilding
the shattered Court and Treasury party on the basis of an alliance between his own and Bute's friends, by ceasing to seek the patronage of
the Elder Pitt, by eschewing mistaken notions of popularity, he could
reasonably have remained the King's minister until his death. If he had

[20] On this aspect of Rockingham's career and character see C. Collyer, 'The
Rockingham Connection and Country Opinion in the Early Years of George III',
Proceedings of Leeds Philosophical and Literary Society, vii (1952–5), 251–75; 'The
Rockinghams and Yorkshire Politics, 1742–61', *Publications of Thoresby Society*, xli,
Thoresby Miscellany, xii (1954), 352–82.

any political talents at all they were those of the party leader – shelving awkward questions, averting divisive quarrels, and generally working through compromise. In administration the role of a Lord Liverpool would have suited him temperamentally and it might well have suited the times. Yet Rockingham clung to his 'principles'. In fact so marked was his contempt for the considerations of expediency urged on him by more pragmatic politicians, that some of his friends, perhaps rightly, came to suspect that he valued his public reputation far more than his ministerial career. 'My Lord Rockingham,' Newcastle wrote in June 1766, 'I believe, wishes to go out, and flatters himself that he shall go out with more *éclat* than any man ever did.'[21] Whatever the truth of this, Rockingham's strange conduct, while reducing his term as Prime Minister, contrived to make him the darling of generations of Whigs, a liberal Victorian before his time.

BIBLIOGRAPHY

Unfortunately there is no satisfactory biography of Rockingham. Albemarle's *Memoirs of the Marquis of Rockingham and his Contemporaries* (London, 1852) is useful only for the extracts from Rockingham's correspondence printed, though even these are often inaccurately reproduced and badly edited. G. H. Guttridge, *The Early Career of Lord Rockingham: 1730–65* (University of California Publications in History, xliv, 1952), deals only with Rockingham's younger days. The two Rockingham ministries are covered respectively by P. Langford, *The First Rockingham Administration, 1765–6* (Oxford, 1973), and J. A. Cannon, *The Fox-North Coalition* (Cambridge, 1969). Among the many monographs which touch on aspects of Rockingham's years in opposition, the following are particularly useful: G. H. Guttridge, *English Whiggism and the American Revolution* (Berkeley and Los Angeles, 1963); J. Brooke, *The Chatham Administration, 1766–8* (London, 1956); B. Donoghue, *British Politics and the American Revolution* (London, 1964); I. R. Christie, *The End of North's Ministry, 1780–2* (London, 1958). I. R. Christie's *Myth and Reality in Late Eighteenth-Century British Politics and Other Papers* (London, 1970) has invaluable essays on the Rockingham party in opposition. Finally, though there are very many articles that cast light on various aspects of Rockingham's career, three deserve a special mention. L. S. Sutherland, 'Edmund Burke and the First Rockingham Ministry', *English Historical Review*, xlvii (1932) 46–72, identifies the precise role of Burke and Rockingham in relation to the commercial interests. C. Collyer, 'The Rockingham Connection and Country Opinion in the Early Years of George III', *Proceedings of Leeds Philosophical and Literary Society*, vii (1952–5), 251–75, and 'The Rockinghams and Yorkshire Politics, 1742–61', *Thoresby Miscellany*, xii (1954), 352–82, reveal the importance of Rockingham's Yorkshire background.

[21] Newcastle's *Narrative of the Changes in the Ministry*, p. 75.

9

WILLIAM PITT, EARL OF CHATHAM

BY

STANLEY AYLING

William Pitt, born 15 November 1708, younger son of Robert Pitt, MP, and Harriet Villiers. Educated at Eton, Oxford and Utrecht. Cornet of Dragoons 1731. MP for Old Sarum 1735–47; Seaford 1747–54; Aldborough 1754–6; Okehampton 1756–7; Bath 1756–66. Dismissed from cornetcy by George II and Walpole 1736; Groom of the Chamber to Frederick, Prince of Wales 1737–45; Commons spokesman for Prince 1737–41. Unsuccessfully demanded action against Walpole on his fall in 1742; inherited £10,000 from the Duchess of Marlborough for opposing Walpole 1744. First acute depressive attack 1744. Excluded from Pelham's government of 1744; Paymaster 1746. Second breakdown 1751–3. Married 1754 Lady Hester Grenville; three sons (including William, second son, later Prime Minister, born 1759), two daughters. Denied Commons leadership 1754. Secretary of State, November 1756 (dismissed April 1757); Pitt–Newcastle coalition 1757–61 (resigned and accepted pension and peerage for wife 1761). Supported repeal of the Stamp Act 1766; formed ministry (Lord Privy Seal) and accepted Earldom of Chatham 1766. Resigned 1768 following third breakdown. On recovery opposed Grafton and North governments. Collapsed while opposing American independence in the Lords, April 1778, and died on 11 May 1778.

WILLIAM PITT, EARL OF CHATHAM

'The first question I shall ask when I go to town,' wrote Horace Walpole in June 1768, 'will be, how my Lord Chatham does. I shall mind
his health more than the stocks. The least symptom of a war will
certainly cure him.' Walpole was always amused to wonder 'how much
the mountebank had concurred to form the great man', and his uncharitable scepticism that summer, when a desperately ill Chatham lay
torpid under his depression, was justified at least to this extent: it was
the threats and opportunities of war that had always brought out the
best of his ferocious energies. He had first gained prominence in the
1730s, demanding war with Spain: 'When trade is at stake . . . you
must defend it or perish.' He had saved his country at a moment of crisis
in the subsequent war with France. He had gone on to demand war *à
outrance* when the nation, sated by his victories, had had enough of it.
And after the peace of 1763, nothing roused his energy and eloquence
more than the fear of another war that might bring disaster in America
and revenge for France.

From the beginning he had claimed to represent 'the voice of
England', and there were times – certainly between 1756 and 1760, and
perhaps even as early as 1739 during the clamour against Spain – when
the claim was reasonable. The source of Britain's greatness, he always
maintained, lay in overseas trade. Her interests were hence global rather
than continental; and for many years he preached that her policies ought
not to be tied to Hanover's tail – thus by the offence given to George II
long precluding himself from major office. Sir Robert Walpole held that
commerce would flourish best in peace; Pitt that it required a constant
readiness for war. Over Spain, the more vulnerable Bourbon power, his
views fluctuated as the years passed; during the fifties he was anxious to
secure her neutrality. But towards the formidable power of France he
never wavered. Britain's trade, her prosperity and that of her colonies,
would not be secure until the French were mastered.

Blackballed by the King and belonging to no parliamentary connection once he had parted company with the 'Patriots' and the Prince of
Wales, Pitt until the beginning of the Seven Years War spent his

energies either in opposition or in minor office only. During that time the Spanish war ('of Jenkins's Ear') was succeeded by the general European war ('of the Austrian Succession'). Then came a breathing-space with the Peace of Aix-la-Chapelle which, except for Italy, settled nothing. While in Europe preparations continued for a renewal of the war, on the disputed frontier of North America and along the Bengal and Coromandel coasts of India the contest never ceased, as British traders, regardless of the quarrels between Prussia and the Habsburg Empire, or of the necessity of protecting Hanover from the French, fought to secure or enlarge their interests.

This was the struggle that absorbed Pitt's attention. The strategy with which to wage it was developed, in the light of his contacts with merchants trading with the West Indies and America and along the shores of Africa and India, during the long years in which he built up his reputation in the Commons and with the public, ostentatiously waived the customary substantial perquisites of the Pay Office, and manoeuvred fruitlessly for high office. All this time he conducted his fluctuating personal battle with physical illness and mental instability, either (for two prolonged periods) in his private hell of acute depression, or in the public theatre of the Commons, huge-booted and flannelled against his gout, often looking ill enough to convince many he was dying.

During his nine years as Paymaster, Pitt laboured to deserve the promotion that he never doubted ought to be his. Sometimes in the cause of loyalty – and perhaps self-advancement – he sacrificed his better judgement, though he could not resist standing firm against Pelham's naval economies. Several times he earned, and accepted, charges of inconsistency. He had to admit modifying his views on Hanover; he conceded the need for subsidising Britain's European allies; and in 1751 he spoke in favour of a peace with Spain which left Britain miles short of those minimum claims he had earlier laid down as prerequisites for peace. Still George II maintained his ban, and the Pelhams did not labour over-strenuously to break it. Indeed, when Pelham died in 1754, Newcastle, succeeding him, first attempted to manage the Commons through a minor second-rate politician, and then, when this broke down, chose Henry Fox rather than Pitt to lead the House.

Meanwhile events pointed clearly to an early resumption of war, and Newcastle's attempts to avoid it aroused Pitt's scorn only a little less than his subsequent efforts to wage it. For a time a second prolonged mental and physical breakdown held Pitt back. Then the blessing of his marriage, and the access of vigour that coincided with it, helped to make once again a formidable man of him. Released from obligations to Newcastle, appealing now in a torrent of speeches not only to the Commons but over the heads of King and Government to the nation at large, he hammered away from the outset of the 1755 session at the unpreparedness and incompetence which, he claimed, looked like losing command of the seas, sacrificing 'the long injured, long neglected, long forgotten people of America', and frittering away an empire. An electric presence, with his hawk nose and scorching glance, he was mordantly sarcastic at ministers' expense, mournfully eloquent at the nation's plight, arrogantly yet soberly convinced that he and only he could save the country. While 140,000 men were ready to defend Hanover, only 'two miserable battalions of Irish' had been sent to America. We were sending our money abroad 'to buy courage or defence' when we should have been 'like Athens putting ourselves aboard our fleet', reinforcing the American colonies, and building up a militia at home. He prayed to God, he said, the King might not 'have Minorca, like Calais, written on his heart'. When Minorca (the principal Mediterranean base) was indeed lost, followed by the British forts at Oswego on Lake Ontario, and the French finally signed their alliance with the Habsburgs, a Pitt ministry began to look the only alternative to national humiliation. The one possible alternative, which the King would have preferred as the lesser of two evils, a ministry led by Fox, was put out of court by Pitt's refusal to have any truck with it. Pitt held out for his own terms. He must have an inquiry into the late ministry's conduct, have personal access to the King, and be 'in the first concert and concoction of measures'. The 'succour and preservation of America' must have priority, while a home militia must be established. Not specifically demanding the right to name his Cabinet colleagues, he nevertheless tendered his draft list, excluding Newcastle and all his recent chief lieutenants, and suggesting a figure of dignified rank, the Duke of Devonshire, for the Treasury. Pitt himself, in the office of Secretary of State, was of course to be *de facto* Prime Minister.

In one sense it was a false start. 'Great genius,' Lyttelton observed of him, 'is not conducted by the rules of common prudence'; and Pitt, strongly as he enjoyed the support of the merchants and professional classes, and backed though he was by many independent country-gentlemen members, by Tories, and of course by his own family connection of the Grenvilles, had neglected to provide himself with a parliamentary majority. He spurned Fox and the Cumberland connection; he had ousted Newcastle and Hardwicke, who led the main Whig group. Devonshire had accepted the Treasury with mixed feelings and was soon anxious to resign. The King described his ministers as scoundrels. Even the city merchants and public opinion grew cooler in their praise of Pitt when he courageously opposed sacrificing Admiral Byng as a scapegoat for Minorca. Finally Cumberland refused to act as commander-in-chief while Pitt remained chief minister.

Declining to resign, Pitt was dismissed in April 1757, after less than five months in office; but even in that short time the conduct of the war was given a new spirit. The Hessians and Hanoverians whom a scared Newcastle had imported for defence were sent back to Germany, and against the opposition of the Lords a militia was established. New battalions were raised, old regiments expanded, and two new ones formed from recently rebellious Highland clans. (It would 'gain the Scotch', Pitt hoped – and happily they might settle in America at the end of the war.) He husbanded his ships as well as the precarious situation allowed, and immediately laid down an ambitious building programme, with heavy emphasis on a new class of fast frigates. Working with furious energy, and in practice dictator of the Admiralty and War Office as well as both the Secretaries' offices, he set an urgent and novel atmosphere of 'action this day'. He planned general strategy, giving priority to the attack on Canada; but no detail was too small for his attention. He always delegated as little as possible; he himself must attend to the arrangements for convoys, to the preparation of siege trains, even to the condition of a consignment of ammunition flints. His under-secretaries he treated as clerks. Once a dragoon himself, he had studied war, and understood logistics; in contact too over many years with merchants at home and abroad, he was well instructed in the geography and economics of America and the Caribbean. His colleagues found him impressive, but overbearing and more than a little mad. Indeed he never recognised colleagues but only subordinates: as Newcastle was later to complain, 'such treatment cannot be borne . . . he will be Treasurer, Secretary, General, and Admiral'. Towards those inferiors who protested that impossibilities were being asked of them, his scorn could be annihilating. 'Sir,' he said to one, indicating the crutches his gout required, 'I walk upon impossibilities.'

The public support he had accumulated was demonstrated during the eleven weeks when George II looked fruitlessly for a new administration. It 'rained gold boxes', and nineteen of the nation's chief cities offered the discarded minister their freedom. As Johnson remarked, Pitt was 'a minister given by the people to the King' – in itself a phenomenon of significant novelty. Newcastle, seeing that Pitt was indispensable, negotiated an understanding with him; and the King was obliged to reinstate him. Newcastle, appointed First Lord of the Treasury, while twittering querulously that he 'would not be inferior' to Pitt, was realist enough to accept that 'after near forty years' he would leave 'ordinary business' to others and 'desire the King's permission to trouble him only twice a week'. He was quite aware that 'if he whispered in the Closet or gave any disturbance in Parliament . . . he might expect all kinds of hostilitys from Mr P'. In fact, he was to play his part to the general satisfaction and even to Pitt's. Attending to parliamentary management, conferring regularly with Pitt on matters of supply, fretting constantly over the war's expense, chronically alarmed at the rashness of sending so many troops abroad, he privately considered that Pitt's notion 'of being able to extirpate the French from North America' was 'the idlest of all imaginings'. But he soon accommodated himself to the badgering and bullying; and recognising, however ruefully, Pitt's qualities, he was ready to support him even when he was being most outrageous – for example in 1759 when Pitt provoked a crisis by forcing the King to bestow the Garter upon his insufferable brother-in-law Temple. From his side Pitt proceeded on the assumption that his monopoly of policy was absolute. Even in financial matters he was by no means prepared to leave things to Newcastle, especially where the King's German troops were concerned. 'The demand of forage for the Hessians' was 'preposterous'; and how possibly could he persuade the Commons to budget for 'another 38,000 Germans'? 'In the name of God, my Lord, how came such an idea on paper?' In fact the Commons was ready for three years and more to eat out of his hand. 'Mr Pitt declares only what he would have them do,' wrote Chesterfield, 'and they do it *nemine contradicente*'.

Hard as he looked at continental commitments, Pitt had moved a long way from his earlier contempt for Hanover and hostility to the King's 'German business'. He was now ready to contribute a containing force of British or British-hired troops to the continental army led by Ferdinand of Brunswick, and for the rest of his life he was to be a champion of the Prussian alliance, with its wartime obligation of subsidies for Frederick the Great. He was also committed to some much criticised diversionary raids on the French coast. But of the main targets he was never for a moment in doubt – mastery of the seas and, by means of that, the conquest of French overseas trade. Even supporting Prussia was only to 'conquer America in Germany'. Territory in itself, without strategic or commercial advantage, possessed no attraction. It was still arguable in Pitt's day whether the single sugar island of Guadeloupe or the whole of Canada should be reckoned the richer prize – and Pitt himself contended that victory in Canada would be thrown away if it did not carry with it the Newfoundland cod-fishing monopoly, which was worth as much as the rest of Canada's wealth combined. Taking Goree, off the Senegal coast, was a necessary step to damaging the French silk industry (through the trade in gum) and denying France the benefits of the slave trade upon which in turn the sugar trade rested. The capture of Mauritius (contemplated but never actually undertaken) would have undermined the whole French trading position in India. Nothing was more distant from his ambitions than an extensive territorial empire in India; indeed the very successes there of Clive and Eyre Coote were later to cause him problems to which he had no answer. Trade was the goal. The sacrifices involved in its pursuit were an investment for future wealth and greatness.

After two years of setbacks and disappointments but also of wide-ranging and ambitious preparations, in 1758 the tale of victories began to come in. 'God send a miracle to save old England at last,' Thomas ('Diamond') Pitt, then Governor of Madras, had written home to his son – Pitt's father – in 1704, before the news of Blenheim could reach India. By the summer of 1758, and increasingly during 1759, it looked as though his prayer was being posthumously answered, and ironically by one of his own 'cockatrice brood of Pitts', against whom he had railed so constantly. Apart from Clive's extraordinary performance at Plassey, news of which was long delayed, the first successes of this new (so-called Seven Years) war were Prussian – Frederick's defeat of the French at Rossbach and the Austrians at Leuthen. Then in July 1758 Louisbourg, the gateway to the St Lawrence and the strongest fortress in North America, fell to the combined sea and land assault of Boscawen and Amherst. Pitt's reputation as miracle man was established. Thanksgivings in St Paul's, bonfires and illuminations in the City, celebrations throughout Britain and British America greeted the event and its architect. 'Nothing but congratulations to you my dear brother

Louisbourg', wrote Temple, 'I shall never call you by any other name except that of Quebeck in good time.' On the mainland Fort Duquesne on the Ohio was next taken and renamed Fort Pitt; it is the modern Pittsburg. In December Goree was captured. During 1759 the tempo quickened. The French lost Guadeloupe. The continental army defeated them at Minden. Boscawen destroyed part of the Toulon fleet at Lagos Bay – in neutral Portuguese waters; but it would be rather easier, Pitt considered, for Britain to satisfy the Portuguese Court than for the French to replace their battleships. In September the assault on Quebec which Pitt and his advisers had first envisaged a dozen or more years earlier was at last brought to success by Wolfe; and to close a triumphant year came news of Hawke's no less daring victory over the Brest fleet in Quiberon Bay. Naval supremacy, the *sine qua non* of all Pitt's enterprises, was by then secured, and Garrick's company at Drury Lane could celebrate the achievement that New Year's Eve with a popular new number:

> Come cheer up my lads, 'tis to glory we steer. . . .
> Heart of oak are our ships,
> Heart of oak are our men. . . .
> We'll fight and we'll conquer again and again.

By September 1760 Montreal had fallen, and with it in effect all Canada. Of major British objectives only Minorca, Martinique and Mauritius remained unattained.

Widely differing circumstances combined at this stage to weaken Pitt's position, public idol though he had become. Two royal deaths contributed. Abroad, Ferdinand VI of Spain, who had pursued neutrality, was succeeded in 1759 by Charles III, who prepared to reactivate the Bourbon Family Compact. At home, George III, succeeding his grandfather in October 1760, was under the influence of Lord Bute, once Pitt's tactical ally but now his most dangerous rival; and Bute stood for peace. George III, wishing to install him as chief minister, looked forward to the day when he could be rid of many of the presiding group of Whig politicians, including both Newcastle, his grandfather's 'knave and counsellor', and 'that mad Pitt', who had treated both Bute and George himself with scant regard and had apparently forgotten that 'a day must come when he must expect to be treated according to his deserts'.

George III did not, however, dismiss Pitt. Pitt dismissed himself.

That this could be accepted without overmuch dismay was partly because, by 1760, he had in large measure performed what the nation had
asked. There was little fear now of invasion. Choiseul's new plans for
yet another attempt inspired no anxiety, except in the breast of Newcastle, where anxiety was endemic. The overseas empire had been
saved, and enough new bargaining counters won to be put into peace
negotiations against the return of Minorca – with ample to spare, both
for glory and the balance-sheets. Most country gentlemen felt it was
time to think of reducing the Land Tax down. Some even of Pitt's
City supporters were nervous about going for a colonial grand slam.
Might not a flood of sugar bring a slump in profits? Influential voices in
the Cabinet and outside spoke of the likelihood of a great European
coalition against Britain if victory was pushed too far. Exploratory
negotiations with France were begun in March 1761, and more than
once Pitt was outvoted in Cabinet on the projected terms. He still
wanted 'the total destruction of the French in the East Indies', and
refused to accept sharing the Newfoundland fisheries with the French.
Now that the French navy had been mastered, he considered that a
Franco-Spanish alliance and an extension of the war could be confidently faced. The Spanish Empire was infinitely more vulnerable in
1761 than the French had been in 1755: 'You are prepared, and she is
not.' In any case, Pitt argued, it was better openly to fight France and
Spain than to be faced by France aided by Spanish money, ships, and port
facilities, which was the likely alternative. When his intelligence sources
told him that Spain's decision to declare war was taken, he argued in the
Cabinet for a pre-emptive strike against her, before her home-coming
treasure fleet could make port. Only Temple supported him – and
resigned with him when the rest of the Cabinet decided to await Spanish
action. He would go on no longer, he declared, since his advice was
spurned. He would be responsible for nothing he did not direct.

The impetus of his direction carried over into the last phase of
hostilities. Belle Isle had been taken a little before Pitt's resignation,
and the great prize of Martinique soon after it; and when the Spaniards
entered the war they were defeated in Cuba and the Philippines. Yet
the peace which Bedford was already negotiating in Paris on behalf of
a government in which Bute was now dominant, restored so much to
France and Spain that the mercantile community was outraged; and
Pitt, pallid and emaciated, gloved and bandaged, was carried into the
Commons to denounce for three and a half hours – much of the time

sitting, and in low spectral tones – our 'treacherous' desertion of Prussia, the abandonment 'of all the Spanish treasure and riches that lay at our feet', and above all the neglect

'of the great fundamental principle that France is chiefly, if not solely, to be dreaded by us in the light of a maritime and commercial power – and therefore by restoring to her all the valuable West Indian Islands, and by our concessions in the Newfoundland fishery, we have given her the means of recovering her prodigious losses. . . .'

For the next three and a half years, while George III struggled with the Whig factions, Pitt stayed in the shadows, invalid but still ambitious and redoubtable; aloof, oracular, unpredictable, and unbending. He could still compel in the Commons the sort of attention given to no one else so intensely, as when he pleaded for the repeal of the Stamp Act and a policy of conciliation towards the Americans. When, however, on repeated occasions negotiations were begun with him upon his conditions for re-entering the King's service and so lending this or that administration the strength and stability his name might bestow, Pitt's responses were devious and ambiguous. He was a master of the opaque rigmarole. He mystified and exasperated. And his ever-shifting relationships with his brothers-in-law, George Grenville and Lord Temple, added fresh dimensions of complication. When all the provisos and qualifications were at last translated into intelligible statements, these usually amounted to a refusal to consider any terms other than those that would make him dictator of policy.

When, after years of ministerial confusion, he finally returned to office in 1766, it was at the head of a government hand-picked to do his bidding; three of his own followers in Grafton, Camden, and Shelburne, and the rest chosen one or two from this group and one or two from that, with the deliberate intention of breaking parties and the spirit of party – 'to root out the present method of banding together', as George III hopefully expressed it. It was to be a government of patriotic renewal. There was certainly no doubt who was to be Prime Minister – few ministers have ever been quite so 'prime' as Pitt in the summer of 1766 – but the post of First Lord of the Treasury (after Temple had bad-temperedly refused it) went to the Duke of Grafton. Pitt knew that his own health was too precarious to be burdened with the weight of Commons business. He had, moreover, never lacked a desire for rank or an esteem for wealth and grandeur. (Since inheriting a large estate in Somerset from an admirer he was during these years overspending wildly and perhaps pathologically upon it.) So now, becoming Lord Privy Seal, he accepted the Earldom of Chatham, and thus at a stroke destroyed one pillar upon which his strength had rested – the magic he could wield as the Great Commoner. As Walpole coolly observed, 'The silence of the House [of Lords], and the decency of the debate there, were not suited to that inflammatory eloquence by which Lord Chatham had been accustomed to raise huzzas from a more numerous auditory.'

Chatham's ministry, declared Burke, the great subsequent champion of party, was 'a tessellated pavement without cement'; and very soon the tesserae began to work loose. The Prussian Ambassador noted how at the King's levee Pitt held his own 'levee' in the ante-room, handing ministers a note as they left him, with their instructions written on it; and Charles Townshend was not the only minister who resented Chatham's style. It proved, moreover, even more difficult to compel policies than men. None of the three major concerns that exercised Chatham at this time, conciliation of the Americans, limitation of the East India Company's powers, and an Anglo-Russo-Prussian alliance against the Bourbons, proved amenable to his efforts. Reasonably fearing French preparations for a counter-stroke, he plunged into the project of the anti-Bourbon alliance as though war were imminent; but neither Frederick nor the Tsarina Catherine showed interest. And the Americans, whom Chatham hoped to be able to treat as patriotic Englishmen happening to live overseas, proceeded to present demands that so dedicated an imperialist could not possibly entertain. The merchants of New York, he was pained to observe, 'disobedient', 'irritable and umbrageous', were 'quite out of their senses'.

Within a few weeks of taking office Chatham had retired to Bath for a month to nurse an attack of gout which had among other things incapacitated his writing hand. During the autumn he was back in London, forcing himself and others along with all his old drive, though the total of his attendances in the Lords during his whole ministry amounted to two only. By Christmas 1766 he had returned to Bath, and only after two abortive attempts managed to get himself back to London by March, when immediately he collapsed again. That he was very sick there is no doubt; but a fair relative appraisal of physical and psychological factors in his complicated and erratic infirmity is not to be determined. Shrewd, but not shrewd enough, Horace Walpole wondered if the 'master dissembler' was being 'extravagant by design'. Many, including the King, for a time suspected some malingering, the more so as he was occasionally reported out horse-riding. But undeniably by the spring of 1767 Chatham was the pitiable victim (it was the third time for him) of what contemporaries sometimes knew as 'gout in the head', their euphemism for madness. He was suffering from fever, digestive disorders, insomnia, giddiness, and palpitations; from irrationality, mental confusions and distortions; and for long stretches from a paralysing stupor that robbed him of the will to move or eat or speak – the extreme depressive stage of his psychosis. His doctor and his devoted wife, who was his secretary, nurse, and guardian angel, hopefully awaited a good strong return of the gout, which it was believed would expel these evil humours.

For the rest of 1767 and throughout 1768 he remained in a generally poor state, sometimes being driven out or even riding, but mostly unable to concentrate, and sometimes almost comatose. Meanwhile his ministers pursued policies and imposed measures – in particular concerning the East India Company and American taxation – which a Chatham in control would not have approved.

In 1766 the East India Company's charter was due for statutory renewal. Chatham had for some years been 'uneasy' over India, as he had told Clive, and even before his collapse the vast recent acquisitions were the subject of Cabinet disagreements. The trade in sugar and slaves by which many of Chatham's City supporters grew rich never roused a whisper from him; but the grandson of 'Diamond' Pitt spoke strongly against those East India merchants who 'lived in riot and luxury' upon 'the ignorant, the innocent, the helpless'. He had never accepted that British conquests in India belonged wholly, by right, to the Company. It would be fanciful to suppose that he ever envisaged any future British *raj* in India; but he did wish to see some of the Company's territorial revenues surrendered to the State. The quarrels, principally with Townshend, had arisen over how, and how much. As Chatham sank into inactivity all he would say was that 'he would make no plan', and that the matter should 'find its way through the House'. It was plain that British-controlled India had become too big to be managed by a body of merchants but, as Rockingham wrote to Burke in 1772, 'In regard to what Lord Chatham's ideas may be on East Indian matters': I am not sure that his Lordship has had *or ever had any* fixed plan or idea on that subject.'

Chatham summoned the strength to resign – or as George III saw it, finally to desert – in October 1768. By then he was on the way to as good a recovery as his battle-scarred constitution was ever likely to manage. By mid-1769 a visitor discovered him 'high in spirits and in fury' at the Government. He was soon in a mood to be 'a scarecrow of violence', to try anything that might topple first Grafton (who had of course originally come in as Chatham's nominee) and then North, who took over as chief minister in 1770 and behind whom stood the King, stubborn as ever but by now experienced too, and determined not to be outmanoeuvred either by Chatham, that 'trumpet of sedition', or by the Whig clans. The combination of the Rockinghams with a Chatham who was now busily repairing his family alliance with Temple and Grenville did indeed sound formidable, but Burke and Rockingham had no mind to accept this cuckoo in their nest.

For two years Chatham attacked on all fronts, echoing the virulence of 'Junius', even on one occasion, like 'Junius' again, unmistakably attacking the King himself. He fulminated against those who had 'laid the axe to the tree of liberty' by expelling Wilkes from the Commons – not that by this time he had any more respect for Wilkes than Wilkes for him ('flint-hearted' Chatham). Upon the newly raised topic of parliamentary reform he would not advocate abolishing rotten boroughs – for several of which he himself had sat – lest, as he said, amputation of dead limbs should kill the tree; but with the Whigs he denounced the 'corrupting' power of royal influence and supported an increase in the representation of what he took to be the uncorrupt counties. He called, too, for triennial rather than septennial general elections. On India, he called vehemently for intervention against 'the lofty Asiatic plunderers of Leadenhall Street'. And on eight occasions he factiously and fierily attacked the North ministry's quiet settlement of the Falkland Islands dispute with Spain. He loved peace, so he protested, but 'if our honour is to be the expense of our tranquillity, let discord reign'.

The American problem remained, and dominated Chatham's last years, while his powers ebbed. Though he unequivocally affirmed Britain's right to regulate imperial trade and impose 'external' taxation, he continued to deny her right to tax 'internally' – a distinction which sounded constructive until an incident such as the Boston Tea Party exposed its limitations. He had once claimed to 'rejoice' at the resistance of the Americans, yet he deeply dreaded the consequences. To safeguard and strengthen the colonies of the western hemisphere had always been at the top of his priorities; and now, partly through the umbrageousness of the Americans but, he considered, vastly more through the blindness of the British, the whole edifice was in danger. Worse, France, rebuilding her navy, was preparing to seize her moment of revenge. In his now rare descents upon Parliament Chatham made repeated pleas for some show of 'affection' to which the English in America might respond. In 1774 he took the Protestant New Englanders' side in their resentment against the Quebec Act, a measure designed to increase the 'affection' of French Americans for British rule. Any concession to the French appeared to him a dangerous mischief.

A Chatham in full control over the years from 1763 could probably have done no more than delay the revolt of the Americans. For all his willingness to 'be to their faults a little kind', and despite his ability to see that even victory must mean defeat ('You cannot *make* them buy your cloth'), his views remained rooted in the old colonial system. The colonies beyond the Atlantic were 'the fountain of our wealth, the nerve of our strength, the nursery and basis of our naval power'. He would never concede that America, in the process of becoming a nation, must sooner or later wish for independence. To accept *that* – he would as soon, he declared, swallow trans-substantiation. When in April 1778 the Duke of Richmond moved that the King withdraw his troops from the revolted provinces, Chatham's concern was 'unspeakable'. Infirm and agitated, he had insisted on travelling to Westminster. He spoke, faltered, and resumed 'with shreds of eloquence' protesting against ignominious surrender, before he suffered his final and fatal collapse. To the last he sustained what Horace Walpole called his one style, the epic; 'the multiplication table' was not for him.

BIBLIOGRAPHY

Brooke, J., *The Chatham Administration of 1766–8* (London, 1956)

Corbett, Sir J. S., *England in the Seven Years War* (2 vols, London, 1907)

Eyck, E., *Pitt versus Fox, Father and Son* (London, 1950)

Hotblack, K., *Chatham's Colonial Policy* (London, 1917)

Kimball, G. S., *Correspondence with Colonial Governors* . . . (2 vols, New York, 1900).

Macaulay, Lord, 'William Pitt' and 'The Earl of Chatham', in *Essays* (London, 1834, 1844)

Namier, Sir L., *England in the Age of the American Revolution* (2nd edn, London, 1961)

Plumb, J. H., *Chatham* (London, 1953)

Robertson, Sir C. G., *Chatham and the British Empire* (London, 1946)

Rosebery, Lord, *Chatham, his Early Life and Connections* (London, 1910)

Sherrard, O. A., *Lord Chatham* (3 vols, London, 1952–8)

Taylor, W. S. and Pringle, J. H. (eds), *Chatham Correspondence* (4 vols, London, 1839)

Tunstall, B., *William Pitt, Earl of Chatham* (London, 1938) (the best one-volume biography)

Williams, B., *William Pitt, Earl of Chatham* (2 vols, London, 1913) (the standard Life)

10

THE DUKE OF GRAFTON

BY

PETER DURRANT

Augustus Henry Fitzroy, born 28 September 1735, elder son of Lord Augustus Fitzroy (d. 1741) and grandson of the 2nd Duke of Grafton, whom he succeeded in 1757. Educated at Peterhouse, Cambridge, 1751–3. Married (1) 1756 Anne Liddell (Div. 1769); three sons, one daughter. (2) 1769 Elizabeth Wrottesley; five sons, eight daughters. MP for Bury St Edmunds 1756–7; Lord of the Bedchamber to the Prince of Wales 1756–7; Lord Lieutenant of Suffolk 1757–63, 1769–90; Secretary of State for the Northern Department 1765–6; first Lord of the Treasury 1766–70; KG 1769; Lord Privy Seal 1771–1775, 1782–1783. Died 14 March 1811.

THE DUKE OF GRAFTON

Grafton's appointment as First Lord of the Treasury in July 1766 was unusual in that he was not thereby appointed Prime Minister. Traditionally the First Lord of the Treasury had assumed the leadership of administration; but in 1766 the King had summoned William Pitt, not Grafton, to form a government. Pitt, however, regarded with distaste the prospect of involvement in the day-to-day business of administration, and he retired to the House of Lords, as Earl of Chatham, to direct affairs from the less demanding post of Lord Privy Seal. Grafton was appointed, in effect, as Chatham's man of business. Not until twelve months later did he assume the leadership of the ministry.

Chatham pressed Grafton to accept office because he realised that in few others was proven ability coupled with such considerable devotion to himself. The Duke had first established himself in politics as a leader of the 'Young Friends' of the Duke of Newcastle in opposition to Bute and Grenville. Such diverse people as George III, Burke and Charles James Fox testified to his ability in debate.[1] He had, moreover, some experience, albeit limited, of office, under Rockingham in 1765–6. Above all he possessed a high personal opinion of Chatham, believing that Chatham's leadership was vital to a successful administration.[2] When Chatham threatened to retire from politics unless Grafton joined him, the Duke had little option but to agree.

It was nevertheless with great reluctance that Grafton accepted the appointment. His early enthusiasm for politics, manifested in 1762–3, had not endured, and he accepted in 1766, as he had done a year earlier under Rockingham, without eagerness and more from a sense of duty than from delight. He much preferred the life of a country gentleman, and he was invariably happier in the country than in London. There he could indulge in pursuits that really interested him: farming, hunting,

[1] George III to Grafton, 15 Feb. 1768, Grafton MSS 120; Burke to Charles O'Hara, 11 Mar. 1766, *The Correspondence of Edmund Burke*, ed. T. W. Copeland (10 vols, Cambridge, 1958–70), i, 244; C. J. Fox to Sir George Macartney, 14 Mar. 1766, BM Add. MSS 47568, f.8.
[2] Grafton had resigned from the Rockingham administration in May 1766 on these grounds.

racing (his fondness for horse-racing, though greatly criticised, was not really exceptional by the standards of the day), and, more unusually, collecting and talking about books. His friends were drawn from men who shared these interests, rarely from the political world.[3] And he greatly preferred to enjoy their company in the relaxed atmosphere of Euston Hall, his Suffolk home, than to immerse himself in the tensions and perplexities of public life.

In unfamiliar society, Grafton seems generally to have been shy and uneasy. His 'dislike of anything of a public nature' had been noted in Italy in 1762;[4] nor had his feelings changed with the passing years. He still disliked the ceremonial aspects of his office, and he was glad to be excused attending Court functions.[5] He could command tact and delicacy in his dealings with people, but he lacked charm and was inclined to seriousness. Under stress he could be short-tempered and irritable, even among friends.[6] Nor was his private life beyond reproach.[7] Casual associates received little encouragement to improve their acquaintance with him, and enemies found him easy material for criticism.[8]

[3] His friends included, for example, Earl Spencer, his neighbour in Northamptonshire; racing men such as Hugo Meynell and the Earl of March; and scholars and intelligent men such as John Symonds, Professor of Modern History at Cambridge; John Hinchcliffe, Bishop of Peterborough and Master of Trinity College, Cambridge; Richard Watson, Bishop of Llandaff and Professor of Chemistry at Cambridge; and Arthur Young, the agriculturalist. The only significant friendships he made through politics were with Camden and Northington.

[4] Sir Horace Mann to Horace Walpole, 12 June 1762, *The Correspondence of Horace Walpole*, ed. W. S. Lewis (24 vols, Yale, 1937–65), xxii, 40.

[5] T. Bradshaw to S. Martin, 4 July 1767, BM Add. MS 41354, f.107; George III to Grafton, 15 Sept. 1768, *The Correspondence of King George III*, ed. Sir J. Fortescue (6 vols, London, 1927), ii, 651.

[6] J. Cradock, *Literary and Miscellaneous Memoirs*, ed. J. B. Nicholls, (4 vols, London, 1828), i, 106.

[7] Grafton's difficulties were considerably increased by domestic unhappiness. Differences with his first wife had led to separation in 1764, when Grafton had taken a mistress. At times of stress, Grafton was prone to be unusually careless of conventional decorum. But it is unjust to call him profligate. He was loyal to his mistress, until his divorce enabled him to remarry. With his second wife he enjoyed more than forty years of contented married life.

[8] He suffered a good deal of adverse criticism, particularly from 'Junius' and Horace Walpole, who between them created a legend of profligacy and indolence which too many historians have been prepared to accept. A man is seldom pictured fairly by his enemies, and much of the criticism they and others levelled against him is merely malicious invention.

Impelled by duty, but hindered by lack of ambition, Grafton never really made a success of his political career. Though he spent most of his life in politics, he was not a career politician. He was a conscientious administrator,[9] attending most of the Treasury Board meetings, and occasionally taking work away with him to Suffolk – where in ten days 'his Grace did more real business than he would have been suffered by solicitors to do for a month in London.[10] He could be resolute and decisive, but his enthusiasm was sporadic, and he very often lacked conviction when dealing with political issues. Partly perhaps because he was pursued by domestic problems, partly because his real interests lay elsewhere, Grafton never really put his heart into politics.

Significantly, he never attached to himself a group of political adherents: when he left the Treasury in 1770 few men followed him. This was partly because his was not an immediately attractive personality: his public aspect did not invite close friendships. But it was also because his own attitude was antipathetic to groups. He was, for example, not interested in building up a following by extending his electoral interests. His only real associates were generally personal friends. During his career he was associated with several political groups, but never as a fully committed member. He was always a little apart. Like his first idol, Chatham, he was something of a solitary figure in politics.

For his first few months in office Grafton relied entirely on Chatham for direction, and would scarcely take even the smallest decision without Chatham's approval. And indeed he was given little encouragement to act independently; for Chatham could be devastatingly critical of anyone who deviated from the path laid down by himself.[11] Yet Chatham's leadership was inadequate from the very beginning. He spent long periods in Bath, too far removed from the centre of affairs to exercise detailed control. By March 1767 he had been overtaken by illness and was completely incapable of political activity. Grafton, who

---

[9] Except in the matter of electioneering, which he found distasteful and tended to neglect. This admittedly was a considerable failing in a prime minister.

[10] T. Bradshaw to S. Martin, 25 Sept. 1767, BM Add. MS 41354, f. 111. And when in 1782 The King criticised North for being two years behind in completing the quarterly account books of the secret service, he added: 'The Duke of Grafton never let a month elapse after the quarter without getting the book finished and delivering it' (J. Brooke, *King George III* (London, 1972), p. 235).

[11] For example in the case of Charles Townshend over the East India Company business in 1766–7.

[159]

had not been appointed to direct affairs, was reluctant to take responsibility, as long as there was a chance of Chatham's recovery. But such a lack of direction was almost disastrous for the ministry. Opposition built up during April and May, and Grafton was faced with the very real prospect of defeat. When the ministry's majority in the House of Lords, normally the stronghold of administration, sank to three (on 26 May 1767), Grafton was very close to resignation. After seeing Chatham – incidentally for the last time in private interview – Grafton resolved to patch up and continue for the rest of the session. But his loyalty to Chatham had almost disappeared. The highhandedness and lack of sympathy that Chatham had shown throughout the preceding year had disgusted Grafton; and by his totally unco-operative response to the King's solicitations during June,[12] Chatham finally forfeited the Duke's regard.[13]

Far from feeling free to retire, however, Grafton felt compelled to carry on by a new loyalty which overpowered his reluctance – a loyalty to King George III. Grafton had always felt a sense of duty towards the Crown; but now this was overlaid and strengthened by a more personal loyalty to the King. And in return he was rewarded with a degree of friendship and support which neither Rockingham nor Grenville had enjoyed. George III and Grafton had been in a similar position *vis-à-vis* Chatham during the preceding twelve months. Both young men who had been in politics for a comparatively short time – and for the King a particularly trying time – they had handed over an unusual degree of authority to Chatham; and he had failed them. Perhaps in this lay the origins of the good relations which indubitably existed between King and minister; relations that were confirmed by Grafton's behaviour at this crisis. For by staying in office he almost certainly averted a political upheaval similar to those of July 1765 and July 1766 – occasions that the King looked back on with dread and that he desperately wished to avoid being repeated. Despite Grafton's faults and even their disagree-

[12] See the letters between George III and Chatham in Fortescue, op. cit., i, 523-4, 530-3, 535-8.
[13] Grafton had no further contact with Chatham except when it was politically unavoidable. He endeavoured to stop Chatham resigning in October 1768, but largely because he feared the effect it would have on Camden, at that time his closest Cabinet colleague. In February 1770, Grafton delivered a blistering attack on Chatham during the debate on the State of the Nation. See Horace Walpole, *Memoirs of the Reign of George III*, ed. G. F. R. Barker (4 vols, London, 1894), iv, 63.

THE DUKE OF GRAFTON

ments, the King's goodwill continued until the Duke resigned in 1770.[14]

Grafton needed considerable resolution to abandon the pleasant prospect of retirement and to face the daunting task of rebuilding the ministry. His situation in July 1767 was altogether unenviable. The pressures of opposition were bad enough; but the situation in the Cabinet was yet worse. Grafton had scarcely one colleague on whom he could absolutely rely.[15] Eventually he turned to Lord President Northington, an old political campaigner who had saved the King during the negotiations of the previous summer. With Northington's agreement, Grafton determined to attempt a showdown with Chatham. Together they insisted to the King that it was essential

'that Lord Chatham should either appear and assist in filling up the vacancies that must immediately happen, or otherwise quit any thoughts of being Minister, as it was impossible to continue longer in this state of suspense, or prevail with men of abilities to undertake a temporary plan, which might be totally reversed whenever Lord Chatham's health permitted him to act.'[16]

The measure of Grafton's courage and resolution at this time – unsurpassed in his career – may be taken from his decision to continue even though Chatham ignored the ultimatum, and remained in office as a permanent embarrassment to the administration. By remaining Grafton had in effect accepted responsibility for the administration. Still only thirty-one, he was *de facto* Prime Minister – the youngest Prime minister, with the single exception of the Younger Pitt, in the 250 years between Sir Robert Walpole and the present day.

The negotiations of July 1767 are important not merely because they

[14] In August 1769 the King, conferring the Garter on Grafton, wrote: 'I can with great truth declare that I never gave a Garter with more pleasure and that it is one of the very few I have given unsolicited' (George III to Grafton, 26 Aug. 1769, Grafton MSS 538).

[15] Indeed, he drew up the King's speech for the end of the session with Marchmont and Dyson, neither members of the Cabinet. See G. F. S. Elliot, *The Border Elliots and the Family of Minto* (Edinburgh, 1897), p. 402n. Of the Cabinet, Conway and Northington were anxious to resign, Camden and Shelburne were devoted Chathamites, Townshend was totally untrustworthy, and Granby and Hawke were service chiefs and political nonentities.

[16] Sir Gilbert Elliot's Memorandum, G. F. S. Elliot, op. cit., pp. 402-3.

mark Grafton's arrival as Prime Minister. Together with those of December 1767 they represent a critical point in the emergence of political stability in the 1760s; and they are crucial for an understanding of the nature of political organisation. Grafton had two fairly straight-forward objectives: to increase the support his administration enjoyed in Parliament, and – more important – to bring into his Cabinet some colleagues on whom he could rely. As a disciple of Chatham, Grafton had quoted the master on the subject of forming a ministry composed of the best men from all parties. But experience had not confirmed his belief in this approach. Politicians did to a large extent work in groups. This is not to suggest that parties were fixed and rigid in membership, or that they were the sole units of political organisation. The career of Grafton himself is a denial of this. But parties did exist, and it was necessary in any political calculation to take them into account. Chatham's attempt to build a non-party administration had failed: the Cabinet was in pieces within twelve months of its formation. Grafton had discovered the reality of political grouping in his two unsuccessful attempts to detach individuals from the Bedford coterie. In July 1767 the remains of non-party doctrine were perhaps just evident. Had it been possible, Grafton would have liked to detach support from among the followers of both Bedford and Rockingham – though more to break opposition than to strengthen government. But such a scheme did not preclude the possibility of absorbing a group. Grafton's chief success in July was in dividing the Opposition more firmly into its constituent groups (in itself a useful achievement). That he accepted the fact of party is shown by his willingness in December to take in the Bedfords.

In December 1767 a political party was admitted to administration; but this did not mean that the ministry had become a party ministry. Indeed, one of its chief weaknesses lay in the fact that the Cabinet continued to lack cohesion and unity. In some ways it was as much a collection of individuals as had been Chatham's Cabinet in 1766.[17]

[17] The Cabinet (excluding Chatham) consisted of Grafton himself and nine colleagues. Of these only two, Gower and Weymouth, were from the Bedford group (though the Bedfords had in addition several non-Cabinet posts). North and Hillsborough were primarily king's men. Shelburne remained a Chathamite, and Granby was rapidly becoming one. Camden retained his allegiance to Chatham, but he was wavering, and in October 1768 he declared his support for Grafton, only to return to Chatham in January 1770. Conway was discontented with Grafton, but more inclined to follow his line than any other. Hawke was a nonentity who followed Grafton.

Grafton certainly had colleagues who were thoroughly reliable in their own departments, as Weymouth showed by his handling of the riots in the spring of 1768. But the Cabinet collectively suffered from an inability to make decisions. This weakness was already apparent in February 1768, when the Cabinet failed to give an opinion on the establishment of a legislature in Canada.[18] In part this was undoubtedly due to a genuine divergence of opinion; but to a great extent it was also due to Grafton's failure to give a decisive lead in policy matters.

Within a few weeks of its formation, Grafton's new administration was put to the test by the re-emergence of John Wilkes on to the political stage. Though still outlawed, Wilkes had returned to England in February 1768. The following month he stood as candidate for the City of London in the general election. Defeated but undaunted, he tried again in Middlesex, where, to the accompaniment of much riotous behaviour, he came top of the poll. The ministry was faced with two problems: one was the preservation of public order; the other, a much more delicate political question, was what to do with Wilkes.

On the question of public order, Grafton was quite prepared to back strong measures, as soon as they were seen to be necessary – though he had been reluctant to give the impression of 'finding fault only with the People for their Joy too riotously testified at the late Election'.[19] It was the duty of government to keep order and to preserve society and the Constitution. Though Grafton took little active part in arranging measures – this was Weymouth's department – he gave his approval to a policy of vigour.[20]

In the case of Wilkes himself, Grafton's natural reaction was one of caution. Remembering the trouble that Wilkes had caused Grenville in 1763–4, he had no desire to give gratuitous offence by ill-advised intervention. But those who had pressed for vigorous action against the rioters were anxious to punish Wilkes. The King adopted a similar attitude. Considering his conception of duty to the King and his natural reluctance to assert himself, it is perhaps surprising that Grafton went as far as he did to avoid the application of hard-line measures against Wilkes.

The suggestion that Wilkes be expelled the House of Commons was raised almost as soon as he was elected, and it met with widespread

18 George III to Grafton, 18 Feb. 1768, Grafton MSS 510.
19 Grafton to George III, 31 Mar. 1768, Fortescue, *The Correspondence of King George III*, ii, 605.
20 Grafton to Weymouth, 9 May 1768, Longleat MSS.

approval. The King supported the measure, and 'the ideas of the ministry' also went to expulsion.[21] A meeting of the principal men of the House of Commons independently approved the idea.[22] Nevertheless, Grafton avoided implementing such a course of action. Wilkes had appealed against his outlawry, and Grafton realised that if he was expelled, and then cleared in the courts of law, administration would be very embarrassed; while if his outlawry was upheld, Parliament could most justifiably take action against him. In the event the outlawry was quashed, but a fine and imprisonment substituted for his several offences. Grafton would have been quite happy to leave the matter there; and in spite of the earlier approval for expulsion, he might have succeeded. The matter remained untouched over the summer recess, and the Cabinet was far less sure in October than it had been in April whether to proceed to expulsion.[23] But Wilkes would not accept oblivion. In November, he prepared to present a petition to Parliament. Grafton, hoping to avoid a revival of the problem, endeavoured to dissuade Wilkes by promising that expulsion measures would be dropped if he obliged.[24] But Wilkes refused. The presentation of the petition was the signal for anti-Wilkes speeches in the House of Commons. Barrington, whom Wilkes had particularly libelled, attacked him strongly. Grafton found little support for his attitude.[25] On 3 February 1769 Barrington moved the expulsion of Wilkes. It was carried, and so the farce of the Middlesex elections began.[26]

[21] George III to North, 25 April 1768, Fortescue, op. cit., ii, 613; Rigby to Bedford, 23 April 1768, Bedford MSS, lvii, f.54.

[22] Bradshaw reported to Grafton that the meeting had not been informed that the Government had taken any resolution on the subject of Wilkes (T. Bradshaw to Grafton [25 April 1768], Grafton MSS 309), though those present presumably had some idea of the Government's attitude.

[23] Rigby to Bedford, 31 Oct. 1768, Bedford MSS lvii, f.206.

[24] J. Almon, *The Correspondence of John Wilkes* (5 vols, London, 1805), iii, 293–4.

[25] 'As the times are, I had rather pardon W[ilkes] than punish him. This is a political opinion, independent of the merits of the cause' (Camden to Grafton, 9 Jan. 1769, *Autobiography of the Third Duke of Grafton*, ed. Sir W. Anson (1898), p. 201). But Camden seems not to have supported Grafton in the Cabinet. See H. Walpole, *Memoirs of . . . George III*, iv, 58–9.

[26] Wilkes was expelled on 3 February. He was twice re-elected and twice the elections were annulled by Parliament. After his third re-election in April, the Commons decided that votes cast for Wilkes were invalid, and that Henry Luttrell (defeated by 1,143 votes to 296) had therefore been duly elected. See G. Rude *Wilkes and Liberty* (Oxford, 1962), chapters 3 and 4.

The other major issue that Grafton's administration faced concerned the attitude to be adopted towards the American colonies, which had offered severe provocation during 1768.[27] Grafton was again somewhat awkwardly placed. On this issue the Cabinet was more definitely polarised into authoritarian and conciliatory camps than it had been over Wilkes. Grafton once again favoured moderation, and once again faced a strong force of hard-liners. He certainly cannot be accused of failing to offer a solution to the problem: he had one prepared in November 1768.[28] But it met with little enthusiasm in the Cabinet, and Grafton, though disappointed, did not press it. The crucial decision came in the summer of 1769 when the Cabinet met to decide on the proposals offered by Hillsborough, the Colonial Secretary. They were passed by five votes to four – with Grafton in the minority.[29]

Grafton's failure to provide a commanding leadership in the Cabinet was apparently considerable. The Cabinet clearly had some responsibility for deciding measures. But the extent of the Prime Minister's responsibility for directing policy within the Cabinet was much less clearly defined. Certainly he was not appointed with a 'programme' of measures to put into effect; though it is arguable, with the advantage of hindsight, that the country would have been better served had Grafton pressed his own opinions harder. The Government was the King's Government, carried on with his appointed servants, and Grafton saw his main role as sustaining the King's administration. When it came to negotiation, for example, he was generally prepared to take responsibility; but when it came to deciding policy, he was much less ready to assert himself. Measures had to be favoured by both King and administration before they were possible.[30] The issues facing the administration in 1768–9 were genuinely divisive and Grafton's approach, admittedly not very forcefully presented, failed to find acceptance. But he did not therefore feel it necessary to retire. If the Bedfords gained ascendancy over Grafton – which in itself is doubtful – they did so because they listened more closely to the King.

[27] Hillsborough to George III, 19 and 22 July 1768, Fortescue, op. cit., ii, 637, 638.
[28] Grafton to George III, 29 November 1768, ibid., ii, 673.
[29] Gower, Weymouth, North, Hillsborough and Rochford favoured the measures; Grafton, Camden, Conway and Granby disapproved. Hawke was absent. (Rochford had replaced Shelburne in the Cabinet in October 1768.)
[30] The agreement of both Houses of Parliament was also necessary; but the Court usually had had a potential majority, which only needed cultivating. Grafton was less skilful at this than North.

Grafton left office in January 1770, less because he lost his nerve than because he lost heart. The Rockinghams, who had been involved during the preceding autumn in collecting support outside Parliament, in the form of petititions against the Government's action in the Middlesex election dispute, launched a strong attack on the ministry at the opening of the new session in January 1770. The re-emergence of Chatham on the political stage, now however in opposition, gave courage to the Opposition, and severely discomfited the ministry. The divisions in the Commons showed but a slender majority for the administration. And in the Cabinet Grafton faced desertions: Camden resigned, and then Granby, after wavering, followed suit. The attempt by Grafton and the King to replace Camden with Charles Yorke failed when Yorke died within three days of his appointment. Grafton's half-hearted (and unsuccessful) attempt to persuade the Attorney-General, William de Grey, to accept, strongly suggests that he had had his fill of political responsibility.[31] He knew moreover that he had a potential successor of considerable ability in North. The King considered his resignation a desertion, and it was widely expected that the ministry would fall. But North survived. Grafton had done what he conceived to be his duty. He had served the King in 1767 and for two and a half difficult years since then, and he left his successor a ministry that formed the basis of the most secure administration since the death of Henry Pelham.

Though Grafton resigned office in 1770 he had not done with politics: indeed he was still active thirty years later. He supported North until 1775, when he resigned because he could no longer support a policy of coercion towards America. His support continued to be held valuable, and it was sought by both North (in 1779) and Pitt (in 1784). Grafton took office once more, under Rockingham and Shelburne in 1782–3. But he maintained all the time his old independence of political groups, a detachment that enabled him, towards the end of his life, to achieve something of the reputation and eminence of an 'elder statesman'.

BIBLIOGRAPHY

Though written late in his life and in places coloured by hindsight, *The Autobiography and Political Correspondence of the Third Duke of Grafton*, ed. Sir W. R. Anson

[31] Grafton's *Autobiography*, p. 245–50; Lord Hardwickes 'Memorial of Family Occurrences', BM Add. MS 35428, folios 116–21; George III to Grafton, 15 Jan. 1770, Grafton MSS 543; Jenkinson to [Lowther], 18 [Jan. 1770], BM Add MS 38206, folios 197–8.

(London, 1898), remains the principal and indispensable source for a study of Grafton's career. It includes many letters from the Duke's correspondence: there are, however, several important unpublished letters among the Grafton Manuscripts in the Bury St Edmunds and West Suffolk Record Office. Further letters from Grafton are published in *Correspondence of William Pitt, Earl of Chatham*, ed. W. S. Taylor and J. H. Pringle (4 vols, London, 1838–40), and in *The Correspondence of King George III, 1760–83*, ed. Sir J. Fortescue (6 vols, London, 1927–8); and there are unpublished letters among the Chatham Papers in the Public Record Office. J. Brooke, *The Chatham Administration* (London, 1956), is invaluable for the period 1766–8; there is, however, no adequate survey of the ministry for the period 1768–70. The ministry's attitude to Wilkes is discussed briefly in G. Rude *Wilkes and Liberty* (Oxford, 1962).

11

LORD NORTH

BY

JOHN CANNON

Frederick North, 2nd Earl of Guilford, but styled Lord North from 1752 to 1790, born 13 April 1732, first son of Francis, 1st Earl of Guilford. Educated at Eton, 1742–8, and Trinity College, Oxford, 1749. Married 1756 Anne, daughter of George Speke; four sons, three daughters. Succeeded as 2nd Earl, 1790. MP for Banbury 1754–90; Lord of the Treasury 1759–65; Joint Paymaster-General 1766–7; Chancellor of the Exchequer 1767–1782; First Lord of the Treasury 1770–82; Home Secretary 1783. PC 1766; KG 1772; Chancellor of the University of Oxford 1773–92; Lord Lieutenant of Somerset 1774–92; Lord Warden of the Cinque Ports 1778–92. Died 5 August 1792.

LORD NORTH

Frederick, Lord North, has an unenviable reputation as the worst prime minister of all time. It is an assessment with which, in his more sombre moments, he might have inclined to agree. His continuation as First Lord of the Treasury, he told the King at the crisis of the American war, was 'to be reckoned among the principal causes of the present dangerous position of this country'.[1]

To defend a man from his own strictures may seem unduly zealous. At first sight the case against Lord North is overwhelming. He is the only prime minister to be associated with failure in a major conflict: in 1783, for the first and last time in modern history, Britain tasted the full bitterness of defeat. 'It is a paltry eulogium for the prime minister of a great country,' observed Horace Walpole sourly, 'yet the best that can be allotted to Lord North is that, though his country was ruined under his administration, he preserved his good humour.'[2]

But this is a verdict which is bound to be affected by the lengthening perspective of history. To Lord North's contemporaries the loss of the thirteen American colonies was an unprecedented calamity: it is hardly surprising that most people regarded it as the consequence of gross political blunders. But when independence for the American states was followed in turn by the emancipation of Latin America from Spain and Portugal and by mass de-colonisation in the twentieth century, the broader trends of historical explanation emerged and human culpability diminished: the American revolt then appeared as the first in a series of national colonial risings rather than the unique occurrence it had once seemed. In the same way, it was natural enough for Horace Walpole to assume the ruin of the commonwealth: on this occasion he was in agreement with George III who wrote that the peace settlement completed 'the downfall of the lustre of this empire'.[3] In fact Britain stood on the threshold of those industrial changes that were to give her unimagined political and economic power.

[1] *The Correspondence of George III*, ed. Sir J. Fortescue (London, 1927), iv, no. 2692.
[2] *Memoirs of the Reign of George III*, ed. G. F. R. Barker (London, 1894), iv, 55.
[3] Fortescue, vi, no. 4470.

The shadow of defeat falls so heavily over Lord North's career that it becomes necessary to emphasise how successful were the early years of his administration. After a spell of two years as Chancellor of the Exchequer, North took over the premiership from the Duke of Grafton at a moment of acute crisis. Grafton's ministry had staggered from disaster to disaster since its formation in 1766. First Lord Chatham, the great man on whom all was to depend, went to pieces under the strain of responsibility and for months was totally incapable of conducting business: in October 1768, much to the King's dismay, he insisted on resigning. During 1769 the ministers were plagued by the complications arising out of the Middlesex election and tormented by the dexterous Wilkes and his savage henchman 'Junius'. The Opposition succeeded in drawing together its forces to form a working coalition and, to the amazement of the political world, was joined in January 1770 by Chatham himself, an apparition from the past, miraculously restored and belabouring his former colleagues as enemies of the Constitution. Chatham's first salvo carried away the ministry's Lord Chancellor, Camden, and his successor, Charles Yorke, died after only three days in office. A week later Grafton tendered his resignation and the Opposition seemed on the brink of success. To North the King confessed that there was no peer who could be placed at the head of the Government should he refuse to serve.

Within a few months of Lord North's taking office, the situation was transformed. The Government's majority, down to a mere 40 odd in January, was up to 97 four weeks later. In March the Opposition overplayed its hand with a violent remonstrance from the City of London, which produced another government victory by 271 votes to 108. Before the year was out the Opposition was in complete disarray: there was not 'the least glimmering of hope', Burke warned Lord Rockingham in December 1770.[4]

Circumstances undoubtedly favoured the ministers. The deaths of William Beckford and George Grenville within five months of each other removed two formidable opponents. The opposition alliance had always appeared fragile: it was not easy for the Rockinghams, with their train of pocket boroughs, to collaborate enthusiastically with a group preaching radical reform of Parliament. The excesses of the Wilkite agitation produced a conservative reaction which assisted

[4] *Correspondence of Edmund Burke*, ed. L. S. Sutherland (Cambridge, 1960), ii, 176.

government supporters to recapture some of the ground they had lost in city politics.

Nevertheless, North's own contribution was important. Though still a young man, he was portly in build and his flabby cheeks and protruding eyes gave him, according to one witness, 'the air of a blind trumpeter'.[5] But he was a hard-working and capable administrator with ten years' experience in office behind him. He rarely attempted wit, his delivery was portentous and his articulation far from distinct, but his speeches were relevant and seldom tried the patience of the House. Not least among his political assets were his good humour and imperturbability. He was a cultivated and agreeable companion: 'Never was a first minister,' wrote Wraxall who knew him well, 'less intrenched within the forms of his official situation. He seemed, on the contrary, always happy to throw aside his public character.'[6]

His humour was admitted on all sides. He seems to have felt a sense of professional pride in his performance in the House of Commons: the burdens of his private misfortunes were rarely allowed to show through and he possessed a remarkable resilience, bobbing up under pressure like a cork. Two examples must suffice, from the dark days after Saratoga when a joint Franco-Spanish invasion seemed a possibility. He turned on Charles Fox who was eking out an evidently underprepared speech with a good deal of synthetic abuse: it reminded him, said North gently, of those maps by ancient geographers who concealed their lack of knowledge with pictures of elephants and other strange beasts. To Temple Luttrell, a noisy and pertinacious critic of the administration, North was sharper: when Luttrell, in a burst of false candour, hoped that his remarks would not clog the activity of government, North waved him aside with contempt – no more than the fly which, landing on the wheels of a chariot, 'thought she raised the dust with which she was surrounded'.[7]

It was also much to North's advantage that he was a member of the House of Commons. In view of the administrations of Lord Liverpool at the beginning and Lord Salisbury at the end of the nineteenth century it would be idle to claim that a seat in the Commons was an essential condition for successful premiership. Nevertheless it was useful, as Sir

[5] Walpole, op. cit., iv, 52.
[6] N. W. Wraxall, *Historical and Posthumous Memoirs*, ed. H. B. Wheatley (London, 1884), i, 361–2.
[7] *Parliamentary History*, xx, 336; xix, 1387.

Robert Walpole's career had demonstrated, and the point had been re-inforced by the difficulty that subsequent first ministers in the Lords had experienced in obtaining suitable deputies in the Commons. The Duke of Newcastle had found Sir Thomas Robinson useless – the Duke 'may as well send his jackboot to govern us,' Pitt had remarked – while Henry Fox proved demanding. George Grenville, appointed to lead the Commons during the Bute ministry, was not long in discovering his own power and aspiring to first place. The ignorance of Commons manage-ment shown by Lords Chatham and Shelburne contributed substantially to their political failures. But North was in a position to keep an eye on those independent members whose support was so necessary to him and his affability ensured that he remained sensitive to changes of opinion in the House.

No less important was the extremely good understanding that North soon reached with the King. The Grenville administration five years earlier, though strong in other respects, had broken down on this very point, the King confessing that he would 'rather see the Devil in his closet than Mr Grenville'. North, by contrast, was on the most cordial terms with the King. In 1771 George wrote offering him the Garter – the first time a commoner had been so honoured since Sir Robert Wal-pole – and by 1775 could refer to him as 'my sheet anchor'. Two years later he intervened to pay Lord North's personal debts, amounting to some £18,000, putting the proposal in a letter of great kindness and delicacy. 'You know me very ill,' wrote the King, 'if you do not think that of all the letters I have ever wrote to you this one gives me the most pleasure, and I want no other return than your being convinced that I love you as well as a man of worth as I esteem you as a minister.'[8]

The Government's policy during North's early years as first minister was moderate and conciliatory. Though he had taken the lead in the Grafton administration's prosecution of Wilkes, he saw the wisdom of allowing the matter to drop, and when Wilkes took his seat in the House of Commons in 1774 North treated him jocularly: 'He agreed entirely in opinion with the counsellor, whoever he was, that might think one Wilkes sufficient: for indeed he thought that it was one too much in any well-regulated government; though, he said, to do him justice, it was not easy to find many such.' The same cool approach appeared at first to have restored harmony in the American quarrel, which North in-herited from previous ministries. By removing all taxes except a small

[8] Fortescue, iii, nos. 1742 and 2059.

one on tea, North hoped to appease the colonists while keeping a token of control to satisfy opinion at home. In April 1771 he could claim that 'the American disputes are settled and there is nothing to interrupt the peace and prosperity of the nation'.[9] His handling of the nation's finances was approved even by his critics and the crisis over the East India Company in 1772 served merely to confirm his resourcefulness and adaptability: though the limitations of his Indian settlement were soon apparent, North's appointment of a Governor-General was an important extension of the principle of public responsibility.

The first few years saw Lord North's administration established almost beyond overthrow. Horace Walpole thought that the session of 1773 had been the most triumphant ever known, with the Opposition itself nearly abandoning the game. 'This is an epoch,' wrote Thomas Dampier in February 1775, 'which will render Lord North's name immortal in our English history.' Though this testimony from the tutor of North's sons in a letter to Lord Guilford may not be wholly disinterested, it is confirmed, if in less ecstatic terms, from other sources. Henry Cruger, newly elected for Bristol and a 'hot Wilkite', admitted in his maiden speech in December 1774 that 'the abilities of the minister it seems are universally acknowledged'.[10]

In presenting his budget of May 1772 to the House of Commons North allowed himself the guess that there was 'the fairest prospect of the continuance of peace' that he had known in his lifetime. The following month a gang of Rhode Island radicals seized the revenue cutter *Gaspée*, wounded the captain and burnt the vessel. The British ministers retorted by authorising the Governor to seek out those responsible and present them for trial. It is not easy to see what else they could have done short of admitting that the British had no authority in the colonies. The Governor failed to discover the culprits. Many Britons concluded that the Americans were incorrigible; many Americans concluded that the British were feeble and despotic. The Boston tea party a year later repeated the affront on the grand scale and the ministry responded with four coercive acts designed to bring the colonies back to obedience. The dispute, North declared, was no longer about taxation: it was whether the British retained any power in America – 'it is very clear

[9] *Parliamentary History*, xviii, 1013; xvii, 165.
[10] *Last Journals*, i, 179; Dampier to Guilford, 6 February 1775, Bodleian MSS North d. 16, f.7; *Parliamentary History*, xviii, 67.

we have none if we suffer the property of our subjects to be destroyed'. North misjudged the situation completely: four or five frigates, he assured members, would be sufficient to do the business without any military force.[11]

The rest of North's ministry was played out in the context of these momentous decisions. Before 1774 was over the first continental congress had been summoned to co-ordinate American resistance. British patriotism rose in reply to American intransigence and left North little room for manoeuvre. 'It was not in the power of the minister to sit still and take no measure,' he admitted, and it is significant that the Opposition did not dare to risk a division on the Boston Port Bill. North and his step-brother Lord Dartmouth battled hard in the Cabinet against the fire-eaters and he took his political life in his hands by pushing the conciliation proposals of February 1775. Indeed, the charge against North might well be the reverse – that his reluctance to abandon plans for retrenchment and economy sent Britain into the struggle less well prepared than she might have been. December 1774 – a month after the King had written that 'blows must decide' – was a strange time for North to move the retention of the Land Tax at three shillings in the pound, together with a naval establishment 4,000 fewer than for the previous year. Two months later the number of seamen had to be increased, but the Land Tax was not raised to four shillings until 1776.[12]

The first two years of fighting in America passed without any decisive encounter. North survived two unpleasant Cabinet crises in late 1775 and 1776 over the conciliation proposals and his parliamentary majority held firm. In 1777 the British devised a plan to end the conflict by splitting New England, the heart of resistance, from the rest of the American colonies: Burgoyne's army, marching south from Canada, was to effect a junction with General Howe, marching northwards from New York up the Hudson river. Throughout the autumn of 1777 North and his colleagues waited anxiously for news. The King's Speech for the parliamentary session, due to open in November, had to be drawn up without their knowing which way the issue had gone. In October came heartening reports that Howe had captured Philadelphia, headquarters of Congress and the largest American city: on 2 December Lord Sandwich wrote to acquaint the King that Burgoyne and his entire army had been

[11] *Parliamentary History*, xvii, 489, 1167, 1172.
[12] ibid., p. 1187.

forced to capitulate at Saratoga. 'The consequences of this most fatal event,' wrote North, 'may be very important and serious, and will certainly require some material change of system.'[13]

Saratoga was Lord North's political death warrant. It was to him what the Norwegian campaign proved to Chamberlain or the Somme to Asquith. Yet circumstances combined to give him a stay of execution that lasted more than four years. The Opposition, of course, professed no doubt that his majorities were sustained by corruption on a massive scale and generations of historians accepted the legend of the King's Friends, oblivious to everything but the service of their master. In fact it is clear that the influence of the Crown was already beginning to shrink.[14] North's survival was in part the work of the Opposition itself which had adopted so extreme a line that it fell into discredit. He was, in addition, the victim of his own remarkable popularity, which gave him a fund of goodwill to draw upon in the moment of crisis. But the essential factor was the King's determination under no circumstances to part with North.

After Saratoga began a tragi-comedy unsurpassed perhaps in British history as the first minister, his nerve gone, begged piteously to be allowed to resign and was refused on literally dozens of occasions. In letter after letter North pleaded his total incapacity to cope with the demands of the situation. 'The anxiety of his mind,' he told the King in January 1778, 'has deprived Lord North of his memory and under-standing.' Capital punishment, he wrote two months later after the King had dropped hints that he might be the first victim of any new political arrangement, 'is preferable to that constant anguish of mind which he feels from the consideration that his continuance in office is ruining His Majesty's affairs'. 'Let me not go to the grave,' he beseeched George, 'with the guilt of having been the ruin of my king and country.'[15]

Each effort the hapless man made to escape was stymied by fate or by the King. In the spring of 1778 he urged George to come to terms with Lord Chatham in the desperate hope that the miracle he had wrought during the Seven Years War might be repeated. If Chatham were not brought in, North wrote on 30 March, the nation was undone.

[13] Fortescue, iii, nos. 2092 and 2095.
[14] I. R. Christie, 'Was there a "New Toryism" in the earlier part of George III's reign?', and 'Economical reform and "the influence of the Crown", 1780', in *Myth and Reality in Late Eighteenth-Century Politics* (London, 1970).
[15] Fortescue, iv, nos. 2179, 2228 and 2329.

A week later Chatham suffered a fatal collapse while speaking in the House of Lords. 'May not the political exit of Lord Chatham,' inquired the King without any elaborate show of grief, 'incline you to continue at the head of my affairs?' After further months of negotiation with the Opposition, North attempted to pass the poisoned chalice to a member of his own Cabinet: 'The person best qualified for that station appears to him to be Lord Suffolk,' he wrote on 16 November. Lord Suffolk, doomed by North's good opinion, keeled over and was dead within three months, at the age of 39.[16]

To all of North's entreaties the King turned a deaf ear. For years he kept him in harness with a subtle mixture of encouragement and reproach. His strongest card was the appeal to North's honour. Was he really prepared to desert his sovereign in the hour of need as the Duke of Grafton had done? Had not the King demonstrated in every possible way not merely his trust, but his affection for his minister? Was the King to be rewarded by being handed over to his political enemies? 'Common honesty and that sense of honour which must reside in the breast of every man born of a noble family' should compel North to stay.

Why was George III so desperately anxious to keep North's services? It would certainly not have been difficult to find people who would have conducted the war with more vigour, and unquestionably more enthusiasm, than North showed. It was not, as was often suggested, that the King had found a first minister pliant and obedient in all things, a willing tool. The fact is that Lord North, for all his limitations which the King knew full well, was an indispensable political asset. It was of critical importance that the chief government spokesman in the House of Commons should be a man of cheerful and amiable disposition, fat and sleepy, demonstrably unwarlike in his conduct and interests, concerned chiefly with retrenchment and fiscal reform – the last man who might be suspected of plunging lightheartedly into conflict. That North, known to stand for compromise and conciliation, should acknowledge the need to carry on the struggle, was in itself a persuasive argument. The Government's case could certainly have been put by tougher and more resolute politicians – Henry Dundas, for instance – but they would have forfeited the reserves of trust that Lord North still commanded. North's character, the source of so many of his misfortunes, was also the source of much of his political strength.

[16] Fortescue, iv, nos. 2257, 2284 and 2452.

North's reasons for continuing were, no doubt, complex. He was by no means indifferent to power and influence and it is noticeable that when the King showed signs of taking the protestations seriously, North was inclined to shuffle. He felt deeply the many favours he had received from the King and particularly the payment of his private debts. But much of the difficulty arose from the ambiguities of the eighteenth-century political system, in which the role of the monarch had never been precisely defined. Where was the line to be drawn between private and public obligations? To what extent was carrying on the government a matter of personal loyalty to the sovereign? In the nineteenth century, Wellington, Peel and Melbourne were all capable of seeing the issue in highly personal terms. 'I am under such obligations to the King,' declared North, 'that I can never leave his service while he desires me to remain in it.'[17] In the context of modern constitutional theory, North's conduct is scarcely defensible: in the eighteenth century, it made some sense.

North's attitude towards the office he held is not easy to ascertain. In public he denied that the Constitution allowed for a prime minister and claimed to be answerable only for his departmental administration of the Treasury: 'He never should be so presumptuous,' he told the House of Commons in May 1778, 'as to think himself capable of directing the departments of others. . . . He did not think our constitution authorised such a character as that animal called a prime minister.'[18] In part this reflected North's reluctance to accept responsibility; in part it was a useful debating ploy and one which the great Sir Robert Walpole, a determined engrosser of power, had not hesitated to use.[19] But in his private letters to the King, North conceded in full the case for a prime minister. 'Whoever may come to the assistance of government,' he observed in the spring of 1778 when overtures were being made to Chatham, 'must be the director and dictator of the leading measures of government. Lord North knows too well his want of ability and decision. . . .' On a subsequent occasion he confessed to the King that he had not that 'authority of character' that the situation demanded: 'In these critical times it is necessary that there should be one directing

---

[17] Egerton MSS 2232, f.11.

[18] *Parliamentary History*, xix, 1173.

[19] In the censure debate of 1741 he declared that he did 'not pretend to be a great master of foreign affairs: in that post in which I have the honour to serve His Majesty it is not my business to meddle with them.' *Parliamentary History*, xi, 1298.

minister, who should plan the whole of the operations of government.' North's experience of his own inadequacy seems to have made a lasting impression on him and convinced him of the need for a prime minister at all times. When he met Charles Fox in February 1783 to negotiate the coalition he was reported to have said that there 'should be one man, or a Cabinet, to govern the whole and direct every measure. Government by departments was not brought in by me. I found it so, and had not vigour and resolution to put an end to it.'[20]

So North stayed for four more years, in receipt of a constant parliamentary buffeting from Fox and Burke – augmented after 1780 by Sheridan and the young Pitt – and threatened continually with impeachment and the block. Politically disastrous, the last years of his ministry revealed courage of a high order. In between parliamentary sessions his subordinates Jenkinson and Robinson worked with the King to keep him going, like seconds trying to get their man into shape to last a few more rounds. In October 1779 Robinson found his lordship 'much calmer than usual': a week later North was in 'a state of mind such as it is melancholy even to reflect on'. Next came a surprising recovery and a month later he was 'in a good deal of Vigour of Mind and Spirits'. Alas, it did not last, and before the month was out North was once more petitioning for release, 'for I must look upon it as a degree of guilt to continue in office while the public suffers and while nobody approves my conduct'.[21]

But he struggled on, surviving, with some dexterity, the crisis over economical reform in the spring of 1780 when the House of Commons, in a spasm of revolt, carried against him Dunning's motion that the influence of the Crown had increased, was increasing and ought to be diminished. The year 1781 even saw a kind of Indian summer with opposition hushed and administration fortified by delusive gleams of hope from America. North was released from his treadmill by the news in November 1781 of the surrender of Lord Cornwallis's army at Yorktown. At last the parliamentary majorities began to melt. Even then it took a blunt and cogent exposition of constitutional realities before North could persuade the King to give way: 'The torrent,' North warned in March 1782, 'is too strong to be resisted. Your Majesty is well apprized that, in this country, the Prince on the Throne cannot,

[20] Fortescue, iv, nos. 2239 and 2446; *Memoirs and Correspondence of Charles James Fox*, ed. Lord John Russell, ii, 38.
[21] Fortescue, iv, nos. 2792, 2807, 2828 and 2845.

with prudence, oppose the deliberate resolution of the House of Commons.'[22]

There is much that might still be said on North's behalf but it forms a plea in mitigation rather than a defence. His personal honesty was un-questioned – no small thing in a period that had seen Sir Robert Walpole and Lord Holland make vast fortunes in the service of the State. He was capable of devising schemes of some ingenuity, though usually under pressure of circumstances: his East Indian legislation was forced upon him by the imminent threat of bankruptcy to the Company, while his financial innovations, considered of some importance, were largely a reply to opposition criticisms.[23] He could respond to events but he had neither the foresight, nor perhaps the time, to anticipate them. It is significant that some of his best and most telling speeches were those delivered in support of the *status quo* – against further concessions to the dissenters and against parliamentary reform. His misjudgement of American affairs was one he shared with most of his generation: he was no wiser than they were, which is in part why they found him so com-fortable a leader. He was essentially a man of business above his station – a truth which his superb debating ability concealed from many of his supporters but never from North himself. The troubles facing the country, he told the King in the summer of 1778, might yet be overcome if affairs of state were well conducted: 'They can hardly be well con-ducted unless there is a person in the Cabinet capable of leading, of discerning between opinions, of deciding quickly and confidently, and of connecting all the operations of government, that this nation may act uniformly and with force. Lord North is not such a man. . . .'[24]

His niche in history is as one of the greatest of all parliamentarians. 'That assembly,' wrote Wraxall, 'presented in fact a theatre on which he acted the first personage.'[25] From beginning to end North maintained that the war against America was a war to uphold parliamentary author-ity. In his final speech as prime minister, after he had announced the resignation of the administration, he turned to his supporters and in

[22] Fortescue, v, no. 3566.
[23] His Indian legislation is discussed in L. S. Sutherland, *The East India Company in Eighteenth-Century Politics* (Oxford, 1952), and his financial policy in J. E. D. Binney, *British Public Finance and Administration, 1774-92* (Oxford, 1958).
[24] Fortescue, iv, no. 2334.
[25] *Historical and Posthumous Memoirs*, i, 369.

thanking them showed his awareness of the source of his influence. He wished, he said, to acknowledge

'the very kind, the repeated and essential support he had for so many years received from the Commons of England, during his holding a situation to which he must confess he had at all times been unequal. And it was . . . the more incumbent upon him to return his thanks in that place because it was that House which had made him what he had been.'

BIBLIOGRAPHY

Butterfield, H., *George III, Lord North and the People*, 1779–80 (London, 1949)
Cannon, John, *The Fox–North Coalition* (Cambridge, 1969)
—, *Lord North: The Noble Lord in the Blue Ribbon* (Historical Association pamphlet G 74) (London, 1970)
Christie, I. R., *The End of North's Ministry, 1780–2* (London, 1958)
Lucas, R., *Lord North* (2 vols, London, 1913)
Pemberton, W. B., *Lord North* (London, 1938)
Valentine, A., *Lord North* (2 vols, Oklahoma, 1967)

12

THE EARL OF SHELBURNE

BY

FRANK O'GORMAN

William Petty Fitzmaurice, born 13 May 1737, the son of the Hon. John Fitzmaurice, 1st Earl of Shelburne. Educated privately and at Christ Church, Oxford and served in the Seven Years War. Succeeded to the earldom 1761 and in 1784 became Marquess of Lansdowne. Married (1) 1765 Lady Sophia Carteret; (2) 1779 Lady Louise Fitzpatrick. MP for Chipping Wycombe 1760–1; First Lord of Trade 1763; Secretary of State for the Southern Department 1766–8; Secretary of State for Home Affairs 1782; First Lord of the Treasury 1782–3. Died 7 May 1805. He was succeeded as Marquess by his son by his first marriage, John Henry Petty; the second marriage was childless. Petty was the name adopted by the first Earl on succeeding to the estates of his uncle.

THE EARL OF SHELBURNE

Shelburne's political career was one of the most remarkable in eighteenth-century history. His tenure of office was not uneventful but it was brief and it ended in failure and humiliation. The measure of his failure is difficult to grasp, tantalisingly elusive to explain. For Shelburne was perhaps the most brilliant intellectual in politics in the second half of the eighteenth century after Burke. He was also the most hated of all politicians. The political career of this curious man spanned the first half of the reign of George III and in a very real sense he was one of its most complete casualties.

Of his intellectual brilliance and personal charm there can be no doubt. Those close to him testified constantly to the generosity of his private manner, his kindness, his wit and his patience. Yet Shelburne was a complex person who may perhaps be described as a compulsive intellectual. He took few ideas for granted and subjected prevailing ideas and institutions to constant analysis. Furthermore, he rather enjoyed making a show of his intellectualism. He must have been one of the very few eighteenth-century statesmen to have enjoyed the services of what the twentieth century would term a 'think tank' in the little coterie of intellectuals which he patronised at Bowood, and to have established a formal secretariat to facilitate his political activities. To his contemporaries, therefore, Shelburne appeared to be something of a 'character'. At the same time, there can be no doubting the sincerity of his involvement in intellectual life. He had a brilliant mind, kept abreast of current developments in a wide variety of subjects and made himself an authority on several. Men of the calibre of Price, Priestley and Jeremy Bentham, while owing much to his patronage, were ready to respect the man himself. The Bowood circle, indeed, pioneered many of the reformist ideas which were to agitate British political life until and after the first Reform Bill. Shelburne strongly supported the notion that the intellectual had an important role to play in politics. The Members he returned in his boroughs – Calne and High Wycombe – were men of a very high calibre. In the whole of the eighteenth century there is no party to compare with his brilliant group of men who sat in the Commons, including Isaac Barre, John Dunning, John Calcraft and Lord Mahon.

Even more remarkable than his intellectual gifts and pursuits, however, is the fact that he was universally detested by his contemporaries. Posterity has not been able to provide satisfactory explanations for it. Historians have usually ascribed it to certain aspects of his personality. Men hated Shelburne because they felt that they could not trust him. They regarded him as utterly without principle and thus completely unreliable. It was not just the fact that he became a 'King's man' in 1782 after he had espoused popular causes for over a decade. Widespread distrust of him antedates the Rockingham-Shelburne ministry of 1782. Essentially, Shelburne lacked the ability to communicate his whole personality to others. He was remote and unreachable, never at ease and never relaxed. His efforts to appear so gave him an air of inconsistency and unpredictability which was exaggerated by his effusive bonhomie. In his desire to present his pleasantest face to the world he indulged in lavish flattery and obsequious ingratiation whose transparent insincerity was manifest. Shelburne, then, was a lonely and isolated individual who did not understand others, and lacking the ability to understand men, their emotions and their motivations, he was perhaps unsuited to politics. But there was more than this to Shelburne's unpopularity. Contemporaries constantly (and completely without foundation) accused him of corruption, immorality, and even subversion. Because he was not trusted, his 'advanced' ideas were treated with fear and scepticism. An aura of secrecy and sinister mystery surrounded Shelburne. It was entirely characteristic of his career that his London residence in Berkeley Square had once belonged to Lord Bute.[1] When the radical reformer of the 1770s became the 'King's man' of 1782-3 contemporaries were shocked but they were not surprised. It was exactly the sort of behaviour they expected from 'the Jesuit of Berkeley Square'.

In 1760 Shelburne launched himself into his political career. His family was Irish and he thus felt no inclination to associate himself with the great Whig aristocracy led by the Duke of Newcastle. Indeed, his earliest political associates were Henry Fox and Lord Bute, and he participated in their endeavours to destroy the political world of the

[1] Bute's abiding influence with the King was constantly assumed by political observers until the end of the 1760s. Shelburne's association with Bute thus provoked comment and raised the issue of his political integrity.

Pelhams. He acted in 1762–3 as a go-between for the King with Fox (whom the King detested) and Bute (whom he loved). He was rewarded with the gratitude of George III but he paid dearly for it. (Already he was beginning to acquire that reputation for intrigue which dogged his whole career.) Shelburne was further rewarded by his appointment as President of the Board of Trade during the ministry of George Grenville. Although he attended assiduously to his departmental duties he revealed qualities of weakness and indecision which, together with his own unpopularity, deprived him of any influence on policy. His resignation in September 1763, less than six months after taking office, created neither surprise nor regret.

It was just at this moment in his life that he came under the influence of William Pitt. For the next five years at least Shelburne was to live under his shadow. Accepting Pitt's principle of 'Measures not Men', he followed his lead over the issue of general warrants in 1763–4 and over his refusal to join the Rockingham ministry of 1765–6. Shelburne's loyalty was rewarded when he received Cabinet office in the Chatham administration of 1766–8. Although he kept something of the spirit of Chatham alive while the ostensible premier nursed his gout at Bath he was unable to persuade his colleagues to follow the policies of the Great Commoner. He was unable, for example, to stop Charles Townshend from pushing through his disastrous scheme to tax the American colonists. Indeed, he became increasingly isolated within the ministry. Differences over policy and patronage led to his resignation in October 1768. Shelburne's future looked bleak. His affection for Chatham was not reciprocated. The early respect of the King had not been maintained. Shelburne had kept aloof from the Rockingham Whigs, the largest opposition party. Fortuitously, the Petitioning Movement of 1769 rescued him from political isolation and gave a new twist to his hitherto wholly unremarkable political career.[2]

Shelburne involved himself in the movement initially because of his desire to follow Chatham's lead[3] but he also wished to preserve the

[2] The Petitioning Movement of 1769 was organised by a temporarily united opposition of Chatham, Grenville and Rockingham protesting against the actions of Grafton's ministry over the Middlesex election, the unseating of Wilkes and the seating of his defeated opponent, Luttrell.

[3] Nevertheless, it was in 1769 that Shelburne began to shake himself free of his subordination to Chatham. Although he remained respectful and even obsequious towards him until his death in 1778 Shelburne emerged as an independent political figure at this time.

[187]

following which he had painstakingly built up for himself in commercial circles, particularly inside the East India Company, during the last few years. His support of Wilkes opened up contacts with the radicalism of the metropolis and he threw himself wholeheartedly into the radical movement, playing an essential role in forging a link between the metropolitan radicals and the parliamentary politicians. At this time, too, he came under the influence of the radical ideas of English Dissent. Through the influence of Price and Priestley he came to appreciate the currents of reformist thought which went back to the seventeenth century. After the failure of the Petitioning Movement in 1770 Shelburne remained in opposition, in uneasy alliance with the Rockinghams, dedicated to radical reform of British political institutions.

Conflict with the Rockingham Whig party was to be the dominant theme of the rest of Shelburne's active political career and disputes and disagreements had already begun to manifest themselves in 1769. Fundamentally, Shelburne's reforming principles were different from those of the Rockinghams. They continued to proclaim the traditional complaints of opposition against corruption and secret influence and asserted that these could only be cured by party government. It is doubtful if Shelburne believed, with the Rockinghams, that since the beginning of the reign of George III a deliberate policy of corruption had been undertaken by the Court which had for its object the establishment of an inner Cabinet (whose existence undermined the authority and responsibility of the official Cabinet) and the silencing of Parliament as an organ of protest and opposition. The Rockinghams thought in terms of establishing a different system of government. Shelburne was more radical than the Rockinghams.[4] He was, at the same time, more loyalist than they were. He wished to improve the King's service, not to weaken his ministers. Shelburne objected less to the political role of the Crown than to waste and inefficiency of government. Unlike the Rockinghams, he was concerned with comprehensive administrative reform and bureaucratic efficiency.

Shelburne's economic and imperial thinking was also at odds with that of the Rockinghams and far in advance of it. After he left office in

---

[4] Although Shelburne's acceptance of parliamentary reform remained largely theoretical it offended the Rockinghams. He advocated an additional Member for each county, but even this very moderate proposal was regarded by them as proof of his readiness to listen to the popular voice. They constantly suspected his 'popular' politics. They found his defence of the Gordon rioters in 1780 distasteful.

1768 he came under the influence of Adam Smith and Dean Tucker and adopted their free trade ideas.[5] He thus came to question the rigid, mercantilist structure of the Empire.[6] He embraced the vision of an abiding imperial partnership and a federal alliance with the Americans based upon voluntary agreement. Consequently, he found the notion of complete American independence unacceptable in the 1770s and was distressed when the Rockinghams began to accept it in 1778. Shelburne perceived that the old imperial system was breaking down and that a new kind of imperial relationship would have to replace it if the Empire were to survive at all. Simply to accept American independence, as the Rockinghams seemed content to do, was to preside over the liquidation of the Empire, and this Shelburne refused to do.[7]

Fundamentally, Shelburne's approach to politics was different from that of the Rockinghams. One of the basic elements in the political thought and practical activities of both Chatham and Shelburne was their detestation of party.[8] Neither of them suffered fools gladly. They were too arrogant ever to have considered themselves to be *members* of a party. They wished to retain their freedom of action and to do so they would endeavour to destroy factions. They would consult the national interest and appeal to the country at large to vindicate their conduct. Shelburne believed that Cabinets ought to include the best men of all parties. The Cabinet would be dominated by a great national leader who would enjoy a unique position of trust and confidence with the King. Members of the Cabinet were to be servants of the Crown and the first minister. It was the function of the Cabinet to approve of

[5] In this area of thought he was far in advance of Chatham. (It confuses the biographies of both men to assume that he was Chatham's pupil in everything.) Chatham remained something of a mercantilist and never grasped the significance of the new free trade theories.

[6] In 1765–6 Shelburne had already opposed the internal taxation of the colonies by the British Parliament. Furthermore, in 1775, when hostilities began, he was prepared to abandon all rights of taxation.

[7] Of American independence Shelburne remarked in a debate in July 1782 that 'he had used every effort in public and in private, in England and out of it, to guard it from so dreadful a disaster'. (William Cobbett, *The Parliamentary History* (London, 1806–20), xxiii, 193.)

[8] 'The fact was, that he was, and had through life stood aloof from parties. He was of no party. It was his pride and principle to be of no faction, but to embrace every measure on its own ground, free from all connection. Such had been his political creed; as such he stood before the people, and as such he coveted to be judged by them.' (Ibid., xxvi, 575.)

policy already decided upon between the departmental head concerned and the King. Individual ministers were responsible for their policy not to Parliament, not to the Cabinet, but to the King. It followed that the King must retain the full exercise of his prerogative of appointing ministers.[9] It is important to understand that the protection of the royal prerogative of appointing ministers was a natural consequence of Shelburne's distaste for party.

It is hardly surprising, then, that after the failure of British arms in America and the resignation of North, the King attempted to persuade Shelburne to lead a new ministry. The King reasoned that, in spite of his radical tendencies, Shelburne had no party to impose upon him. Disagree they might over policy, but at least he had no intention of humiliating the monarchy. But Shelburne was too realistic to have believed that he could have survived for long without the Rockinghams, and he persuaded the King to form a ministry around them but including him. Shelburne may well have been worried by his prospective position in the Cabinet in 1782. He disagreed with the Rockinghams on many matters of policy and principle and saw that their party clannishness could leave him isolated and powerless. His major safeguard against that possibility was the protection of the King. For his part, the King needed a friend in the Cabinet to protect him from the Rockinghams and from the earliest days of the ministry used Shelburne as his agent. The royal riposte to the constitutional revolution of 1782, then, was to use Shelburne to weaken and divide the Rockingham-Shelburne ministry.[10] It mattered little that the Rockinghams obtained the Treasury and the bulk of the offices.[11] Shelburne understood what the King was

[9] Shelburne's ideas, 'which for seventeen years he had imbibed from his master in politics, the late Earl of Chatham', included the conviction that he should 'stand up for the prerogative of the Crown and insist upon the King's right to appoint his own servants'; otherwise 'the monarchical part of the Constitution would be absorbed by the aristocracy, and the famed Constitution of England would be no more'. (Ibid., xxiii, 192–3.)

[10] The King even put into writing a promise of 'full power and full confidence' in Shelburne. (Lord Fitzmaurice, *Life of William, Earl of Shelburne*, (2 vols, London, 1912), ii, 89.)

[11] Even so, of the nine members of the Cabinet, Rockingham could only rely absolutely on three, Fox, Cavendish and Keppel. Shelburne could rely upon Grafton, Ashburton and, in most circumstances, upon Camden, Conway, and possibly Richmond. The ninth member was Thurlow, closer to the King than he was to either Rockingham or Shelburne.

about and prepared to co-operate with him in his scheming. Indeed, he even promised his full co-operation and assistance.[12]

There was bound to be trouble in the Cabinet. Shelburne behaved as though he wished to encourage it. He was enjoying his power and his position. He strutted and boasted, revelling in the King's confidence, delighting in his new-found importance, scorning the Rockinghams and making it very clear to them that although Rockingham might have the Treasury, the King wished the ministry to be one in which 'all ecclesiastical and civil preferments should be jointly recommended'.[13] Furthermore, the King supported Shelburne in his Chathamite conception of the workings of the Cabinet over and against Rockingham's idea of Cabinet solidarity. He would not entertain the Rockingham's 'practice of discussing business and laying advice before the King unasked'.[14] Even in matters where co-operation ought to have been possible between Shelburne and the Rockinghams it was not forthcoming, and Shelburne was at least as much, and possibly more, to blame than Rockingham.[15] For example, when the Rockinghams brought in their economical reform legislation Shelburne did not lift a finger to help them. It is true that his idea of economical reform was somewhat different from theirs but this fact scarcely warranted his ostentatious scepticism towards the Rockinghams' policy. He confessed that there were parts of it which he did not understand and professed it to be too difficult and daunting an undertaking to be carried out at that time.[16]

The most serious area of disagreement between the two wings of the ministry lay in the problem of making peace with America. As we have observed already, the Rockinghams were much readier than Shelburne

[12] 'I certainly would not run away from any opportunity of serving his Majesty, or the public.' (Fitzmaurice, op. cit., ii, 88-9.)

[13] The King to Shelburne, 5 April 1782. (*The Correspondence of George III*, ed. Sir J. Fortescue (6 vols, London, 1927), v, 443-4.)

[14] The King to Shelburne, 29 April 1782. (Ibid., 504-5.)

[15] Shelburne's political morality can be assessed from a brief glance at his behaviour over the Irish question. Ireland was Shelburne's responsibility, falling as it did within his department. But when the Rockinghamite Lord Lieutenant of Ireland, the Duke of Portland, recommended that Ireland be granted legislative independence, Shelburne refused to commit himself on the subject. He well knew the King's aversion to legislative independence and saw no reason to share in the royal odium which Portland incurred.

[16] Fitzmaurice, ii, 224-5.

to concede American independence. They believed that such a concession would leave England free to take action against her European enemies. Shelburne and the King wished to move more slowly, to make concessions to the Americans but not to go to the lengths of severing all connections and links with them. Shelburne persisted in his opinion that American westward expansion and, to some extent, even American trade, were matters over which the British Government ought to retain some measure of responsibility. It was not just these differences of opinion that wrecked the ministry. The peculiar administrative structure of the times worsened the existing political and personal discord. Charles James Fox was Foreign Secretary and therefore responsible for peace negotiations with the European powers, but Shelburne, as Home Secretary, had responsibility for the American negotiations. Fox feared that Shelburne was attempting to take over the conduct of the negotiations with France. His position grew increasingly desperate. Shelburne's opinions not only had the support of the King but they obtained the approval of the Cabinet. Further, even the European powers came to regard the negotiations with Shelburne as more official than those with Fox. The matter came to a head when Fox brought the dispute before the Cabinet. At its meetings on 26 and 30 June, however, the decision went Shelburne's way. Independence was not to be conceded initially but was to be part of a general settlement. At this, Fox threatened to resign.

At exactly this point, with the ministry on the verge of disintegration, the Marquis of Rockingham died (on 1 July). Even before his death it was clear that Shelburne would be his successor.[17] His appointment was greeted with the resignations of Fox and Lord John Cavendish, the Chancellor of the Exchequer, from the Cabinet, and some few resignations in the lower offices. Fox protested that Rockingham's successor as leader of his party, the Duke of Portland, and not Shelburne, should have been appointed to the Treasury, on the grounds that Shelburne did not have the confidence of the major part of the Cabinet and the ministry.

It is important to be clear about exactly what was at issue in these disputes, for it was largely because of the principles at stake in them that the ministry of Shelburne has its significance. Most contemporaries, even if they disliked Shelburne, thought that he and not Fox was con-

[17] Especially to Shelburne who, as Rockingham lay dying, was already casting around for support.

stitutionally in the right in July 1782. The King had freely chosen Shelburne to lead the ministry and a ministry had been formed. Until it was proved that the ministry did not enjoy the confidence of Parliament the King's choice must be respected. The behaviour of Fox seemed spiteful and full of pique. His claim that the Cabinet and not the King should choose Rockingham's successor was of very doubtful constitutional propriety indeed. Few people took Fox seriously, for he was attacking openly the royal prerogative of appointing ministers.[18] Although there was not much enthusiasm for Shelburne's administration in July 1782 he did appear to be in a strong position. Fox was discredited and Shelburne was a man of far greater talent than the Duke of Portland. He was, furthermore, the heir of Chatham and of his principles and, in the political conditions of the summer of 1782, the defender of the Constitution and, especially, of the monarchy. He clearly had a *prima facie* right to govern.[19]

Shelburne intended to make full use of the political power which was now his and he entertained far-reaching ideas of reform. His two major preoccupations, however, were to be economical reform and the making of peace. The first was to prove a disappointment, the second a disaster.

Shelburne set himself to eliminate waste, extravagance and inefficiency from the machinery of government with commendable enthusiasm and industry. He saw clearly enough that the persistence of useless and outdated offices owed as much to the lingering concept of office as a freehold as to greed and pluralism. This he could not change overnight. He achieved a substantial number of minor reforms affecting the organisation of the Treasury but he went out of office before he could implement many of his schemes.[20] He attempted with little success to reduce the debt on the Civil List. He improved the supervision of the fees system, removing the worst of the abuses. He did something to

---

18 Burke gave Fox some good advice at this point, suggesting that he remain in office until Parliament had had an opportunity to sustain or to defeat Shelburne. Burke's advice would have effectively prevented Fox from seeming factious and, in particular, stirring up the problem of the royal prerogative of appointing ministers. See J. Cannon, *The Fox–North Coalition* (Cambridge, 1969), pp. 21–2.

19 He was also extremely fortunate in that the parliamentary recess began less than a week after he took office. His ministry was bound to survive, therefore, for at least six months, until Parliament reassembled.

20 Shelburne himself asserted that he had many economic reform proposals in preparation when he left office. (*The Parliamentary History*, xxiii, 824.)

rationalise the system of estimating the expenditure of various departments.[21] Further than this he did not have time to go. Many of his
schemes were taken over by the Younger Pitt and gradually introduced
by him but the credit for their initiation really belongs to Shelburne.

The great issue upon which the fate of the ministry hung, however,
was that of peace-making. Shelburne hurried to complete the peace
preliminaries before Parliament met. This he did when they were signed
on 30 November. It should be stressed that for Shelburne to have made
a successful and popular peace was quite out of the question. British
troops had been humiliatingly defeated in America, and if the war had
been lost then the peace could not be won. The British public made a
scapegoat of Shelburne and castigated the luckless premier mercilessly,
especially over his inability to do anything for the American loyalists.
As soon as the preliminaries were made public, Shelburne's ministry
began to look very vulnerable indeed. The peace terms were Shelburne's own. He was an autocratic premier[22] and it was his own
personal stature that was in question. His political future depended
upon his ability or inability to persuade Parliament to approve the
preliminaries. On 17 and 21 February his peace was rejected in the
Commons by divisions of 224 to 208 and 207 to 190 respectively. Three
days later he resigned. What explains his disastrous defeat and his
ignominious departure from office?[23]

To a large extent Shelburne's Chathamite principle of refusing to
organise a parliamentary following went far towards destroying his
ministry. Shelburne had only a small group of followers and he would
have to rely for a majority entirely upon the Court and administration
group. He really believed that this normally loyal body would be sufficient to obtain a majority for the peace. His advisers promised him a
massive majority and he was unwise enough to believe them.[24] Another
aspect of his Chathamite principles contributed to his downfall. Shel-

[21] For his economic reform activities, see the authoritative account in J. Norris,
Shelburne and Reform (London, 1963), chapters 10, 11, 12.
[22] Before the debates on the peace preliminaries Grafton and Keppel had resigned,
the former entirely and the latter partly because of Shelburne's high-handedness.
Richmond had stopped attending the Cabinet and Camden was extremely unhappy
at his own situation.
[23] Ignominious not only because of his apparent cowardice but because during the
debates hardly any members, even among those who normally supported him, had
a good word to say for him.
[24] Cannon, op. cit., p. 30.

burne believed that the confidence of the Crown was sufficient to keep a ministry in office. It was not. Unlike Chatham Shelburne did not have the personal qualities that appealed to uncommitted members. Indeed, it was Shelburne's unpopularity that made possible the Fox-North Coalition which turned him out of office. Shelburne might have saved himself by cultivating North, but his unfounded optimism of the winter of 1782–3 allowed the Foxites an almost free hand in negotiating with North.[25] Even when he did approach North the result was disastrous. He tried to commit him to supporting the peace terms without telling North what they were. Only Shelburne could have been guilty of such an indiscretion. Only Shelburne could have been guilty of the fatal error that precipitated the agreement between Fox and North which was reached on 14 February, just three days before the first of the two Commons divisions. Shelburne attempted to frighten North into remaining neutral on the issue of the peace, a blunder which drove that amiable nobleman straight into the arms of Charles James Fox.

Shelburne's premiership came to an end, then, because of his adherence to Chathamite ideas and his political ineptitude as well as the peace and his personal unpopularity. But ministries could and did survive occasional defeats in the eighteenth century, even on great issues. Why did not Shelburne, who after all had only narrowly lost an unpopular peace against a well organised parliamentary opposition, remain in office? The answer is that he had by this time lost the will to fight. He had no stomach for public, political battles and feared further defeats at the hands of the Coalition. He no longer believed that he enjoyed the unlimited confidence of the King. Indeed, he went so far as to blame his parliamentary defeat upon the King's lack of support. To the end he believed in his own righteousness.

There was something tragic in his isolation. While there was no justification for his conviction that the King had been disloyal to him there can be little doubt that the King's confidence in his minister was beginning to weaken. His radical ideas had never endeared themselves to him and Shelburne was of little use to him if he could not even stave off a defeat in Parliament on a major issue. His Cabinet colleagues provided no support or encouragement. Thurlow had always thought his economical reform ideas to be nonsensical and had little sympathy for him. Conway and Grafton, two of the mildest of men, were offended by

25 Even as late as December it was quite obvious that the Northites and the Foxites were still at odds. Shelburne did nothing to profit from their dissensions.

his high-handedness. Grafton, indeed, resigned because he did not consider himself to be in receipt of 'the fair confidence of the principal
minister', and he accused Shelburne of 'attempting to break through
that system of *general Cabinet advice*, which has been understood by us
all'.[26] In short, his imperiousness had made an enemy of most members
of his own Cabinet. Some of them, Richmond and Keppel, for example,
yearned for a reconciliation with Fox. By February, then, the remarkable situation obtained where Shelburne had not a single friend in his
own Cabinet.[27] Even outside the Cabinet there was no enthusiasm for
him. Such political 'friends' as he had, men such as Pitt the Younger
and Henry Dundas, were uninterested in saving Shelburne. They had
their own careers to look to. It was, perhaps, just as well for Shelburne
that he did resign in February 1783. His political isolation would not
have allowed him to survive for very long even if he had summoned up
the courage to struggle on.

Shelburne left some few constructive achievements to posterity. The
peace treaty was renegotiated by the Coalition but they were hardly
able to improve on it. He did not stay in power long enough to negotiate the kind of free trade relationship with America of which he had
always dreamed. For the same reason his plans for economical reform
remained unfulfilled, his other schemes unrealised.

The story of his premiership, however, is strongly suggestive of the
state of British politics during the constitutional crisis of 1782–4. For a
ministry to survive it was no longer sufficient for the first minister to
enjoy the royal confidence and the patronage which possession of the
Treasury provided. A ministry had to be led in the Commons and sustained there by a party of supporters. A ministry had to command
acceptance among a fairly wide section of opinion and particularly
among the Independents. Those statesmen of eighteenth-century Britain
like Chatham and Shelburne who did not form parties were naturally
more acceptable to monarchs than those who did but they could not
survive without organised parliamentary support. This had been the
lesson of the Chatham administration of 1766–8 and it was the lesson of

[26] Sir W. Anson (ed.), *Autobiography of the 3rd Duke of Grafton* (London, 1898), p.
362.
[27] However, there appears to be no truth in the old tradition that Shelburne's
Cabinet met very infrequently because Shelburne was afraid to assemble it. Between 12 July and 19 December it met at least 26 times. (I. R. Christie, *Myth and
Reality in Late Eighteenth-Century British Politics* (London, 1970), p. 69.)

Shelburne's ministry of 1782-3. Lord Shelburne was the last Prime Minister to attempt to govern without the aid of Party.

BIBLIOGRAPHY

The manuscripts of Shelburne have been much neglected by historians. There is a large deposit at Bowood, Wiltshire, and another at the William Clements Library, Ann Arbor, Michigan, USA. The only modern study of Shelburne is that by John Norris, *Shelburne and Reform* (London, 1963), but it is still necessary to consult Lord E. Fitzmaurice, *Life of William, Earl of Shelburne* (3 vols, London, 1875–6), which includes an invaluable autobiographical fragment. There is valuable material on particular aspects of Shelburne's career in: V. T. Harlow, *The Founding of the Second British Empire, 1763–93* (2 vols, London, 1959–64); J. Cannon, *The Fox–North Coalition* (Cambridge, 1969); D. Jarrett, *The Begetters of Revolution, 1759–89* (London, 1973).

13

THE DUKE OF PORTLAND

BY

E. ANTHONY SMITH

William Henry Cavendish-Bentinck, born 14 April 1738, son of the 2nd Duke of Portland. Educated at Westminster School and Christ Church, Oxford. Succeeded as 3rd Duke 1762. Married 1766 Lady Dorothy Cavendish, daughter of 4th Duke of Devonshire; four sons and one daughter. Lord Chamberlain of the Household 1765-6; Lord Lieutenant of Ireland 1782; leader of the Whig party 1782; First Lord of the Treasury 1783; leader of the Whig Opposition 1783-94; abandoned opposition 1792; joined Pitt 1794; Home Secretary 1794-1801; Lord President of the Council 1801-5; First Lord of the Treasury 1807-9. PC 1765; KG 1794; Lord Lieutenant of Nottinghamshire 1795-1809; Chancellor of the University of Oxford 1792-1809. Resigned as Prime Minister on 6 September 1809 and died 29 October 1809.

THE DUKE OF PORTLAND

If other holders of the office have been nicknamed the 'forgotten' and the 'unknown' prime ministers, William Henry Cavendish-Bentinck, third Duke of Portland, must surely rank as the 'unheard-of' prime minister. Yet he held the post on two separate occasions, no less than twenty-four years apart, and each time he came to 10 Downing Street at the height of a political and constitutional crisis which seemed to threaten the balanced eighteenth-century constitutional relationship between the King and his ministers. In the first instance he came to office as nominal head of the Fox–North Coalition, attempting to assert the supremacy of the Cabinet, backed by a House of Commons majority, over the King's personal will. On the second occasion he volunteered to rescue George III from ministerial domination after the King's quarrel with Grenville's Cabinet on the Catholic question, so repeating the role which Pitt had played against his administration in December 1783. His two periods of office thus offer contrasting views of the constitutional relationship between King and ministers in the late eighteenth and early nineteenth centuries, just at the time when that relationship was passing through a vital transitional period. The decline in the formal 'Influence of the Crown' and the emergence of the new political forces outside Parliament were beginning to change the context of eighteenth-century aristocratic politics, and would eventually transform the Constitution into a parliamentary democracy in which the Crown was to become little more than a figurehead and the prime minister a national as well as a party leader. Portland's career illustrates the limited extent of this development by 1809.

Conscientious and industrious, Portland dedicated himself from the first to the service of the Whig party. 'I consider myself as a servant of the Party,' he wrote to Newcastle in 1766, 'and shall always think it my duty to act in the manner that is most conducive to its support.'[1] Nevertheless, he failed to overcome a natural shyness and dislike of public prominence. He was an affectionate and considerate friend and a devoted family man, but to those who did not know him intimately he

[1] British Museum Additional MS 32977, f.58.

seemed aloof and frigid. Horace Walpole characterised him as 'a proud though bashful man', and a later historian remarked that he was 'an outstanding representative of the aristocratic theories for which he lived'. He was, however, a man of firm principles. Canning called him 'one of the most blameless, and noble-minded of men'.[2] He was one of the few to preserve a spotless reputation in an age when public men were often accused of personal intrigue or underhand dealing, and though he lacked the drive and energy to be a successful party leader in opposition he never lost the respect and, indeed, the devotion of his colleagues. Paradoxically, it was his complete lack of personal ambition that raised him to the premiership. Like Trollope's Duke of Omnium – for whom he might almost have been a model – he became Prime Minister partly because he was a duke, and partly because his appointment to the office enabled other, more vigorous but more abrasive colleagues to serve together under him. In both his administrations the driving force came from others – from Fox and Burke in 1783, from Perceval, Canning and Castlereagh in 1807-9. On both occasions Portland was a 'dummy' rather than a real Prime Minister, but on both occasions the choice met with the general approval of the other ministers. As his grandson Charles Greville later wrote, Portland's election as Whig party leader in July 1782 showed 'how aristocratic that party was, and what weight and influence the aristocracy possessed in those days; they would never have endured to be led by a Peel or a Canning'.[3] Yet Portland's subsequent authority was never questioned by the men of talent in the party.

Despite Portland's election to Rockingham's office as Whig party leader, he did not succeed immediately to the premiership. George III was not yet willing to accept a prime minister at the nomination of a party in the House of Commons, however strong in numbers. The post was offered to Shelburne, who was distrusted by the Foxites. They determined not to serve under him. 'Where there is not confidence, there must be Power,' Fox wrote on 12 July, 'and Power in this country must accompany the Treasury.' He declared to the King that the Whigs would insist on a prime minister of their own choosing.[4] If the King would not accept Portland, he might be forced to do so. In February

[2] A. S. Turberville, *A History of Welbeck Abbey and its Owners* (1939), ii, 319-21.
[3] C. C. F. Greville, *Journal of the Reign of Queen Victoria, 1837-52*, part II (1885), iii, 212-13.
[4] Fox to Portland, 12 July 1782 (*Memorials and Correspondence of C. J. Fox*, iv, 275).

1783 the Government was defeated in the Commons by the Coalition between the two opposition parties of Fox and North. Shelburne resigned, leaving the King to find another combination that could obtain a majority in the Commons. For the second time in the eighteenth century, this requirement dominated the search for a prime minister. Previously, ministers appointed by the Crown had been able to expect support from the Commons almost as a matter of course. In 1782 and 1783 the majority of the Commons was sufficiently intractable and determined to compel the King to submit to their virtual nomination. Fox again declared that the Whigs would not join any government unless Portland were placed at the head of it.[5]

Portland and Fox were not satisfied with a mere commission to form a government. In the first place, remembering the difficulties caused for Rockingham in 1782 by the use of Shelburne as a go-between, they insisted on Portland's receiving the appointment directly from the King. 'If it is his Majesty's pleasure to place me at the head of the Treasury,' Portland wrote, 'it is impossible to suppose that he means to withhold from me any part of his confidence, but it is very necessary that the public should be convinced of that circumstance.'[6] They were also determined that the ministry should institute a new relationship between the King and his servants. At the beginning of the crisis Portland declared: 'If . . . it should be the King's pleasure to place the Government in our hands, the powers of carrying it on must be given to those who are looked upon to be Whigs, and were considered to be such by our late most excellent friend, Lord Rockingham.' In particular, he would not serve unless George abandoned his insistence that Lords Thurlow and Stormont should be in the Cabinet, and when Portland was at last admitted to the royal presence on 23 March he refused to disclose the proposed arrangement of offices except for the Cabinet itself. While giving an assurance that any removals would be made 'as little obnoxious to his Majesty as the case would possibly admit', and in particular that there would be no alterations in the Bedchamber so long as its officers supported the Government, Portland insisted that before he could discuss further arrangements the King must signify his confidence in his ministers by approving the list of the Cabinet and binding himself to accept their recommendations. He therefore submitted only

[5] North to George III, 4 Mar. 1783; George III to Shelburne, 19 Mar. (Fortescue, *Correspondence of George III*, vi, 260-1, 292).
[6] Portland to North, 17 Mar. 1783 (Fortescue, p. 285).

the seven names proposed for the Cabinet. Pitt's refusal to come to the rescue left the King without an alternative and, muttering threats of abdication, George submitted to Portland's demands on 31 March, pleading that only the emptiness of the Treasury prevented him from prolonging the struggle. And if his new minister wished for a free hand in distributing the lesser offices, he should have it. The King insisted on the point that Portland had 'named' rather than 'recommended' the members of the Cabinet, and on 4 April he wrote that he had no desire to interfere with the formation of the Admiralty Board, which Portland could arrange as he liked.[7] On 1 April, the day before the ministry formally took office, the King even wrote to Lord Temple, who had refused to join them, to express the earnest hope that, as William Grenville expressed it, 'those who act with us should hold themselves apart from such a government in order that he may have something else to look to whenever circumstances shall allow it'. In the meantime he declared his resolution to grant no peerages or other honours at the ministers' recommendation, to signal his disfavour to the public at large.[8]

Portland's first ministry set out under conditions unprecedented in the history of British Cabinets, with the sovereign almost publicly avowing his distaste for his ministers, and the events of the next months did not improve the relationship. The settlement of the Prince of Wales's income on his coming of age in August 1783 resulted in a quarrel between Portland and the King when the Duke proposed to allow the Prince – who was associated politically with the Whig party and personally with Fox's circle of friends – an annual sum amounting to double that received by George III when he was heir to the throne, plus a large sum to help pay off his enormous debts. The King refused point-blank so 'to gratify the passions of an ill-advised young man'. 'The reception I met with in the Closet,' wrote Portland to Lord Loughborough, 'was so grievous that I know not how to describe it.' The King threatened to expose the whole affair to the public as a job for the benefit of the

[7] Portland to Temple, 22 Feb. 1783 (*Memoirs of the Court and Cabinets of George III*, ed. Buckingham and Chandos (1853), i, 163); North to George III, 15 Mar., George III to North, 23 Mar., Portland to George III, 23 Mar., George III to Pitt, 23 Mar., to Weymouth, 25 Mar., draft messages of abdication [? 28 Mar.], George III to Portland, 4 April, and his memorandum, 30 Mar. (Fortescue, vi, 280, 298–300, 310, 314–17, 325, 332–3). See also O. Browning (ed.), *Political Memoranda of Francis, Duke of Leeds* (Camden Society, NS xxxv, 1884), pp. 86–7.

[8] George III to Temple, 1 April (Fortescue, vi, 329–30); W. W. Grenville to Temple, 1 April (*Court and Cabinets*, I, 216).

ministers and their friends, and even sent copies of his correspondence with Portland to Lord North in the hope that he and Stormont, both members of the Cabinet, would disavow the Government's policy. Portland had to persuade the Prince to accept his father's offer of half the proposed income plus the Duchy of Cornwall revenues and a capital sum from Parliament to pay his debts. Despite the ministry's parliamentary strength, the King had won a victory, and the Government's life remained precarious.[9]

The fall of the Portland ministry over the India Bill in December 1783 is a story that has often been told.[10] The Bill was a serious attempt to bring the political administration of India under closer public control, but it contained provisions which could be interpreted, like those concerning the Prince of Wales's income, as designed more for the advantage of the ministers than of the Empire. The proposed Commission for the Government of India, to be nominated by Parliament and serving for a fixed term of four years, was to control Indian patronage and administration, and was to consist of close friends and associates of Fox and North. Since the four-year term of office would run beyond the date of the next general election, it was at once assumed that the aim of the Bill was to ensure the ministers' success at the polls in 1786 or 1787 and so to make their tenure of office permanent. It was in response to this threat that Pitt and Temple initiated the well-known plan to secure the defeat of the Bill by the direct use of the King's name with the House of Lords, and to use the defeat as a pretext to dismiss the ministry and appoint a new one under their leadership. On 17 December the Lords rejected the Bill, and on the following day the ministry was dismissed, the King merely sending a messenger to collect the seals of office, 'as audiences on such occasions must be unpleasant'. The ministers considered themselves deceived, as the King had never hinted his disapproval to them; the revelation of the royal displeasure even converted the vote of Lord Stormont, a member of the Cabinet itself, into one against the Bill.[11] The King's action was a foretaste of the tactics which Portland himself was to exploit against Grenville's ministry

[9] George III to Portland, 16 June 1783, and to North, 16 June (Fortescue, vi, 401–3). Portland to Loughborough, 18 June (Portland MSS, PwF 9212).
[10] The most recent account is that of Dr J. A. Cannon in *The Fox–North Coalition* (1969).
[11] George III to North, 18 Dec. 1783 (Fortescue, vi, 476); W. Eden to Morton Eden, 16 Dec. (*Journal and Correspondence of Lord Auckland* (1861), i, 69).

in March 1807 and, as Fox pointed out with some force in the House of Commons, it violated the cardinal constitutional principle of the responsibility of ministers, 'the only pledge and security the people of England possess against the infinite abuses so natural to the exercise of this power. Once remove this great bulwark of the Constitution, and we are, in every respect, the slaves and property of despotism.'[12] If the accession to office of Portland's ministry exposed the limitations of the royal power over the appointment of ministers and determination of policy in face of a strong and determined political party, the manner of its dismissal showed that the King need only find a sufficient degree of support elsewhere in order to recover his position.

Portland remained out of office for over eleven years. In July 1794 the greater part of the aristocratic section of the Whig party joined Pitt, anxious to strengthen the Government's hand in dealing with the twin threats of French aggression abroad and French revolutionary example at home. As Home Secretary, Portland was responsible until 1801 for the maintenance of law and order in the country and the control of popular disturbances. The experience confirmed his strong natural conservatism – he had always been utterly opposed to parliamentary reform and a convinced adherent of the creed of aristocratic Whig paternalism. By 1805, when he went into what he expected to be his political retirement after serving for ten and a half years without a break in the Cabinet, he had come to represent the ultimate in loyalty to King, country and the old Constitution. It was to protect all these that he agreed to assume the burdens of office once more in 1807, nearly a year after Pitt's death.

George III's quarrel with his Ministry of All the Talents over the proposed Catholic Relief Bill came to a head early in March 1807. As in November 1783, the King had given no overt sign of his opinion of the Cabinet's proposal when it was submitted to him for approval, tacitly reserving his freedom of action until the parliamentary situation became clear. On this occasion it was Sidmouth, always a strong anti-Catholic, who became alarmed at the scope of the measure, and his visit to the Palace provided George with evidence that there was a possibility of replacing the ministry with one more agreeable to his own Protestant views. Once again he hinted at the possibility of his using the royal veto against the Bill if it passed both Houses. Such a step, as Lord Mulgrave wrote, would lead to the dismissal or resignation of the

[12] *Parliamentary History*, xxiv, 216–17.

ministry and a dissolution of Parliament, accompanied by 'the greatest agitation . . . both in this country and in Ireland'.[13] To avert the political crisis which would result from the direct involvement of the Crown in a contest with Parliament, the Pittite leaders agreed to offer to form a government, with Portland at its head.

As early as June 1806 the Duke of York had suggested that Portland was the only possible leader of Pitt's former friends, amongst whom there were 'too many persons of the same rank, and nearly the same political consideration', while the King too seemed to regard the Duke as Pitt's natural successor.[14] It was Portland, therefore, who took the initiative when the crisis of March 1807 developed. On the 12th, after consulting Malmesbury, he addressed a long letter to the King, assuring him that 'should . . . the belief I wish to entertain be well founded, and that your Majesty shall not have given your consent to the measure in its present shape, I have little apprehension of disappointing your Majesty when I venture to express my opinion that it may be ultimately defeated . . . in . . . the House of Lords', providing the King's views were made unequivocally plain. He advised George to seek a direct explanation with Grenville, and, in the likely event of the ministry's resignation, declared 'that your Majesty would have an abundant choice of persons capable of managing your Majesty's affairs, and that so circumstanced, those persons would receive the general support of the nation at large'. Finally,' as for myself, incapable as, *I know*, I am from age, infirmity and want of ability to render your Majesty any profitable service, should your Majesty be of opinion that I can be of any use to you, I will do the best I can to serve you to my life's end.'[15]

George III, constitutionally proper as always, sent no formal reply to Portland's letter until after the crisis was over, but there is no doubt that it provided him with the support he needed to act. On the 13th he authorised a message to Malmesbury to declare his unchanged sentiments on the Catholic question. On the same day he saw Grenville, declared his objection to the Bill, and demanded its withdrawal. The Cabinet agreed on 15 March to withdraw, but reserved the right of

13 Mulgrave to Lowther, 11 Mar. 1807 (Lonsdale MSS, quoted in A. Aspinall (ed.), *Later Correspondence of George III*, iv, 525, n.1).
14 Malmesbury, *Diary and Correspondence of . . . 1st Earl of Malmesbury* (1845), iv, 359–61.
15 Portland to George III, 12 Mar. (*Later Correspondence of George III*, pp. 525–8). The King replied on the 22nd (ibid., p. 533).

the ministers as individuals to declare in Parliament their support for the principles behind the Bill. The King demanded in return a pledge that they would propose nothing more to him on the Catholic question, and on their refusal sent for Eldon and Hawkesbury to come to Windsor. They saw him on the 19th, were informed of his wish to change his ministers, and recommended that he should send for Portland, 'as more likely to unite the feelings of persons than any other man'. The King, reported Eldon and Hawkesbury, declared that Portland should have a completely free hand – 'he may dispose of everything'. He was to confer with Chatham and Viscount Lowther, and submit a plan for approval.[16]

Portland accepted the commission on the 20th, though with great reluctance owing to his advanced infirmity. He had been gravely ill for some time, and had only a few months before undergone with great courage the ordeal of 'cutting for the stone'. He realised that the appointment might shorten his life, but, he assured Malmesbury, 'he should by no means regret a few years, or perhaps months, more or less, when he had the inward satisfaction of thinking they were sacrificed in his endeavours to serve his King and his country'. Hawkesbury reported to the King that Portland was 'most ready and willing to lend himself to be the instrument of any arrangement which your Majesty might deem advantageous to your service.'[17] On 25 March Portland and his colleagues were sworn in.

Portland's Cabinet of 1807 was, to appearances, one of the most impressive of the eighteenth and nineteenth centuries. It included three future prime ministers – Perceval, Hawkesbury and Canning – in addition to Eldon and Castlereagh, two of the leading statesmen of the early nineteenth century. Yet it proved to be one of the weakest and least successful of administrations. Portland's continuing and progressively worsening ill health must be held partly responsible for its lack of unity. He had never been an inspiring leader or shown much talent for coordinating the efforts of others when he was at the head of the Whig party. Now he was largely ignored by his own colleagues, and on occasions not even summoned to Cabinet meetings. Malmesbury lamented that the Duke 'had so few, or rather *no* person in the Cabinet he could call his personal friend', and noticed that his colleagues 'take a great

[16] Malmesbury, iv, 373–4, 378–81; Camden to Lowther, 19 Mar. (Lonsdale MSS, quoted in *Later Correspondence of George III*, p. 529, n.1).
[17] Malmesbury, iv, 375; Hawkesbury to George III [20 Mar. 1807] (*Later Correspondence of George III*, iv, 530).

9. William Pitt, 1st Earl of Chatham, by William Hoare

10. Augustus Fitzroy, 3rd Duke of Grafton, by Pompeo Batoni

11. Frederick, Lord North, by N. Dance

12. William, 2nd Earl of Shelburne, from a mezzotint of a group, by Sir Joshua Reynolds

13. William Cavendish-Bentinck, 3rd Duke of Portland

14. William Pitt, 'the Younger', by John Hoppner

15. Henry Addington, 1st Viscount Sidmouth, by George Richmond

16. William Grenville, 1st Baron Grenville, by John Hoppner

deal on themselves, immediately belonging to *him*, and treat him more as a nominal than as a real head of the Ministry'. So, 'if ever he had a point to contend, or ever was disposed to contend one, [he would] be left in a very small minority.' Perceval, as Leader of the Commons, Hawkesbury, Canning and Castlereagh were the major political figures in the ministry, but they were uncomfortable colleagues who failed to work closely together. Unfortunately, too, the remaining members of the Cabinet were less able men who could offer Portland no real support. Portland failed – he did not even try – to weld these discordant elements into a team. The position was summed up by Perceval in August 1809: 'It is not because the Duke of Portland is at our head,' he wrote, 'that the Government is a Government of Departments; but it is because the Government is and must be essentially a Government of Departments that the Duke of Portland is at our head, and is the best head possibly that we could have. I very much doubt us continuing long under any other.'[18] The Cabinet contained a group of self-willed individuals, men of equal importance, so that a 'strong' premier would merely have driven it rapidly to self-destruction. Even Portland's feeble authority could not hold it together when his colleagues began to quarrel amongst themselves. The ministry thus burrowed its way further and further into difficulties, partly of its own making, in the conduct of the war and at home, while the Prime Minister, frequently incapacitated by bouts of agonising pain, was unable to deal effectively with his colleagues. Malmesbury wrote: 'I have often been with him when I thought he would have died in his chair; and his powers of attention were so weakened that he could neither read a paper, nor listen for a while, without becoming drowsy and falling asleep.'[19] He was clearly incapable of handling the dispute between Canning and Castlereagh. Canning's campaign to have Castlereagh removed from the War Office opened in March 1809, and the Duke, instead of stepping in and acting with firmness at the outset, allowed matters to drift on until the end of June, when Perceval found out that Castlereagh was, unknown to himself, virtually under sentence of dismissal. The consequence was a quarrel between Perceval and Canning, and, in September, Castlereagh's resignation and duel with Canning. By then, however, Portland's health had finally given way. In August he had an apoplectic

[18] Malmesbury, iv, 386, 394; Perceval to Huskisson, 21 Aug. 1809 (Perceval MSS, quoted in D. Gray, *Spencer Perceval* (1963), p. 223).
[19] Malmesbury, iv, 413.

seizure on the way to his country house at Bulstrode, and, though he partially recovered his mind and speech, he resigned on 6 September with the Cabinet breaking up around him. He died after a second seizure on 29 October.

If in his first ministry of 1783 Portland represented the Whig claim to the supremacy of Cabinet and party over the Crown, in his second term of office he stood for the preservation of monarchical influence over the rising claims of the politicians. On both occasions he presided over ministries composed of discordant groups and individuals, and he failed to impose a personal authority over them. He allowed Fox to run his first ministry into head-on collision with the King, and Canning to destroy his second. Portland was thus a prime minister in only a limited sense. His role was virtually that of a figurehead for abler men who supplied the real driving power of government, and on both occasions too his tenure of office depended directly upon the King's willingness to allow him to hold it. Portland's career shows that even by 1809 the authority of a prime minister still depended on the personal attitudes of the sovereign and of the individual members of the Cabinet.

BIBLIOGRAPHY

Aspinall, A., (ed.), *Later Correspondence of George III* (Cambridge, 1962–70), vol. iv
Fortescue, Sir J. (ed.), *Correspondence of George III* (London, 1927–8), vol. vi
Diaries and Correspondence of James Harris, First Earl of Malmesbury, edited by his grandson, the 3rd Earl (1845), vol. iv
Welbeck MSS (Nottingham University Library)
Cannon, J., *The Fox–North Coalition* (Cambridge, 1969)
Gray, D., *Spencer Perceval, the Evangelical Prime Minister* (Manchester, 1963)
Turberville, A. S., *A History of Welbeck Abbey and its Owners* (London, 1939), vol. ii

14

WILLIAM PITT 'THE YOUNGER'

BY

PETER DOUGLAS BROWN

William Pitt, born 28 May 1759, son of William Pitt, MP (cr. Earl of Chatham 1766) and Lady Hester Grenville, daughter of Richard Grenville, MP. Educated at Pembroke College, Cambridge; Lincoln's Inn 1778; called 1780; MP Appleby 1781–1784; Cambridge University 1784–1806; PC 1782; Chancellor of the Exchequer 1782–1783; First Lord of the Treasury and Chancellor of the Exchequer 1783–1801, 1804–1806; Lord Warden of the Cinque Ports 1792. Unmarried. Died 23 January 1806.

WILLIAM PITT 'THE YOUNGER'

William Pitt became Prime Minister at the age of twenty-four and proceeded to manage the affairs of a great empire for seventeen years without interruption, an achievement unique in the parliamentary annals of any country. Born during the Annus Mirabilis of 1759 and conditioned by the universal adulation for his father, politics were for him the only concern. Chatham, discerning a true senator, himself trained the boy in oratory. A Cambridge undergraduate at fourteen, William had as tutor the Reverend George Pretyman-Tomline, whom he would one day appoint Bishop of Lincoln. Though he was far from being head of a coterie, a good many of his university acquaintance were destined to serve under him. Granby (soon to be fourth Duke of Rutland), John Pratt, son of Chatham's Lord Chancellor Camden, and the tenth Earl of Westmorland all became Viceroys of Ireland; Althorp as second Earl Spencer would be First Lord of the Admiralty when Nelson fought at Aboukir. Pitt watched House of Commons debates and met Charles James Fox, already prominent in Parliament, but whose unstable ways were a source of alarm to his friends.

With Pitt ebullience took the form of a happy ambition, tempered by a serenity reminiscent of those classical sages whom men of the eighteenth century sought to emulate. In respect of the appetites, his temper had no difficulty in meeting the moderation demanded by his circumstances. Chatham's financial embarrassments precluded provision for a younger son and Pitt would be the first future Prime Minister ever to undertake a profession: Cambridge was followed by practice at the Bar. When in 1780 the King sprang a general election Pitt, just come of age, manifested that optimistic courage which would always be one of the most appealing sides to his greatness. He offered himself for the representation of his university but ended bottom of the count, though not ignominiously. Rutland introduced him to Sir James Lowther, the greatest parliamentary patron in England, and Pitt, after some misgivings about representing a private borough, accepted his nomination for Appleby. What practical advantages membership of Parliament might bring were however far from evident, for North, as the King intended, had held on to a majority in the House of Commons, and for Chatham's son the apostasy of seeking his board from that ministry was unthinkable.

That Pitt should have become Prime Minister scarcely less than three years after entering Parliament was not, and never could have been, due solely to the concurrence of precocious abilities with the public memory of Chatham. So meteoric a transformation could take place only in consequence of a cataclysm so great as to throw party alignments into utter confusion. The American war, whether decided in terms of unity or division between the English-speaking peoples, must dominate allegiances at Westminster. But when Pitt embarked on politics the coming disaster was not in evidence, for the war situation, though unpromising, was not hopeless.

Pitt's sympathies naturally lay with the opponents of the war which his father had deplored. He had a young man's enthusiasm for the re-form of the House of Commons, which his father had advocated and the cause of America had made hugely topical. He was also an admirer of Adam Smith and his free trade principles, which belonged to the generation after Chatham. For Pitt there was an obvious leader in Shel-burne, his father's disciple, the most intellectually pioneering man in the politics of the day. Pitt was welcomed into that eclectic circle of the man who might well be a prime minister for the future. It would not however be correct to call him Shelburne's follower: already his in-sularity matched his gifts. Pitt owed his introduction to the moderate parliamentary reformer Wyvill not to Shelburne, but to his cousin Lord Mahon. In the House of Commons, with the ease of a total unself-consciousness, Pitt established a reputation as a first-class debater. News of Yorktown made certain the opening of a new chapter but the prospects of Shelburne, let alone Pitt, were hard to discern. Shelburne had the asset of Chatham's reputation but also the disadvantage of his very small parliamentary following. Yet while North's ministry was crumbling, Pitt declared before the House of Commons his unwilling-ness ever to condescend to junior office – a most ill-judged essay in conceit from anyone but himself.

True to his word Pitt refused a minor place in the Rockingham ministry. The piecemeal harassment of the Civil List, after the prin-ciples conceived by Burke for limiting the 'influence' of the Crown, could not spark off his enthusiasm. Shelburne became the Secretary of State with the main responsibility for negotiating peace with America, in a most unenviable situation, hated by Fox and Burke. Pitt, acting in concert with Wyvill, called for a select committee of the House of Commons on parliamentary reform. He was beaten 161–141, a respectable defeat which would be the best the reformers would manage in Pitt's lifetime. On Rockingham's death Shelburne was appointed Prime Minister and Fox hastened back to the game of opposition. But Fox was considered even by some of his friends to be resigning on grounds purely personal.

The King would have liked Pitt at the Home Office but for the jealousies so rapid a promotion must arouse. Pitt was happy to be Chancellor of the Exchequer with a seat in the Cabinet. Shelburne had a most ambitious programme to cover the deficiencies laid bare by the war. All depended upon the ministry building a majority and Pitt indicated that, though he would not be a party to a coalition with North, an arrangement with Fox might be palatable. But Fox made clear to Pitt that he would not serve with Shelburne. So Fox and North got together and Shelburne, his plans for peace with America and France thrown out by the House of Commons, resigned. To some extent Pitt, by his obduracy towards North, had been responsible for his chief's downfall, but his subsequent consistency of conduct would redeem him. From Shelburne Pitt had learnt much, above all the ideal of sound administration as an end in itself, and not merely as a means to the diminution of 'influence'. He also recognised that Shelburne had come to grief in part because his plans were far too comprehensive for any House of Commons to swallow at once. Reform would have to be gradual, step by step, and as little alarming as possible to interested parties.

In George III's eyes Shelburne was a broken reed, and as he had no intention of treating with Fox and North, to invite Pitt to become Prime Minister was not so very surprising. But despite the pleas of Shelburne and Dundas, Pitt declined the opportunity, offered twice within a month, because his majority would have to depend upon North's goodwill. He thereby preserved his freedom of action and proved to the world that, unlike Fox, he would not compromise his principles for power. The way was open for the Infamous Coalition of Fox and North with Portland Prime Minister. Pitt stood forth as the champion of parliamentary reform and during May and June put forward a series of resolutions which won moderate support. But the stance of the Government was most impressive and Pitt made plans to resume his Bar career. Then Fox threw the game away by his India Bill, a most unpopular measure which vested Indian patronage in a committee to be nominated by the Coalition's majority in the Commons. Pitt considered Fox's Bill barely constitutional, doubted its passage through the Commons and was certain the Lords would block it. He spoke loud and clear against, and here opened his great parliamentary duel with Fox, 'Cicero in Catilinam', that would last their days. On this occasion Pitt misjudged the Commons, who passed the India Bill by a handsome majority in one of the most important divisions of the century. The King's next line of defence was the House of Lords but the consequences of challenging the Commons had first to be considered. The chances of a new minister establishing a majority were exactly counted, and also the probable outcome of a general election: both calculations were found to leave 'no *manly* ground for apprehension'. Pitt agreed to take the risk, the alternative being to leave the King shackled with Fox and North for ever and so destroy every chance for himself. A message entrusted to Pitt's first cousin, the second Earl Temple, informed the peers that anyone who voted for Fox's India Bill would be considered a personal enemy of the King, and this secured its rejection. On 19 December 1783 George III dismissed the Coalition and Pitt was appointed Prime Minister.

Forming a ministry was not easy; with what Henry Dundas censured as great cowardice, Temple retracted his acceptance of a Secretaryship of State. The Government which emerged was not impressive. Thurlow, so long the King's man, was bound to come back as Lord Chancellor. Lord Sydney, conscientious but rather dull, returned to the Home Office. For Foreign Secretary Pitt took the Duke of Leeds's heir, Carmarthen, indolent and ineffective. The second Earl Gower as Lord President and Rutland temporarily Lord Privy Seal brought borough influence and historic connections. All the Cabinet were peers and, Thurlow excepted, not one a statesman of even second-class rating. Shelburne was not invited into the Government but had to console himself with the marquisate of Lansdowne: Pitt had no wish for a rival. His real trust lay in a circle of close friends, especially his first cousin William Wyndham Grenville, Dundas and George Rose, but at first they could be given only junior places.

Pitt saw that, rather than ask for a dissolution, he would be wiser to face the House of Commons, let members see him in action and for the man he was, pilot through the budget and leave Fox to do his worst. Fox hoped to turn Pitt out by the votes of the existing House of Commons who, he held, had the right to dictate the choice of prime minister. Pitt admitted that a minority government was 'unusual' but upheld the prerogative of the King. In truth his situation was more unknown than 'unusual', and the penalty for losing what was really a fight to the death between George III and Fox could be impeachment. The King, who had soon lived down what unpopularity he had acquired owing to the American war, happily dilated on the rights of the executive in a 'mixed Constitution'. Fox did himself the greatest harm by his dissolute manner of life, his open and constantly reiterated abuse of the King and his association with the open whore-mongering of the Prince of Wales, gleefully reported in the newspapers. The King showed his confidence by the creation of some peers; Lowther became Earl of Lonsdale. The Freedom of London which Pitt received on 28 February was a very distinct mark of popularity. The King and Pitt as champions of the Constitution were far more convincing than 'Carlo Khan', the libertine, who had tried to filch the riches of the East. Fox's Whig friends stayed firm. But North's followers had for years been happy to look to the approval of George III and man by man they deserted to Pitt. Fox dared not lay himself open to the charge of disrupting government by refusing supply. The Mutiny Bill through, the King dissolved Parliament on 24 March.

No eighteenth-century government ever lost a general election but the extent of Pitt's victory was astounding. He had a personal triumph in this time being elected for his university. Fox was again returned for Westminster, but through the country 160 of the men who had voted for his India Bill were thrown out. In the debate on the Address when Parliament met, Pitt's majority was 282–114. It was the coincidence between the King's judgement and that of the electorate that made the decision so complete. The ultimate future lay not with prerogative, but in Fox's concept of the functions of the House of Commons: this however was for the next generation.

In the hour of triumph Pitt made a mistake. Motivated by spite he attempted on a technicality to prevent Fox from taking his seat: the good sense of members prevailed and Pitt met his first defeat. But this was none the less essentially Pitt's House of Commons. The landed gentry would readily support him as representing a stable government and the type of Member desirous of office would rally to his banner. Eden did not heed the charge of tergiversation he was bound to attract on joining Pitt in 1785, and Jenkinson crowned a lifetime of service by his presidency of the Board of Trade, which won him the earldom of Liverpool. Pitt did not attempt to become a party leader in the sense ascribable to Walpole, Pelham and in some respects to North. For the first ten years he was the only member of the Cabinet not to be a peer. His personal following in the House of Commons never exceeded fifty and he depended upon the typical man of goodwill customarily ready to vote for administration. Apart from his natural aloofness Pitt was of the tradition of Chatham, who had thought the idea of party as defined by Burke positively harmful. His interest lay in seeing that the King's Government was carried on, and well; for that he had all the necessary support. By way of paradox Fox, though leader of a permanent minority, played the party game. He held his men together and of those who had survived the general election few deserted. He never forgave Pitt the way of his coming to power and castigated him as the reimbodiment of North's system. Pitt was not completely dependent upon the King, for both knew the alternative might be Fox. But just as the prerogative had been essential for his survival, so the understanding that he had the King's confidence was necessary for keeping his majority together. The King found that generally he and Pitt saw eye to eye over policy, left him to carry on business, and over patronage they compromised.

Pitt's India Act went through comfortably though at the cost of condoning some past abuses. The system of dual control thereby established lasted until 1858. Political power was exercised by the Board of Control in London, whilst on paper patronage stayed with the Company. Cornwallis embarked upon his great career as proconsul by becoming Governor-General, and from home Dundas at the Board of Control gradually established his all-pervasive influence. Though the Company lobby remained important, India ceased to be in the forefront of interest and Fox was completely dished over his pet topic. So far as the affairs of Warren Hastings were concerned neither Pitt nor Fox intervened initially. But Fox, anxious to get his own back, joined the attack as a political manoeuvre. Pitt's vote for a prosecution on the Benares charge, which made impeachment certain, astounded his friends and the King, but he seems simply to have changed his mind in the light of the evidence. At first the trial superficially compensated the Opposition for their ineffectiveness in Parliament, but as time drew on people became disgusted at the perversion of a legal process for party interest and the Whigs lost reputation.

With India out of the way Pitt could turn to the problems bequeathed by the American war. The loss of the American markets and shipyards was expected to be catastrophic. In the opinion of the Emperor Joseph II Britain was a second-class power. With this the views of Pitt and the King coincided in the sense that an adventurous foreign policy was economically out of the question. But Pitt had before him Shelburne's ideal of free trade as the means to recovery. The Americans would have welcomed a trade treaty but Pitt knew the House of Commons would never allow a return to the reciprocities of the old Empire now the political link had gone. Soon the disadvantages of the commercial breach with America would be more than offset by an immense upsurge in British production and trade which continued unbroken even during the French revolutionary wars. In the case of Ireland, constitutionally autonomous since 1782, closer links were imperative. Here Pitt's vision passed beyond the bounds of economics: if reciprocity in trade could be accompanied by an Irish contribution to imperial interests, and some parliamentary reform in Dublin, Britain and Ireland would enjoy a common polity, with domestic concerns left to the local legislatures. The Dublin Parliament substantially cut the proposed contribution to the Navy, and trouble there was not unexpected, but Pitt had not bargained for the storm of protest from merchants and manufacturers in Britain. The concessions to Ireland had to be curtailed so drastically that there was no hope of acceptance in Dublin. The Crown was left the only point of union between the two countries. The peace treaties had required a trade agreement with France, which during 1786 Eden negotiated on highly favourable terms. To Fox's objection that France was the natural enemy of Britain Pitt retorted that 'to suppose that any nation could be unalterably the enemy of another is weak and childish'. The treaty was approved by a large majority.

Pitt, after the manner of Walpole, Pelham, and of North as minister in time of peace, built his reputation upon his mastery of the national finances. At the opening of his ministry the interest on the National Debt, the Civil List and military and naval expenses exceeded the appropriated revenues by £2 million. There was the burden of an unfunded debt of £14 million carrying a discount of 14–15 per cent. Pitt's genius as an administrator was ideally suited to the mood of business optimism. He reduced the duties on those articles most extensively smuggled, cut drastically the duty on tea and substituted a Window Tax graduated to hit large houses. In the year 1787 alone Pitt carried nearly 3,000 resolutions through the House of Commons to remodel the port and excise duties. Already he had built a revenue surplus of nearly £1 million and set up a Sinking Fund for the reduction of the National Debt. Pitt depended very greatly upon his Treasury staff, especially Rose, for his own arithmetical calculations were frequently inaccurate and his immaculately presented budgets were the fruit of much correction. Financial prosperity gave power at the international level and in 1787 Pitt had no difficulty in checking the designs of France upon Holland, and an alliance followed with Prussia, the other interested power. Britain was back in the comity of Europe.

In respect of economical reform Pitt avoided offending interested parties by a sweeping clearance of dead wood. Sinecure offices and pensions were quietly abolished on the death of the holders and the diminution in the 'influence' of the Crown that resulted was an incidental result rather than a publicly declared objective. But in the long term Pitt's reductions were far more extensive and above all administratively efficient than anything Burke had envisaged. So penetrating was Pitt's decomposition of the ancient tissues of reward that he had to resort to peerage creations and baronetcies. He has been held responsible for an alleged decline in the intellectual standards of the House of Lords and for honouring wealth rather than merit, criticisms without foundation. Until 1784 the Hanoverians had been so parsimonious that new creations had barely exceeded extinctions. Pitt's policy, although prompted by the erosion of patronage, also reflected the great expansion of the moneyed class. A House of Lords which comprised Liverpool, Barham, Auckland (Eden), Wellesley and a promotion for Cornwallis cannot be called undistinguished.

The scheme for parliamentary reform which Pitt put forward in the House of Commons on 18 April 1785 turned out to be no more than an episode in his ministry. It was planned to re-allot seventy-two rotten boroughs among the counties and London, by buying the rights of the owners, subject to their consent. Pitt may have been sincere but by this time parliamentary reform stood no chance. The King did not trouble to manifest his opposition; his views were well known and he appreciated that even Dundas, Rose and Grenville were against. There was, as North was quick to point out, little popular demand for change and the measure was defeated 248–174. The men who had voted against reform had no wish for Pitt's resignation. Pitt probably realised that his successes in other fields had assuaged the discontents of the North era. To put forward changes not desired by the King or the House of Commons was a pointless exercise and his was to be a ministry not of reform but of sound government. The nonconformists, closely identified with the movement for parliamentary reform, had with considerable reason expected Pitt to prove himself the Prime Minister who would secure the repeal of their disabilities. Pitt in 1787 and again in 1789 opposed the repeal of the Test and Corporation Acts; there was already liberty of worship and a free Constitution did not call for the abolition of the Anglican monopoly of political power.

Amidst the stubborn conservatism of Pitt's Britain the movement for the abolition of the slave trade was a brilliant beacon of praiseworthy endeavour. Only in this country was the cause taken seriously, in the sense that the Government was committed, which as the trade was a bulwark of the mercantilist economy was all the more remarkable. It was on Pitt's advice that Wilberforce decided to raise the issue in Parliament, though party was not involved for Fox and Burke were equally enthusiastic. In Wilberforce's absence through illness, Pitt on 9 April 1788 introduced and carried a Commons resolution for an investigation as early as possible. Abolition was made a Cabinet matter and over the next two years Pitt and Grenville did all they could. Two great obstacles were that the refusal of the French Government to show interest made any infringement of British mercantilism appear one-sided: also, though the great men were for abolition, the dwarfs were obscurantist. Unfortunately time slipped by until the French Revolution cast its shadow.

Suddenly, in November 1788, Pitt's Government – indeed it seemed possible his whole career – was put to hazard when the King fell dangerously ill. Modern medicine has diagnosed porphyria, but then his delirium was thought to betoken insanity. Evidently a Regency might prove essential, a prospect delightful to the Prince of Wales who would make Fox Prime Minister and then demolish Pitt's power by exactly the same methods his father had used to destroy the Whigs. Acting on impulse, Fox produced the distinctly un-Whiggish doctrine that the Prince had an inherent right to the Regency with full monarchical authority, the function of Parliament being restricted to naming the inauguration date. This turned out to be giving the game to Pitt, who admitted that only the Prince could be Regent but also maintained that Parliament must first nominate him, subject to such restrictions as the precedents might indicate. Superficially it might seem that Pitt and Fox had swapped creeds, with the Prime Minister as the man of 'the people' and Fox the advocate of prerogative. In fact Fox's motives were so obviously selfish and the Prince's deportment so very unseemly that the public preferred Pitt's insistence upon constitutional propriety. But then Fox was convinced that the illness was chronic and a Regency unavoidable. Pitt, who knew the King intimately, was not so sure but some decision could not long be delayed. Already Thurlow was showing himself only too ready to ease Fox's way, provided he remained Lord Chancellor. The conditions embodied in the House of Commons resolutions of 16 December were very restrictive, which would seem to guarantee Pitt's dismissal. Disturbing news came from Dublin, where the Irish House of Commons had offered to acknowledge the Prince as Regent without limitations, irrespective of what might happen at Westminster. Then the King recovered and the air cleared, almost as though nothing had happened.

Pitt's ministry, essentially a one-man government, enjoying a general rather than a party support, emerged unscathed, whilst Fox had lost ground badly. Pitt's character had become set; distant as ever, he reserved his gay side for his small circle and there was no sign of his wishing to marry. The incompleteness of his domestic side perhaps went together with his Philistine blindness in respect of contemporary art and literature. With the King his relations were always formal, but politically as one they embarked upon their glorious autumn and neither perceived the significance of the taking of the Bastille that summer. If Fox thought that event heralded a new era in human relations, Pitt was happy to see France bankrupt and ruined by dissension. In truth the Revolution placed the Whigs in dire peril. Burke's *Reflexions upon the Revolution in France*, though leading directly to a breach between him and Fox, did not at first affect the Whig party. But time would prove that the French Revolution was very different from the Glorious Revolution and the Whigs were in no position to face an event bound to force upon all men a reappraisal of political values. Pitt was happy to fish in troubled waters and already he saw that their divisions would work to his own advantage. At the general election of 1790 Pitt's majority was increased and the opportunity was taken to give a peerage to Grenville, who had never fared outstandingly in the House of Commons and might counteract the sinister machinations of Thurlow. Two years later Thurlow had to be got rid of for attempting to tamper with Pitt's Sinking Fund Bill. He had no parliamentary group to fall back on so with the King's agreement he was succeeded by Loughborough. The old independence of the eighteenth-century Lord

Chancellor was ended and in future he would have to submit to the principle of Cabinet solidarity. The King would always fear a return of his illness and saw the need to take things steadily. Increasingly he settled at Windsor, a willing absentee from London, though he never neglected his dispatch boxes. But he could sometimes be tiresome about appointments, promotions and vacant Garters. One day he would very properly refuse Pitt's request to have the rather secular and, by episcopal standards, unscholarly Tomline translated to Canterbury. Though the King could not save his favourite Lord Chancellor he knew what to look for in his archbishops.

That the embarrassment of the French Court was to Britain's advantage seemed proved when in 1790 a crisis arose with Spain because a British trading station on Nootka Sound in Vancouver Island had been destroyed. Spain regarded the Pacific as her monopoly, a claim Pitt would not tolerate, and in May he obtained a vote of credit for the Navy. The quarrel was similar to that over the Falkland Islands in 1770-1 and France once more was in no condition to back her ally by force. In the event of war Pitt was ready to co-operate with potential rebels in the Spanish Empire by an expedition to Mexico. On 28 October Spain agreed to a Convention by which the Vancouver settlement was allowed and the freedom of British navigation in the Pacific and trade north of California was recognised. Though Pitt's direct interest was only commercial the future existence of the colony of British Columbia was in fact assured.

The Constitution of Canada set up by North's Quebec Act required attention. The influx of American Loyalists had greatly increased the English-speaking population. Though there was an unofficial majority, French and English, on the nominated legislative council, Loyalists who had settled in New Brunswick enjoyed a representative Assembly and Crown Colony government had never been popular with the merchant community. The French might by now be deemed suitable for representation but Pitt was firmly against the hazard of combining the two communities under one Assembly. Grenville, who had succeeded Sydney at the Home Office, had no doubt that the British Parliament was exportable and he drafted the required legislation. There were to be two Canadas, Upper and Lower, each with two legislative houses, one elected, the other nominated. This solution reflected much thought upon the theory of colonial government, for the terrible American example was held to have resulted from too little control, yet regard must be paid to the natural rights of British subjects. Though not entirely satisfactory in practice, the Canada Act of 1791 remained the Constitution until the Durham Report and the changes of 1840.

The continental powers were not deeply concerned about the French Revolution until Louis XVI, by attempting to flee the country, turned his people against him and endangered the dynasty. Tension lay in the east, where Russia, Prussia and Austria were bent upon dividing Poland. There British interests were not affected but Pitt was concerned at the designs of Austria and Russia upon Turkey. In 1790 the Emperor Leopold II agreed to an armistice returning to the *status quo*. But Catherine the Great snubbed Britain and went ahead with the establishment of a naval base at Otchakoff (Odessa) on the Black Sea. On 22 March Pitt obtained the consent of the House of Commons to a naval armament, but finding the prospect of war generally unpopular he decided to back down. The Duke of Leeds, as Carmarthen had become, resigned – no great loss – and Pitt's position was strengthened by the appointment of Grenville, one of the greatest Foreign Secretaries of all time.

At the opening of 1792 Pitt cut taxation and reduced the Navy by 2,000 men. He forecast that in fifteen years a further £25 million of the National Debt would have been paid off, possibly only in ten: 'There was never a time when, from the situation of Europe, we might more reasonably expect fifteen years of peace than we may at the present moment.' But in August France declared war on Austria and Prussia, Louis XVI was deposed and the British Ambassador withdrawn. The French army overran Belgium and the Scheldt was declared an open river. The threat to Holland revived the tensions which had nearly brought about war in 1787. But for the present the Government in Paris was flirting with the idea of an accommodation with Britain as between the free nations of Europe. French agents were in London and Edinburgh spreading revolutionary propaganda, and on Pitt's advice the militia was called out and an Aliens Bill passed, as a precaution against the thousands of émigrés, refugees and agitators entering the country. When in January Louis XVI was executed Grenville ordered the French agent Chauvelin out of the country and a French declaration of war soon followed.

Under the impact of an ideological war Britain became a less free society. Obviously the correspondence between liberal-minded circles in Britain and France as of late had to be suppressed. But also freedom of political association and comment for purposes exclusively British, parliamentary reform included, were severely circumscribed. Fox's Libel Act of 1792, which Pitt had supported, gave some protection to publications of a nature once deemed innocent but now liable to penalties. Pitt's war policy lay in the formation of a grand coalition against France and between March and October 1793 Russia, Sardinia, Spain, Naples and Portugal, moved by fear of the French Revolution, joined Austria and Prussia as England's allies. Pitt thought French finances extremely precarious and expected only a short war. Already he was showing that sanguine over-confidence that marked one of his failings as a war leader. Grenville from the start had few illusions about what the country was up against. To him and also to the King the war was always ideological, a contest between forms of government as well as a clash between the essential interests of nations. Pitt had to keep the House of Commons happy and he always made clear that the war aim was self-preservation and not, as Fox alleged, to foist the Bourbons back onto the French people. But arguments theoretical or material did not serve to keep Prussia or Russia in the field, with the partition of Poland still uncompleted. By the end of 1795 Austria was the only great power actively engaged against France.

To support the war must entail some parliamentary co-operation with the Government, and on this issue the Whig party split. Canning, the great catch among the young generation, whose early friendships had been with Fox and Sheridan, chose to enter Parliament under Pitt's auspices. In July 1794 Portland, with great reluctance, decided to join Pitt's Government, and with him went Spencer, Fitzwilliam and Windham. They had to make a farewell to all the Foxite lore about Pitt acting as the King's tool in undermining the principles of parliamentary government established by the Glorious Revolution. Portland at the Home Office and Spencer at the Admiralty were assets from the administrative point of view. Windham, forceful and versatile, became the first Secretary at War to sit in the Cabinet. Fox was left with a party of only about fifty. British politics would never again be the same, for here was the foundation of the Tory party of the future, leaving Fox and Grey to liberalise the Whigs.

Pitt was the first British statesman whose career would be broken by Ireland. It was the example of the American Revolution, together with economic disadvantages, that had caused the constitutional revolution in Dublin of 1782. Since then the Protestant aristocracy had been in control and for them as well as for the English Whigs the French

Revolution possessed a magnetism. Of British rule only the Crown and the Privy Council's veto remained, but British mercantilism still had a sore edge. The Catholic peasantry in their turn had grievances against Protestant landlordism. Pitt believed the Catholics to be basically conservative and in 1793 Irish Catholics with the property qualifications were given the vote in parliamentary elections, which enfranchised many smallholders. The remaining Catholic disabilities were exclusion from the major offices and from the right to sit in the Dublin Parliament. In 1794–5 Pitt acceded to the request of Fitzwilliam, one of the greatest landowners in Ireland, for the Viceroyalty, though on the understanding that no sweeping changes were to be attempted. Fitzwilliam's instructions were not exact but he exceeded their spirit by dismissing Tory officials and promising full Catholic political rights at once. The King intervened to make clear his opinion that Catholic emancipation would divide rather than unite the two countries, and was in any event a constitutional question beyond the competence of 'any council of ministers'. After only two months Pitt recalled Fitzwilliam, who got a cold reception from Portland. Catholic opinion was deeply exasperated and a train of events set alight which would lead Ireland into a terrible rebellion.

Napoleon's conquest of Italy in 1796 closed any possibility of forcing the French back to their original frontiers. By the end of 1797 the position of Britain seemed desperate. The Navy had mutinied and when in October the Emperor was forced to make peace before Napoleon's army marched on Vienna the fighting on the Continent was ended. But despite disaster Pitt maintained a surface calm, though inward anxiety was undermining his health. The business of managing a war was not his *métier*, for far from being spontaneously exact and prompt he was a terrible correspondent and lacked altogether the natural dispatch required. Fortunately he had no political difficulties, for the 1796 general election confirmed his leadership and Fox unwisely seceded from House of Commons proceedings. The vast sums needed for the war were cheerfully voted, not that Pitt's efforts to meet the bills were uniformly successful. His famous Income Tax, a frightening innovation, yielded only six millions instead of the ten he had expected. His continuation of the Sinking Fund while borrowing at inflated rates has been justly condemned. Where Walpole, Newcastle and North had come to grief over war, Pitt survived the most costly disasters Britain had known that century, and it was universally agreed that provided he and the King stayed together, his administration was as solid as a rock. The country knew that in revolutionary France Britain was confronted by a novel enemy and Pitt was the only man.

The Irish rebellion of 1798 presented Britain with the most mortal threat since the Battle of the Boyne. Pitt thought the British Empire in danger of disruption, and in June reached the conclusion that a union between Britain and Ireland was essential and must be of the closest description, a joining of Parliaments. Often he had speculated in general terms on the possibility of union being produced by the natural course of events and now he made it his policy. The danger that the French might invade Ireland was frustrated by the Navy and instead Napoleon sailed to Egypt. It was a happy moment, for Nelson's victory on the Nile put new heart into Britain and enabled Pitt to build a second coalition with Austria and Russia. When at the close of the year Napoleon as First Consul had the impertinence to write a personal letter to George III suggesting peace, Pitt and Grenville brushed him aside.

The Union with Ireland was Pitt's most controversial achievement. India and Warren Hastings, parliamentary reform, nonconformist relief, even the harsh regulation of the press, pale beside the intensity of the passions aroused then and since by Pitt's failure to secure the right of Catholics to sit at Westminster as a condition of suppressing the Dublin Parliament. To Pitt it was out of the question to allow a Catholic majority to dominate a legislature already practically independent of imperial control. On the other hand to combine a union of Parliaments with Catholic emancipation would present no hazard, because the Protestants must always be in a majority at Westminster. The objections of the Protestant landowners, who since 1782 had had the run of things, at the loss of their legislative independence would have to be overcome. The consideration uppermost in Pitt's mind was imperial solidarity, and he saw a union as incorporating the Irish people in the metropolitan leadership of a great empire, with all the concomitant advantages. He did not consider religion the only issue at stake, or placating the Irish Catholics by full equality the sole advantage. He looked forward to the participation of the Irish nation in a project which he hoped would prove as outstandingly successful as the Union with Scotland. The dimensions of Pitt's thought were not mean or sectarian but conceived in a design of grandeur, to the advantage of the British Isles considered as one.

When Pitt took his decision the Irish rebellion was at its height and the Protestant landowners thoroughly frightened. The first step was to meet Camden's request to be replaced. Cornwallis, whose term in India had been most successful, was appointed Viceroy. The King understood well that union was the objective and made the shrewd suggestion that the panic gave an easy opportunity to overcome any objections in Dublin. At the same time, recalling the Fitzwilliam episode, he made absolutely clear in a letter to Pitt that further concessions to the Catholics were not open to consideration. Pitt knew very well that on a subject of that nature the King would never change his mind, and therefore if Catholic emancipation was presented to the Westminster Parliament as part of the union deal, he would face a crisis. The King's hint to rush matters was not taken. The rebellion was going from bad to worse but Cornwallis pursued a clement policy while, in accordance with Pitt's custom, the practical problems of union were investigated. At the end of December 1798 Pitt and the Cabinet drew up a plan based upon the Scots precedent. By this time the rebellion had subsided and fear of French invasion was no more. When therefore in January that able young man Castlereagh, just become Irish Secretary, presented his proposals to the Dublin Parliament, he was faced with an outburst of nationalist opposition. In the last week of the month Pitt carried his union resolutions through the House of Commons, with practically no opposition. There was not, and never had been, any question of Catholic emancipation being part of the proposed Act but Pitt, while expressly discounting any commitment in point of time, pointed out that the admission of Catholics to full privileges might be agitated with greater safety in a united Parliament. During the autumn of 1799 Pitt authorised Cornwallis and Castlereagh to approach the Catholics in terms suggestive of an early review of their disabilities, once union was secured. Cornwallis also went to work with the Irish Parliament, with promises of peerages and favours. The Irish borough owners were richly compensated. Inevitably the magnates came begging to London and Pitt met their expectations. But only the scale of corruption merits criticism, for the methods were of a kind always required to secure major legislation. During the spring of 1800 Union was agreed in both Parliaments by majorities of 158–118 in Dublin and 236–50 in Westminster.

Soon Cornwallis and Castlereagh were reminding Pitt of his promises. He knew that he would have to confront the King with a united Cabinet. When at a meeting of 28 September he explained his plan to relax the oaths of allegiance in a sense acceptable to the Catholics,

Loughborough alone dissented. The first Parliament of the United Kingdom met on 22 January 1801 and Pitt carried the Address by 245–63; but already the King was contemplating a change of ministry. At the levee six days later he declared to Dundas of emancipation: 'I shall reckon any man my personal enemy who proposes any such measure. The most Jacobinical thing I ever heard of.' Next day the King sent Addington to Pitt with the request that Catholic emancipation be abandoned. Pitt wrote to the King arguing that emancipation would present no dangers, offering his resignation as the alternative and finally deprecating his sovereign's direct employment of his authority. To this the King replied with his favourite argument, that his Coronation Oath precluded his consent to emancipation, but asking Pitt to stay on for the remainder of the reign. Pitt none the less resigned on 3 February and two days later Addington agreed to form a government.

Grenville, Dundas, Spencer and Windham went out with Pitt and in Dublin Cornwallis and Castlereagh followed. Canning too resigned, contrary to Pitt's advice, and constituted of himself a sort of unofficial opposition, more Pittite than Pitt. Of the younger generation Pitt much preferred Perceval and is said to have seen in him the future Prime Minister, although he was an opponent of emancipation. Portland, Westmorland and Chatham were ready to serve under Addington. Hawkesbury succeeded Grenville as Foreign Secretary and embarked upon the course that, as second Earl of Liverpool, would make him Prime Minister. The great Pitt ministry was ended, his parliamentary majority broken up, and he was left with his personal following of around fifty. Pitt's situation was painfully isolated, for Dundas particularly was deeply indignant at his abdication in favour of Addington, whom he thought incapable of maintaining sound government.

The question was what Pitt would do next. Before the end of the month the return of the King's malady promised still greater confusion. The Prince of Wales suggested that this time the attack might be prolonged, which drew Pitt's comment: 'Thy wish, Harry, was father to that thought.' Pitt promised Cornwallis and Castlereagh that he and the outgoing ministers would do their utmost for the Catholics. But only four days afterwards, deeply stung at a spiteful remark by the King that he was to blame for his illness, Pitt gave his famous pledge never again to raise Catholic emancipation during the reign. The King's attack lasted only three weeks but Pitt had fallen into a manifestly contradictory position. Having completed the budget Pitt handed over to Addington on 14 March, ignoring the suggestion of his friends that he might, in view of his pledge to the King, carry on.

Pitt's conduct of the Irish crisis cannot be explained with complete satisfaction. If political circumstances, especially the King's objections, made impossible the achievement of Union with full rights for Catholics, then Pitt's allowing Cornwallis and Castlereagh to promise emancipation was, on the face of it, perfidy. Probably, as during 1784 and 1788, he had meant to feel his way to safety, but he showed none of the buoyancy of his early years. His actions after his resignation, meekly supporting Addington and especially his double pledges to the Catholics and to the King, have no satisfactory explanation in terms of justice to Ireland. But Pitt never looked upon Union in an exclusively domestic context. Imperial interests in time of war were the paramount consideration and to that end the exclusion of the Prince of Wales from power by protecting the King's health was essential. The undertakings to the Irish Catholics were always general and though any reading of Pitt's character excludes trickery, he knew that the political balance at Westminster must condition their fulfilment. The King's distaste for Catholic emancipation and national opinion could well have been at one: Britain was still a Protestant country. Addington's victory at the general election of 1802 and the ease with which, after Pitt's death, the King dismissed his next Prime Minister, Grenville, for demanding Catholic emancipation, would indicate that an attempt to form an opposition party on that issue would have added to political confusion without bringing nearer the ideal of religious equality.

The peace preliminaries agreed by Addington and Hawkesbury towards the end of the year widened the breach between Pitt and his friends. The limitation of France to her 1792 boundaries, let alone a Bourbon restoration, were simply out of the question. Pitt, consulted towards the end of the negotiations, thought the terms 'highly creditable and on the whole very advantageous'. Grenville could not forgive a treaty which abandoned every colonial and maritime conquest except Trinidad and Ceylon. Peace depended upon Napoleon's moderation, and the weakness of the Peace of Amiens concluded in March 1802 was that the independence of the Dutch and Italian republics guaranteed under the Treaty of Lunéville with Austria was not reaffirmed. Soon Napoleon would show all too clearly that these were but client states of France. Pitt, who never attended properly to his household bills or kept an eye on his servants, was racked with anxiety over debt. His health was very poor and had not been helped by heavy drinking sessions with Dundas over the years. Strongly though Pitt disapproved of Addington's budget of 1803, he resisted the entreaties of Canning and Rose to come out into the open against the Government, for he felt his ground far from certain. Dundas, who had vowed never to bow to Addington, had accepted a peerage as Lord Melville. Then in March Addington sent Melville to Pitt as emissary to negotiate a coalition. Pitt had no intention of being less than the head and the comment reported of him was: 'Really, I had not the curiosity to ask what I was to be.' Pitt's terms were that the King, Addington and the Cabinet should give him the undisputed leadership, and that Grenville, Melville, Spencer and Windham be included. But the resurrection of the great Pitt ministry was impossible, partly because he himself would not force Addington's hand. The failure to provide Britain with a strong government was one reason for Napoleon's willingness to reopen the war.

When early in 1804 Grenville reached an understanding with Fox to work for a broad-based ministry, a new party alignment was formed which could not work to Pitt's advantage. That April Pitt decided to form a ministry and would readily have employed Fox, but the King would not listen, which therefore prevented Grenville from serving. So Pitt had to head a ministry which included Addington himself and six ministers who had served under him. A crisis with Spain, whose Bourbon King was ready to be the ally of Napoleon, brought out Pitt's old fire. He retaliated in the way his father had desired in 1761 and had the Spanish treasure ships destroyed on the high seas. The expected Spanish declaration of war placed the entire west European coastline in Napoleon's hands, and the sharp criticisms of Grenville completed the breach of an old friendship. The ministry was under constant strain and though Addington, with some demur, took a peerage as Lord Sidmouth, some of his friends were promoted, to the intense irritation of Rose and Canning. Then in April came the blow of Melville's impeachment for malversation. Two months later Sidmouth and some of his friends resigned because, owing to their attitude to Melville, Pitt refused them advancement.

Pitt had been engaged in negotiations with Austria and Russia which he hoped might lead to a third coalition. He laid down two principles, which were to be the foundation of the peace settlements negotiated by Castlereagh in 1814: France should be surrounded by strong buffer states and the whole guaranteed by international agreement. The talks with Russia nearly broke down owing to Tsar Alexander I's demand for Malta. But then Napoleon, by having himself crowned King of Italy, so provoked Austria and Russia that the coalition came into being. Much depended upon the willingness of Prussia to join but Frederick William III's greedy designs upon Hanover frustrated this. News of the battle of Ulm was soon followed by Trafalgar: Britain could not be destroyed by France but Austerlitz ended the war of the third coalition. Pitt died on 23 January 1806, twenty-five years after he first entered Parliament.

Pitt had been the greatest Prime Minister since Walpole and until Peel no man comparable would appear. In the magnitude and variety of his commission, shouldered over so long a period, he stands alone. Pitt was not the founder of a political party. His government was one of business, based upon a leadership personal rather than of principle. The Tory party which came after him was not of his intention but was forged by war and fear of revolution. It was in the achievements of peace that Pitt's creative powers excelled. Fundamental changes of policy in home finance, overseas trade, colonial government and foreign policy, and finally the Union between Britain and Ireland, all fell within Pitt's compass. During the years of peace fate was on his side. The work of reconstruction following the American war was guaranteed success by the spontaneous and fortunate eruption of industrial enterprise on an unprecedented scale. In terms of constitutional as distinct from administrative reform, directly considered, Pitt in truth achieved nothing at home. The innate conservatism of the eighteenth century and, it might perhaps be suggested, of the British genius, was against Pitt the young reformer. A Prime Minister unable to secure the abolition of the slave trade could not have reformed Parliament. Pitt's great achievement is to be found not in the formal but in the conventional and more important aspect of the Constitution. He established decisively that Britain has a Prime Minister, a description which from being one of doubtful repute came by his example to personify the government of this country.

For the Empire Pitt accomplished much. The East India Company was given a new respectability and the government of India that centralised force which enabled Wellesley to render British supremacy unchallengeable. The government of Canada was established so that the British and French could expand peaceably. The foundation of the settlement of Botany Bay for transported criminals was also an achievement of the great Pitt ministry, though he did not visualise the future Australia. Britain without the American colonies emerged with a new identity, and the optimism which inspired survival from Napoleon and finally glorious victory.

The French Revolution involved the greatest cleavage in European civilisation since the Reformation. The division between revolutionary France and the old Europe was by no means entirely founded upon ideology. French patriotism, hitherto so affronted by the deceits and inefficiency of the royal government, blazed forth with a new confidence and exerted a corresponding attraction over other nations. The Belgians, Dutch, Italians and Germans had in many respects suffered as much as the French by the failure of the ancient governments to meet the aspirations of the peoples. How far Pitt appreciated the importance of nationalism may be doubted. Britain was not seriously affected by a malaise of regime and her citizens for the most part considered King George and the House of Commons to represent their interests. As a war leader Pitt in no way compared with Chatham in strategical concepts or in that determined efficiency essential in mounting military operations. He represented the national will to resist tyranny: 'England has saved herself by her exertions, and will, I trust, save Europe by her example.'

BIBLIOGRAPHY

Aspinall, A., (ed.), *The Later Correspondence of George III, December 1783–December 1810* (Cambridge, 1962–70)

Bolton, G. C., *The Passing of the Act of Union* (Oxford, 1966)

Brooke, John, *King George III* (Constable, 1972)

Coupland, Sir Reginald, *Wilberforce* (Collins, 1945)

Ehrman, John, *The Younger Pitt* (Constable, 1969)

Magnus, Sir Philip, *Edmund Burke* (Murray, 1939)

Marshall, Dorothy, *The Rise of George Canning* (Longmans, 1938)

Mitchell, Leslie, *Charles James Fox and the Disintegration of the Whig Party 1782–94* (Oxford, 1971)

Rose, J. Holland, *William Pitt and National Revival* (G. Bell, 1911)

Rose, J. Holland, *William Pitt and the Great War* (G. Bell, 1911)

Watson, J. Steven, *The Reign of George III* (Oxford, 1960)

White, R. J., *The Age of George III* (Heinemann, 1968)

15

HENRY ADDINGTON, VISCOUNT SIDMOUTH

BY

PHILIP ZIEGLER

Henry Addington, born 30 May 1757, eldest son of Dr Anthony Addington and Mary Hiley. Educated at Cheam School, Winchester and Brasenose College, Oxford. Married (1) 1791 Ursula Mary Hammond; two sons, four daughters. (2) 1823, Mary Anne Townsend; no issue. Admitted to Lincoln's Inn and read for Bar; MP for Devizes 1784; seconded the address 1786; Speaker of the House of Commons 1789–1801; Prime Minister 1801–4; created Viscount Sidmouth 1805; Lord Privy Seal in Ministry of All the Talents 1806–1807; President of the Council 1812; Home Secretary 1812–1821; Member of Cabinet without Portfolio 1821–24. Died 15 February 1844.

HENRY ADDINGTON,
FIRST VISCOUNT SIDMOUTH

When Addington became Prime Minister in March 1801 he took the place of William Pitt; when he resigned in April 1804 William Pitt replaced him. When he took office the Napoleonic wars were spluttering on, when he left it the brief truce was over and we were at war again. All that had changed significantly in the intervening years was Addington's own reputation. When his ministry began he was generally esteemed if not revered, a man of honour and proven ability whose new appointment seemed surprising but not absurd. When it ended he was derided where he was not detested, his government dismissed as a catastrophic failure. Whether either or both these judgements were correct is the most important question that the student of Addington must answer.

The most remarkable feature of Addington's life is that a man whom not even the most benevolent critic could credit with transcendent talents should have risen from bourgeois origins to supreme office in an intensely aristocratic society and under a king who felt few things to be more detestable than the middle classes. The Addingtons were yeomen farmers who, over the previous century, had edged nervously into the minor gentry. Henry's father, Anthony, chose medicine as his road to fortune and mental illness as his particular field of expertise. The choice was a shrewd one. Few ailments were more fashionable than insanity and it was not long before he was established in London and a regular visitor at many of its greatest houses. By the time Henry was born on 30 May 1757, his father had become a Fellow of the College of Physicians and had built up a most lucrative practice.

Addington's education – Cheam, Winchester, and Brasenose, Oxford – was conventional and notable, principally, for the energy with which he built up the circle of loyal friends who were to remain closely linked with him throughout his political life. Four members of his first administration were at the same preparatory school as himself, two more were added at Winchester. None of them was of outstanding quality yet none of them was less than competent. Divided they would have been of trivial importance, united they formed the Addingtonian Interest in Parliament and were a force to be reckoned with. It is a curious paradox that a man whom all agreed to be devoid of personal magnetism or outstanding charms should nevertheless have commanded and retained the loyalties of this far from inconsiderable band.

But Dr Addington gave his son more than a sound education and a useful if unspectacular circle of acquaintances; he gained him also the patronage of Lord Chatham and the comradeship of Henry's contemporary, William Pitt. Dr Addington had graduated from the role of medical adviser to that of Chatham's confidant and counsellor. The two families saw much of each other. At first Henry, the successful schoolboy home on holiday, tended to patronise his shy and sheltered friend, and for the first year or two in which they were reading for the Bar in London and were much in each other's company, he seemed still the more mature and independent of the two. It was not to last. Pitt flourished, moved into a more brilliant and sophisticated circle and, finally, 'went into the House of Commons as an heir enters his home'. Addington dwindled into a dowdy country cousin, dependable and decent enough, but to be tolerated rather than courted. Still, they remained close to each other, and when at the election of March 1784 Pitt shattered the Foxites and Addington entered Parliament for the first time as Member for Devizes, no one doubted that the ranks of the Pittites had received a staunch and potentially valuable recruit.

It cannot be said that Addington's early years in Parliament were crowned with glamorous success. It was nearly two years before he spoke at all, and then only because Pitt forced his hand by choosing him to second the Address. 'He was *very* little embarrassed,' wrote his brother Hiley approvingly; 'Not destitute of grace and dignity,' noted Wraxall; but he was not encouraged to repeat the effort. It was more than a year before he spoke again and then only briefly on a technical point connected with the Horse Tax. But he did not waste his time. He was sensible and industrious on committees; indefatigable in widening his acquaintance, even among the Opposition; and renowned as an expert on the rules and precedents of Parliament. It was his reputation as a good House of Commons man that emboldened Pitt to give him dramatic promotion in 1789.

The Speakership had fallen into sad disrepute over the last decade, culminating in Charles Cornwall who had kept a supply of porter underneath his chair and sipped it noisily during debates. When Grenville was elected early in 1789 it was felt that things were looking up, but, arrogant and ambitious as all his clan, he stayed in the post only long enough to savour the quality of the perquisites and was then on the way to replace Lord Sydney as Home Secretary. Was the Chair, demanded Burke, to become 'a succession house, a hot bed for statesmen'? He spoke for many members, and the general indignation convinced Pitt that he must find a safe man for the post – a man who would be free from higher ambitions and prove himself a devoted servant of the House. Addington's eligibility seemed obvious. Not everyone agreed. The Whig candidate for the Speakership wrote with disgust: 'Pitt could not have made a more obnoxious choice. . . . He is the son of Lord Chatham's physician and is in fact a sort of dependant to the family. The Chair has hitherto been filled by persons of quite a different description.' But Elliot was exceptional in his judgement. Most people thought Pitt had chosen well and though the Whigs dutifully divided against him it was done with little animosity. 'We were all very sorry to vote against you,' Sheridan told him affably.

Whatever strictures may be passed on other stages of his career, no one can deny that Addington proved an uncommonly good Speaker. He was patient, diligent, invariably courteous, well versed in the rules of the House and yet aware that sometimes they must be ignored, a thoughtful negotiator when disputes threatened the smooth running of affairs. Above all he was impartial, a quality today taken for granted in the Speaker but in 1789 an agreeable rarity. Only in one way were his future prospects damaged by his incumbency of the Chair. Any chance there ever was that he might become a competent parliamentary debater now disappeared. His latent vices of pomposity and prolixity flourished horrifyingly in this sympathetic atmosphere; free from heckling he never learnt to think on his feet or to deal with interruptions. Most dangerous of all, he lost all capacity to see when he might make himself absurd: the notes he prepared for a debate in 1800 on the corn shortage, in which he extolled the virtues of bran as opposed to grain and dwelt lovingly on 'the rarefying warmth, the solvent moisture and the grinding action of the stomach', show either that he did not know his nickname was 'The Doctor' or that he was disastrously unaware of the damage that could be done by ridicule. Such indifference was endearing, admirable even, but it boded ill for his future if he ever stepped outside the parliamentary asylum offered by his present office.

In every other way his stature grew during his twelve years in the Chair. His friendship with Pitt grew close again and his influence increased, so that he formed with Granville, Dundas and Loughborough an informal inner council which the Prime Minister found convenient to consult on many issues. Such conduct may not seem wholly Speaker-like but he justified it by the paramount needs of the war. Indeed, by 1794 all but a tiny rump of Whig irreconcilables under Fox had rallied to the Government. Often these latter did not attend debates at all; when they did their very weakness made it easy for Addington to defend their interests without damage to the cause he had espoused. Without shame he vowed allegiance to his glorious friend. Pitt and he dined together, talked together, drank far into the night together. On one occasion they were almost mobbed together. After a banquet at Canterbury a hostile crowd booed them heartily. 'A pretty story will this make in the papers,' said Pitt. 'The Minister and the Speaker dined with the corporation, got very drunk and were hissed out of town!'

Towards the end of 1793 Pitt offered Addington Dundas's seat in the Cabinet. Addington refused; he was quite happy where he was. Then in 1797 Pitt contemplated resignation on the grounds that a new prime minister could more easily reach a settlement with the French. In such a case his successor, it was secretly agreed, would be the Speaker. This too came to nothing but it is of importance as showing that, to the King and Pitt at least, the idea that Addington might one day head the Government was not a sudden whim but a long-meditated project. In 1799 another link in the chain was forged. The Bill for the Union of Ireland and England was debated in the House of Commons. Pitt believed that a Union would be disastrous unless swiftly followed by Catholic emancipation; Addington would not wholly commit himself but argued that emancipation would be unthinkable in present circumstances and hinted strongly that he could not imagine what might occur to make him ever change his mind. At Windsor the words made pleasant hearing; one follower of Pitt's at least would oppose a step which George III considered would be not merely dangerous folly but in violation of his Coronation Oath.

In October 1801 Pitt decided to force the issue. If the King would not accept emancipation for the Catholic Irish then he would have to find a new prime minister. 'Is such an enterprise necessary?' asked Auckland in dismay. 'Is it expedient a *Cui bono*? With what view? To what end?' Many of Pitt's followers were asking the same questions and the King now called on Addington to 'open Mr Pitt's eyes on the danger arising from the agitating of this improper question'. Dutifully Addington laboured to avert the crisis but Pitt proved implacable. The King's riposte was to send for the Speaker and ask him to form an administration. Addington, with patent sincerity, pleaded that Pitt must be prevailed upon to stay and that, even if he did not, someone more worthy should be found to fill his shoes. 'Lay your hand upon your heart,' said the King grandiloquently, 'and ask yourself where I am to turn for support if *you* do not stand by me.' Pitt now added to the pressure. Addington *must* take his place, no one else would be generally acceptable. He would urge his supporters to serve in the new administration and, for himself, pledged 'the most uniform and diligent support'.

Whatever Pitt might urge, however, not many of his former ministers were prepared to take jobs under Addington. Men like Dundas, Spencer and Windham felt themselves committed to the principle of emancipation while the smaller fry such as Canning could not bring themselves to desert their beloved chief. Addington quickly found that he would have to make do with the rump of the old Government – including Pitt's elder brother Chatham as a testimony of continuing goodwill; a handful of new recruits of stature like St Vincent and Hawkesbury, later to be Lord Liverpool; and a topping up of friends and relations from the 'Addingtonian Interest'. 'The Goose Administration', Canning called it. 'Wretched, pusillanimous, toad-eating . . .' Yet in fact it promised to be business-like enough. In Portland, Perceval and Hawkesbury it contained three future prime ministers and its law officers were of impressive quality. The average Member thought well of it: 'Thank God for a government without one of those damned men of genius in it,' as a Tory squire is said to have exclaimed. At any rate, it promised well enough for Addington to report optimistically to George III. 'The King cannot find words sufficiently expressive of His Majesty's cordial approbation of the whole arrangements,' wrote the delighted monarch. 'Addington', he told his new Prime Minister face to face, 'you have saved the country!'

Not everyone was satisfied with the official account of Pitt's resignation. 'Pitt went out,' judged Malmesbury, 'because he felt himself incapable either of carrying on the war, or of making peace.' This is not the whole truth, but there is still something in it. Military disasters and the defection of his allies had left his European policies wholly barren. Near starvation, mutinies and discontent at home completed the pattern of a war which it seemed could never be won and yet might well be lost. Pitt's earlier efforts to make peace had failed dismally and several of his ministers would have opposed any new negotiation. Part of the heritage he passed on to Addington was the need to bring about an honourable peace and the assurance that, from him at least, the Prime Minister could count on every help to make it possible.

In his first speech in the Commons the new minister pledged himself to take all possible steps to secure a peace. It can be argued that he was in too great a hurry, that he allowed his perception of his own problems to blind him to the still greater difficulties of the French, but it is hard to see that further delay would have done more than prolong the agony. Addington's belief was that Britain needed a truce more than France so as to rebuild the economy and allow its continental allies a breathing-space in which to recover their strength and their will to fight. The argument was a reasonable one and, if it be accepted, then the case for urgent negotiations needs no further defence.

Once begun, the discussions with the French were carried through with commendable secrecy and speed. By the beginning of October the preliminary terms had been worked out. It was clear that we were to give away a lot in the way of wartime conquests but Addington was not alone in attaching little importance to colonial kickshaws which could anyway be quickly retaken when and if war broke out again. More important was the proposal to abandon Malta. 'I have no idea how the effect of this measure is ever to be recovered,' wrote Windham. 'Chance may do much, but according to any conception I can form, the country has received its death blow.' Nelson supported the Government's decision but Addington himself had doubts and it is noteworthy that it was the British failure to evacuate Malta, in defiance of our treaty obligations, that eventually gave Napoleon his most justifiable complaint against us. All criticism of the peace was, anyway, of trivial importance. Pitt himself was satisfied and the people were delighted. The carriages of the French emissaries were towed in triumph from St James's Square to Downing Street and all the cows, calves and asses of Falmouth were bedecked with ribbons. Addington's stock was high.

Behind the euphoria, however, certain built-in weaknesses persisted. Addington as prime minister suffered from three handicaps which were to cripple and, in the end, destroy him. He was not an aristocrat, he was not an orator and he was not William Pitt. It was surprisingly common for an industrious young man from the middle or lower-middle classes, with luck and an influential patron, to break through into the ruling elite, but to be prime minister was another matter. On top of this there was the freakish fact that for a prime minister to be a doctor's son was not only socially unpardonable but irrepressibly comical as well. 'The Doctor', with flowing coat-tails and clyster pipe sticking from his pocket, became the cartoonist's butt, and the sniggers of smart society rippled out throughout the country until the idea that the Prime Minister was at least faintly ridiculous became common currency in every home.

Addington's second handicap, his lack of oratory, at first seemed almost an asset. The House of Commons was sated with fine speaking. 'At the close of every brilliant display,' wrote Sydney Smith of Pitt, 'an expedition failed or a kingdom fell. God send us a stammerer!' Now the stammerer had come. But the charm of Addington's stumbling sentences soon passed and when the House cried out for inspiration and leadership nothing was offered them. The contrast with his great predecessor was nowhere more striking.

And in the continued and conspicuous existence of this predecessor lay Addington's most considerable handicap – not the Pitt of reality but a larger-than-life, an infallible, a dream Pitt. The redeeming feature about John Brown was that, though his soul might go marching on, his body at least was safely mouldering in the grave. The unfortunate Addington had to compete with a rival who enjoyed all the privileges of a sanctified spot in the obituary column and yet was evidently and embarrasingly alive. For the moment he might be benevolently disposed towards the new administration, but not all his benevolence could curb the malicious mischief-making of his young acolyte Canning. In the end it was the benevolence that was to be eroded.

For the moment, however, all seemed set fair. The King treated Addington with singular affection, installed him in a handsome house in Richmond Park and sent him seven cows from the royal herd as a special mark of his esteem. The Prime Minister was conscious, however, of the weakness of his ministers in debate. He made tentative overtures toward the Whigs: 'Sheep that he is,' wrote Canning fretfully, 'he is calling in the wolves to his assistance.' But the wolves would not answer the call and on the whole Addington was more relieved than sorry. A union with the Whigs would not have pleased either Pitt or the King and in them lay his sure support. As George III had put it: 'If we three do but keep together all will be well.'

The period from the announcement of the Preliminaries of Peace to the signature of the formal treaty was Addington's golden age. His first budget, in which the ending of the war allowed him to abolish the 'monstrous', 'inquisitional', 'boldly tyrannical' Income Tax, was a triumphant popular success. The election that followed also went well; Pitt's massive majority was retained even though the master himself was absent from the field. 'It was the fashion at first to say *that it would not do,*' observed Wilberforce. 'I always maintained the contrary, and the event has justified my expectations.' Yet in Addington's very success lay danger. It is one thing to protect and patronise a failing government, another oneself to be patronised by one's prosperous successor. After eighteen months in retirement Pitt seemed further than ever from a return to office, and Addington took less trouble to cajole and propitiate his former master. Pitt was too big and honest a man to turn against Addington simply because he felt an itch for office, but it became more and more certain that he would look with suspicion and disfavour on any action of the present Government. His friends fostered the conviction that, if war broke out again, his leadership would be indispensable. Canning hailed him as 'the Pilot that weathered the storm', to whom the nation would turn as soon as the winds began to blow again. The analogy was perhaps flattering to Pitt who had committed the offence, surely reprehensible in a pilot, of abandoning his vessel in mid-tempest, but it reflected the feeling of many who were still numbered among the Government's vociferous supporters.

In the autumn of 1802 the storm began. Napoleon complained about the activities of the royalist emigrés in Britain and the excesses of the London press; then, in October, marched his troops into Switzerland. With the resumption of war appearing ever more inevitable Addington introduced a sensible but conservative budget and looked hopefully to his friend for support. He looked in vain. Pitt sulked in Bath while his minions in London fed him with slanted reports of the Government's ineptitude and hostility to their predecessors. Addington's followers behaved little better, his brother Hiley, in particular, excelling himself in the venom of his attacks on the Pittites. By January 1803, when the two men met again, Pitt had almost been persuaded that it was his duty to strike down his unworthy surrogate and take back the reins of power.

For a man who was well pleased with his own performance Addington proved astonishingly ready to adopt the same point of view. He knew as well as anyone how much of his parliamentary support depended on Pitt's goodwill and was quite prepared to sacrifice his own position in the interests of a settlement. First he proposed that both men should serve under a third party – perhaps Pitt's elder brother Chatham. Pitt dismissed the idea out of hand. 'Really,' he commented disdainfully, 'I had not the curiosity to ask what I was to be.' Then Addington went still further. He and his most intimate cronies would resign to make way for Pitt – his only condition was that some of the other ministers should survive and a few of his most embittered enemies be, temporarily at least, excluded from office. This too Pitt rejected: he must have absolute freedom to reshape the ministry as he chose. Negotiations broke down. 'It was a foolish business from one end to the other,' grumbled the King. 'It was begun ill, conducted ill and terminated ill.'

So the resumption of war in May 1803 found Addington still in office. His conduct of the war has been much criticised, both at the time and by posterity. Such criticism rests for the most part on the assumption that he was trying to wage the same sort of war as Pitt before him by launching – usually futile – forays in every direction and welding France's continental enemies into new coalitions against Napoleon. But this was not Addington's policy. He believed that the conditions which had made stalemate inevitable in 1801 still obtained. Whoever took the initiative would court disaster; victory would go to the side that remained inactive longest. Napoleon's Army, staring in frustration across the Channel, would either take to the sea and be dealt with by the British Navy or remain ashore and suffer in health and discipline. The strategy was hardly a noble one, nor free from risks, but it was still reasonable and consistent with the view of affairs which had led Addington to conclude the Peace of Amiens. The history of the next few years was to suggest that it was at least as successful as any alternative Pitt had to offer.

On the economic side, certainly, the Prime Minister coped with striking competence. In his budget of 1803 he introduced a new-styled Income Tax based upon fundamentally new principles, introducing a daring innovation which was to survive to the present day and to be known as 'Taxation at the Source'. The results were electrifying. Pitt's Income Tax, at 2 shillings in the pound, had yielded some £5.3 million in 1800; in its first year Addington's new tax, at only 1 shilling in the pound, produced £4.7 million. Though Pitt deplored the innovation in the debate in the House of Commons he made no important changes in his own budget the following year. Addington had laid the economic foundations of the system that was to carry Britain to victory.

Nevertheless, from the moment war was declared, the only question was how long Addington's administration would survive. It is easy to chart the course of the illness, the gradual ebbing away of strength, the phases of fitful recovery, the inevitable relapses and the sudden, catastrophic deterioration which heralded the end. But diagnosis is another matter, for though it was clear that the Government was dying it was harder to understand exactly why.

One problem was that, though its strengths and successes were inconspicuous and slow-maturing, its blunders and weaknesses were embarrassingly obvious. The pattern was set by Addington's pitifully inept performance when he broke the news to the House of Commons that war had been resumed. At such moments a parliament demands inspiration; it got a trickle of stumbling platitudes. Instead Pitt seized the occasion to make one of his greatest speeches – so much so that even Fox had to declare: 'If Demosthenes had been present he must have admired, and might have envied.' Worse followed when the time came to enlist the armies needed for Britain's defence. The Government recruited far more men than it could arm or train and was forced into a humiliating reversal of policy. No other single misfortune could so immediately have diminished its reputation in the eyes of the people at large.

In the last resort, however, it was a question of confidence. All government rests fundamentally on an act of faith: the belief of ministers that they have a right to command and of the people that they have a duty to obey. From Addington's administration the faith had seeped away. 'They are, upon my soul, the feeblest – lowest almost – of men, still more so of Ministers,' wrote the choleric Creevey. It was an absurd misjudgement, but increasingly ministers behaved as if they believed it to be correct. Though the King was still loyal to his favourite prime minister not even he could protect the Government from a combination of Whigs and Pittites, and though Pitt still hesitated to commit himself to all-out assault, Fox's offer to join him in 'solemn union against the Doctor' was a temptation which could not long be resisted.

It was the desertion of Addington's Lord Chancellor, Eldon, that precipitated the end. Acting as self-appointed representative of certain disaffected ministers he opened private negotiations with Pitt and offered to act as intermediary between him and the King. When the keeper of the royal conscience cast himself in such a role, Pitt could hardly be blamed for assuming that the Government was doomed. With every vote Addington's majority in the Commons crumbled further. On 29 April 1803 he told his Cabinet that he could no longer carry on. 'Why are we to part?' asked the King in anguish. 'Can I do nothing to reconcile you and Mr Pitt?' The answer was too obvious to need spelling out; Addington's Government was at an end.

Addington himself claimed to believe that, if he had dissolved Parliament, he could have won an election by a large majority. He did not do so only because he feared to throw the country into confusion while invasion still threatened. His prediction was the less convincing for the care he took not to put it to the test, but it was not wholly ridiculous. There was still much goodwill in the country towards the Doctor and his ministry. Addington had proved himself an honest and usually competent administrator; his conduct of the nation's finances had been always capable and sometimes masterly; his foreign policy and direction of the war had been uninspired but far from disastrous.

Yet few governments can have been more generally denounced or have lost the confidence of so many of their closest supporters. It is this contrast between performance and reputation that provides the most intriguing feature of Addington's administration. His failure, one can only conclude, was primarily a failure of communication, a failure to put himself across so that his authentic talents could be as readily remarked as his equally real but, on the whole, less significant defects. In all he did he seemed to exude an aura of pettiness – 'the indefinable air of a village apothecary inspecting the tongue of the State' was Rosebery's vivid phrase. It was the conviction that he was too small for his job that drove his peers into irrational opposition. His failure was not so much one of achievement as of personality and of will. He was not a bad prime minister but he was bad at behaving like a prime minister and at convincing others that he was an effective prime minister. In the end he could not even convince himself.

In 1803 Addington was forty-six years old. As Lord Sidmouth he had more than thirty years of active political life ahead of him. The supine and fatuous Doctor, butt of the political cartoonists, the 'pitiful, squirting politician . . . not fit for anything but a shop' was to be mysteriously transformed into a harsh and fanatical reactionary who honeycombed Britain with a network of spies and whose policy of repression and persecution drove his country to the verge of revolution. Sidmouth of the Six Acts, of Oliver the *agent provocateur*, of Peterloo, was rivalled only by Castlereagh in the rogues' gallery of the Radicals:

> . . . two vultures sick for battle,
> Two scorpions under one white stone,
> Two bloodless wolves whose dry throats rattle,
> Two crows perched on the murrained cattle,
> Two vipers tangled into one.

It would be out of place to examine here Sidmouth's record as Home Secretary or in the other posts which he filled before his final retirement. A man of deeply conservative disposition with an exaggerated reverence for law and order, it was inevitable that he would gain – and indeed largely earn – the label of diehard reactionary. With no conception that the hideous poverty and misery of the working classes could be in any way the responsibility of government, it would have been futile to look for even a glimmering of reforming zeal. And yet within the moral code of his time he was a humane man, benevolent whenever benevolence seemed in order, fair and, on the whole, moderate where he felt repression was essential. His caricature as a cruel and evil tyrant was still less convincing than the earlier version of a flabby puppet who sprang into political motion only when the strings were pulled by William Pitt.

Indeed, it is his consistency that impresses. At every point in his career his deficiencies were obvious. He lacked imagination and a broad grasp of policy; he lacked flexibility; he lacked enterprise; above all he lacked grandeur and the art of kindling enthusiasm in the public. But he had qualities too. He was determined; he was courageous; he was thorough; he could command the devoted loyalty of his closest friends and allies. And among his qualities were several which are not invariably associated with the trade of politics. Integrity can be a dangerous asset and Addington's inability to conceal or compromise his often wrong-headed principles won him many enemies and little respect. Courtesy is frequently taken as the defence of the feeble and he was often dismissed as a flatterer and a hypocrite. Consideration for others is a grave handicap for the ambitious and he found himself ruthlessly thrust from the path of those with a clearer eye for the main chance. 'I am not aware', he wrote in old age, 'of having ever wilfully injured or given pain to any human being.' It is hardly the boast of a successful politician but it is not a bad epitaph for all that.

BIBLIOGRAPHY

The only recent biography of Addington is Philip Ziegler's own: *A Life of Henry Addington, First Viscount Sidmouth* (London, 1965). George Pellew's three-volume *Life and Correspondence* (London, 1847) is the only other full-scale biography. It is neither stimulating nor reliable. F. O. Darvall's *Popular Disturbances and Public Order in Regency England* (Oxford, 1934), Professor Feiling's *Second Tory Party* (London, 1938) and Steven Watson's *The Reign of George III* (Oxford, 1960) provide useful background to Addington's career. *The Diary and Correspondence of Lord Colchester* (London, 1861) is probably the most relevant of the innumerable biographies and autobiographies which relate to the period.

16

LORD GRENVILLE

BY

PETER JUPP

William Wyndham Grenville, born 24 October 1759, third son of George Grenville (q.v.) and Elizabeth, daughter of Sir William Wyndham. Educated at Eton and Christ Church, Oxford. Married 1792 the Hon. Anne Pitt, elder daughter of Thomas, 1st Baron Camelford. PC 1783; created Baron Grenville 1790. MP for Buckingham 1782–4 and Co. Buckingham 1784–1790. Chief Secretary 1782–3; Paymaster-General 1783; Joint Paymaster-General 1784–9; Board of Control 1784–90 (President 1790–1793); Vice-President of the Board of Trade 1786–9. Speaker of the House of Commons 1789; Home Secretary 1789–91; Foreign Secretary 1791–1801; Auditor of the Exchequer 1794 until death in 1834; First Lord of the Treasury 1806–7. Chancellor of the University of Oxford 1810 until death on 12 January 1834.

LORD GRENVILLE

The news of Pitt's death, as it sped through London on 23 January 1806, cast gloom upon a dim and uncertain future. The Government, as it confronted the opening of Parliament on the 26th, was weak and in need of reinforcement; the continental situation, in the wake of Ulm, Austerlitz and the capitulation of Prussia, was perilous. Lord Grenville, Pitt's cousin, heard the news at Camelford House on the corner of Oxford Street and Park Lane. Deeply saddened, he scribbled a note to his brother, the Marquis of Buckingham, that he was retiring immediately to Dropmore, his country residence in Buckinghamshire, where he hoped to 'restore my mind tolerably to its level'; he added that he would return to London in two or three days 'at latest'.[1]

Grenville's concern to return to London reflected the general view that he would be involved in any negotiations leading to the formation of a new government. Together with the 'Grenvilles' (the thirty or so relations, friends and supporters who looked to him for political guidance), he was associated with the Foxite whigs in a loose opposition coalition formed in March 1804 to urge more effective measures of domestic policy. With more than a hundred supporters, the coalition was, after the Pittites, the largest single party in the Commons. Furthermore, his long service under Pitt until 1801 and the sincere respect between the two men since then, encouraged some Pittites to regard him as only temporarily estranged from their cause and as a likely future ally. Finally, few could match his administrative experience, particularly in the field of foreign affairs. In terms of his political pedigree and the strength of his party associations he had strong claims to office and perhaps, to the premiership. As an individual, however, he possessed qualities of character and ability, which at both the private and public levels made these claims less formidable.

In public Grenville appeared (as in his portrait) to be of singularly strong, self-willed and independent character: cold and distant and deserving of the nickname 'boguey' or bugbear.[2] This exterior, however,

[1] Huntington Library, Stowe MSS, STG Box 41 (4).
[2] Applied as early as 1787. See Countess of Minto, *Life and Letters of Sir Gilbert Elliot* (London, 1874), i, 140.

concealed tensions between his personal instincts and proclivities and the normal demands of public life. The main feature of his private life was his dependence upon a narrow family circle in which he neither assumed nor aspired to a dominant role. The youngest of three sons, his parents died when he was a young boy and he soon fell under the influence of Buckingham, to whom he was to accord constant gratitude and deference. In the world beyond his relation's homes and estates he was ill at ease and insecure. His marriage to a distant cousin in 1792, and their move to a small estate in Buckinghamshire, has therefore a special significance. Dropmore became an increasingly welcome retreat from public life – a sanctuary where he could develop his strong inclination for the private study of classical literature and religion. Within a year or two of leaving office in 1801, domestic habits had taken a firm root. In October 1803 he wrote: 'I can hardly keep wondering at my own folly in thinking it worthwhile to leave my books and garden, even for one day's attendance in the House of Lords.'[3]

The main feature of his public life was his relatively modest ambitions. His decision to enter politics was the inevitable choice of a younger son of no estate and with a very small income.[4] Later, as he scaled the political ladder, he was continually torn between settling for financial security in a modest political backwater and the more glittering prospects that went with the key offices of state. By 1794 political independence had come with a peerage while financial security had been achieved with the sinecure office of auditor of the Exchequer. His course thereafter was beset with fears of the effects of office upon his health and his domestic life. These fears persisted after his resignation in 1801 and were a reason for his unwillingness to adopt the role of a party *leader* with any vigour. As he put the matter to his banker in April 1805: 'I deprecate any event which would again impose on me the burthen of fatigue and disquietude inseparable from a public situation.'[5]

Grenville's political thinking was strongly conservative. With regard to the Constitution he believed that measures of economical reform had, by the beginning of 1783, produced a reasonable balance between the powers of the Crown, executive and Parliament. Government, he thought, was best conducted by a strong Cabinet system and he dis-

[3] The Duke of Buckingham, *The Court and Cabinets of George III* (London, 1855), iii, 331.
[4] Approximately £1,500 in 1782.
[5] Coutts MSS 1090: Grenville to Thomas Coutts, 28 April 1805.

approved strongly of 'the wretched system of a Cabinet of cyphers, and a government of one man alone',[6] which he deduced was a feature of Pitt's last ministry. As for MPs and their attitude to political issues, he believed that actions should be guided by informed considerations of policy and took the view that 'systematic' opposition was foolish and dishonest. After 1801 he eschewed such a course and insisted upon purely 'prospective' opposition.

Abroad he looked to a stable Europe and an expanding Empire. He thought that the first objective was best achieved by the subduing of Republican France by continental armies subsidised by Britain, a policy he had pursued as Foreign Secretary and which was hotly opposed by Fox. As for the Empire, he believed that its future depended upon the success of his European policy but that in the interim, policies should be governed by the requirements of security. Thus in the case of Ireland he supported the Union and Catholic emancipation as ways of quietening a troublesome dependency.

As for his authority in the political world, it rested almost entirely upon his prodigious capacity for hard work, his experience in nearly every department of state, and hardly at all upon a personal magnetism. After 1801 his prominence derived from his trenchant attacks upon government policies and his view that Britain's future depended upon an ordered policy in which the priorities were: first, a union of political parties headed preferably by Pitt – a ministry of all the talents; second, the stabilisation of Ireland by Catholic emancipation and the strengthening of Britain by a reorganisation of her armed forces and a reform of her national finance. These were the qualities which enabled his friends and relations and the Foxite Whigs to look to him for their future. For the arts of leadership and the managing of policy he had little aptitude. His preference, as he said himself, was to 'rather follow than lead',[7] and when confronted with the problem of finding the means to suit the ends of policy he had often displayed an inflexibility of mind and a weakness of spirit.

As Grenville mourned, the King consulted his ministers in the hope that they could reshuffle their pack and continue in office. They refused, arguing their weakness in the Commons; instead they advised the King to consult Grenville. He was their obvious choice for of the other party

[6] *Court and Cabinets*, iii, 422.
[7] Fitzpatrick, W. (ed.), *The Dropmore Papers* (HMSO, 1892), i, 194.

leaders Fox, as Pitt's bitterest enemy, and Sidmouth, who had recently resigned from the Government, were out of the question. In addition, many Pittites recognised that Grenville's views upon foreign policy were similar to their own, and some predicted that if this were to break the loose coalition between the Grenvilles and the Foxites then he would have to look to them for support.[8] Grenville simply appeared the best insurance for the survival of Pittite policies and, perhaps, their return to office. The King reluctantly accepted their advice and on 27 January asked Grenville to prepare a plan of government 'without exclusion', thereby recognising that the serious situation demanded that he accept Fox into Cabinet rank.[9]

In the construction of the Government during the following three weeks Grenville's initial steps were hesitant. The King asked him to plan, not to form, a government and he initially expressed his reluctance to take the position of First Lord and urged the claims of Lord Spencer.[10] His reasons were an unwillingness to take the lead and a concern that by so doing he would be obliged to resign his auditorship of the Exchequer, leaving him in the situation in which 'I should in fact receive no addition to my present income and must incur a very great additional expense'.[11] When pressed by his brothers and by Fox, who agreed to introduce a Bill enabling the auditorship to be conveyed to a trustee, thus guaranteeing Grenville's financial security, his reluctance to take the lead was assuaged. From that moment (30 January) his course was more determined and he set about trying to form a government which in terms of both policy and personnel would have some flexibility in the future. The King's objections to the Government's plan to reorganise the administration of the Army and do away with the power and patronage of the commander-in-chief, his son the Duke of York, were firmly resisted. On 3 February, having agreed to the first list of recommended appointments, the King expressed himself as satisfied with Grenville's insistence that he and his colleagues required time to prepare measures

[8] See e.g. Rev. L. V. Harcourt, *Diaries and Correspondence of George Rose* (London, 1860), ii, 313; Scottish RO, Melville MSS: Robert Dundas to Melville, 11 Feb. 1806.
[9] It is interesting that on the morning of 22 Jan. the King held a long conversation with Buckingham's close friend, W. H. Fremantle, about the Grenvilles and their likely course in office. (Huntington Library, Stowe MSS, STG Box 33 (17): Fremantle to Buckingham, 24 Jan. 1806.)
[10] *Court and Cabinets*, iv, 15–16; *Dropmore Papers*, vii, 346–7: Auckland to Grenville, 28 Jan. 1806.
[11] Stowe MSS, STG Box 41 (5): Grenville to Buckingham, 30 Jan. 1806.

in detail and that they recognised his right to veto any they submitted to him.[12]

As to the political character of the Government Grenville believed that in view of the 'evils and dangers' that faced the country, it should rest ideally 'upon the most extended basis' and include all four political parties.[13] The obstacles in the way of achieving such a policy immediately were certainly forbidding. The opposition of the Foxites to a Commons vote of funeral honours to Pitt on 27 January had indicated their hostility to such a course and determined some Pittites that they could not take a part. In addition, it was doubtful whether the number of offices available could accommodate the pretensions of more than three of the parties. Nevertheless if Grenville had been in a vigorous frame of mind he could have set himself above the claims of his immediate colleagues and made the attempt. He did not. Instead he adopted the more modest course of trying to persuade some junior members of the old Government to stay in office and to keep the door open for future admissions by insisting upon 'no proscription' against Pittites in matters of patronage and a benevolent attitude to their past conduct in government.[14] Even this proved too modest a policy to succeed and when Grenville made firm offers, to Lord Bathurst to remain at the Mint and to Charles Long to stay in Ireland and become Chancellor of the Irish Exchequer, they were refused as not being sufficient to attach the Pittites as a body to the Government.[15] Only a pale reflection of the policy remained. Fox intimated that it might be a good idea to admit Pittites in the future and a few of their number, including Canning, Castlereagh and Perceval, felt that enough had been done to determine them not to refuse to take a hand when the right opportunity arose.[16]

The Government was therefore constructed from three of the four parties. Lord Sidmouth and his thirty or so Commons votes were taken in because this step was warmly recommended by the Prince of Wales (who regarded himself as guardian to the new administration), and

[12] *Dropmore Papers*, viii, 8–9: the King to Grenville, 3 Feb. 1806; Northants RO, Fitzwilliam MSS: Grenville to Fitzwilliam, 3 Feb. 1806.
[13] *Dropmore Papers*, vii, 332: Grenville to Wellesley, 23 Jan. 1806; British Museum Additional MS 41852, folios 213–16: Grenville to T. Grenville, 24 Jan. 1806.
[14] Public Record Office, Granville MSS: Morpeth to Leveson Gower, 7 Feb. 1806; *Dropmore Papers*, viii, 44–5.
[15] BM Fortescue MSS: Bathurst and Long to Grenville, 7 Feb. 1806.
[16] *Diaries and Correspondence of George Rose*, ii, 246–51; Countess Granville, *Private Correspondence of Lord Granville Leveson Gower* (London, 1916), ii, 178.

because it suited Grenville's desire for a comprehensive government.[17] Sidmouth became Lord Privy Seal, and his acolyte Lord Ellenborough Lord Chief Justice with a seat in the Cabinet, an appointment which, as it united judicial and excutive functions in one person, caused a minor storm in the Commons. The remaining Cabinet posts and the bulk of the junior appointments were dealt out amongst the Foxites and the Grenvilles in a proportion to their voting strength in the Commons which favoured the Grenvilles. Five Cabinet posts went to the Foxites, Fox at last becoming Foreign Secretary, and three, including Spencer at the Home Office and William Windham as Secretary at War, to the Grenvilles. A number of critics concluded that this was 'a Fox or a Sidmouth Government with a little of Lord Grenville', but this was far from the truth.[18] Admittedly the omission of Grenville's brothers appeared a sign of weakness but then Buckingham made it clear that he did not want to load 'a cart already too heavily charged', while Tom Grenville had no wish to attend Parliament with any frequency.[19] However, the notion rested upon little more than a casual glance at the list of appointments. Close study would have revealed that while Fox and his friends were strong in the Commons and clearly dominated foreign affairs, the Grenvilles controlled the efficient offices connected with domestic policy. As First Lord of the British and Irish Treasuries, with a (Foxite) Chancellor of the Exchequer in Lord Henry Petty who at twenty-six was too young and inexperienced to stray far from his orbit, and with friends taking two of the three junior lordships of the Treasury, the senior and vice-presidencies of the Board of Trade and the Irish Exchequer, Grenville took a firm control of financial policy. With Spencer at the Home Office he had the last word in Irish and, as it transpired, Scottish affairs, including the all-important question of the distribution of patronage. And finally there was Windham who, as an old colleague under Pitt and an early associate in opposition to Addington, was at least within Grenville's sphere of influence if not a slavish Grenvillite. In terms of numbers and debating strength the Government was largely Foxite; in terms of decision-making Grenville's influence was certainly as strong as that of Fox. Further, Grenville was regarded by his colleagues from the outset as the effective head of the Government.

Of more accuracy were the gibes that this was far from being a

17 Devon RO, Sidmouth MSS: Sheridan to Sidmouth, n.d. (30 Jan. 1806).
18 Carlisle R.O., Lonsdale MSS: Robert Ward to Lonsdale, 1 Feb. 1806.
19 Bucks R.O., Cottesloe MSS: Buckingham to Fremantle, 27 Jan. 1806.

ministry of all the talents. The absence of the leading Pittites made that inevitable but Grenville had at least kept the door open for them. The omission from high office of those peacocks in the Whig camp – Sheridan, Tierney and Whitbread – was certainly striking, and can be accounted for by Grenville's distaste for them and their pretensions and Fox's instinctive preference for men of more considerable social standing. However, in filling up the sixty or so vacancies and dealing with the flood of applications for favours, Grenville looked to talent and efficiency rather than to ornamental qualities. He deliberately kept his Cabinet as slim as possible, did his best to avoid the appointment of nonentities to junior posts, and took little interest in creating peers, baronets and privy councillors. He even eschewed an earldom for himself.[20] Nevertheless it was not a ministry of *all* the talents as Grenville had initially hoped and what talent it precisely possessed was yet to be discovered.

The main lines of policy were established by the end of March at a series of Cabinet meetings which exhibited 'the most perfect and cordial harmony'.[21] One reason for this unexpected feature was the division of responsibilities between Fox and Grenville. The other was that in the field of foreign affairs the differences between the two men had dissolved under the hammer blows that Bonaparte had inflicted upon the third coalition. By the end of December 1805 France had occupied large portions of the Austrian Empire, given Russia her marching orders from Moravia, Hungary and Galicia and had forced Prussia to a treaty. The differences between Fox and Grenville over the virtue of fighting the war with continental allies became merely 'speculative'.[22] In addition, the previous Government left little behind it in the way of contingency planning and Grenville was thus able to lend himself in mid-February to Fox's attempt to negotiate peace. His view was that any terms agreed by the French would prove unacceptable to Britain, but that sufficient time would be bought to consolidate the country's strength for the inevitable struggle ahead. Fox, for his part, proved to be more than the submissive negotiator that Grenville had feared. He agreed that the basis of any terms should be '*uti possidetis*', and that

---

[20] BM Add. MS 41852, folios 225–6, 251: Grenville to T. Grenville, 30 Jan., 26 Mar. 1806.

[21] *Dropmore Papers*, viii, 107–8: Grenville to Fox, 19 April 1806.

[22] *Court and Cabinets*, iv, 12–13: Grenville to Buckingham, 14 (not as printed 13) Jan. 1806.

Britain should insist upon a joint negotiation with her ally Russia, as a means of laying the basis for future continental co-operation against France. Further, he entered fully into the measures taken against Prussia as a result of her annexation of Hanover in February 1806. Thus until Fox's health deteriorated in late June there were few differences in the Cabinet upon foreign affairs,[23] leaving Grenville able to concentrate upon the cultivation of what he was later to refer to as a 'defensive and husbanding system' on the domestic front.[24]

Grenville's strong preference for a 'system' that emphasised the need for domestic security flowed from a number of considerations. It derived from his view that Britain was in a perilous position; it built upon the basis of the co-operation established between the Foxites and the Grenvilles; it demonstrated his anxiety to obtain a political consensus and it reflected his instinct for 'systematic' government. Its central features were as follows. First, a reorganisation of the armed services which Grenville, in the company of others, had been urging since the renewal of the war with France. Second, a reform of national finances so as to deal with the recurring problem of raising enough money to pay for the war. Third, a policy of 'conciliation' towards Ireland in terms of both political management and measures, combined with a strengthening of the Union. Grenville's reasoning as to management was that the traditional distribution of Irish offices upon political grounds strengthened divisions within the Protestant ascendancy, alienated Catholics from the administrative system and made the task of managing the Irish MPs in the interest of government more difficult. Fourth, the adoption of the similar principle of 'moderation' with regard to Scottish patronage in order to unite the Scottish MPs in support of government and as a means of ensuring that 'the administration of Scotland should no longer be considered as separate from the rest of the Empire'. And, finally, the avoidance of measures that would force the Pittites into active opposition. In short, Grenville had in mind a United Kingdom prepared for the vicissitudes of war if Fox failed to secure an honourable peace.[25]

[23] See e.g. BM Add. MS 47569, folios 275–8: Fox to Bedford, 26 April 1806.

[24] BM Fortescue MSS: Grenville to Fitzwilliam, 9 Jan. 1809 (copy).

[25] This view of Grenville's policy depends upon a quantity of documents too numerous to mention here. For Ireland, however, see in particular BM Add. MS 47569, f. 284: Fox to Bedford, 13 May 1806; for Scotland, Scottish RO, Melville MSS: Robert Dundas to Melville, 26 Feb. 1806; BM Add. MS 41852, f. 241: Grenville to T. Grenville, 6 Mar. 1806; BM Fortescue MSS: Grenville to the Marquis of Douglas, 27 June 1806.

When the parliamentary session ended on 23 July, Grenville had failed to impress this cautious programme upon the minds of his colleagues as a blueprint for positive action. This was one reason for its general lack of success. He simply had no experience of firm leadership. In earlier days Pitt had solved the problem by restricting his Cabinet confidants to less than a handful and, in order to concentrate upon essentials, had often dropped whole areas of policy. Grenville, on the other hand, in conformity with his expressed hostility to government 'by one man alone',[26] took everyone into his confidence, and while allowing departmental heads a fair degree of independence, attempted constant supervision of all their activities. Moreover, rather than adopting a policy of supervision by a few brisk directives, Grenville preferred to cosset and coddle. He even moved from Oxford Street to 10 Downing Street in order to be close at hand, a move which he regarded as 'irksome' and which annoyed the Chancellor of the Exchequer who argued that the house was annexed to his office and not that of the First Lord.[27] The result was that instead of impressing the overall strategy of government upon his colleagues, he found himself attending to the details of its individual components. This diffusion of energy was carried further by his taking up matters that were extraneous to his real purpose, such as the reform of the Scottish court of session, the giving of statutory permanence to a proclamation prohibiting the importation of African negroes into colonies acquired during the war, and, throughout June, the investigation into the conduct of the Princess of Wales, the report of which he largely wrote himself. He therefore indulged his capacity for business and neglected its management with the result that few, if any, of his colleagues were given a clear idea of the direction in which they were travelling.

The other reasons why government measures failed to impress the parliamentary public lie more with lack of time to prepare them properly and the weaknesses and inexperience of individual ministers.[28] The reorganisation of the armed services amounted to no more than an

---

[26] See p. 255.
[27] *Dropmore Papers*, viii, 20-1; BM Fortescue MSS: Grenville to the Bishop of Lincoln, 15 April 1806. He moved to 10 Downing St, in April. There he found Hoppner's portrait of Pitt and hung it in a place where it would escape dust.
[28] A detailed study of the Government's measures can be found in A. D. Harvey, 'The Talents Ministry', *Historical Journal*, xv (4), 619-49. I have therefore only provided references for details or interpretations not found there.

increase in Navy pay and Windham's army plan which was novel only in that it dealt at a stroke with all three forces – the militia, volunteers and regular. Its central features were a pruning of the militia and the volunteers and the application of the long-discussed principle of limited service to the Regular Army in order to improve recruitment. Lack of time to prepare the measures properly and Windham's inability to think a problem through produced measures which reduced the volunteers but failed to increase recruitment into the regulars. Further, Windham's slackness in presenting his plan in the Commons, combined with his caustic criticism of the much loved volunteers – 'painted cherries', he once called them – alienated the country gentlemen and the Pittites.

In the financial sphere, where Grenville's authority was strongest, the Government proved to be unprepared for an immediate comprehensive measure. The budget had to be presented quickly and as a result Grenville and Petty fell back upon measures largely foreshadowed by their predecessor. Two acts improved methods of public accounting: the treasurership of the ordnance was regulated and a watchful eye kept upon the matter of reversionary offices. As to the budget, the property tax was raised, as had been widely expected, and in order to meet the remaining deficit the assessed taxes were raided after an attempt to produce the money from two alternative sources had been beaten off in Parliament. This package, which tended to underline the need for comprehensive reform, again led to severe Pittite criticisms.

As to Ireland, Grenville's policy prevailed, although only after a Foxite shot across its unionist bows. Immediately prior to the Government's taking office, Fox had inferred in the Commons that he would like to repeal the Union. Passions in Ireland waxed warm[29] until Fox, when in office, retracted. This conversion symbolised Grenville's control over Irish affairs. When the new Viceroy, the Duke of Bedford, left for Ireland in March, he had agreed to pursue the 'system of conciliation' in matters of patronage[30] and although Fox later lamented his acquiescence, it was largely upheld.

In the case of Scotland, the prospect of a Whig manager of patronage was killed and Pitt's friends were assured that in that sphere Grenville

[29] Dublin SPO, 531/225/3: Charles Long to Marsden, 17 Feb. 1806; BM Fortescue MSS: Lord Glandore to Grenville, 27 Feb. 1806.
[30] Durham University, Grey MSS, Box 6, file 17 (8, 9): Bedford to Howick, 5 Jan. 1807 and reply on 15 Jan.

and Spencer would have the last word.[31] Scottish party politics, however, proved more difficult to manage than the Irish, and by July the
policy was beginning to creak and groan under the weight of the
mutual suspicions of both the Whigs and the Pittites.

In several respects, therefore, Grenville's plan had come to very
little. This, together with the fact that the conduct of government
business was admitted by even a junior minister to be 'loose and
desultory'[32] led the Pittites to abandon their policy of 'forbearance' and,
in June and July, to enter into spirited opposition.[33] Throughout this
campaign the Government maintained sufficient majorities but it was
generally admitted that it could not take on another session without
some addition to its debating strength. It was reported that Lord
Lowther told Grenville to his face that 'the weight of debate (Fox of
course excepted, but Fox only) was wholly on the side of the Opposition', that 'the Government was thought and felt to be exceedingly
inadequate; that upon this point country gentlemen and others not
politicians, felt sore and ashamed; and were obliged to confess, that the
Opposition made the Government appear weak and ridiculous.'[34]

Thus by the end of the session Grenville was confronted with severe
problems. His 'system' had made little impression upon his ministers,
and they in turn had hardly made a favourable impression upon Parliament. He was no doubt aware of his difficulties. As early as May he had
confessed to Buckingham that he did not believe his continuance in
office could do much good and might well 'destroy my own happiness'.[35]
His confidence might well have declined further had it not been for the
steady deterioration in Fox's health during July and the fact that the
full control of the Government fell into his hands. By force of circumstance, Grenville's attention was diverted from domestic security
and the difficulties he had encountered, to strengthening the Government in the House of Commons and the direction of foreign policy.

On 16 July he adopted the comforting but hardly imaginative policy
of introducing his brother Tom into the Cabinet as President of the
Board of Control. During August he negotiated with George Canning of the Opposition, but finding him unwilling to act separately

[31] See p. 258.
[32] *Dropmore Papers*, viii, 285: Auckland to Grenville, 16 Aug. 1806.
[33] Welbeck MSS: Canning to Titchfield, 26 April 1806.
[34] Harewood MSS: Canning to his wife, 16 June 1806, reporting Lowther's remarks.
[35] *Court and Cabinets*, iv, 29-31.

from his colleagues decided (after some wavering) that he could not introduce the Pittites as a party into the Government. When Fox died on 13 September Grenville was therefore forced to reshuffle his Cabinet from the three parties in the Government.[36] His real hope was to put Windham out of harm's way by elevating him to the Lords and thus allow Tom Grenville to take one of the two remaining secretary-ships of state that could be held in the Commons, thereby strengthening his own influence. Windham refused, however, and Grenville did not insist. Instead he fell back upon putting Lord Howick into Fox's place and Tom Grenville into that of Howick at the Admiralty. As his brother was not regarded as a first-class debater, the accession of strength was minimal.

On the continental front Grenville began to broaden the range of policy to the point where a basis for comprehensive allied action was its main aim. On 4 September, having heard that the Tsar had rejected any possibility of a separate treaty with France, he put Britain's negotia-tions in Paris upon a footing in which the accommodation of Russia was a priority. In the instructions sent to Paris, emphasis was placed upon the need to recognise Russia's special interests in the Adriatic and the Mediterranean; in particular, a firm resolution was taken that as Russia requested, Britain would insist that Sicily be retained by the King of Naples. Further, the terms of 'uti possidetis' were added to by the inclusion of Buenos Aires, the news of whose capture by a free-booting British force arrived on 12 September. When it became known that Prussia was showing a determination to resist Bonaparte's encircling movements, Grenville requested that the Foreign Office consider the formation of a Northern League to which Britain would be a party. On 20 September the Cabinet decided to open negotiations with Prussia for the restitution of Hanover and the establishment of a general con-

---

[36] A warm feeling had existed between Grenville and Fox since their political association in 1804. However, Grenville never found it easy to deal with friends outside his family circle and he was never upon intimate terms with him. The nature of the relationship is captured by a few words he said to Lord Lauderdale on 31 July just as that close friend of Fox was leaving an interview he had had with the Prime Minister. He said that 'he had many times abstained from going to Stable Yard (where Fox lived), from an apprehension that if Mr Fox should know he was there, he might suppose he was come upon business and make an effort to see him, which might do him harm; but that if he followed the dictates of his own inclination, he should be there every day.' (The Earl of Ilchester, *The Journal of Lady Holland* (London, 1908), ii, 171.)

cert. On 3 October, two days after Prussia presented France with an ultimatum, he was willing to consider a Prussian subsidy, a matter which he concluded would certainly require endorsement by Parliament before Christmas. And finally, a fresh look was given to the feasibility of putting a British force upon the Continent.[37]

As Grenville took these tentative steps forward, news arrived in London on 8 October that the Paris negotiations had broken down over the question of Sicily. In view of this and the outbreak of the Franco–Prussian war, he concluded that 'vigorous resolutions' might be called for, which, if taken, would require the sanction of Parliament. The question was therefore raised of the Government's security in the existing House of Commons. Despite the fact that it had enjoyed sufficient majorities in June and July, Grenville concluded that it was less than gilt-edged. His reconstructed Cabinet desperately needed a boost to its strength and authority. Further, there were persistent rumours that members of the Opposition were to be seen at Windsor and were undermining the King's confidence in his ministers. Grenville therefore decided to seek a general election. As governments did not lose general elections at this time, it would increase the Government's strength and, as the power of dissolving Parliament rested with the King, would, if granted, demonstrate clearly his support of the Government. In short, Grenville sought absolute security at home before venturing abroad. On 12 October he requested, and the next day received, the King's agreement to a dissolution of Parliament.

In principle his policy was safe and sound. In practice, however, while it increased the Government's strength by about forty votes, it diverted Grenville's attention still further from the overall direction of policy. He took upon himself the management of the election campaign in which, in conformity with his earlier policy of 'moderation', he attempted to see that government favour was given to those who were generally in support of the Government rather than simply to thick and thin party men.[38] This ensured that the campaign was particularly complicated and onerous. As Bonaparte followed up his decisive victory

[37] *Dropmore Papers*, viii, 312 (Cabinet minute), 324–6, 352–5; A. Aspinall (ed.), *The Later Correspondence of George III* (Cambridge, 1962–70), iv, 471–5; Durham University, Grey MSS, Box 21, file 2: Grenville to Howick, 27 Sept., 3, 11 Oct. 1806, which indicate Grenville's superintendence of foreign affairs.
[38] For the 1806 general election consult M. G. Hinton, 'The General Elections of 1806 and 1807', an unpublished University of Reading PhD thesis.

over the Prussians at Jena on 14 October, the British Prime Minister threw himself into decisions about the merits of this or that electoral interest in a hundred and one far-flung places.

Thus when the new Parliament assembled on 15 December, Grenville was mentally tired and in no mood to spirit his Cabinet into the 'vigorous resolutions' that the allies were now demanding in the wake of the French occupation of Berlin on 25 October. Prussia requested a subsidy; Russia, extended credit; and Sweden some money to strengthen her forces at Stralsund, a port that gave British commerce access to northern Europe and could be used as a springboard for a military adventure in Bonaparte's rear. Throughout the period during which the Cabinet considered these matters (until 18 March), it was strongly affected by Grenville's gloom and despondency at the failure of Prussia and his view that without more independent resolution on her part 'a complete submission of the Continent under the name of peace' was likely before the spring.[39] Thus instead of making a warm response to outstretched hands, he allowed arguments against positive action to prevail and showed more enthusiasm for what were essentially diversions, such as the recapture of Buenos Aires, which had been lost almost as soon as it was won, various schemes that the Board of Trade put forward for enriching colonial trade, and, to some extent, a naval attack upon Turkey, then at war with Russia. A mere pittance was offered to Prussia; suspicions that Russia would be unable to meet the interest upon British credit, and fears that Parliament might not sanction what might amount to a loan resulted in an offer that proved offensive to Russian dignity. As for the Baltic, consideration of the fact that British action at sea or upon land would require warm weather and either Denmark's co-operation or defeat led to indecision. And finally, the question of military action at any point on the Continent was complicated in the minds of ministers by fears of the cost and the likely drain upon defensive forces which they still regarded as inadequate. It is true that some of Grenville's colleagues were opposed almost as a matter of principle to both continental alliances and the prospect of military action in Europe, and that if he had decided upon vigorous measures, he would have had to battle hard in the Cabinet. However, the firm conclusion to be drawn from the evidence of the Cabinet's deliberations is that numbed by Prussia's defeat, Grenville failed to bring his colleagues to clear-cut decisions. Once again he chose to concentrate upon domestic

[39] *Court and Cabinets*, iv, 127.

security. Here the burden upon Grenville proved considerable and under its impact his thinking narrowed to the point at which he became convinced that security depended upon the success of his policies in two of the three remaining areas that he had regarded as government priorities on coming into office: national finance and Ireland.

Since his resignation in 1801 Grenville had become increasingly interested in the question of political economy, and upon taking office in 1806 had looked for a comprehensive answer to the question of raising money for an extended war. During December and January he produced with the advice of Petty and others 'our great plan', which sought to peg war taxes at an acceptable minimum through the creation of an extra Sinking Fund.[40] Although a lively debate upon its merits took place over the next six years, it seems likely that if it had been put into full operation it would not have succeeded.[41] However in the first two months of 1807 the important fact is that it was not received with any enthusiasm in Parliament and in fact was virulently attacked by Canning and Castlereagh in the middle of February. One of the bases upon which Grenville hoped to make Britain capable of extended offensive or defensive action was thereby undermined. This seems to have stiffened his resolve, at a critical time in the life of the Government, that in Ireland his policies had to succeed.

In the case of Ireland it was characteristic of Grenville's thinking that he was to regard the policy he eventually decided upon as the solution to a range of problems that the Government confronted in its quest for security. In the autumn of 1806 serious disturbances occurred in the midland and western counties and there was some evidence that they were connected with republican feeling and French agitators. At approximately the same time the Catholic leaders in Dublin intimated that they would seek to petition the new Parliament for Catholic emancipation. For a long time Grenville had believed that stability in Ireland was essential to Britain's security; he also knew that the King would not countenance Catholic emancipation and that a Catholic petition would be likely to divide and destroy his Cabinet. For the

[40] BM Fortescue MSS: Grenville to Wellesley, 26 Jan. 1813; the collection also contains a file of papers relating to the plan, in which it seems likely that David Ricardo had a hand.
[41] Its main defect was to fix war expenditure at an annual sum of £32 million, which was soon exceeded. For a lengthy discussion of the plan see A. Alison, *History of Europe* (London, 1848), x, 198–208.

future he therefore looked to a comprehensive (but diversionary) policy comprising tithe reform, an increase in the parliamentary grant to the Roman Catholic College at Maynooth, state provision for the Catholic clergy and a reform of the Established Church.[42] For the present he decided upon extending to the United Kingdom the Irish Act of 1793 which allowed Catholics to hold commissions in the Army up to the rank of general. To Grenville's mind this measure would kill three birds with one stone. It would pass as a limited concession to Catholics and perhaps forestall the presentation of a petition. It would, by enabling Catholic officers to serve in Britain, solve some of the problems created by the failure of Windham's Army plans.[43] Finally, as Catholic regiments were to be raised in the west of Ireland, it would curb the disaffection there without recourse to the proclaiming of whole areas under the terms of the dreaded Insurrection Act.

If Grenville had decided upon the extension of the precise terms of the Irish Act (a measure which it could be argued was complementary to his general policy of completing the Union), then the Government would have survived longer into history. He did not. Instead he decided in the first week of February, as a result of sustained pressure from the Catholic leaders in Ireland for a substantial concession, that the terms of the Act had to be added to so as to enable Catholics to be generals on the staff.[44] As a result of that decision he was confronted over the next five weeks with two main problems. The first was that when the matter was brought to the King's attention, he was to be persuaded to agree to an extension of the terms of the Act to Britain but not to any addition to them. The second was that Lord Sidmouth threatened his resignation if the terms were added to, while Lord Howick appeared destined to leave the already fragile Treasury bench for the House of Lords in view of the imminent death of his father.

Grenville did not choose to meet any of these problems head on. He

[42] *Dropmore Papers*, viii, 486–8: Grenville to Bedford, 29 Dec. 1806, which should be compared with Lord Holland's memorandum of ministerial discussions on the Irish question of 17 Dec. 1806 in the Holland House MSS.

[43] As early as August Grenville had calculated the likely deficit in the regular forces and had concluded that extra Catholic troops would be required for overseas duties. (Huntington Library, Stowe MSS, STG Box 170 (12), 7 Aug. 1806.)

[44] Detailed narratives of the crisis over the Irish question can be found in M. Roberts, *The Whig Party 1807–12*, pp. 7–34; M. G. Hinton, 'The General Elections of 1806 and 1807', and A. Aspinall (ed.), *The Later Correspondence of George III*, iv, xxxviii–xli.

did not clarify to the King the situation with regard to the Catholic question, partly as a result of a genuine misunderstanding as to the King's views, and partly because of his fears of the King's likely reaction. As to the problems of the Cabinet, he once again threw out a lifeline to Canning, although on this occasion he considered broadening the base of the Government to include both Pittites and radical members of the Whig party.[45]

Neither parry succeeded. The King was forced to clarify the Catholic question to the Cabinet by making it clear on 13 March that he would not accept a measure that did not conform exactly with the terms of the Irish Act of 1793. The following day Canning threw back the lifeline and urged upon Grenville the general view of the Opposition that he should drop the Catholic measure (now in the form of a Bill) and stay in office.[46] Thus when the Cabinet met on 15 March neither the King nor the Opposition was pressing for the Government's removal. In order to stay in office Grenville had to choose between two alternatives, neither of which was particularly attractive. He could either modify the Bill until it conformed exactly with the terms of the Irish Act or drop it altogether. In either case he would have to confront the wrath of those in the Cabinet who were now determined to stand by the enlarged measure and that of the Catholic leaders in Dublin. On the other hand, neither course would be opposed by the King and most of the Pittites. However, Grenville was in no mood to take on a struggle with his friends. Constant participation in the problems of every government department, and the piloting through the Lords of new measures to reform the Scottish court of session and to abolish the slave trade had borne him down. To be confronted now with the problem of managing a policy he regarded as essential to his whole 'defensive and husbanding system' proved too much. On 7 March he had informed Buckingham that he longed 'daily and hourly' . . . 'for the moment when my friends will allow me to think that I have fully discharged (by a life of hitherto incessant labour) every claim that they, or the country can have upon me'. He continued with a thought prompted by problems elsewhere but which well applies to those he confronted with his Cabinet: 'I want one great and essential quality for my station, and every hour increases the difficulty . . . I am not competent to the

[45] Harewood MSS: Canning to his wife, 4, 7, 11–14 Feb. 1807, are particularly valuable sources.
[46] ibid., Canning to his wife, 17, 18, 20 Mar. 1807.

management of men. I never was so naturally and toil and anxiety more and more unfit me for it'.[47] In this mood Grenville sought for himself and his friends an honourable release. On 17 March the Cabinet agreed to drop the Bill but reserved the right to express their views as individuals on the Catholic question, a move that given the King's sensibilities was tantamount to asking him to look for another government. On 18 March, having asked and been refused the Cabinet's agreement not to raise the Catholic question to him again, this is exactly what the King set about doing. In his resolution to retire from office, Grenville had sought to secure a politically face-saving dismissal.[48]

Having therefore failed to achieve the security he believed necessary to his country, Grenville returned quickly to Dropmore. On 20 March Lord Howick requested him to attend a meeting to discuss measures of opposition. He replied: 'I feel very repugnant to any course of active opposition having been most unaffectedly disinclined to take upon myself the task in which I have been engaged and feeling no small pleasure in an honourable release, I could not bring myself to struggle much to get my chains on again.'[49] Nor did he, although for the next ten years he lingered on in public life as an ill-fitting and ever-drooping figurehead to the Whig party.

Five days after he had replied to Howick's letter, he surrendered his seals of office. On the same day the royal assent was given to the measure that would stand to the lasting credit of the ministry of 'all the talents' – the abolition of the slave trade. Ironically it had never been sponsored by Grenvilles's Cabinet.

BIBLIOGRAPHY

Alison, A., *History of Europe, 1789–1815* (London, 1848), x, 168–249

Aspinall, A. (ed.), *The Later Correspondence of George III* (Cambridge, 1968), pp. 26–41

Fitzpatrick, W. (ed.), *The Dropmore Papers* (HMSO, 1912) viii, 7–49; (HMSO, 1915), ix, 7–26

Harvey, A. D., 'The Ministry of All the Talents', *The Historical Journal*, xv, no. 4 (1972), 619–49

Roberts, M., *The Whig Party 1807–12* (London, 1939), *passim*

[47] *Court and Cabinets*, iv, 132–3.

[48] In a letter to Lord Derby on 24 March Grenville made it clear that the Cabinet had not resigned but had been 'turned out'. (BM Fortescue MSS.)

[49] Durham University, Grey MSS, Box 21, file 2.

17

SPENCER PERCEVAL

BY

JOYCE MARLOW

Spencer Perceval, born 1 November 1762, second son of the 2nd Earl of Egmont and Catherine, daughter of Charles Compton. Educated at Woolwich, Harrow, Trinity College, Cambridge and Lincoln's Inn. Married 1790 Jane Spencer-Wilson; six sons, six daughters. Joined Midland Circuit 1786; Deputy Recorder Northants 1787; Junior Counsel Crown prosecution of Tom Paine 1792 and of Horne Tooke 1794; KC 1796. MP for Northampton 1796; Solicitor-General 1801–1802; Attorney-General 1802–1804; again Attorney-General 1804–1806; PC 1807; Chancellor of the Exchequer 1807; Prime Minister 4 October 1809 till 11 May 1812, when murdered in the lobby of the House of Commons.

SPENCER PERCEVAL

When the Duke of Portland's administration staggered to its close in the early autumn of 1809, there was one seeming front runner for his job, the brilliant, wayward Canning. But Canning had intrigued too many times, he had alienated too many people, he had wanted the highest office too obviously and too passionately, and the unsavoury scent of the duel with Castlereagh hung too closely over him, for sufficient support to be forthcoming. The man for whom adequate factional support was eventually fashioned was Spencer Perceval. It was the combination of professionalism (although it is doubtful whether his contemporaries would have recognised it as such) and the sound reactionary views that led to sufficient backing for his candidacy. And to George III, Perceval was eminently acceptable because of his proven championship of the Crown and Constitution and his opposition to Catholic emancipation.

Spencer Perceval ranks high among Britain's unremembered prime ministers, but he has two distinct claims to fame that posterity might recall. He remains the only man to have held the offices of Solicitor-General, Attorney-General and Prime Minister; and the sole man holding the last office to have been assassinated. His ability to survive politically is also worthy of more attention than it has generally been accorded.

Perceval was born in London in 1762. He was the second son of the second marriage of the second Earl of Egmont, which meant his inherited financial prospects were never good and he always needed to earn a living. As a young man he showed no outstanding qualities. Samuel Romilly, who liked him, described him as a person 'with very little reading, of a conversation barren of instruction, and with strong and invincible prejudices on many subjects'. But if he was not an intellectual Perceval had a mind capable of absorbing and utilising facts, he had application and he had an equable temperament. After leaving Cambridge in 1781 he entered Lincoln's Inn and then joined the Midland Circuit as a barrister. By the early 1790s he had begun to establish himself, and he attracted Pitt's interest. The attention was not

[273]

gained by any brilliant performances at the Bar but by steady, plodding industry and by the soundness of his invincible prejudices.

From childhood Perceval had been deeply religious, and he matured with a fervour that was evangelical in its attachment to the Church of England, both as a religious creed and as the lynch-pin of the Constitution. His fervent Anglicanism meant that he was opposed to Catholic emancipation, and he therefore appealed to an influential sector of the ruling elite. On the question of the war with France he proved himself equally sound. Perceval believed as absolutely as he disbelieved in Catholic emancipation that the war must be fought to a conclusion. Unless Napoleon could be brought to his knees, the British way of life was doomed. All reasonable men of whatever class must grasp this obvious fact. They must accept that the prosecution of the war to final, decisive victory was the first priority of the age. As this was the view held by a majority of those possessing power and influence, Perceval's appeal grew wider.

In 1796 he was invited to stand for Parliament as a Tory candidate, and was duly returned without difficulty. Initially Perceval attended the House of Commons infrequently, concentrating on his legal career to obtain the necessary money to support a large family. When he did attend he was not at first a success. In court he could deliver his thoroughly prepared briefs to a captive audience whereas in Parliament he was shouted down and forced to extemporise. Such experiences left him stuttering and stammering. But Perceval was a worker by temperament and circumstance, and he had acquired a leech-like tenacity, probably more through the circumstance of having to earn a living than from inherent character. During Addington's brief reign as Prime Minister, it was chiefly he who defended the shaky administration with a mounting skill and confidence. It was during Addington's tenure of office that he was offered, and accepted, first the post of Solicitor-General, then of Attorney-General. He continued to hold the latter post in Pitt's last administration.

When Pitt died in 1806, Perceval had built up a solid reputation, as both lawyer and politician. (In the former capacity he was extraordinarily successful, earning 5,000 guineas a year at his peak.) Generally his reputation was solid. His private life was exemplary. He was a devoted father and husband, and unlike many of his parliamentary and legal colleagues he neither gambled nor drank. He had demonstrated his soundness on the entwined subject of the Constitution and the

Church of England and on the subject of the French war. But he had also shown that he could fight for an unpopular view if he believed in it, and that he was nobody's puppet. As Attorney-General he had refused to equate the Government with the masters in the growing volume of trades union disputes. He had sponsored a Bill to alleviate the horrors of the convict passage to New South Wales, and he had been a consistent supporter of Wilberforce in his anti-slavery campaign.

The quality that was increasingly impressing his contemporaries was his integrity. When bribery and corruption were such integral parts of the power structure, a man who was relatively indifferent to the lure of money and position in return for vote or support was exceptional, but useful. With Perceval's relative disinterest in patronage went a positive distaste for intrigue which again was useful for those manipulating the eternally shifting sands of parliamentary alliance. Once Perceval committed himself to a man and his policies, it was a safe assumption that his allegiance would be retained, as it had been by his first patron and hero, Pitt.

Perceval's unusual qualities of industry, integrity, loyalty and commitment were based on the fact that he was of an emergent species. He was a professional in the last full tide of the amateur, a man who got on with the job in dedicated, earnest fashion when to be seen to be earnest or dedicated was regarded as un-English and un-gentlemanly. Perceval can be viewed as an early Victorian, a herald of a new approach to the business of governing the country. However, this was only in respect of his approach to earning a living and concentrating on the job. In other ways he remained solidly eighteenth-century. He had no sympathy with or understanding of the ideas that had already germinated and were increasingly to preoccupy his descendants. He did not believe in corporate responsibility for the less fortunate members of society or that the Government should interfere in trade, industry, education or any facet of the average citizen's life. For him, as for many others, there was an ordained hierarchy. Some were born rich, more were born poor, a few intelligent, the majority stupid. He believed that one should be personally kind and considerate, and accept responsibility for one's immediate inferiors; but to contemplate interfering by legislation in the way a man conducted his estate or factory, to consider upsetting the preordained natural structure of life, was both dangerous and sacriligious.

Despite the King's approval and the promises of parliamentary support, it was with extreme difficulty that Perceval formed a government. MPs might in theory be prepared to accept him as the least objectionable candidate of ability but in practice few of any calibre were willing to serve under him. Canning refused, certain Perceval could not function without him; the small band of Canningites therefore also refused; Castlereagh held aloof; Addington, now Lord Sidmouth, refused; and he failed to enlist the Whig support of Grey or Grenville. But eventually Perceval succeeded in filling his vacancies, his strongest ministers being Lord Wellesley at the Foreign Office, Lord Liverpool at the War Office and Lord Eldon as Lord Chancellor. However, in the first week of its life Perceval's administration was defeated four times, and Canning was not alone in considering him the most compromise of candidates and his ministry the most stop-gap of measures.

The problems facing Perceval as he became Prime Minister and First Lord of the Treasury were daunting. Britain had already been at war with France, apart from the brief respite of the Treaty of Amiens, for seventeen years. The economy was consequently stretched to its limits. In fact he assumed office at a moment when trade was enjoying a boom because of the opening of the South American markets, but this boom proved as temporary as the Peace of Amiens. Behind him, and mountingly ahead of him, stretched the adverse effects of Napoleon's Berlin and Milan decrees which had closed continental markets to British goods; the equally adverse effects of the retaliatory British Orders in Council which had imposed a blockade on Napoleon's Europe; and the closing of the United States markets by the Americans, who had become entangled in the European embargoes and sanctions.

As a result of the trade war, large sections of the population had already suffered greatly, no sections more disastrously than the new manufacturing districts in the North and Midlands. It was these areas that were also, obviously, bearing the brunt of the Industrial Revolution. But that there had been any sort of revolution was scarcely recognised. The effects of a changing life-style, a booming birthrate, the new concentrations of population, the inevitably new relationships between masters and men, the shifts of wealth and emphasis, were being largely ignored. The country was still being ruled by its old system or lack of system; a totally unrepresentative Parliament, an anomalous jumble of local government, a creed of vague paternalism based on a policy of *laissez-faire* and non-interference by the State.

The problems of the year 1809 would have daunted a better man than Spencer Perceval. On the one hand there was an apparently endless, economy-draining war that had to be fought to a conclusion; on the other hand there was a divided, restless, distressed country. Moreover, as Perceval assumed office, the consequences of unplanned industrialisation allied to the economic stresses of the French war were patently building to a head that could burst at any moment. It was not expected that he would long survive such a combination of problems and pressures.

But Perceval astonished everybody, initially by remaining in office longer than the predicted few months, then by surmounting a succession of difficult or potentially disastrous situations that should in theory, without doubt, have toppled him. He survived George III's ultimate descent into madness and the passing of the Regency Act, the latter of which events should definitely in theory have removed him from office. The newly empowered Prince Regent was supposed to be a friend both of Canning and the Whigs, and furthermore Perceval had earlier alienated the Regent by defending his wife, Caroline, in the 'Delicate Affair' of her supposed pregnancy. But Perceval's tenacity won the day, and the Prince Regent did not dismiss him. He went on to survive the disastrous economic effects of the collapse of the briefly opened South American markets, followed by the United States Non-Intercourse Act which finally closed their markets to British goods and thereby plunged the manufacturing districts into even greater distress. He survived the Luddite Riots, those potentially so dangerous eruptions of the long-simmering discontent which first surfaced early in 1811 and were still flaring at the time of his death. He survived a monetary crisis involving the mounting National Debt, the absence of a gold standard and the value of paper money. And he survived the resignation of Lord Wellesley, the elder brother of the Duke of Wellington, from the Cabinet.

Part of the reason why Perceval not only survived, but was beginning to show signs of prospering when the assassin's bullet cut short his life, lay in the qualities that had led him unspectacularly but doggedly upwards: the determination, the dedication, the professionalism, the will and ability to fight that so many had underestimated. Grattan said, 'He is not a ship of the line, but he carries many guns, is tight-built, and is out in all weathers.' He also survived and started to prosper for the very reason that he was *not* 'a ship of the line', because he was a mediocrity when placed alongside the foremost politicians or statesmen.

Ideally, the times needed a man of genius – and on the military front they got one in Arthur Wellesley, soon to be created Duke of Wellington. But torn by internal dissensions and jealousies, with the shadow of the French Revolution looming over them, fearful that a similar event might happen in England, the ruling classes did not really want a man of genius on the home front. They wanted somebody who would not rock the boat. Perceval might be castigated as 'a little man with a little mind' by a few, but for the majority of those wielding power in and out of Parliament he fought for what was desired – victory over Napoleon; and delivered what was required – a preservation of the *status quo*. Certainly Perceval endured because of his own tenacity and determination, but the strength of his reactionary beliefs, reflecting the mood of the ruling classes, played its part in his survival.

The strength of Perceval's beliefs has since led him to be listed among the most repressive and reactionary of nineteenth-century prime ministers. It is true that he sat on the keg of gunpowder known as the Luddite Riots and did nothing other than have them put down by the use of troops, transportation to New South Wales and executions. Retrospectively, the eruption of Luddism is the most crucial event of Perceval's tenure of office. At the time, despite the French revolutionary fears, it was remarkable how little governmental interest was shown in the riots. The surprising indifference arose basically because of the lack of centralised government in England. The Home Office obtained information and received cries for help from the local magistrates in the disturbed areas; but these same magistrates were empowered to call for military aid without sanction from Westminster; there was no central body collating the extent of the disturbances. The fact that 12,000 troops were used in suppressing the Luddite Riots – more than the future Duke of Wellington had at his disposal in Spain – was never commented upon, if indeed realised. Further, although it was appreciated that distress caused discontent, it was felt there was nothing the Government could do to ameliorate conditions. Time, the recovery of trade, sensible arrangements by the masters, would eventually effect improvements. In the meantime the only course of action for the good of the country was to suppress the discontent as evinced in the machine-breaking and general rioting, in piecemeal fashion when and where it occurred.

The causes of Luddism – why the riots were occurring – never impinged upon Perceval. He never began to appreciate that the severe distress was linked to the growing dependence of an industrial economy on the reaction of world markets. Nor did he realise that Luddism had much deeper roots, that the breakdown of the old quasi-paternalist system and the onset of industrialisation demanded a new approach to the country's government, political and social as well as economic. But then the causes of Luddism did not penetrate the minds of other members of the Cabinet or of Parliament or of the ruling classes as a whole. Again Perceval reflected the prevalent atmosphere. Some governmental action was taken against the riots – frame-breaking became an offence punishable by death early in 1812. But on the whole, ironically if disastrously for the starving stockingers of Nottinghamshire, the hosiers of Leicestershire, the hand-loom weavers of Lancashire, and the croppers of Yorkshire, Perceval and the country bobbed up from the shock-waves of Luddism because nobody in power took them too seriously. The outbreaks had to be put down, and if some men had to be hanged that was a necessary measure 'called for by the circumstances of the time' (as Perceval had earlier said of Pitt's Gagging Acts). If 12,000 troops were required in the process that was a surprising but again unfortunate necessity. It was ostensibly on the grounds that Perceval was starving his brother of sufficient troops and supplies to conduct the Peninsular campaign that Lord Wellesley resigned. But in the resignation there was no hint that one of the reasons Wellington was being starved of troops and supplies was because they were tied up on home duty, suppressing the Luddite Riots.

Had a man of greater vision, comprehension or social conscience been Prime Minister at the period, the sufferings of the new working classes might have been less prolonged, the future social struggle less traumatic, but such men are not thick upon the ground in any era and they were not conspicuous in the early 1800s. Any man who had grasped the implications of industrialisation, and had been able to read the storm warnings of Luddism clearly, would also have needed to have been a master politician and tactician to have carried extensive remedial legislation through a Parliament consisting of country gentlemen and the scions and protégés of the great landed families. Perceval obviously did not possess such attributes. Given the existing circumstances and political and social climate, his basic achievement was to have survived. Perhaps his second achievement was to have pumped sufficient troops and supplies into Spain to have allowed Wellington to consolidate his position. Whatever Lord Wellesley claimed when he resigned, between 1809 and 1812 the Peninsular campaign more than got off the ground. Napoleon's troops were for the first time defeated on land by a British-led force, and the seeds of victory were planted. After two decades of war there was little likelihood of serious attention being given to the distress at home until Napoleon had been finally defeated. Of its own volition the war had become the first priority, and Perceval was probably right to pursue it as such. Up-ending the priorities at this stage could have created even greater problems.

Allowing that the war had to be fought to the bitter end, Perceval could and should have taken some remedial measures at home. His record as Prime Minister was essentially negative. But if he had a little mind it was not a mean one, and he did much to encourage young politicians – Palmerston and the young Peel were among his notable protégés.

Had Perceval not hung on, would the situation have been any better for the distressed masses? If Perceval had fallen within the predicted few months would a man with a broader, more comprehending mind have been likely to assume office? The answer is almost certainly, no; and Perceval's successor, Lord Liverpool, did not noticeably change tactics or alter policies. But when Lord Liverpool became Prime Minister there was greater political stability than there had been three years previously. This surprising stability, however unsurprisingly repressive it was, can be attributed to Perceval's capacity for survival. If his Government had collapsed within the predicted few months, the consequences would undoubtedly have been a succession of squabbling ministries. Confidence abroad would have been undermined, trade would have slumped deeper into the mire, the task of rallying the anti-Napoleonic forces in Europe would have been more difficult than it was, and the war would have dragged on longer than it did. The alternative was home-brewed revolution, a doubtfully beneficial occurrence when successful. As the forces of radicalism and discontent lacked a great leader in the same measure as did the ruling classes, anarchy or greater repression would have been the more likely outcome. It can be said that Perceval's negative, repressive three-year tenure of office provided a framework for stability.

Despite the repression, it was not a starving weaver or a revolutionary idealist who cut short the life of the Prime Minister who had survived against the odds. It was a man called John Bellingham. He had been arrested and imprisoned while trading in Russia and when eventually released became convinced that the British Government owed him financial redress for his sufferings. Failing to obtain satisfaction from various ministers, he transferred his obsessional sense of grievance to the Prime Minister. On 11 May 1812, Bellingham stationed himself in the lobby of the House of Commons, a revolver hidden in the specially tailored pocket of his coat. The only connection with the economic distress that had surrounded Perceval's administration was tangential and unrelated to the assassin. When Bellingham shot him, Perceval was on his way to attend a session of the committee that had finally been appointed to inquire into the adverse trade effects of the Orders in Council. Bellingham shot at point-blank range, and Perceval died almost immediately.

Bellingham was brought to trial on 15 May. His counsel's plea of insanity was rejected and on 18 May he was hanged. His counsel's was one of the very few voices to protest at the unprecedented speed of the proceedings. Perceval was eulogised as 'the model of a high-minded, high-principled, truthful, generous gentleman, *sans peur et sans reproche*', and Parliament voted large sums of money to support his widow and family. There were some murmurings about a revolutionary plot, and some vague attempts to tie up the assassination with the Luddite Riots. On the whole life in the country continued as before, singularly unaffected by the first – and hopefully the last – assassination of a British prime minister. That life did continue without interruption, that neither the Radicals nor the distressed masses utilised the melodramatic event, can be viewed as proof of the stabilising effect of Perceval's capacity to survive, or evidence of the law-abiding nature British discontent had already acquired.

BIBLIOGRAPHY

A Full Report of the Trial of John Bellingham (London, 1812)
Darvall, F. O., *Popular Disturbance and Public Order in Regency England* (Oxford University Press, 1934)
Gray, Denis, *Spencer Perceval* (Manchester University Press, 1963)
Treherne, Philip, *The Rt Hon. Spencer Perceval* (London, 1909)
Walpole, Sir Spencer, *The Life of the Rt Hon. Spencer Perceval* (London, 1874)
Williams, C. V., *The Life and Administration of the Rt Hon. Spencer Perceval* (London, 1872)

18

THE EARL OF LIVERPOOL

BY

NORMAN GASH

Robert Banks Jenkinson, born 7 June 1770, son of Charles Jenkinson (created Baron Hawkesbury 1786 and Earl of Liverpool 1796). Educated at Charterhouse and Christ Church, Oxford. Married (1) 1794 Lady Louisa Hervey and (2) 1822 Mary Chester. MP for Appleby 1790–96, Rye 1796–1803; India Board 1793; Master of Mint 1796; Foreign Secretary 1801–3; called to the Lords as Baron Hawkesbury 1803; Home Secretary 1804–6, 1807–9; succeeded as 2nd Earl of Liverpool 1808; Secretary for War and Colonies 1809–12; Prime Minister 1812–27. Died 4 December 1828.

LORD LIVERPOOL

Who was prime minister at the time of the Battle of Waterloo? The question is rarely asked. Robert Banks Jenkinson, second Earl of Liverpool, is one of the least known and most underrated prime ministers in British history. When his name is recalled, it is more often in the depersonalised phrase 'the Liverpool administration', a label of a government rather than the evocation of a personality. Even contemporaries felt this anonymity. The savage caricatures of the period seized on Castlereagh, Sidmouth and Eldon, hardly ever on Liverpool. When his premiership ended abruptly in 1827, the dominant feeling was not a sense of personal loss but a realisation that an era in British politics had come to an end. Liverpool had been Prime Minister for fifteen years, longer than all his successors and all but one of his predecessors. He had gathered round him an unsurpassed array of talent. Castlereagh and Canning were his Foreign Secretaries; Wellington was a member of his Cabinet; Peel was his Home Secretary; Huskisson his President of the Board of Trade; Robinson – 'Prosperity Robinson' – his Chancellor of the Exchequer. Of the next ten prime ministers, six had served his administration.

His early career seemed almost a curriculum for the premiership. His father had held office under Grafton, North and Pitt, made a position for himself as one of George III's most trusted political servants, and was rewarded with an earldom before the end of the century. The education of his eldest son – Charterhouse, Oxford, and the Grand Tour – was conventional, though the additional grounding in French, history, mathematics and political economy prescribed by his father opened up to young Jenkinson a wider intellectual horizon. The man who told the House of Lords in 1815 that he 'had been bred up in a school where he had been taught highly to value the commercial interest', and the King in 1824 that the steam engine was 'the greatest and most useful invention of modern times', possessed from the start a more open mind than most of the squirarchy from which his family came. Elected for a pocket borough in 1790 before he came of age, he was appointed by Pitt to the India Board three years later. After that he was never out of office, except for the thirteen months of the Grenville administration in 1806–7. By 1809 he had held all three secretaryships – Foreign, Home and War – and was the anchor man of any ministry formed on Pittite–Tory principles. Only accident and his own native caution had kept him from even greater eminence. George III had wanted him to be chief minister in 1806 and again in 1807. If in 1809 Perceval and Canning could have agreed to serve together under a peer, Liverpool would have been their choice. Few prime ministers have made such a measured ascent to supreme office or been prepared for it by such comprehensive experience. Nothing could have been more natural after Perceval's assassination in 1812 than the view of the Cabinet that if they were to continue, it must be under his leadership.

Long before that date age and office had enabled Liverpool to master his highly-strung temperament. The awkward, bookish undergraduate, alternating between shyness and pomposity, had turned into a modest, conciliatory politician. The irresolution and procrastination that marked his early career had been replaced by calmness and resolution. The lanky, shambling, melancholy figure depicted in Hickel's picture of the House of Commons in 1793 was becoming the stout, serious, ungraceful and reflective man of the Lawrence painting in the National Portrait Gallery. The public did not realise, as his colleagues did, that the imperturbability and courtesy of his outward manner concealed a tense personality. He had, wrote his biographer C. D. Yonge, 'an anxious temperament'. His patronage secretary Charles Arbuthnot, who knew him more intimately than possibly any man, spoke of 'a most nervous mind'. Consciousness of impending difficulties tended to throw him into what Huskisson called his 'grand fidgetts'. His agitation over the Cabinet changes in 1822 at some stages, reported Canning, 'amounted almost to illness'. He was profoundly distressed by personal conflict and unkindness. He had few relaxations; he lacked sociability. He had, wrote Henry Hobhouse, Under-secretary of State at the Home Office, 'fewer personal friends and less quality for conciliating men's affections than perhaps any Minister that ever lived'. Politically he was always a solitary person. 'I feel,' he wrote in 1820 in a moment of depression, 'I have few, very few publick friends in the world.' To his wife, who died in 1821 after twenty-seven years of married life, he was devotedly attached; but it was perhaps indicative of his need for domestic comfort that he married again almost immediately. Hardly any of his correspondence with his wives exists because he was hardly ever separated from them.

To his public life, however, he brought qualities which in aggregate few prime ministers have equalled. In grasp of principles, mastery of detail, discernment of means, and judgement of individuals he was almost faultless. Cautious and unhurried in weighing a situation, he was prompt and decisive when the time came for action. In debate he was not only informed, lucid, and objective, but conspicuously honest. It was said that you could make a speech against him and leave the Chamber, knowing that in his reply he would state your arguments as fairly as yourself and probably more clearly. Though his colleagues might occasionally disagree with him, he never lost their respect or their trust. He repaid them in full. He never dismissed a minister; he was never ungrateful or disloyal. Kind by temperament, he had an instinctive tact in dealing with others. His conciliatory manner smoothed away innumerable personal difficulties. He was a man whom it was almost impossible to dislike; and he himself could find something to like in almost everyone. Few, for example, who had to work with Wellington's vain and pompous brother, Lord Wellesley, had much good to say of him. But, Liverpool wrote characteristically to Arbuthnot in 1823, 'the truth is, he is a great *compound*, and if one is to have the use of him, it must be by making as little as possible of some of his absurdities. . . . A man may be wise in some things & most foolish in others.'

Yet intellectually he could be as hard as rock. 'We wish,' he wrote to Castlereagh, when discussing plans for the disposal of Napoleon after Waterloo, 'that the King of France would hang or shoot Buonaparte as the best termination of the business.' He refused to interfere with Ney's execution since he thought that Louis would never be safe on his throne 'till he has dared to spill traitors' blood'. In the less sanguinary field of British domestic politics he did not hesitate to make an example when clemency would have been taken as weakness. The Earl Fitzwilliam was removed from his lord lieutenancy for identifying himself with radical protests after Peterloo; and the riotous scenes which turned the Queen's funeral in 1821 into a political demonstration were answered by the dismissals of an Army officer and a metropolitan magistrate. On patronage, which he administered with puritanical integrity, he could be immovable even against the highest suitors. He rejected Wellington's solicitations for a bishopric for his brother, a married clergyman living apart from his wife. He refused to allow Lord Conyngham, husband of the King's favourite, to be made Lord Chamberlain, or to sanction a canonry at Windsor for Sumner, a curate who tutored the Conyngham children. When in 1823 Arbuthnot warned him of the royal displeasure and urged him to conciliate the Court by making Knighton, the King's private secretary, a Privy Councillor, Liverpool's reply was brusque and uncompromising: 'The K. will find himself very much mistaken if he supposes that if he dismissed me . . . Canning, Peel or anyone of my colleagues would remain behind. . . . Let the K. take care that he does not make the close of a reign which has been hitherto most glorious, & on the whole most prosperous, stormy and miserable.'

As Prime Minister he maintained the integrity both of his own office and of the parliamentary Constitution over which he presided. When Castlereagh, despite his description of the Holy Alliance as a piece of sublime mysticism and nonsense, suggested that the Prince Regent might sign the document as an 'autographic avowal of sentiment between him and the sovereigns, his allies', Liverpool was adamant. For the Prince to sign the Act of Accession, he wrote back, would be 'inconsistent with all the forms and principles of our Government'. Within the Cabinet he permitted no cabals or divisions. When Wellesley complained in 1812 of not having the weight he expected in the Government, Liverpool told his brother that Wellesley on his side had failed in his obligations as a colleague: 'Government through a Cabinet is necessarily a Government *inter pares* in which every man must expect to have his opinions and despatches canvassed.' Eleven years later when the alliance with the Grenvillites had been cemented, Liverpool flatly refused to allow Buckingham to enter the Cabinet as their representative: 'I cannot bear the idea of the Cabinet being a connection of little knots of parties.' On the other hand he maintained stubbornly the right of the prime minister to choose the men he thought fittest for any particular post. When the King in 1821 seemed to be putting an absolute ban on Canning's return to the Cabinet, Liverpool was prepared to use the ultimate sanction at his disposal. 'Upon such a principle, so applied,' he wrote to Arbuthnot, 'I cannot agree to remain at the head of the Government.'

The traditional interpretation of Liverpool's administration divided it into two contrasting phases: 'reactionary Toryism', dominated by Castlereagh, Sidmouth, Eldon, and Vansittart; and 'liberal Toryism', dominated by Canning, Peel, Huskisson and Robinson. The ministerial reconstruction of 1821-2 marked the division and provided the explanation. On this analysis Liverpool's role was that of a neutral chairman, taking his colour from his colleagues. Such a view will hardly survive even a cursory examination. Liverpool was never a mere chairman presiding over a Cabinet of superior talents. Disraeli's disparaging epithet of the 'Arch-mediocrity' was as shallow as most of his historical judgements. The precise influence of a prime minister over his colleagues is always difficult to assess. But it is clear that the guiding lines of policy were always firmly in Liverpool's hands, in consultation with an inner ring of ministers: Castlereagh and later Canning, the successive leaders in the House of Commons; Bathurst, the influential elder statesman of the Cabinet; and Wellington, whose unique standing in politics transcended any particular office. Liverpool himself kept a close supervision of all the main departments, including the Foreign Office; and in matters of trade and finance was always the dominating figure. Commenting on the new Chancellor of the Exchequer in 1823 Wynn observed casually that 'Robinson will be a decided improvement on poor Van, both in manner and popularity with the House, but as to measures, Liverpool must of course give the orders, and he obey'. To make the Cabinet reconstruction of 1821-2 the dividing-line in the history of the Liverpool administration is to distort it in another way. It leaves in the background the first four years of his premiership, which were occupied in winning the war against Napoleon. Lord Liverpool is unique among British prime ministers in that he not only led his country to victory in the greatest and most expensive war it had ever fought, but grappled with post-war economic and social difficulties of a kind that were not to recur for another century, and finally won through to years of prosperity and social stability.

The achievement is more remarkable since Liverpool had to face a Parliament which had lost most of the apparatus of eighteenth-century administrative influence without gaining the discipline of nineteenth-century party organisation. The regular Government supporters in the Commons were hardly more numerous than the permanent Opposition, and the balance was held by a heterogeneous mass of Independents whose support fluctuated with the measures proposed and the mood of the country. For most of his premiership Liverpool had to reckon with an unstable, critical and occasionally hostile House of Commons. The ministry itself had a sickly birth. It could only exist at all by agreeing to shelve the major issue of domestic policy, Catholic emancipation; and for a while it seemed a caretaker government, holding office while the grandees in opposition considered on what terms they might consent to take power. Only the necessities of war enabled Liverpool to survive his first testing years. It was an additional misfortune that the administration was particularly weak in the Commons. In the absence of able and experienced politicians, Liverpool had (as he modestly wrote) 'no recourse but to bring forward the most promising of the young men . . . I should be most happy to see another Pitt amongst them. I would willingly resign the government into his hands for I am fully aware of the importance of the minister being if possible in the House of Commons.'

Fortunately for the ministry, Liverpool's four years as war leader saw the military success that had defied his predecessors. The Spanish revolt in 1808 for the first time enabled British sea power to be translated into effective operations on the continental mainland. But everything depended on the ability of the Government to discern and their will to exploit the opportunity. As soon as he became Secretary for War in 1809 Liverpool concentrated on success in the Peninsula. 'I laid it down as a principle,' he wrote, 'that if the war was to be continued in Portugal and Spain, we ought not to suffer any part of our efforts to be directed to other objects.' As prime minister three years later he maintained the Peninsular strategy unflinchingly against the defeatist criticisms of the Whig Opposition. From the start he realised that in Spain, unlike the states of central Europe, Napoleon was faced with the opposition of an entire people. He was equally quick to appreciate the strategic effect of Napoleon's disastrous expedition to Russia. 'The Spanish War,' he wrote to the British Ambassador in Moscow in 1812, 'is the only national war in which Buonaparte has been engaged before the present. The Russians have therefore the example of Spain and the success of Spain before their eyes.' To his own commander in the field he gave unwavering political support, unprecedented financial backing, and the widest latitude of action. The alliance of Wellington, Liverpool, and Bathurst, his successor at the War Department, was in fact the most efficient combination the country produced in twenty years of conflict.

But the financial cost had been enormous. After Waterloo the Government faced a House of Commons clamouring for instant tax reduction and a public that complained of the inflation of the war while resenting the economic adjustments to the peace. 'The country at the moment is peace mad,' the Prime Minister wrote to Castlereagh early in 1815, 'Many of our best friends think of nothing but the reduction of taxes and low establishments.' The refusal of Parliament in 1816 to renew the Income Tax left the ministers to meet an expenditure of £30 million with a revenue of £12 million and made inevitable the ruinous policy of borrowing and raids on the Sinking Fund from which they did not extricate themselves for another five years. It was not a defeat for the Government; only for its policy. The independent MPs did not wish to displace Liverpool and his colleagues. But they were determined to set limits to government expenditure and insist on administrative economies beyond anything that the ministers themselves thought reasonable or even practicable. In 1817 and 1818 the Cabinet found itself fighting desperately not merely to preserve a minimum revenue for its ordinary needs but to safeguard the basic administrative structure of the State. Savage reductions in military and naval establishments, a drastic over-haul of civil offices, a cut in the Civil List, and a 10 per cent deduction from official salaries in 1817 merely fed the appetite for economy in the country without curing the Government's weakness in Parliament.

What paradoxically helped to maintain the ministers in office was the widespread disorder and violence, and the semi-seditious activities, which marked the economic depression of the post-war period. Liverpool himself was convinced that what confronted the Government was a dangerous combination of economic distress and revolutionary doc-trine which would not have emerged but for the example of the French Revolution. In one who had witnessed the storming of the Bastille in 1789 it was not a surprising attitude; and it was shared by most of his class. It is easy in retrospect to criticise the Government for reacting too strongly to casual disorder and for believing too easily in the exist-ence of a genuine revolutionary spirit in the country. But the emblems and vocabulary, and occasionally the actions, of many extreme Radicals after Waterloo gave colour to that belief. The Government had no organised police at their disposal; they found it difficult to get exact information; and they were dependent on the support of an unpaid, amateur magistracy. Nevertheless, unlike his more alarmist advisers, Liverpool always tried to distinguish between distress and agitation. The repressive legislation passed in 1817 and 1819 was only that which he thought any responsible government ought to undertake; and it was based in good faith on such evidence as the Government could collect.

If he erred, he did so in good company; and the House of Commons supported him with sweeping majorities. His prime object was to isolate the agitators, support the magistracy, and protect law-abiding subjects from intimidation. He was defending, not bending, the Constitution. 'Fear of the mob,' he told the House of Lords, 'invariably led to arbitrary government.' It was this fear he wished to dissipate; arbitrary government he wished to avoid. Moderate firmness at the start would, in his view, prevent more brutal measures later. Like most Englishmen of his generation, he had learnt from France how easily timidity of authority in the face of disorder can lead to anarchy.

For a prime minister who sought to separate economic grievance from political agitation, there was a further handicap. The accepted doctrines of political economy – and Liverpool was above all a political economist – taught that government could do little to remove the causes or alleviate the effects of economic distress. 'There was a doctrine that could not be too often or too strongly impressed on the people of this country,' he observed bravely in 1819. 'They ought to be taught that evils inseparable from the state of things should not be charged on any government.' Even if government sought to intervene, he believed that the effects would at best be short-lived; at worst positively harmful. 'I am afraid,' he wrote, 'that government or Parliament never meddle with these matters at all but they do harm more or less.' Nevertheless, though imbued like most educated men of his generation with *laissez-faire* philosophy, he was not a doctrinaire and was prepared to break with theory if circumstances made it necessary. The piecemeal measures passed by the Government in 1817, including a Poor Employment Act sanctioning state loans for promoting useful works, at least indicated the Government's awareness of the social problem and their readiness to consider short-term palliatives. To the working classes Liverpool's attitude was paternalistic. His million-pound Church Building Act in 1818 was the first time for a century that the central government had acknowledged direct responsibility for the spiritual needs of the growing urban population. He supported efforts to improve educational facilities for the poor. He favoured a reform of the Game Laws and welcomed the elder Peel's Factory Bill to protect children in the cotton industry.

Liverpool in fact was a conservative statesman in the fundamental sense. He wished to avoid organic change by pursuing administrative reform. But he was neither a bigot nor a reactionary. He was opposed to Catholic emancipation because, as he put it with unusual bluntness in 1825, 'the Protestant gave an entire allegiance to his sovereign; the Catholic gave a divided one'. But the issue for him was political, not religious: the future of the Irish Union. The previous year, when Lansdowne had introduced Bills to enfranchise English Roman Catholics and admit them to the magistracy, he had both spoken and voted in favour. In the same spirit, though he refused to repeal the Test and Corporation Acts, he had passed a Relief Bill for dissenters in 1812 which was hailed by many of them as a second Toleration Act. 'An enlarged and liberal toleration,' he told the Lords, 'was the best security to the Established Church.' He disliked any general scheme of parliamentary reform but was prepared to support the disfranchisement of individual corrupt constituencies. In such cases he preferred to transfer the seats not to the populous towns, whose representatives were 'least likely to be steadily attached to the good order of society', but to the counties. The county MPs, he observed to his Cabinet, 'if not generally the ablest members in the House, are certainly those who have the greatest stake in the country and may be trusted for the most part in periods of difficulty and danger.'

Yet all this, as he realised, was only scratching the face of the main problem. The real solution lay in a return to general prosperity which would benefit poor as well as rich. By 1819, dissatisfied at the slow recovery of the national economy, Liverpool was ready to give a lead to the country. The 1819 Currency Commission and the return to the gold standard provided the necessary financial stability and Vansittart's budget of that year marked a real attempt to end the chronic post-war insolvency and initiate a constructive financial policy. More would have been done in 1820 had not the Government been paralysed by the Queen's divorce. After that the work was resumed and gained momentum with the ministerial changes of 1821–2. The importance of those changes has, however, been both exaggerated and misinterpreted. They were in fact part of a regular process of renewal which had been both checked and made more urgent by the depressing effects on the Government of the Queen's trial. The considerations that weighed with Liverpool were personal rather than political. He wished to improve the parliamentary efficiency of the ministry, strengthen the House of Commons front bench, and deny the King the nucleus of an alternative administration. But the shift of policy had already started. The substitution of Canning merely meant the continuation of the new line in foreign affairs which had been emerging before Castlereagh's death. The first of Peel's legal reforms had been prepared under Sidmouth. Before Robinson became Chancellor of the Exchequer, Liverpool and Vansittart were already laying the foundation of the new financial policy and Wallace, the able Vice-president of the Board of Trade, was initiating the changes in the commercial code later identified with Huskisson.

What was cardinal to the changed direction of government in the 1820s was the great commercial policy which had been signalled in 1819 and received its first authoritative exposition in Liverpool's speech on free trade in 1820. His purpose was threefold: to move from a high tariff to a low one; to modify the rigidity of the Navigation Acts in favour of a more flexible mercantile system; and to substitute for the monopolistic Corn Law of 1815 a protection that would recognise agriculture as one, but only one, of the great interests of the country. The essence of the new approach was that it took into account not only the needs of the producer but the interests of the consumer. What the farmers needed, Liverpool told the House of Lords in 1822, was not high protection but a market. The low prices of which they complained, he added pointedly, did in fact benefit the great majority of the people. Before the end of his ministry he was planning the significant modification of the Corn Laws which issued in the Act of 1828. Even in 1825, with the confidence of success, he was able to enunciate with authority 'the general principle of free trade as the great foundation of national prosperity'.

For the 'unprecedented, unparalleled prosperity', as he described it, in which the country was basking in 1825, Liverpool could legitimately take much personal credit. The new commercial policy of the 1820s owed everything to government initiative, nothing to external pressure or parliamentary tactics. Had he been given time and opportunity, he would have gone further. By 1824 he was convinced that tax reduction had gone too far and what was needed was a substantial surplus to make possible further tariff reforms. If ministers did what they ought to do, he told Canning ('Do not be alarmed, I am not going to propose it') they would increase direct taxation by £2 million and reduce tariffs by double that amount. He had always regretted the abolition of the Income Tax; nothing that could be substituted for it, in his view, was 'so equal and just'. But it was not until after his death that ministers could even talk of reviving it; and not until 1842 that Peel was able to accomplish it. At this, as at almost every other point, Liverpool was faced with unsurmountable limitations on his freedom of action.

Within the Government his difficulties were ironically greater than before. The Queen's divorce case in 1820 had been forced on the Cabinet by the intransigence of both parties. Once the peaceable compromise for which he had worked proved unattainable, Liverpool's conduct of the Bill in the House of Lords was exemplary in its fairness and dignity. But the collapse of the proceedings created a resentment in the King which threatened the actual existence of the Government. Only the lack of a congenial alternative deterred George IV from inaugurating his reign with a change of ministry. Much of his anger was directed against Liverpool personally and the friction continued in later years. Within the Cabinet the old harmony broke down after 1820 and was never restored. 'Ours is not, nor never has been a *controversial* Cabinet,' said Wellington in 1821; but everything seemed to change with the return of Canning. There were conflicts over his flamboyant diplomacy and irritation at Liverpool's apparent subservience to his old college friend. Many of his colleagues thought Canning was a disloyal intriguer; and though their suspicions were usually baseless, the distrust which Canning engendered was a political reality. It was only Liverpool who kept the discordant elements together.

Liverpool's partiality derived, however, as much from intellectual conviction as personal friendship. On foreign policy there was a clear identity of minds. Though Liverpool had admired and trusted Castlereagh – 'the right arm of the administration', as he called him – he himself was always insular rather than European. His constant argument from 1815 onwards was that Britain could not enter into further engagements with her wartime allies and that the nature of British parliamentary government put it in a class apart from the autocracies of Europe. One of the difficulties with Wellington was that he was heir to the Castlereagh tradition. 'He is rather *more continental*,' Liverpool wrote in 1822, 'than we either are or ought to be *permanently*.' His support for Canning's South American policy was based on an appreciation of the commercial advantages for Britain; and his forceful reaction to the threatened Spanish attack on Portugal in 1826 showed how far he was from being a reluctant follower of his Foreign Secretary. Nevertheless, Canning, by his restlessness, his badgering of the Prime Minister, and his advocacy of Catholic claims, was a continual drain on Liverpool's emotional strength. Canning's move in 1825 to make the Catholic question no longer an open one almost broke up the Cabinet; and only the reluctance of his 'Catholic' colleagues to support him saved the day.

As it was the Prime Minister felt that the end of his ministry was approaching. Early in 1827 he told Arbuthnot that he had made up his mind to retire and leave to others the inevitable settlement of Catholic claims. By that date he was a tired and prematurely aged man. The strains of the 1820–2 period had brought him to a pitch of nervous frustration from which he never fully recovered. The irritability, pessimism, and unusual bursts of temper noted by observers in those years were probably the marks of physical deterioration. Increasingly he began to speak of his declining health and inability to continue in office. 'It is not affectation in me to say that I am ill in body, as well as in mind,' he wrote to Arbuthnot in June 1821. It is possible that it was at this time that he suffered the organic heart damage indicated by his later symptoms. Lassitude and a disquietingly low pulse rate caused him to take a cure at Bath in 1824. At the end of 1826 renewed illness again turned his thoughts to resignation. His doctors sent him off for a month to Bath but the effects were brief. The stroke which in February 1827 ended his career was, as far as can be diagnosed, the result of a chronic hypertensive condition. He lingered on, a mental and physical wreck, until December 1828.

By that date he was already a figure of the past; and in a few more years a gulf seemed to have opened up between the Age of Reform and the Age of Peterloo. Yet the more the nineteenth century is put into perspective, the more significant does Liverpool's role appear. It was not merely that his political skill had kept an administration together so long or that his sheer professionalism as an administrator had enabled him to master all the diverse needs of government between 1812 and 1827. Even more important is that in the face of enormous practical difficulties he opened up the road along which early Victorian Britain was to travel with increasing certainty and profit in the next generation. The work of Peel's great ministry of 1841–6, for example, can only be appreciated when it is seen as a conscious resumption of the principles and policies initiated in 1819–27. Liverpool was the pioneer who prepared the ground and provided the training for his greatest pupil. In his emphasis on the need to promote general prosperity, in his insistence that agriculture and industry were not conflicting but interdependent interests, in his determination that executive government should follow a national and not a class policy, he laid down the maxims that Peel was to follow fifteen years later.

BIBLIOGRAPHY

Aspinall, A., *Correspondence of Charles Arbuthnot* (Camden series, lxv, 1941)
—, (ed.), *Letters of George IV* (3 vols, Cambridge, 1938)
Brock, W. R., *Lord Liverpool and Liberal Toryism, 1820–7* (Cambridge, 1941)
Buckingham, Duke of, *Court and Cabinets of the Regency* (2 vols, London, 1856)
—, *Court and Cabinets of George IV* (2 vols, London, 1859)
Petrie, C., *Lord Liverpool* (London, 1956)
Yonge, C. D., *Life of Lord Liverpool* (3 vols, London, 1868)

19

GEORGE CANNING

BY

ELIZABETH LONGFORD

George Canning, born 11 April 1770, only son of George Canning and Mary Anne, daughter of Jordan Costello. Educated at Eton and Christ Church, Oxford. Called to the Bar 1791. MP for Newport, Isle of Wight, 1794. Married Joan Scott (a wealthy heiress) 1800; four children of whom the third became Earl Canning, Governor-General of India. Foreign Secretary 1807. Fights duel with Castlereagh 1809. Rejected Foreign Office 1812; Ambassador to Lisbon 1814; Foreign Secretary 1822; Prime Minister and First Lord of the Treasury 1827. Died 8 August 1827.

GEORGE CANNING

Canning, like Anthony Eden, is a Prime Minister chiefly remembered for having been Foreign Secretary. To this paradox is added an enigma. Was he – would he have become – a great all-round statesman? For he succumbed to the illness which afflicted him throughout his brief premiership, and died at the politically youthful age of fifty-six.

A special dazzle still hangs about Canning, recognisable to this day. There is the Canning Club, to which Tories are proud to belong. He is seen, rightly or wrongly, as an innovator. He is looked to as the prophet of British nationalism. Because he was held to be 'of the people', and knew how to win popularity while never idolising the people, he is popular still.

George Canning was born in London on 11 April 1770, the same year as his future Cabinet colleagues, Henry Huskisson and Lord Liverpool; a year after Wellington, Castlereagh and Napoleon. His early childhood was passed in harsh circumstances. His father, who came from Northern Ireland, having quarrelled with his family, died in penury on 11 April 1771. His mother, also Irish, went on the stage to keep herself and married a villainous actor who set young George 'on the highroad to the gallows'. Rescued by his uncle, Stratford Canning, a City banker, George found himself enjoying an elitist education: preparatory school near Winchester, followed by Eton. He shone as a scholar, debater and model pupil. From the experiences of a childhood so nearly wrecked he must have gained his determination to succeed, and to succeed through the most single-minded dedication to hard work and what passed in those days for abstinence.

His uncle, being a prominent Whig, introduced him to Whig politicians like Burke and Fox, whose cause he ardently espoused. At Oxford he made friends with young Tories until, with the coming of the French Revolution, he was converted by William Pitt, the Prime Minister, to Toryism. As a frequenter of the London debating clubs, Canning was noted for his elegant figure, expressive face and air of perfect breeding. But his enemies would never accept him as a gentleman. The murk of his childhood stuck, down to the unprepossessing name of his second stepfather, a silk mercer called Hunn; for the rest, the man was just too sharp. He revelled in vituperation, invective and satire. In ridiculing the Philosophic Radicals of the 1790s, he threw off many verses which, though now rendered innocuous in the anthologies, were then the cause of much pain and anger:

> But of all plagues, good Heaven, thy wrath can send,
> Save, save, oh! save me from the *Candid Friend!*
> (*New Morality*)

Yet these 'candid friends' were the very Whigs whose principles Canning had once so volubly defended. Now he was excoriating them, together with the philosophy of the French Revolution, in a fortnightly publication, the *Anti-Jacobin*. Canning had done what Winston Churchill was to do: changed sides, not gravely like Mr Gladstone, but impudently, with wicked laughter. Young George, like young Winston, could be represented by critics as something of a bounder.

Canning entered Parliament for a Tory pocket borough in January 1794 and for two years supported Pitt and the war against France from the back benches. This entailed supporting the Aliens Act and the suspension of Habeas Corpus. It was observed that the youthful orator put on an 'air of surprise' when defending the indefensible. He was rewarded in 1796 with a government post: Under-Secretary at the Foreign Office. So successful was he that a leading Whig, the future Earl Grey, took to quitting the Chamber ostentatiously when Canning was up.

By 1800 Canning had also established his material and emotional life. He married Joan Scott, an heiress. The marriage was idyllic; indeed, but for this unruffled zone of happiness, he might not have lived as long as he did.

The delicate role he had to play as liaison officer between Pitt and Grenville (Foreign Secretary) aroused some suspicion. His refusal after Pitt retired to serve under Grenville and Charles James Fox in the coalition ministry of 'All the Talents' (1806) changed suspicion into pronounced distrust. His game seemed to be too clever by half. In justifying Pitt's war policy, Canning inevitably slashed at Fox's attempts to make peace. His vehemence may have helped to drive Fox to his death, much as Grey's hostility was to hound Canning to death some twenty years later. Poetic justice destined Canning to die in the same house as Fox. When George III brought down the 'Talents' ministry by his refusal to consider the Catholics' claim to equality of civic status, Canning celebrated the ministers' demise with his usual joky rhymes:

> Though they sleep with the devil, yet theirs is the hope,
> On the downfall of Britain to rise with the Pope.

The real joke was that Canning himself was eventually to 'rise with the Pope', for he was later to lead those Tories who advocated Catholic emancipation.

The aged Duke of Portland now formed a purely Tory government (1807) with Catholic emancipation forgotten and only the war against Napoleon pursued. It assembled many of the great Tory names of the next twenty years: Canning as Foreign Secretary, Castlereagh at the War Office, Liverpool at the Home Office, Wellington as Irish Secretary. Just before taking office again, Canning had been described by a diplomat as 'very clever and very essential to government; but . . . *hardly yet a statesman*' because of 'his dangerous habit of *quizzing*'. Canning's reputation for quizzing (destructive criticism), in addition to Portland's somnolent senility and the exigencies of the war, soon dragged the ministry into fierce trouble. Castlereagh's handling of his department, culminating in the disastrous Walcheren expedition, had convinced Canning that the War Minister ought to be moved to a different post. Instead of acting at once, Portland let the plan leak out and haughty Castlereagh, hearing of it, regarded it as a typically low intrigue prompted by Canning's plebeian ambition. Tempers flared, and in one of his rare waking moments Portland joined Canning and Castlereagh in resigning. The latter two fought a duel in which War slightly wounded Foreign Affairs; Portland expired. Yet still the blight seemed to hang over politics and the war. Portland was succeeded as Prime Minister by unexciting Mr Spencer Perceval, who ended his tenure after two and a half years with a burst of uncharacteristic melodrama: he was assassinated in the House of Commons.

There followed a prolonged spasm of manoeuvring by the Prince Regent (later George IV) and elbowing by the politicians, in which Canning's staunch ally, the Marquis Wellesley, tried and failed to form a government. Possibly because he thought the Government which Lord Liverpool then constructed would not last, Canning declined to serve the new Prime Minister as Foreign Secretary, a refusal he soon came to regret. This fresh eclipse was the worst, and from 1814 to 1816 he was an expatriate. When he returned to the Cabinet it was only to the Board of Control, the Government's liaison office for Indian affairs. Even from this peripheral position he once more had to resign in 1820. King George IV had forced the Cabinet to bring Queen Caroline to trial, and she had been friendly with Canning and his wife. The new hiatus, it was proposed, should be filled by appointing him Governor-General of India. Suddenly this came to nothing by the most unexpected turn of the political wheel. Lord Castlereagh, Foreign Secretary since 1812, committed suicide in August 1822. And despite Canning's past mistakes and consequent effacement, it seemed to those in the inner circles of power that he must be his former enemy's successor.

His record so far was marked by many signs of potential and not a few of actual distinction. In 1807 his bold initiative had pre-empted Napoleon's secret plot to seize the Danish fleet – a drama not altogether unlike the Norwegian campaign of 1940, but with very much more skill and luck on the British side. Moreover Canning understood economic and currency questions far better than any ministers before Peel and Huskisson, and was able to make riveting speeches even about bullion. The work he put into his speeches and dispatches was immense. 'Nothing can be done without a great deal of pains,' he once said. 'I prepare very much on many subjects; a great part of this is lost and never comes into play, but sometimes an opportunity arises when I can bring in something I have ready, and I always perceive the much greater effect of those passages upon the House.' His constituency from 1812 to 1822 was the great and growing city of Liverpool. It taught him to appreciate the commercial middle classes. In their interest he spouted eloquently and frequently at democratic meetings, a quirk not shared or approved by most of his colleagues. His reconciliation with Castlereagh after their duel showed that he had charm and no vindictiveness. His loyalty to strange characters like the Marquis Wellesley and Queen Caroline went deep, as did his faithfulness to the principles of his political preceptor, the younger Pitt: only after George III's mind and health went completely in 1811–12 did Canning feel himself absolved from Pitt's promise not to raise Catholic emancipation during the old King's lifetime. His sympathy for the country's industrial classes brought him into alliance with a like-minded statesman and economist, Henry Huskisson. Together they recommended greater freedom in trade and a modification of the Corn Laws for the sake of cheaper bread. Along

17. Spencer Perceval, by G. F. Joseph

18. Robert Jenkinson, Lord Liverpool, by Sir Thomas Lawrence

19. George Canning, by Sir Thomas Lawrence

20. Frederick Robinson, 1st Viscount Goderich, Earl of Ripon, by Sir Thomas Lawrence

21. Arthur Wellesley, 1st Duke of Wellington, by J. Jackson

22. Charles, 2nd Earl Grey, by Sir Thomas Lawrence

23. William Lamb, 2nd Viscount Melbourne, by J. Partridge

24. Sir Robert Peel, by John Linnell

with these signs of liberalism went contempt for what Canning called the 'proud combinations' of aristocrats. He abused Britain's most powerful vested interest as 'our agricultural grandees'.

He was none the less a Tory. When the 'discontented and restless spirit of the age' (to quote his words) expressed itself in the march of the Blanketeers, followed by the 'Peterloo massacre' and finally by the Cato Street conspiracy, Canning was in full agreement with the repressive severities of his fellow Tory ministers. Though he had indeed supported Catholic emancipation since 1812, he was never willing to liberate Protestant dissenters by repealing the Test Acts. As for a parliamentary Reform Bill, he regarded this like any regular die-hard as a recipe for revolution.

So now the complex problems arising in 1822 after Castlereagh's suicide had to be solved. Was it to be the viceroyalty of India for Canning, or the European influence of the foreign secretaryship boosted by leadership of the House of Commons into the foremost power in the State? On the King's side, was not HM in honour bound to turn down the man who had been his detested wife's friend? 'You hear, Arthur,' he huffed and puffed to his closest adviser, 'on my honour as a gentleman?' But Arthur Duke of Wellington would have none of the royal posturing. Firmly he insisted that Canning must be Foreign Secretary. When Canning kissed hands in September 1822 his final struggle with King and countrymen had begun. He likened his appointment by the reluctant sovereign to receiving an entry card to Almack's most gentlemanly club and finding written on the back, 'Admit the rogue'.

There were political as well as personal reasons why George IV should not welcome his new Foreign Secretary. Canning had no use for Europe's congresses. Starting with the Congress of Vienna in 1814 and reaching the last in the series at Verona in 1822, to which he must unwillingly send a British delegate, Canning had no use for the methods which monarchical Europe had chosen to organise peace since the late war. What came to be known as the 'Congress system' was initially intended to supply 'the sovereign remedy' for all the ills thrown up by revolution and Napoleonic empire. From it arose a number of alliances, among which the Quadruple Alliance between Britain, Austria, Russia and Prussia was the most effective. England was not a member of the Holy Alliance, rightly described as a piece of 'sublime nonsense' by Lord Castlereagh. The Quadruple Alliance of 1815, by way of contrast, had his and Wellington's full support, including as it did in its aims the saving of Europe from revolution. Canning also wanted to be saved from revolution, but not to be saved by Congress. In his eyes Britain, having saved Europe by her exertions and example (to telescope Pitt's famous words), stood in mortal danger of losing her proud independence from the Continent, now represented by absolutist emperors and kings. An outpost of liberty, she was forced to watch the autocratic dynasts suppress the constitutional urges of their peoples, wherever a Habsburg or Bourbon, a Romanov or Hohenzollern bore sceptre and crown.

As disciples of Pitt, Castlereagh and Canning were agreed on restoring the European balance of power. This, in economic terms, was always the least costly foreign policy as long as Britain's maritime rights remained intact. But whereas Castlereagh hoped to safeguard that balance through alliances, Canning was resolved to disengage his country from all European entanglements, and then re-enter the arena to mastermind a balance on his own terms.

He therefore had no intention whatever of attending the Congress of Verona in person, as Castlereagh had planned to do, albeit with misgivings. He sent Wellington instead. His final instructions to the great European commander were such as only a soldier trained in implicit obedience to the civil power above him could carry out. Wellington had to inform Congress that British policy in Europe was – non-intervention. This, to a Congress waiting hopefully to sanction, with British backing, a French invasion of anti-Bourbon, extremist Spain, was a bombshell. The invasion did indeed take place in 1823 and was swiftly successful; but with Britain opposed to it, it could no longer be promoted as a European crusade to rescue the King of Spain from his subjects. Canning, speaking ironically enough through the mouth of Wellington, had torn the old system to shreds. 'So things are getting back to a wholesome state again,' he wrote, well pleased. 'Every nation for itself and God for us all.' God and Canning had cast England in the role of 'spectatress'. Exit the Concert of Europe: 'For *Europe* I shall be desirous *now and then* to read *England*'; 'For "Alliance" read "England"', and you have the clue to my policy.' Canning's was not to be a Little England, however, but an England-on-top.

His nationalism belonged to a brand of patriotic thinking always acceptable to the offshore islanders, and it was at once hugely popular. Significantly, Castlereagh had believed 'unpopularity to be the more gentlemanly fate for a politician'. If Canning was a populist, Castlereagh was an 'unpopulist'.

Meanwhile the pro-Europeans, ranging from Wellington and the foreign ambassadors at the Court of St James to Metternich on the Continent, battled against Canning for possession of the King's soul. What was known as the 'Cottage Coterie' was formed among the diplomats who visited George IV in his luxurious *cottage orné* at Windsor. Their object was to jockey the King into making Lord Liverpool dismiss Canning. Wellington for one did not rate their chances of success high. As a prematurely aged man who was said to need a whiff of ether before making a speech, Liverpool was bound to depend more and more on the glamour and vigour which Canning's oratory had brought to his wilting Government in place of Castlereagh's 'gentlemanly' coldness. Once or twice the Duke was heard to say that Liverpool was behaving towards Canning like a 'spaniel' or a 'common prostitute'.

In minor ways, moreover, Canning had made progress with the King himself. That bored old voluptuary was kept awake and amused by Canning's tangy wit. He also appreciated Canning's tactful use of Foreign Office patronage on behalf of the royal circle. Lord Francis Conyngham, son of Lady Conyngham the royal favourite, was given a post there; in return, Lord Francis kept Canning informed of the Cottage Coterie's machinations. Later on, one of Lady Conyngham's ex-lovers, Lord Ponsonby, was posted to South America, a removal for which the suspicious King was duly grateful.

South America, in Canning's political vision, was no mere oubliette for the King's supposed rivals. It was the positive reverse of his European negative. Spain's South American colonies had broken away from the mother country. In doing so they offered rich markets to any country in either hemisphere which would recognise their independence. Castlereagh had desired a slow approach towards *collective* recognition by the European alliance. Not so Canning. His aim was immediate and unilateral recognition by England, so that England's commercial classes could snatch the lion's share of trade. His dynamic policy was more than welcome to the country, where he put it across in public meetings fully reported by the press. This 'speechifying', as his detractors called it, temporarily lowered his stock once more with the King, who asked Liverpool to call the Foreign Minister to heel. (Half a century later Queen Victoria was to make similarly fruitless efforts to curb Gladstone's whistle-stop oratory.) At the same time the diplomats' Cottage Coterie, the ultra-Tories in Parliament, the Duke of York's cronies and other reactionary groups were trying out new ways of poisoning the King's mind against Canning's South American policy. If successful, they hoped to resuscitate the moribund Congress system at the eleventh hour.

The battle over South America, however, could ultimately be won or lost only in the Cabinet. Here, Canning had a secret weapon: he threatened to expose in Parliament the attempts of foreign diplomats to interfere. And stage by stage, with verbal blows given and taken in an orgy of mutual colleague-bashing, Canning pushed his policy through. By July 1824 the sending of commercial attachés to the South American republics was agreed upon. By December there was a Cabinet majority for full diplomatic recognition. Canning was exhausted and exalted. 'I am really quite knocked up by it', he wrote. 'The fight has been hard, but it is won. The deed is done. The nail is driven. Spanish America is free; and if we do not mismanage our affairs, she is English.' Two years later, when the forcibly restored King of Spain was threatening constitutional Portugal, England's ancient ally, Canning brought off a triumphant parliamentary double. In words that link him with Palmerston, he thrillingly announced military aid for the potential victim: 'At this very hour . . . British troops are on their way to Portugal!' The House burst into a roar of astonishment and applause. As for Spain, continued Canning in response to a heckler, even if she did commit aggression (in fact she withdrew) Spain was no longer the awesome imperial power which had loomed so large in our island story. If the invasion of 1823 had won back Spain for despotism, at least it was not 'Spain with the Indies'. To a House electrified by his eloquence Canning declared: 'I called the New World into existence to redeem the balance of the old.'

During this same glorious year, 1826, Canning made his leap back into Europe. He sent Wellington to Russia with an offer of British mediation between the Tsar and the Sultan of Turkey, on behalf of the Turks' oppressed Greek subjects. (Up to now, Canning had merely recognised Greek belligerency, while aiming to 'stay the plague both ways'.) A protocol was signed in St Petersburg which set on foot the liberation of Greece.

But what if there still remained certain benighted Europeans who ignored the lead Britain was giving in freer trade as well as free institutions? When the Dutch minister, M. Falck, persistently rejected a reciprocal lowering of shipping duties, the irrepressible Canning

cyphered a dispatch to his Ambassador at the Hague, ordering re-
prisals – in verse:

> In matters of commerce the fault of the Dutch
> Is giving too little and asking too much;
> With equal advantage the French are content,
> So we'll clap on Dutch bottoms a twenty per cent.

> *Chorus of Douaniers:* Twenty per cent,
> Twenty per cent,
> Nous frapperons Falck with twenty per cent.

Canning's last year, 1827, opened with a royal death which, on
paper, removed yet another obstacle from his victorious path. The Duke
of York had recently proved himself the most effective and bigoted
opponent of Catholic emancipation. He died in January. His state
funeral took place at Windsor in dark and deadly cold. Canning was
among the many who caught severe chills. While still convalescing at
Brighton in February, he heard that the Prime Minister had suffered a
totally incapacitating stroke. There seemed only one possible successor
to Lord Liverpool. But this time Wellington did not tell the King that it
must be Canning. On the contrary, Canning's commitment to Catholic
emancipation ruled him out in the view of Wellington and Peel, as
well as of all the 'right wing'. It was the 'right wing' nevertheless that
finally, though unwittingly, fixed the King's choice upon Canning. A
group of ultra-Tory peers made their way into the King's presence and
urged him to choose Wellington. As soon as Canning heard of this
little expedition he astutely appealed to the King's pride: 'Sir, your
father broke the domination of the Whigs; I hope your Majesty will
not endure that of the Tories.' The King replied promptly, 'No, I'll
be damned if I do.' On 10 April he commissioned Canning to form a
plan for reconstructing the Government, and on the 12th Canning
received loud cheers as Prime Minister.

At once a new crisis broke. The King might be damned if he'd submit
to ultra-Tory pressure; the ultra-Tories, who for this purpose included
Wellington, Peel and half the previous Government, were damned if
they'd serve under Canning. All the old mistrust of the abrasive *parvenu*,
heightened by the recent split over foreign policy and topped up with
the conviction that Canning would sooner or later introduce Catholic

emancipation – these things combined to produce massive resignations. Still racked by rheumatic pains, Canning turned perforce to the highways and hedges and filled up the gaps in his Government with Whigs. Even here the spectre of past animosities arose to damage him. Lord Grey, the ill-tempered leader of the Whig Opposition who long ago had walked out of the House rather than listen to Canning's barbs, now attacked the Prime Minister with every species of virulence, personal and political. Deeply wounded, the victim considered taking a peerage in order to refute Grey face to face.

Furthermore, what Canning called his two 'buggaboos', Catholic emancipation and Corn, were holding up progress on the domestic front. Emancipation had already been defeated in the Commons by four votes on 7 March, and was consequently 'out' for that session. Through a misunderstanding between Wellington and Huskisson exploited by Grey, the Government's attempt in May to liberalise the Corn Laws was thwarted. Only one major undertaking was Canning able to fulfil. In July he drove through a treaty between Britain, France and Russia by which the Sultan of Turkey, unless he accepted an armistice with the hard-pressed Greeks, would be forcibly prevented from destroying them. Three months later, though Canning was not there to hear it, news reached England that the Turkish fleet was at the bottom of Navarino Bay and Greece saved.

Parliament had been prorogued on 2 July. That same month the King, who had come greatly to enjoy the prestige with which Canning's foreign policy invested His Britannic Majesty, wrote sincerely hoping that the Prime Minister was 'rapidly recovering from the odious lumbago'. Far from it, alas; at the beginning of August Canning was lent the Duke of Devonshire's villa in Chiswick where Fox had died. Huskisson visited him and was shocked to see his yellowing complexion. Though Canning assured his friend that it was only a reflection from the bedroom curtains, he died soon after 4 a.m. on 8 August 1827.

From 12 April to 8 August was exactly one hundred days. When measured by the magnitude of Canning's power and glory throughout Britain and Europe, they were days of consummate greatness. But they were only days. If he had lived for a normal span of years, could he have converted the King and the Tory party to Catholic emancipation, and himself to Reform? We shall never know. Nor is it possible to judge how far his hitherto somewhat narrow patriotism, with its passing jingoist undertones, could have developed into a broader states-manship. He had always derided any politician who was internationally-minded:

> A steady patriot of the world alone,
> The friend of every country but his own

– which was a long way from Dr Johnson's 'Patriotism is the last refuge of the scoundrel'. Canning certainly did much for his own country; much also for Greece and Portugal. If he tangled needlessly with the United States over 'calling the New World into existence', this was partly due to his distrust of their republican influence. Perhaps his place among British prime ministers is best symbolised by an incident after his death. He was buried in Westminster Abbey at the feet of his master Pitt; Canning's disciple Gladstone came as a boy to pray and meditate beside the grave.

There was a febrile streak of irritability in the man Canning which ultimately consumed him. It separated him from the giants. Beyond this temperamental defect lay a further weakness. Style, corrosive wit and vivid imagery are no substitutes for the passion that profoundly moves. Canning could play the kettle-drum but not the deep music of humanity. He supported popular movements but not the 'sovereign people'. He used the media of press and publicity but saw nothing whatever wrong beneath the surface of English life. Yet if Peel, Palmerston, Gladstone and Disraeli all looked up to him for inspiration, as they did, he surely belonged to the great liberal–conservative tradition.

BIBLIOGRAPHY

Arbuthnot, *The Journal of Mrs Arbuthnot*, ed. Francis Bamford and the Duke of Wellington (2 vols, London, 1950)
Aspinall, A., *The Formation of Canning's Ministry*, Camden 3rd Series (London, 1937)
—, *The Letters of George IV* (3 vols, Cambridge University Press, 1938)
Bagot, J. F., *George Canning and his Friends* (2 vols, London, 1909)
Briggs, Asa, *The Age of Improvement* (London, 1965)
Gash, Norman, *Mr Secretary Peel: The Life of Sir Robert Peel to 1830* (London, 1961)
Hinde, Wendy, *George Canning* (London, 1973)
Longford, Elizabeth, *Wellington: The Years of the Sword* (London, 1969)
—, *Wellington: Pillar of State* (London, 1972)
Marshall, Dorothy, *The Rise of George Canning* (London, 1938)

Petrie, Sir Charles, *George Canning* (London, 1930)
Rolo, P. J. V., *George Canning* (London, 1965)
Stapleton, A. G., *George Canning 1822–7* (3 vols, London, 1831)
Temperley, H. V., *Life of Canning* (London, 1905)

New Cambridge Modern History, ix, 1793–1830 (Cambridge, 1965)

20

VISCOUNT GODERICH

BY

JOHN DERRY

Frederick John Robinson, born 30 October 1782. Educated at Harrow and St John's College, Cambridge. Married 1814 Lady Sarah Hobart, daughter of the 4th Earl of Buckinghamshire; one surviving son, George Frederick Samuel, later 1st Marquess of Ripon; one son and one daughter died in childhood. MP for Carlow 1806 and for Ripon 1807; Vice-President of the Board of Trade 1812; President of the Board of Trade 1818; Chancellor of the Exchequer 1827; Colonial Secretary and Leader of the House of Lords 1827; Prime Minister and First Lord of the Treasury 1827–8; Colonial Secretary 1830–4; President of the Board of Trade 1841; President of the Board of Control 1843–6. Created 1st Viscount Goderich 1827 and 1st Earl of Ripon 1833. Died 28 Jan. 1859.

VISCOUNT GODERICH

The brief premiership of Frederick John Robinson, Lord Goderich, which lasted for a mere five months, has become notorious as a futile episode in the confusion that followed the retirement of Liverpool and the death of Canning. For most of his administration Goderich was preoccupied with trying to keep it together, and his failure is often cited as evidence of his own ineptitude. While Goderich fell below the standards of management set by Liverpool it is erroneous to suppose that only his limitations prevented the formation of a stable ministry. The behaviour of the King, dissensions within the Tory party, disagreements over Catholic emancipation and foreign policy, and the unreliability of several members of the administration, all contributed to Goderich's discomfiture. Goderich contributed little to the development of the premiership, but his abortive ministry throws light on the state of party politics in the late 1820s and reveals the ambivalent nature of the premiership at that period.

Goderich owed his appointment to the favourable reputation he had built up throughout his political career. He was respected as a man of considerable administrative experience, whose integrity, common sense and fair-mindedness were never in question. He was a good, if not a brilliant, debater, and he was a popular parliamentarian. He was acceptable to most of the factions within the Tory party, while being identified with none. For this reason it was hoped that he would be able to emulate Liverpool in holding disparate elements together. High Tories remembered Goderich's links with Castlereagh; Canningites recalled his sympathies with those commercial policies which were coming to be described as liberal. At the Board of Trade Goderich had played a significant part in the move towards freer trade, though he was never a doctrinaire free trader. His contribution to the nation's growing prosperity had earned him the nickname 'Prosperity Robinson', but the recession of 1825 tarnished his reputation, somewhat unfairly, and what had originally been meant as a tribute came to be regarded simply as proof of his good-natured optimism. His cautious advocacy of Catholic emancipation was cited as further evidence of his ability to see both sides of most political questions. He was never afraid to change his opinions, and although his reasons for doing so were not always clear to his contemporaries he usually succeeded in convincing them of his sincerity without giving offence. It was, therefore, wholly reasonable that there should be widespread agreement that he was as well qualified as anyone to hold together a party which had been shocked by Liverpool's stroke and Canning's death, and which was divided over the Catholic question and uncertain about British policy in the Near East. Goderich's acceptability to the Tory party is a reminder of the mediating role of the premier, who was expected to reconcile conflicts within a government rather than impose policies of his own upon a ministry. Prime ministers habitually conceded a wide discretionary freedom to their colleagues, and ministers regarded themselves as colleagues of the prime minister rather than subordinates. Though Goderich failed to fulfil the expectations which his previous record inspired this does not alter the character of the role he was expected to play. There were some reservations about his capacity to head an administration, and these were notably expressed, with characteristic firmness, by Wellington, but nevertheless no one in the Government expected him to be a dominant prime minister.

Goderich's appointment was also an indication of the continued importance of the King in politics. When George IV chose Goderich to succeed Canning everyone respected the King's right to choose his first minister. Though George IV was in a weaker constitutional position than his father had been forty years earlier he was expected to take the initiative in forming a new government. The King was also able to lay down conditions which he considered binding upon his new minister. No members of Lord Grey's group of Whigs were to be admitted to the ministry, and although George failed to impose stricter limitations on the question of Catholic relief than those that had operated under Canning, he was able to ensure that the issue would remain an open question in the new government just as it had done in the old, and this favoured the anti-Catholic party. The King made suggestions to Goderich affecting several of the most important appointments. Goderich's freedom in choosing his colleagues was therefore severely limited, and in his attempts to broaden the base of his administration he was constrained by the King's prejudices. The appointment of Herries as Chancellor of the Exchequer posed special problems, and it was only with difficulty that Lansdowne, who distrusted Herries as an anti-

Catholic Tory, was prevailed upon to serve as Home Secretary. Goderich was dependent on the King's confidence, and when this was withdrawn his ministry collapsed. Yet the price of the King's support was the exclusion of several moderate Whigs who would have been preferred by Goderich if he had been in a position to press for their appointment. Lord Holland, a Whig favourable to Catholic relief, was kept out of the Government, and from the beginning the Catholic question ominously heightened suspicions which various members of the administration entertained towards each other. The King and the High Tories were determined to prevent any accession of strength to the emancipationists in the Cabinet. There was general respect for Goderich, but little enthusiasm, and he could not rely on the committed personal loyalty of his colleagues.

It was soon evident that without a strong personality at its head the ministry was vulnerable to all the rivalries and confusions within the Tory party. Goderich presided over a ministry which lacked party discipline, essential agreement on fundamental issues, and a sufficient measure of internal harmony to enable it to withstand unforeseen embarrassments. Co-operation was possible only by agreeing to differ, but should any issue provoke major disagreement or any resignation disturb the balance of the ministry it would be difficult for the premier to maintain his position or for the Government to continue. Anti-Catholic Tories regarded Goderich's open-mindedness as a liability. He was thought to be too sensitive to changing circumstances, too willing to accede to reformist policies, too unsound in his commitment to Toryism of the more traditional type, and too generous in his attitude to moderate Whigs. Goderich was a victim of circumstances outside his control. If the King wavered he would be in an impossible position, since he would then be unable to withstand internal criticism. Goderich's ministry was virtually a prolongation of the Canning administration, but the fundamental tensions within the Tory party remained unsolved, and those qualities which had made Goderich acceptable as a prime minister eventually made it impossible for him to reconstruct his ministry on a sounder basis.

He soon found that his ministry was under strain because of dissensions over foreign and domestic policy. When Herries threatened to resign as Chancellor of the Exchequer the King's confidence in Goderich collapsed. But initially improving trade suggested that Goderich might be able to carry out further fiscal and commercial reforms, while a

[317]

conciliatory policy in Ireland was contemplated. Unhappily the critical situation in the Near East, reaching as it did a climax at the Battle of Navarino in October 1827, heightened the stresses within the ministry. Huskisson was sympathetic to Russia but uneasy about Codrington's destruction of the Turkish fleet. Herries was opposed to any action that might damage Turkey still further. Goderich was proud of Codrington's victory but uncertain about the direction of British policy over Greece. Mistrust between ministers over foreign affairs spilled over into other matters. Herries and Huskisson became involved in a dispute about the appointment of Althorp as chairman of a financial committee. Goderich failed to restore discipline and his reputation with both sides slumped. Goderich sought desperately to strengthen his ministry, but the Huskissonites and Canningites feared any extension of High Tory influence while the more conservative Tories remained bitterly suspicious of the more liberal wing of the Government. When Goderich suggested bringing in both Lord Wellesley and Lord Holland the King rejected the proposal.

By the middle of December 1827 Goderich was exhausted and depressed. In addition to his public worries he was tormented by anxieties about his wife's health. When Goderich wrote to the King, seeking to explain his own feelings of inadequacy, George IV's confidence in his minister was sapped still further. Later the King chose to regard this letter as an offer to resign. Nevertheless Goderich still sought a way out of the impasse. With the support of Huskisson he pressed for Holland's inclusion in the ministry, putting forward Wellington's name in addition to that of Wellesley in the hope that this would make Holland's admission less objectionable to the King. The King consulted Huskisson about the possibility of his taking over as prime minister, but when Huskisson refused it seemed that Goderich might, after all, be able to continue. Though the Prime Minister's morale fluctuated he began to think of preparing for the meeting of Parliament that was due early in the new year, but the King was intransigent in his opposition to Lord Holland's appointment.

Rumours about the disagreements within the ministry were rife, and Huskisson's nerve collapsed. No sooner had he asked leave to resign than the unfortunate Prime Minister was faced with a deliberate challenge to his authority. On 21 December Herries revived the dispute about Althorp's chairmanship of the financial committee and threatened to resign if Althorp were appointed. Huskisson reiterated that he would resign if Althorp were not appointed. Other members of the Government became uneasy and there was talk of other resignations. Goderich was blamed for the breakdown of the Government's will to survive. But when he made another attempt to reconcile the discordant factions within his Cabinet he found Herries obstinate and unyielding. Goderich visited the King on 8 January 1828, intending to inform him of the deadlock within the Government, but he found that George IV already regarded the ministry as dissolved, referring to Goderich's earlier letter as tantamount to resignation. There was nothing for Goderich to do but accept the inevitable.

Though Goderich lacked the strength of personality to pull through the governmental crisis he had been unfortunate in facing a foe as malevolent as his Chancellor of the Exchequer. He was unlucky in that so many of his colleagues were deficient both in loyalty and firmness of purpose. Even Huskisson had been less than consistently reliable. Called to the premiership by the King Goderich had also been deprived of assured royal support. Prepared to broaden his ministry by admitting Whigs he had not only found the King hostile to Holland's admission, he had found Grey hostile and aloof. Goderich had inherited a difficult situation; it soon became an impossible one. The Catholic issue exercised a baleful influence upon the conduct of both pro-Catholic and anti-Catholic Tories.

Goderich's experience demonstrated that the premiership did not, of itself, confer pre-eminent leadership or control in the circumstances of the 1820s. The difficulties encountered by Wellington echoed many of the problems that had forced Goderich out of office. Only a stronger sense of collective responsibility within the Cabinet and a growing appreciation of party loyalty in the Commons eventually made it easier for premiers to avoid Goderich's humiliating experience. Yet, though Goderich did not create the divisions that had brought about his downfall, he was reluctant to place party priorities above more traditional ideas of public service. Goderich later served under both Grey and Peel, his career illustrating how loosely he regarded party ties and how deferentially he placed the service of the Crown first in his concept of political duty. The frustrations of his premiership were themselves evidence of the way in which his outlook was becoming inadequate. Sadly, Goderich's premiership showed that integrity, open-mindedness and loyalty to the service of the Crown were incapable of resolving the tensions that were destroying the Tory party, and that finally brought Grey into office in 1830.

BIBLIOGRAPHY

The definitive modern work on Goderich's political career is Wilbur Devereux Jones's *Prosperity Robinson: The Life of Viscount Goderich 1782–1859* (London, 1967), which is based on thorough primary research. But for those interested in the background to the formation of Goderich's ministry G. I. T. Machin, *The Catholic Question in English Politics 1820–30* (Oxford, 1964) is essential reading.

21

THE
DUKE OF WELLINGTON

BY

JOHN CLARKE

Arthur Wellesley, born c. 29 April 1769, fourth son of the 1st Earl of Mornington and Anne Hill, daughter of the 1st Viscount Dungannon. Educated at Eton and at Angers. Married 1807 Catherine Pakenham, daughter of 2nd Earl of Longford. MP for Trim 1790. Aide-de-camp to the Lord Lieutenant of Ireland 1790; major and then lieutenant-colonel of the 33rd Foot, 1793; Flanders campaign 1794; major-general 1799; KB after the Battle of Assaye 1804. MP for Rye 1806. Chief Secretary for Ireland 1807. Copenhagen expedition 1807. Spanish Peninsula 1808. Created Viscount Wellington 1809. Entered Madrid 1812. Field-Marshal and KG 1813. Victorious in Peninsular War 1814. Created Duke and Ambassador to Paris 1814. Waterloo 1815. Joined Liverpool's administration as Master General of Ordnance 1817. Congress of Vienna 1820; Congress of Verona 1822. Resigned from government 1827. Resumed command of the Army 1827. Prime Minister 1828–30, Lord Warden of the Cinque Ports 1829. Failed to form a government 1832. Took over government 1834 pending Peel's return; Foreign Secretary 1834; Leader of the House of Lords 1841; reappointed to the command of the Army 1842. Died 14 September 1852.

THE DUKE OF WELLINGTON

WELLINGTON THE SOLDIER

Arthur Wellesley, first Duke of Wellington, was born in Dublin on 29 April 1769. As fourth son of the Earl of Mornington, Wellesley became a part of the 'Protestant Ascendency' or small minority which had monopolised all power and influence in Ireland since the end of the seventeenth century. After a short, unhappy and impoverished stay at Eton, it was decided that 'ugly boy Arthur is fit food for powder'. Wellesley was sent to Pignerol's military academy at Angers; he was just in time to experience life in France before the Revolution. After joining the British Army in March 1787, Wellesley was made aide-de-camp to the Lord Lieutenant of Ireland and in 1790 he was elected to the Dublin Parliament as member for Trim, County Meath.

In 1794 Wellesley joined the Duke of York's ill-fated expedition to the Low Countries, but most of his military experience was acquired in India where his elder brother, Richard, was Governor-General. Wellesley was soon given the command of the Army of Mysore and later directed the campaign against the Mahrattas. He returned to England in 1804 to defend his brother's expansionist policy, but in 1807 he was appointed Chief Secretary of Ireland. Wellesley combined this job with an active military career. In July 1807 he was sent to Spain with a force of 8,000 men and given instructions to collaborate with those Spaniards who were opposed to the regime of Joseph Bonaparte. In the early years of the Peninsular War, Wellesley was hampered by inadequate numbers of troops, a great deal of ill-informed criticism in England and the incessant quarrels of his Spanish allies. Gradually things improved and Wellesley's objective of driving the French out of Spain was achieved by the victories of Salamanca and Vitoria.

After the abdication of Napoleon, Wellesley, already a marquis, was made Duke of Wellington; hosts of foreign honours were poured on him. In the short period before Napoleon's return he was British Ambassador in Paris and attended the closing stages of the Congress of Vienna. The Battle of Waterloo, Wellington's most famous victory, ended Napoleon's bid to regain power. Wellington was now given command of the Army of Occupation and for three years was the effective ruler of France. At the end of 1817 Wellington joined Lord Liverpool's Cabinet as Master-General of Ordnance; many thought him the most reactionary member of a very conservative government. He despised politicians who tried to obtain 'vulgar popularity', he thought that newspapers abused their relative freedom of comment, he frequently declared that the admission of Roman Catholics to Parliament would mean the end of British greatness and was a strong supporter of Sidmouth's Six Acts. The Duke represented the British Government at the Congress of Verona in September 1822, and in 1826 he was sent to St Petersburg in an attempt to avert war between Russia and Turkey. Wellington's sympathies were with the Holy Alliance powers and he frequently found himself at odds with the liberalising policies of Canning. Disagreements over Spain, South America and Greece brought Wellington close to resignation.

When Canning became Prime Minister in April 1827, Wellington did resign – because he believed that Canning was motivated by hatred of the landed aristocracy and was certain to upset Liverpool's careful balance between those who were in favour of Catholic emancipation and those who opposed it. Wellington also resigned as Commander-in-Chief, a move which was bitterly resented by George IV. After Canning's death, Wellington agreed to resume the command of the Army but made it clear that he did not support Lord Goderich's coalition Government of progressive Tories and Whigs. It was clear that the ineffective and often tearful Goderich could not last long. He resigned on 8 January 1828 and the King invited Wellington to form a government.

WELLINGTON THE PRIME MINISTER

The Duke of Wellington had some important advantages as premier. Above all he was the national hero who had beaten the French. In political terms this meant that he enjoyed the respect of the ordinary people he so much despised. The House of Lords deferred to his every word and was unlikely to make the sort of difficulties that often wrecked the governments of lesser men. The King, whose influence in politics was still enormous, treated him as an equal. Wellington was universally admitted to be a man of high principles and great energy. He was a hard worker and would not spare himself in his determination to master all the details of government. For a man who had little contact with commerce, he was surprisingly expert in financial matters.

These advantages were balanced by serious weaknesses. Now that Tories like Peel, who had once seemed even more conservative than Wellington, were beginning to pay lip service to the ideas of progress, the Duke appeared to be hopelessly out of touch with the mood of the age. Napoleon's doubts whether a man who had enjoyed so much power could ever be content to relinquish it were shared by many Englishmen. Some Whigs like Brougham claimed that soldiers were naturally contemptuous of constitutional government and inclined to tyranny. In fact, no one could have had a more exaggerated respect for the British Constitution than Wellington, but unscrupulous opponents realised that 'liberty in danger' was always a powerful slogan. Wellington's manner sometimes gave colour to these allegations; he seemed to behave with an aloofness more appropriate to a monarch than a subject. Even the King resented this aspect of Wellington. George IV was not a man whose friendship and support could be relied upon; joking references to 'King Arthur' contained a strong element of jealousy.

Wellington's real trouble was that he had come to politics late in life. He was still fundamentally ill at ease in political circles and his apparent aloofness was really more due to shyness than hauteur. It is absurd to say that Wellington was not a politician. No man can become prime minister without being a politician but no other British prime minister has owed his position more to what he did outside politics. Wellington was still a beginner; he had not even learnt the art of deception properly and so was to be caught out more often than his highly professional colleagues. Unlike most premiers, he had only limited experience of the House of Commons, he took no joy in the rough and tumble of debate and had no 'feel' for the mood of Parliament. He was a poor speaker; when nervous he was liable to keep up his own courage by making more and more extreme statements – without the usual qualifications and escape routes. In short, his whole outlook was very different from that of the men with whom he would have to work.

Wellington disliked coalition governments as 'unprincipled' and disapproved of members of the previous administration who had sacrificed traditional loyalties to their desire for office. Even if the Whigs had been prepared to go on, Wellington was right in thinking that a coalition would have been an unstable affair; Lansdowne and Holland were already under strong pressure from Lord Grey to go over to active opposition. But equally Wellington had no desire to form an extreme conservative, or 'Ultra' government. He wanted to restore the position of Lord Liverpool's time when the progressive and conservative wings of the Tory party had been equally balanced.

At the cost of disappointing some close friends, like Harriet and Charles Arbuthnot, who were expecting a more decidedly conservative Cabinet, Wellington succeeded in his objectives – although it was dangerous to upset the King by refusing to recall the Ultra, Lord Eldon, to the Woolsack. Despite the *Manchester Guardian*'s complaints of 'an utter ignorance of the principles of philosophical legislation', it was a strong Cabinet. With Peel as Home Secretary, Huskisson at the Colonial Office and Palmerston Secretary at War, no one could pretend that the administration lacked talent. Whether it possessed unity was another matter. Wellington had complained about Canning's lack of principle but there was scarcely anything important that his own ministers could agree upon. The best thing that could be said was that there was a precarious agreement to disagree on a number of fundamental questions, notably Catholic emancipation and the redistribution of seats. Wellington could only lead a secure government so long as these issues were kept under the carpet. Both the Ultra and Canningite sections of the Cabinet were led by men who were much concerned with their own dignity and very sensitive to imagined insult. A word or even a gesture implying too much support for one side or the other could produce wholesale resignations. Army life was not the best training for such a delicate situation.

Although Wellington was naturally inclined to the Ultras, he was politician enough to appreciate that some progressive measures were essential. Apart from a sop to the Ultras in the King's speech regretting the Battle of Navarino – which effectively secured Greek independence – the record of the first few months was astonishingly liberal. When the House of Commons approved Lord John Russell's motion to repeal the Dissenters Disabilities Acts – against government opposition – Wellington changed his mind and announced that he would now support repeal. These Acts were the last pieces of serious discrimination against Protestant dissenters. Nonconformists in public office had to endure the humiliation of an annual Act of Indemnity to protect them from the penalties of holding an official position without being practising Anglicans. Few now imagined that the dissenters presented any threat to the Constitution, but once Nonconformists were admitted to full equality with Anglicans it would be much harder to defend the con-

tinued exclusion of Roman Catholics from Parliament. To Ultras like
the King's forceful brother the Duke of Cumberland, this concession
was an obvious thin end of the wedge tactic. It is possible that Wellington was already beginning to contemplate Catholic emancipation, but
at least for the moment, he could argue that satisfaction of Nonconformist grievances would make influential dissenters less eager to support the Catholic cause. At the same time, the Prime Minister bowed to
Canningite pressure in the Cabinet and agreed to a modification of the
1815 Corn Laws in an attempt to lower the price of bread in years of
bad harvest. Despite his reputation for bigotry, Wellington had achieved
two important reforms; a sensible observer would have said 'so far so
good'.

A number of influential government supporters had voted against the
repeal of Dissenters Disabilities; if Wellington's balancing act was to
continue, it was quite sensible to follow the reforms with a period of
caution. Wellington was not sympathetic to the demand that the seats
of Penrhyn and East Retford, two notoriously corrupt boroughs, should
be transferred to Birmingham and Manchester, which were still without parliamentary representation. With some logic, the Prime Minister
argued that it would be wrong to penalise all the voters in a constituency
because some had taken bribes, and that an enlargement of the number
of voters by incorporating surrounding villages was the best way to
defeat corruption. Huskisson spoke against this reasoning in Parliament and after an undignified squabble as to whether he had or had not
asked to resign, the three leading Canningites, Huskisson, Charles
Grant and Palmerston, left the Government. Experienced politicians
would have realised that a little loss of face was necessary to preserve
the balance of the administration. Wellington was either too vain or
too unsophisticated to appreciate this. Endless wrangling in the Cabinet
had weakened his fragile temper. Wellington took the easy way out,
but by letting the Canningites go, he drastically curtailed his own freedom of action.

CATHOLIC EMANCIPATION

The usual picture of Wellington as military genius but peacetime
Blimp is unfair. The Duke may have wanted to be a reactionary but he
recognised that he could not be. Despite his general hostility to change,
his approach to the problem of Catholic emancipation was empirical.
Unlike George IV and Cumberland, he did not look at 'The Protestant

Constitution' through a reverential mist of pious observanticism. His ideal solution would have been one of gradual concession; complete equality had to be contemplated but with good management the evil, if inevitable, day might be postponed.

For some time Wellington had been toying with the idea of a Concordat with the Papacy which would admit Catholics to Parliament but give the British Government a veto over the choice of Irish Catholic bishops. If the bishops were safe men who could be relied upon to use their great influence to prevent the election of those who would destroy the Union and threaten property itself, then emancipation might not be a complete disaster. On 10 June 1828 Wellington appealed for tranquillity in Ireland and hinted that if this condition was fulfilled, then something might be done. Events were overtaking the Prime Minister.

Most of the places left by the departure of the Canningites were filled by 'non-political' soldiers. The one progressive appointment was the choice of Vesey Fitzgerald, an untypically good Irish landlord and a supporter of emancipation, to succeed Grant at the Board of Trade. Fitzgerald sat for County Clare and on accepting office would have to fight a by-election. As Wellington was generally believed to be absolutely opposed to the admission of Catholic MPs, his Government was extremely unpopular in Ireland. On 24 June the Catholic leader Daniel O'Connell decided to contest the Clare seat himself. Although a Roman Catholic could not sit in Parliament, there was nothing to prevent him from standing. If O'Connell was elected and then refused admission to Westminster, the always difficult Irish situation was certain to become explosive.

Even if O'Connell could be excluded, the long-term prospects were grim. The franchise in Ireland was surprisingly wide. Roman Catholics could vote and the 40 shilling freehold qualification meant that many voters were practically paupers. This group had little to lose. Even in the 1826 election the Catholic voters had rebelled against the nominees of the Beresford family – probably the most influential in Ireland. At the next general election it was likely that a large number of men like O'Connell would be elected and unable to take their seats because of their religion. There was a danger that this group would form an unofficial Parliament, destroy the Union and encourage popular revolution against the landlords. The best way of meeting this danger would be to take the vote away from those who had no real interest in the preservation of property. This is what Wellington decided to do. He saw that he might be able to trade Catholic emancipation in return for a reduction of the electorate. Like the Concordat scheme this would have the advantage of keeping out extremists. Wellington was not a cynic but a cynic might add that the scheme also had the advantage of opening up a difference of interest between the Catholic peasantry and the Catholic middle classes. As far as Wellington was concerned, although Catholic emancipation was unfortunate, the damage it would cause to the Constitution was minimal compared to that which would result from its continued refusal.

It was an act of statesmanship to decide on emancipation but it was a question of politics to persuade many important people that Wellington was not planning an abject surrender but merely a calculated strategic retreat. O'Connell had been elected but the obstacles facing Wellington were formidable. The Cabinet presented less of a problem than might have been expected. After much agonising, the leading anti-Catholic, Robert Peel, accepted Wellington's arguments. Cabinet ministers are by nature sympathetic to arguments of necessity and expediency. Others can afford to be more inflexible. For the moment Wellington was able to allay Ultra fears by dismissing the pro-Catholic Lord Anglesley from his post as Lord Lieutenant of Ireland.

The main obstacle to emancipation was expected to be the King; it seemed likely that the issue would expand into a trial of strength between royal influence and that of the Prime Minister. In most previous contests the King had won. Despite his general indifference to religion, George IV had frequently declared that if he accepted Catholic emancipation he would be breaking his Coronation Oath, and because of this appalling blasphemy would cease to be King in the sight of God. To Wellington's great surprise, George seemed to agree to his plans. The King was naturally lazy and wanted a quiet life; by the autumn of 1828 he was also a sick man who had to take heavy doses of laudanum to relieve the pain of prostate trouble. It is likely that when George seemed to agree to emancipation, he had not fully appreciated the significance of his actions. The problem for Wellington was whether the Duke of Cumberland would return to England from Berlin in order to open the King's eyes. Cumberland had great influence with his brother so it was vital to keep him out of the country. Wellington was guilty of obvious deception when he wrote to Cumberland that emancipation was not even contemplated when, in fact, plans were well advanced.

Emancipation, combined with proposals to increase the property qualification for Irish voters from 40 shillings to 10 pounds, was announced in the King's speech of 5 February 1829. The King's apparent acquiescence in alliance with the Duke's enormous influence meant that a surprisingly large number of bishops, peers and MPs persuaded themselves that a measure of emancipation from Wellington and Peel was less dangerous than one from genuine pro-Catholics. Drastic changes are more likely to gain acceptance when introduced by conservatives than by those notoriously committed to change. With royal support, Catholic emancipation would have been easy, but it was still not quite clear whether the King's influence would be behind Wellington or Cumberland.

Cumberland returned to England, explained to the King that Wellington had deceived him and obtained an opinion from Lord Eldon that it would be constitutionally proper for George to veto emancipation even if a Relief Bill was passed by both Houses of Parliament. Wellington could only respond with an ultimatum that he would resign unless he received royal support. On 4 March 1829 the King was forced to give way. Despite a rather unnecessary duel between Wellington and Lord Winchelsea the issue was no longer in doubt. For a very short time the Prime Minister became the hero of progressives.

Wellington had exploited his position with the King very cleverly. The Ultra party was essentially one of backwoodsmen. The only member of the Cabinet who supported them was the Attorney-General, Sir Charles Wetherell. They simply did not possess sufficient talent or experience to form a government; their leader, the Duke of Cumberland, would never have been acceptable as Prime Minister – not only because he was a Royal Duke but also because there had been some highly questionable episodes in his past.

Cumberland had probably been the greatest single danger, but his opinion was by no means untypical. There were a number of influential peers, led by Lord Winchelsea, who felt that emancipation must be resisted at all costs. Peers were influential in their own right and often controlled the votes of a number of MPs. When the Catholic Relief Bill eventually passed through the Commons, no fewer than 112 members voted against. Even this represented only a shadow of the anti-Catholic feeling in the country. Emancipation was not a popular cause; hosts of ordinary people believed that a single Catholic in Parliament would mean the end of British freedom. It was only fifty years since the Gordon Riots and if the matter had been decided by referendum, it is certain that there would have been an enormous majority against. Catholic emancipation was one of the many reforms carried through by a fairly enlightened elite against public opinion; with a wider franchise, the measure might have been delayed for some years.

Although emancipation was well received in Ireland, much of the political capital Wellington had made was forfeited by the unnecessary insult of refusing O'Connell admission to Parliament unless he stood for re-election. Obviously the measure prevented the realisation of Wellington's nightmare of a separate Parliament. It was certainly an enormous step forward for religious liberty but, whatever else it did, it did not solve the problem of Ireland. In many areas violence remained almost a way of life. An enormous number of practical grievances remained. Emancipation was really 'too little, too late'.

REFORM

It is a matter of some debate amongst historians whether Wellington's downfall in 1830 is best explained in terms of the Prime Minister's failure to reunite his party, or in terms of the profound social changes which were taking place in a country in the throes of industrialisation. Both were important but the first explanation seems to fit the facts better than the second.

Wellington had now succeeded in alienating both left and right wings of the Tory party. The Whigs were still the largest opposition group in Parliament, but they seemed unlikely to achieve much unless they could make a common cause with the Ultras and Canningites. The Prime Minister's task was to prevent the emergence of such a common cause but, as the two-party system had disintegrated in 1827, any grouping was now possible. The Whigs and Canningites had supported the Government over emancipation; the Prime Minister believed that neither group really wanted to replace him. Wellington strongly disliked Huskisson and hoped that the Canningites would remain quiet even if their leaders were not invited to rejoin the Cabinet. Any formal alliance with the Whigs was ruled out because the King had made it clear that he would never accept Lord Grey as a Cabinet minister. Wellington had been hurt by Ultra allegations of 'betrayal' in 1829 but his natural sympathies were still with this group. At the beginning of 1830 the Prime Minister thought that, by demonstrating his hostility to further change, he could bring the Ultras back to their party allegiance.

The Prime Minister had made two mistakes. He had underestimated the Canningites' desire for office; they were essentially career politicians who felt that their superior talents and experience gave them a natural right to ministerial rank. Unless Wellington was prepared to offer clear-cut terms, he was certain to find the Canningites voting with Grey who would be forced to give them important positions if he ever came to power. Similarly Wellington did not understand the Ultras; he sympathised with them but his thought processes were not the same as theirs. A group of about forty hard-line Ultras were now the Government's most violent adversaries in Parliament. Unlike the Canningites, few of them were professional politicians; they were not interested in being bought off with offices. Wellington's overtures were rejected; regardless of any other considerations, the Ultras wanted revenge for emancipation.

Some of the Ultras can be safely dismissed as 'blockheads' (Peel's contemptuous description) but there were intelligent men amongst them. In fact, there was more in common between the Ultras and groups to the left of the Government than might seem possible. The Ultras were essentially rural landowners but landowners who were very dissatisfied with the depressed state of agriculture. The gentry felt that Wellington had betrayed them, not only by emancipation, but also by his relaxation of the Corn Laws, his deflationary tax policy and his refusal to consider giving up the gold standard as a means of raising agricultural prices. In this sense, the gentry were almost a Radical group; even more important, their belief in inflation as a means of curing distress was shared by many manufacturers and provincial bankers – of whom Thomas Attwood of Birmingham is the best example. Thus the links between rural and urban discontent were surprisingly close.

Wellington was wrong in thinking that he could regain the Ultras by resolute hostility to a reform of Parliament. It was already clear that a wider electorate might have delayed emancipation; men like Sir Richard Vyvyan and Sir Edward Knatchbull seriously believed that Reform might retard rather than accelerate the dreaded 'march of progress'. Many country gentlemen came to the conclusion that their economic ills could not be cured without a drastic reduction in taxes, and that the best way to achieve this was to make MPs more directly responsible to the taxpayers. The demand for Reform had been fairly dormant since the early 1820s; it is important to appreciate that its rather unexpected revival in 1830 was essentially a by-product of a demand for economy. Advocacy of economy and denunciation of 'government waste' are splendid weapons in politics; more than any other issue they have the advantage of appealing to a wide range of opposition factions who can agree on little else. This is what Wellington was now up against.

Seen in this light, many of the traditional explanations of the demand for Reform look unconvincing. The campaign was already well under way before there was news of a revolution in France. Reform was certainly not a contest between town and country, middle class and landowners. In fact all sectors were divided on the issue. It is probably far better to see Reform as yet another round in the endless battle between 'Court and Country'. The sort of redistribution of seats and extension of the franchise contemplated by most people was much less drastic than the proposals introduced by the Whigs in 1831; a very moderate Reform Bill would have satisfied the country and probably destroyed the Whig party for ever. Perhaps Wellington showed that he was fundamentally Irish, not English, by his correct appreciation of the issues of emancipation and his failure to understand the forces at work over Reform. Why was he so wrong?

Towards the end of 1829 it seemed that the economic difficulties that produced discontent were disappearing. Government revenue is a good indication of the level of economic activity; arrears of taxes were being reduced and there was a general building boom. Unfortunately, these signs of recovery were destroyed by an appalling winter, the worst for nearly a century. With so large a proportion of people working out of doors and so much of industry dependent on canal transport, a prolonged period of ice and snow was bound to result in massive unemployment. In January 1830 it was certainly true that 'what was happening at Westminster or in the City was of small account compared to what was happening in the heavens'. Instead of decreasing, discontent was spreading. To make matters worse, it was clear that George IV could not live much longer, and opposition politicians were beginning to step up their attacks on the Government in readiness for the general election which would follow the accession of the new King. It was clear that ambitious men like Henry Brougham would be prepared to inflame opinion out of doors and inject an artificial element of class hatred which grass roots discontent had hitherto lacked.

In the eighteenth century, governments did not lose elections; administrations whose record was far worse than Wellington's could expect a handsome majority. By and large prime ministers only fell when they lost the King's confidence, and William IV quickly indicated that he was satisfied with the ministers he inherited from his brother who died in June 1830. Wellington may have been in favour of old-fashioned policies but his views on political morality were modern. He did not believe that prime ministers should use public money to ensure the election of government candidates and was opposed to the use of sinecure offices to buy the votes of MPs and peers.

Much government patronage had been reformed away in the 1820s; in 1828 Wellington himself complained that he could offer potential supporters nothing more tangible than 'smiles and a dinner'. The Duke did not appreciate, however, that a certain amount of corruption was necessary for political stability, and that the fragmentation of the Tory party was, in part, attributable to the decline in 'places'. Wellington was too idealistic; despite the urgent appeals of the Chief Whip, William Holmes, he did not even utilise the patronage that remained. The Duke fought the election following the death of George IV with one hand tied behind his back.

This election of July 1830 was a muddled affair; it is even an over-simplification to say that the Government was defeated. In the absence of party discipline many 'neutrals' were returned; William Holmes thought that most of the neutrals could be turned into government supporters and calculated that, with good management and sensible policies, the Duke would increase his majority by seventeen seats. It was still not too late – although the fact the new King had no personal animus against Grey meant that Wellington no longer enjoyed a virtual monopoly of the premiership. The election had increased the members who believed that economic distress could be cured by Reform; discontent which had been largely rural was now echoed by a revival of agitation in the towns. For the first time since 1820, Radical demagogues like Cobbett, Carpenter and Hunt, with their talk of Revolution commanded a sizable following.

The Government was in for a difficult time but it is nonsense to suggest that Wellington should have resigned before Parliament met. The Duke could certainly have 'hooked' the Canningites. Huskisson's tragic death at the opening of the Liverpool to Manchester Railway in September 1830 meant that the group was leaderless and seemed ready to return to the Tory fold. Wellington did approach Palmerston who said he would join the Government if another two Canningites were approached as well. Wellington's rejection of these reasonable terms was his fatal mistake – the last chance to restore a 'balanced' Tory party. Again his motives were too honourable; the appointment of three Canningites would mean the dismissal of three loyal supporters – Murray, Beresford and Calcraft. Orthodox politicians would not have been troubled by such scruples but it is not surprising that the Canningites lost patience and finally cast their lot in with the Whigs. There remained only the Ultras.

At the end of August 1830, rural discontent exploded into the Swing Riots. Landowners who attempted to fight falling profit margins by cutting back their wage bill and replacing men with threshing machines saw their machines destroyed by the rioters. Wellington and Peel received hundreds of panic letters from squires declaring that England was on the brink of anarchy and revolution. The Swing Riots do not receive much mention in most histories of Reform. It is true that the farm labourers' cause had little in common with that of the urban middle class, but Swing was crucial to what happened later. The Prime Minister took his cue from the countryside, not the towns. Wellington did not understand the new manufacturing areas; indeed, in 1830 there were not that many factory towns in existence. Wellington saw Swing as conclusive proof of the fragility of civilisation; the smallest concession to popular pressure would lead to anarchy. Conviction was strengthened by political considerations. Swing would have the beneficial effect of bringing the rural Ultras to their senses and make them realise the folly of their flirtation with Reform.

With these two reinforcing considerations in mind, Wellington faced Parliament on 2 November 1830. His speech was a sensation; he went so far in his denunciation of Reform that he declared that even if he were asked to design a Constitution from scratch, he would still incorporate in it all the apparent anomalies of the existing British system of representation. The message was clear: Reform was the same as Revolution. At the end of his speech even Wellington realised that he had probably gone too far. The last bid to gain Ultra support failed. Wellington was wrong; conviction and interest were not the same. The Whigs, now sure of the Canningites, were bidding hard for the vital Ultra vote. Lord Grey announced that the first priority on taking office would be the relief of distress: he opposed the Government's moves towards free trade and had an 'open mind' on the gold standard question. This was insincere pandering to obscuranticism of a kind Wellington would never have stooped to; it was none the less effective. The

[335]

decision of much of the Tory right to support Grey was strengthened by the conviction that Swing demonstrated not the danger but the necessity of Reform.

Wellington's speech had a bad effect 'out of doors'. The Funds fell, there was sporadic rioting in London and a royal visit to the Guildhall had to be cancelled for fear of an attempt to kidnap the King. The fury had arisen very suddenly. When the Civil List was discussed on 15 November the Government was defeated by 233 votes to 204 – 34 Ultras voted with the Opposition. The Duke was glad to take the opportunity to resign.

Wellington was never again Prime Minister; in May 1832 he made an unsuccessful attempt to form a government and in November 1834, when William IV dismissed Melbourne, he was acting Prime Minister for three weeks before Peel returned from Italy. Between 1830 and 1834 Wellington was something of a bogeyman who was seen as the embodiment of all reactionary prejudice. Analysis of the Duke's premiership shows that this picture is wrong. His failures can usually be attributed to excessive high-mindedness. Catholic emancipation made the idea of changing the Constitution really respectable for the first time; to some extent it made Reform possible. Whether willingly or not, the Duke of Wellington speeded up these two most important changes. When he died, on 14 September 1852, he was again a national hero.

BIBLIOGRAPHY

Best, G., 'The Protestant Constitution and its Supporters 1800–29' (*Transactions of the Royal Historical Society*, 1958)

Bird, A., *The Damnable Duke of Cumberland* (London, 1966)

Davis, R. W., 'The Strategy of Dissent in the Repeal Campaign 1820–8' (*Journal of Modern History*, 1966)

Flick, C., 'The Fall of Wellington's Government' (*JMH*, 1965)

Foord, A. S., 'The Waning Influence of the Crown' (*English Historical Review*, 1947)

Longford, E., *Wellington: Pillar of State* (London, 1972)

Machin, G. I., 'The Duke of Wellington and Catholic Emancipation' (*Journal of Ecclesiastical History*, 1963)

Moore, D. C., 'The Other Face of Reform' (*Victorian Studies*, 1962)

Palmer, A., *George IV* (London, 1972)

22

EARL GREY

BY

GEORGE WOODBRIDGE

Charles Grey, born 13 March 1764, eldest surviving son of General Sir Charles Grey, afterwards 1st Earl Grey. Educated at Eton and Trinity College, Cambridge. Married Mary Elizabeth Ponsonby 1794; fifteen children. MP for Northumberland 1786–1807; Appleby 1807; Tavistock 1807. Succeeded as 2nd Earl Grey 1807. First Lord of the Admiralty 1806; Foreign Secretary 1806–7. Succeeded Fox as leader of Foxite Whigs 1806 and became Whig leader 1821. Prime Minister 1830–4. Died 17 July 1845.

EARL GREY

———

Charles, second Earl Grey, was born 13 March 1764 into a long-established Northumberland family. His uncle (whose property he ultimately inherited) was a baronet; his father became an earl. At the age of six he was sent to a boarding preparatory school in Marylebone, entering Eton at the age of nine. After eight years there (1773–81) he went on (aged 17) to Trinity College, Cambridge. Apparently a competent but not an outstanding student, he did not take a degree. He went on a Grand Tour in 1784 to 1786, mostly to southern France, Switzerland, and especially Italy. His education at least gave him a real knowledge of Greek, Latin, French, and Italian; the latter two he could speak as well as read.

At a by-election in July 1786, while he was still on the Continent, he was elected (aged 22) a county Member of Parliament for Northumberland. He first took his seat in the House of Commons in January 1787, and continued to sit for that county until defeated in 1807. He then successively represented two boroughs: Appleby, May to July 1807, and Tavistock, July to November 1807. After his father's death on 14 November 1807, he took (aged 43) his seat as the second Earl Grey in the House of Lords, and, of course, remained in that House until his own death (aged 81) on 17 July 1845.

He married Mary Elizabeth, daughter of William Brabazon (Ponsonby), first Baron Ponsonby, on 18 November 1794. He was thirty; she was twenty; they had fifteen children. His wife and almost all of his children survived him. His married and family life seems to have been unusually happy. He may, on occasion, have been stiff in his social and political relations, but never with his family. It is noteworthy that, despite the evidence of Jane Austen and others regarding contemporary practices, his wife did not address him as Mr Grey or Earl Grey; rather she referred to him by the affectionate nickname of 'Car' both in letters to him and to their children. There is no doubt that he thoroughly enjoyed family life and life at Howick in Northumberland (perhaps three or four days' journey from London). This was not always a help to his political career.

When he took his seat in the House of Commons in 1787 his family political connections, if any, were probably moderately Tory. However, he was attracted by the views of Charles James Fox, and their relationship ripened into friendship. Grey became and remained a Foxite Whig. He was throughout his political career a competent speaker and on occasion a very good one.

In 1788 he became associated with Burke, Fox, and Sheridan in the management of the impeachment of Warren Hastings. On 12 April 1791 he moved, 'That it is at all times, and particularly under present circumstances, the interest of the country to preserve peace.' The avoidance of war, if at all possible – in the age of the French Revolution and Napoleon it was not easy – remained a consistent political view.

In 1792 Grey and other young associates founded the Society of the Friends of the People with, among others, the avowed purpose of forestalling radical reform by introducing moderate reform. In this area it achieved no success. Nevertheless, its relatively brief existence had some important permanent results.

It was the last straw that led to the secession of the Portland Whigs. They were opposed to any reform and objected to the Society and its aims. Fox, who was not a member of the Society but was the acknowledged Whig leader, supported the Society, so Portland and his followers left the party to join Pitt and the Tories. The Society collected and published a report on the manner by which members were 'elected' to the House of Commons (more details on this below). This report became a mine of factual information for reformers then and for historians since. Finally, the Society established the Whigs as the party of moderate reform and Grey as the leader of the moderate reform movement. As such, several times in the 1790s he introduced what may be called embryo Reform Bills; all were rejected on first reading.

After 1800, however, Grey seemed to lose his active interest in reform. He did not support various radical proposals, generally involving a wide extension of the franchise. He became (aged 42) in 1806 a member of the Ministry of All the Talents as First Lord of the Admiralty and in September, after the death of Fox, he succeeded him as Secretary of State for Foreign Affairs. He carried to a successful conclusion Fox's Bill for abolishing the slave trade. When the Government fell, he left office and did not again hold a position in the Government until 1830.

Having succeeded Fox as leader of the Foxite Whigs in 1807, Grey became the Whig leader in 1821 when Grenville and his followers left the party, some (but not Grenville himself) joining the Liverpool Government. During the whole period from 1807 to 1830 Grey was only occasionally an effective leader of the Opposition. From time to time, he offered to withdraw, and often seemed reluctant to visit London. He was firm in his opposition to the restrictive legislation of 1819; he did maintain a 'pure' Whig image by refusing to consider entry into the Canning Government, though he raised no serious objections when some of his followers did.

During this period various Reform Bills were proposed to Parliament, by Burdett, Lambton (later Baron then Earl of Durham), and, especially in the 1820s, by Lord John Russell. Grey made it clear, as did the Whigs as a group, that he would not support proposals for universal manhood suffrage. Since none of the Bills ever got beyond first reading in the Commons, none ever reached the Lords, so Grey had no occasion to support them and did not. Interest in reform, both in the country and in the Commons, waxed and waned in the 1820s, but waxed again at the end of the decade. The Marquis of Blandford introduced Reform Bills in June 1829 and February 1830, as did O'Connell and, once again, Russell, in May 1830.

George IV died in June 1830. Wellington, at odds with the Ultra Tories ever since his Government had passed a Catholic Emancipation Bill in 1829, was only uncertainly supported in the Commons. Accordingly, though he could have waited up to six months, he called for elections in July. Then, and even now, there was no agreement as to the results: had Wellington gained or lost? It seems clear that after the election, as before, he needed additional support to maintain a firm Government.

The new Parliament was formally opened on 26 October 1830. The King's Speech was delivered, and the Address Debate began on 2 November. Many, including Peel (who was to oppose vigorously the Reform Bills), assumed that reform would be a principal topic of debate during the session, but no mention was made of it in the King's Speech. In the debate on that speech, Viscount Althorp in the Commons, and Grey in the Lords, both raised the question. They referred to the disturbed conditions of the country and stressed the urgency of some measure of reform to preserve the Constitution. Wellington made his famous reply, insisting that the existing Parliament answered all good purposes, that he was not prepared to bring forward a reform measure, and that he would resist any such measure proposed by another. This statement almost certainly ensured the defeat of his Government.

On 15 November it was beaten, 233 to 209, in the Commons on a motion to refer the Civil List estimates to a committee. The majority was made up of a motley group of Whigs, Canningites, Ultra Tories, and Members who simply did not like Wellington. He seized the opportunity to resign and wrote that he did so to prevent consideration of a motion for reform submitted by Brougham.

The King sent for Grey. He became Prime Minister (aged 66) on 16 November, remaining in that office until his resignation (aged 70) on 8 July 1834, a period of just under four years. During this period his Government passed a number of very important legislative acts. Of these, however, by far the most important, and the one that most involved Grey, was the Reform Act of 1832. Grey's reputation as a Prime Minister rests largely on his handling of the various Bills leading to this Act. While this is not the place to discuss in detail the long efforts to secure passage, attention must be focused on the part played by Grey. It was his finest hour. It may be said that the frequent nervous illnesses that had plagued him during London visits in the 1820s never troubled him in this period. He was healthy, buoyant, and energetic, and he seemed to enjoy the exercise of power, at least until the Bill that was his personal concern became an Act.

His first task was to put together a Cabinet. This he did in a few days. He included Whigs of his generation – Lansdowne and Holland; younger Whigs – Althorp, Stanley, Graham, and Russell (the last not at first in the Cabinet); Canningites – Melbourne, Palmerston, Goderich, and Grant; Radicals – his son-in-law Durham (Hobhouse, also a Radical, later became Secretary at War but was not in the Cabinet); and even an Ultra Tory – Richmond. His most difficult problem was Brougham, fresh from a great election triumph in Yorkshire. Althorp was to be Chancellor of the Exchequer and Leader of the House of Commons. He was very effective in the latter capacity. Brougham, a more brilliant speaker, wayward, and independent, would certainly have been a difficult colleague. After one false start, Grey solved the problem tactfully by persuading Brougham to become Lord Chancellor.

This Cabinet was very mixed, as indeed was essential if a majority was to be obtained in the Commons. (There was certainly no clear Whig majority.) Goderich had already been Prime Minister; Melbourne, Russell, Stanley, and Palmerston were to be. Stanley and Graham were to become Tories and were to serve under Peel. Grey is said to have boasted that his Cabinet owned more acres of English land than any preceding Cabinet. It was emphatically 'aristocratic'. There were different views, stresses, and strains, but tactful and firm leadership held the members together, in spite of recurrent threats of resignation, until much important legislation had been accomplished.

When Grey took office the southern counties were troubled by the Captain Swing Riots, handled firmly, even severely, by Melbourne. In the winter of 1831-2 there was a cholera epidemic. The autumn of 1831 saw riots in Nottingham, Bristol, and elsewhere, and trade and agriculture were depressed in the winter of 1831-2. Not until the summer of 1832 could the country be said to enjoy peace, order, and some measure of prosperity. Abroad, the Government inherited a Belgian crisis, well handled through the winter of 1830-1. Thereafter the international scene was comparatively peaceful.

Grey made his first speech as Prime Minister on 22 November 1830. He said he had been allowed to indicate that he had the King's approval to introduce a Reform Bill. During the next few months his Cabinet survived rather than governed. Budget changes were forced upon it; minor measures were lost. But the Opposition, indeed the whole country, waited for the Reform Bill and tolerated, if they did not endorse, the Government. In the matter of reform Grey moved ahead early and steadily, but not unduly rapidly. He had many problems with which to contend, problems of which he was always keenly aware but which were often overlooked by partisans for or against reform and even sometimes by subsequent commentators.

The resultant Act, by modern democratic standards, was, of course, a moderate, indeed a very moderate, measure. It must, however, be considered in the historical context. The existing parliamentary system had been crystallised about the middle of the seventeenth century. Thereafter there had only been very few and very minor changes. On the whole, certainly until the advent of the Industrial Revolution, it had worked well. The great challenges of France, for example those of Louis XIV, the French Revolution and Napoleon, had been contained and beaten. For all the poverty and misery that existed in it, England had nevertheless become the richest and most powerful nation in the world. The existing system – and Grey certainly planned to make changes within the existing system and not by revolutionary measures outside it – gave much influence to those who controlled it. Any changes, except the most minor, were bound to excite firm resistance.

[343]

Among the problems that faced Grey were, first and foremost, what should be the nature of the Reform Bill? Second, Cabinet solidarity; third, the King; fourth, at least at the outset, the Commons; fifth, the Lords; and sixth, the public or at least that portion of the public (skilled workers, masters, the middle classes) that had the greatest interest in the subject. The Bill had to be acceptable to all, or at least to a majority. Some of the Cabinet, the King, and the Lords wanted little; some of the public wanted much – both sides had to be satisfied and convinced. Though now discounted by some historians, the threat of disorders and even revolution could not be ignored by a responsible government.

Before considering the nature of the Bill that Grey wanted, it is necessary to sum up briefly the existing parliamentary framework. There were rotten boroughs, in which the population had dwindled to little or nothing, and pocket (or nomination) boroughs, where one or very few men controlled elections, in effect appointing Members of Parliament. The report of the Society of the Friends of the People indicated that 154 individuals sent 307 (out of 658) Members to the Commons. In the late 1820s, Croker, a Tory opposed to reform, concluded that at least 276 (out of 489) English Members were returned by patrons. There was a very uneven distribution of Members in relation to population. For example, more Members were elected in the two counties of Cornwall and Wiltshire than in the five counties of Middlesex, Somerset, Warwickshire, Worcester, and Yorkshire, though the latter had a combined population of more than ten times that of the former. The franchise, with few exceptions, was very limited. Even in Westminster, generally considered a very democratic constituency, less than one quarter of adult males could vote. Though county constituencies enjoyed a uniform franchise, there was no uniformity in the borough constituencies in which about 82 per cent of the English Members were elected. These were the main features that the Government set out to alter.

Shortly after taking office Grey appointed a committee, consisting of Durham, Russell, Graham, and Duncannon, to prepare a Bill. He instructed them that their proposals should be based on property, existing territorial divisions, and fundamental forms, but should be inclusive enough to forestall further demands for reform. He wanted, it may be said, a Bill with the minimum that would satisfy the reform-demanding public and the maximum that would be acceptable to both Houses of

Parliament and the King. The committee completed its work by the end of 1830 and its proposals were discussed by the full Cabinet in January 1831. There some slight changes were made, generally in a conservative direction. When there were disagreements, decisions were apparently taken by Grey.

Next, he personally took the proposed Bill to the King; it was essential for its passage that the King should agree with it or, at least, not strongly oppose it. Through the whole course run on three Bills, it was Grey who always handled the King. He kept William IV fully informed; he was careful to record their conversations and agreements in letters to the King, written immediately after every meeting; he always replied immediately to any letters or comments of the King. In his first interview on the Bill Grey used a technique he was to use on other occasions. He discussed with the King not only the proposed provisions but also those more radical proposals that he and the Cabinet had rejected, thus suggesting that if the King did not go along with the proposals, he might have to put up with something more extreme. While the King, with one possible exception, behaved loyally to his ministers, his personal entourage was always opposed to reform and continually worked on him to oppose it. This was just one of Grey's many problems.

The long-awaited Bill was at last presented to the Commons on 1 March 1831 by Russell. The Bill proposed the complete elimination of about sixty boroughs. This was the famous Schedule A that caught most attention, winning the approval and support of the Radicals and exciting the greatest opposition from opponents. It also proposed the elimination of one Member from a number of boroughs (Schedule B); the redistribution of seats taken from these boroughs, some to go to counties, some to hitherto unrepresented boroughs, both more or less in proportion to population; a slight extension of the county franchise by including some leaseholders; and the establishment of a uniform borough franchise for residents (the famous 10 pound householder vote). Though the number of voters might be reduced (for example by the exclusion of non-resident voters) in a few boroughs, it was increased in most. (All, however, who had the right to vote but did not qualify under the new dispensation, retained the right for life, if residents.)

After an unprecedentedly long debate lasting several sittings the first reading was carried without a division. After further debate, in an all-night sitting, 22–3 March, the second reading was carried in an unusually large house by 302 to 301. Thus the first hurdle – perhaps the most important – was surmounted by one vote.

Shortly thereafter in committee stage a crippling amendment, designed to destroy the Bill, was carried. Grey immediately asked the King for a dissolution and persuaded him to grant one.

In the subsequent election the reformers achieved a substantial victory. The new Parliament was opened on 21 June. Six days later, with no waste of time, a new Reform Bill was introduced. The second reading was carried 6 July by 367 to 231, a majority of 136. Thereafter Grey had no problems with the Commons. He had timed the election well.

The committee stage lasted the whole summer. The third reading was not carried until 21 September. In the Lords the first reading was not opposed. Debate on the second started on 3 October and lasted for five sittings. It was concluded on the night of the 7–8th, in another all-night session. Grey opened and closed the debate for the Government and made at least one significant statement: he indicated that he would accept minor changes but warned the Lords that if they rejected the current Bill, they would sooner or later have to accept a Bill at least as 'efficient'. In spite of accusations made then and later that he was willing and even anxious to weaken the Bill, in fact he never departed from his demand for a Bill as 'efficient' as the one he was proposing. In the early hours of the 8th, the Lords rejected the Bill, 199 (including 49 proxies) to 158 (30 proxies), a majority of 41.

The next day the King asked Grey not to resign. He also indicated, however, that he was not surprised by the rejection (suggesting, no doubt, that he thought the Bill had gone too far), and affirmed that it could not be passed by the creation of new peers. Grey undertook to remain, provided he was allowed to proceed with another Reform Bill basically similar to that rejected. After the Commons had expressed approval of the Government's reform policy by a majority of 131, Grey and Althorp announced in their respective Houses that they would remain in office only if there were reasonable hope of passing an effective Reform Bill. Parliament was then prorogued.

For the next eight months Grey personally assumed most of the responsibility and work in connection with the progress of another Bill. Immediately he was confronted with two problems: a divided Cabinet and unrest in the country.

The Cabinet was divided and remained divided, first on the reform issue and later on other issues, but knowledge of this was fairly well kept from the country. There were those, in the autumn of 1831, who recommended a weakened Bill that would be acceptable to the Lords. On the other hand, there were those who demanded an immediate and firm request for more peers. Somehow Grey kept them all together.

The unrest in the country was potentially dangerous. There were riots in Derby, Nottingham and elsewhere, and a three-day destructive riot in Bristol. Although largely resulting from local issues, they were not entirely divorced from the popular demand for reform. At the same time the existing political associations (the Birmingham Political Union was the most influential of them) renewed their activities and new ones were formed (in London the National Political Union under the leadership of Francis Place). If the unrest got out of hand, it was likely to destroy support for an effective Reform Bill. Alternatively, if repression were too severe, it would forfeit support for the Government. Grey resolved the problem by issuing a royal proclamation declaring illegal those associations with a military character. This satisfied the King, who disliked all political unions and hoped they would be suppressed. Through intermediaries the Birmingham Political Union was asked to refrain from some contemplated activities that might have brought it under the ban. It and others complied. The unrest died down; the unions were not prosecuted and continued their work.

While no problem was expected with the Commons, difficulties with the Lords were certain if another Bill as 'efficient' as that rejected in October were to be passed. Four possibilities were open to Grey:

(1) He could weaken the Bill sufficiently to satisfy the Opposition. This he never considered.

(2) He, and others, could talk to individual peers, including bishops, with the object of converting them. This was actually done with some success. (In October there were only two bishops for and twenty-one against; in April there were to be eleven for and twelve against.)

(3) Discussions could be held with groups of peers. Perhaps not enthusiastically but with the clear intention of satisfying the King that he was trying all possible approaches, Grey negotiated, in two separate periods, with Wharncliffe and Harrowby and their small following, known as the Waverers. (They got no encouragement from the opposition leaders; Peel wrote a strong letter to Harrowby urging him not to compromise and firmly to resist a new Bill.) The first discussion, held late in 1831, produced no agreement. The Waverers really had little to

offer for the concessions they wanted. Grey was adamant on Schedule A, on the proposed new London metropolitan boroughs, and on the 10 pound householder franchise; but he was willing to discuss alterations in Schedule B and some in the proposals for redistribution of seats. Although no agreements were reached in the second discussions in 1832, the Waverers indicated that they would support the second reading, while preserving the right to try to amend the Bill in the committee stage and to vote against it on the third reading if suitable changes were not made.

(4) Grey's fourth option was to push for the creation of more peers. Some of his Cabinet were very eager for this approach, but there were serious difficulties. At that time, the accepted interpretation of the Constitution held that the final decision in this matter rested not with the ministers but with the King, who had already indicated his lack of enthusiasm. There was the question of how many would be required. The second Bill had been beaten by forty-one votes. In March 1832 Grey was to estimate that if slightly more than that number were created (certainly an unprecedentedly large creation – Anne's famous new creations, the one precedent, had involved only twelve), some who had voted for the Bill would turn against it, while others who had not voted would also vote against it. He concluded, therefore, that many more than forty would be required and that the King's consent would be unlikely. But in January 1832 he approached the King in somewhat vague terms since he himself was uncertain as to how many new creations he would need. At one time about twenty-one were suggested; later a number not greatly exceeding that amount. By the end of January the King agreed, in principle, to an unspecified but clearly not to an unlimited number of new creations provided that they were, for the most part, limited to eldest sons and other heirs of existing peers.

Somewhat unexpectedly Grey reconvened Parliament on 6 December 1831. A third Reform Bill was introduced on the 12th and the second reading was passed on the 17th. The committee stage occupied some weeks after the Christmas recess and the third reading was passed, by a majority of 116, on 22 March 1832. There had never been any doubt of the result. But the resistance of the Lords remained.

Early in March Althorp decided that immediate creation of peers was required and threatened to resign if Grey did not present a firm request to the King. Grey wrote him a masterly letter, arguing against such a precipitous step. This letter has sometimes been interpreted as revealing Grey's basic conservatism and a willingness to compromise. In fact it was intended to soothe the King, who had indicated that he might retreat from his promise of some new creations. To him a copy of the letter was sent. The letter accomplished exactly what Grey wanted: the Cabinet was held together and the King was persuaded that Grey was a right-minded man who would not request extreme measures unless their use was proved absolutely necessary. But Grey staked his political fortune on the prediction that the Bill would pass the second reading in the Lords without new peers.

In the House of Lords the first reading passed unopposed on 26 March. The debate on the second reading began on 9 April and occupied four sittings, being concluded on the night of 13–14 April. Grey again opened and closed the case for the Government. He concluded with a highly political and very clever speech, suggesting that all that was at stake was the acceptance of the principle that there should be some reform, leaving the exact details and the degree of reform to be settled in the committee stage. Still another all-night sitting resulted in a victory by a majority of nine (184, including 56 proxies, for; 175, 49 proxies, against). Grey's work and judgement were justified.

On 7 May a crippling amendment was carried in the committee. The next day Grey offered the King two choices: immediate creation of new peers or his resignation. The King chose the latter but asked Grey to remain in office until a new government had been formed. Grey, of course, consented. A week later Wellington informed the King that he could not form a Government. The King, then, had no choice; he had to retain Grey.

On 18 May the reluctant King at last agreed to the creation of the necessary number of new peers. That evening Grey and Althorp announced to their respective Houses that they were staying in office because they had been assured of the necessary means to pass the Bill. The Opposition concluded that further resistance was futile and all but a few die-hards withdrew from further sittings concerned with the Bill. It passed rapidly through the committee stage in the Lords and on 4 June the third reading was carried 106 to 22. The next day the Commons accepted some minor amendments. On 7 June the Royal Assent was given by Commission and the Bill became the Reform Act of 1832.

Thanks to Grey's steadiness, good judgement, and firm but tactful handling of the King, his Cabinet, and the political unions, the country had, if not exactly the first Bill, which had been subject in the second and third versions to many minor revisions, nevertheless, in terms of 'efficiency' and impact, what may justly be termed the Bill, the whole Bill, and nothing but the Bill. Scottish and Irish reform Bills were passed during the summer.

It may be suggested that the next two years, so far as Grey personally was concerned, were anti-climactic. His great work was done. Rifts in the Cabinet became greater and harder to heal; his London ill health again began to plague him.

The only serious foreign affairs problem that confronted the Grey Government had in fact started before he came to office: the Belgian revolution. It was, on the whole, favourably received in England. Grey's Government and the public were not prepared to have the Russians, Prussians, Austrians, or even the Dutch re-establish Dutch rule, but neither were they prepared to allow France, either directly or indirectly, to establish its control over Belgium or any part of it. The British negotiations were conducted primarily by Palmerston, the Foreign Secretary, but with the help and the constant personal interest and assistance of Grey. With the co-operation of Talleyrand, whom Grey frequently saw, a successful and peaceful solution was reached.

The first election held under the terms of the Reform Act took place in December 1832 and resulted, on the surface, in a victory for the Government or at least a defeat for the conservative Opposition. The Government's nominal supporters were, however, divided between those who wanted a vigorous programme of reforms and change and those who wanted only a moderate programme. Satisfying both groups was to prove impossible.

In spite of constant difficulties with the Irish question, which in the end led to Grey's resignation, the accomplishments of his Government in 1833 were considerable. The evidence indicates that they were not, as the Reform Act certainly was, Grey's own measures in which he took a strong personal interest and for which he exercised vigorous leadership. Nevertheless, it was his Government that was responsible.

Among the more important accomplishments was, first, the abolition of slavery throughout the British Empire. Grey had played an important role in the ending of the slave trade, and his son, Howick, did the same in the ending of slavery. Also in 1833 a Factory Act was passed; it was associated with Ashley, though in its final phase it was piloted through the Commons by Althorp. It was important because it established inspectors. In the same year the Government of India Act eliminated the last vestiges of the East India Company's trade monopoly, and established the great principle that government offices in India were to be open to qualified persons without regard to race, creed, or colour. An Irish Church Bill, which did not, due primarily to opposition in the Lords, go as far as the Government had hoped, at least relieved the Irish people from the necessity of paying 'vestry cess' to support the established Protestant Church. A Bank Charter Act helped modernise the banking system. Two law reform acts, especially that establishing a permanent judicial committee of the Privy Council, likewise modernised and improved the handling of justice. A grant for education, though small, marked the beginning of a development that would lead to a national system of free primary education for all. The following year the Commons passed a significant Poor Law Reform Act that was not completed in the Lords until after Grey's resignation.

Throughout its life, the Grey Government struggled with Irish problems. It hoped to mitigate them by reform of the (Protestant) Church of Ireland. Some members of the Cabinet were anxious to move far and vigorously on this path; others hardly at all. Grey hoped to keep them together. Shortly after Russell took a public and strong position on the issue, Stanley, Graham, Richmond, and Ripon (Goderich) resigned. Soon thereafter Althorp and others were unable to persuade Grey and the Cabinet to support modifications, which had been leaked to O'Connell, of a proposed Bill. Althorp resigned and Grey also, on 9 July 1834. Grey in fact had already resigned in January when the Cabinet would not support his Portuguese policy, but had been persuaded by the King and the Cabinet to continue. However, the divisions on Ireland and the Church were too great.

Grey was, perhaps, not a great Prime Minister. Others held the office for longer periods. Others played a more active role in developing parties, programmes, and legislation. He was, however, responsible for what one of its chief opponents, Sir Robert Peel, called the most important Act passed by Parliament in more than a hundred years. Because of Grey's leadership in connection with that Act, it has been said of him that he justly deserves to be 'renowned through all English history'.

BIBLIOGRAPHY

The standard life of Grey is still G. M. Trevelyan, *Lord Grey of the Reform Bill* (London, 1920). The standard account of the Reform Act has for a long time been J. R. M. Butler, *The Passing of the Great Reform Bill* (London, 1914). It has now been superseded by Michael Brock, *The Great Reform Act* (London, 1973). There is a short account by George Woodbridge, *The Reform Bill of 1832* (New York, 1970). For a different interpretation, see the articles of D. C. Moore, especially 'The Other Face of Reform', *Victorian Studies*, ii (1961), 7–34. Professor Moore's other articles are listed in the bibliography of Woodbridge, op. cit. Probably the two most important printed sources are the appropriate volumes of *Hansard's Parliamentary Debates* (3rd series, 1830 onwards), and *The Correspondence of the late Earl Grey with his Majesty King William IV and with Sir Herbert Taylor*, edited by Henry, Earl Grey (2 vols, London, 1867). The works of Butler, Brock, and Woodbridge listed above all have bibliographies.

23

VISCOUNT MELBOURNE

BY

DOROTHY MARSHALL

William Lamb, 2nd Viscount Melbourne, born 15 March 1779, second son of Peniston Lamb, 1st Viscount. Educated at Eton and Trinity College, Cambridge. Called to the Bar 1804. Married 1805 Lady Caroline Ponsonby, only daughter of the 3rd Earl of Bessborough; separated 1825; MP for Leominster 1806–1812; Northampton 1816; Hertford 1819–25; Secretary for Ireland 1827–8; entered Lords 1828; Home Secretary 1830; Prime Minister 1834 (dismissed same year); Prime Minister 1835–9 and 1839–41; stroke ended political career and died 24 November 1848. No surviving children.

VISCOUNT MELBOURNE

The life span of William Lamb, second Viscount Melbourne, who was
born in 1779 and died in 1848, covered some of the most formative years
in English history, when a hierarchical, pre-industrial society was moving irrevocably towards one dominated by urban and industrial pressures. During this period Lord Melbourne was Prime Minister for
seven years, from 1834 to 1841 except for the break of a few months.
How important was his ministry? This depends on the angle from
which it is viewed. Melbourne's direct influence on national policy and
constitutional developments was curiously negative. Yet his name is
more widely known than is that of some prime ministers whose tenure
of office yielded more positive and visible results because to Melbourne
fell the task of smoothing the path of monarchy for the young Victoria
when she became Queen in 1837. Any assessment of his premiership
therefore falls into two parts, the first from 1834 to 1837, the second
from 1837 to 1841.

The negative quality of the earlier period was inherent in William
Lamb's personality and background. As a second son he had not been
intended for a political career, and after Eton and Cambridge had been
called to the Bar in 1804. A year later his elder brother died leaving
young William heir to the viscounty and, as was customary for the
eldest sons of peers, he gave up the Bar in favour of politics, being
returned for the Whig interest as MP for Leominster in 1806. His
brother's death had equally important consequences for his private life;
it made him an eligible match for that wayward, passionate character
Lady Caroline Ponsonby, better known under her married name as
Lady Caroline Lamb. June 1805 saw the beginning of their storm-
tossed marriage. In contrast his years in the House of Commons were
calm. Though he could speak well on occasion he never had the 'feel'
of the House that Lord North had possessed, and though he was a
Member from 1806 to 1812 and again from 1816 to 1829, when on his
father's death he went to the Lords, so far his political career had been
undistinguished. It was not until 1827, at the age of forty-six, that
he first held office as Secretary for Ireland in Canning's short-lived

administration. This was in part due to the political set-up of the inter-vening years. A Whig by tradition he could not have held office under the Ultra Tories led by the Duke of Wellington. His opportunity came when, on the death of Lord Liverpool, the Tories split into two oppos-ing camps, the Ultras under the Duke and the moderates under Can-ning, whose middle-of-the-road politics in domestic affairs seemed to Lamb to hold out the best hope for stable government, always his prime and possibly his only political objective. Accordingly when Canning asked both him and Lord Palmerston to join the Government William, though without undue eagerness, did so.

His first taste of office was short. On Canning's death in 1828, after the brief and inglorious premiership of the tearful Goderich, the Ultra Tories came back under Wellington. Nevertheless it had been an en-couraging and revealing experience. As far as anyone in the perpetually troubled state of Ireland could be successful William Lamb could be so counted. For this his personality was largely responsible. His methods of doing business were informal, as indeed they were to be throughout his official career. He would on occasion even interview his callers while shaving, or in his bedchamber, arguing that they would probably prefer to be seen thus than not at all. This lack of ceremony, a willing-ness to welcome all shades of opinions to his house and his apparently unflappable easy manner commended him to the Irish. Melbourne was a man of few positive political views but an inborn scepticism inclined him to the virtues of tolerance. He had little use for bigoted Protestants and was sympathetic towards Roman Catholic emancipation. This in itself was a useful attribute in an Irish Secretary and one likely to make him popular in Dublin. Nevertheless he left Ireland in 1828 with few illusions. When later faced with the problem of Irish unrest, both as Home Secretary and as Prime Minister, he had little faith in the remedies pressed upon him by either O'Connell or his own colleagues. Roman Catholic emancipation, granted in 1829, had merely led to further demands and Melbourne's growing conviction was that 'it was the natural disposition of the people' and not specific grievances and mis-government that lay at the root of the Irish problem.

After a brief period out of office, during which Wellington and his right hand man, Peel, tried to stem the rising demand for parliamentary reform, the Whigs came back under the leadership of the ageing Lord Grey. In the new ministry Lord Melbourne was Home Secretary. On the surface it was a surprising choice for a ministry pledged to reform.

In no sense was Melbourne a reformer. His first instinct was to leave everything alone in the belief that to right a minor wrong, or to remove a minor injustice, was more than likely to create worse problems than it solved, and that to tinker with either the existing state of society or with existing constitutional arrangements might bring everything crashing down. In these views he was far from unique. Though the eighteenth-century Whigs had campaigned for parliamentary reform their aim had been to curb the power of the Crown in favour of the aristocracy, not to usher in popular democracy. Only the Radicals cherished any such aspirations. But by 1830 the demand of the middle classes, who felt that their wealth and material and intellectual contributions to society en-titled them to a greater share in the running of the country and in the shaping of policy, combined with the resentful mass of the working population, who had come to see in parliamentary reform the best solution for their economic ills, had produced a restlessness that threatened to slip into revolution. To Melbourne and his contemporaries this was something to be avoided at all costs. This fear, combined with the memory of the excesses of the French Revolution, provides the clue to much of the politics of the post-war decades and explains why the aristocratic Whigs placed themselves at the head of the demand for reform on the well-known principle, 'If you can't beat them join them'. Melbourne therefore joined Lord Grey's ministry partly because during his period as Irish Secretary he had discovered an unexpected scope for his very genuine abilities and partly because, though he disliked reform, he realised that in some shape it had become politically necessary, and that it was better to ride the tiger than be eaten by him, a principle to which he adhered throughout his career.

In the fight for the Reform Bill Melbourne himself played very little part. His responsibility was not so much to steer it through the Lords as to back up the forces of law and order at a time when these seemed to be threatened by a new militancy on the part of the masses. Though their misery could be, and to some extent was, exploited by radical re-formers and hotheads, the economic lot of the average landless country-man in overpopulated rural areas was stark enough to explain the waves of agrarian unrest that marked 1830, when the sky was lit by burning ricks and unpopular farmers and landowners were harassed by mobs demanding better wages. The immediate repression of such riots was the business of the local magistrates and the courts but clemency lay with the Home Secretary. It would be unfair to say that this was not exercised. In accordance with common practice, of those condemned to death only the ringleaders were actually hanged, though many of the rioters were transported, but Lord Melbourne put the full weight of his authority behind the work of suppression. He was to do the same in 1834 when the labourers of Tolpuddle strove to emulate the widespread formation of trade unions by the new type of industrial workers. In spite of a petition reputed to have been signed by some quarter of a million persons the Dorset labourers, convicted under an anti-revolutionary law of 1799 against illegal oaths, were transported. Lord Melbourne's view of society remained hierarchical; he was willing to do his duty by his inferiors who accepted their traditional place within it, but he had neither liking for nor understanding of the new middle classes and the desperate workers who swarmed beneath them. Within his own circle he was tolerant, kindly, even sentimentally emotional and sensitive, but the plight of people in the mass, whose lives lay outside his own experience, left him unmoved. His duty as he saw it was to stamp out and extinguish revolutionary fires even by blood if necessary, a duty made easier for a man of his temperament by the fact that it was his role to issue impersonal orders in London without having to come face to face with the personal anguish that resulted. Thus, in spite of his position as Home Secretary in a ministry that not only brought in the great Reform Bill but also passed the first effective Factory Act in 1833 and the Poor Law Amendment Act of 1834, his contribution was largely negative. He stamped out disorder: he suggested no innovations with which to deal with its causes.

By the spring of 1834 Lord Grey's ministry was in difficulties. Once again Irish affairs were producing divergent views within the Cabinet over the form that a renewed Coercion Bill should take, and as a result of intrigues and counter-intrigues Lord Althrop, the indispensable leader of the Commons, resigned. Lord Grey, whose enthusiasm for office after the strain of the last four years was low, declared it impossible to carry on without him and also resigned. It was not easy for William IV to find a replacement. The Whigs still had a majority in the Commons and therefore, though the King would have preferred Wellington and Peel, the new prime minister must be a Whig. The choice was not great. Both Lord John Russell and Lord Brougham would have been unacceptable to important elements in the party, if any group of men so weak and so divided can be dignified by that name. Melbourne seemed the best choice. William IV disliked him rather less than he did his other possible choices and his appointment seemed unlikely to upset the rest of the Cabinet. Melbourne himself is reported to have described the prospect as 'a damn bore' and hesitated as to whether to accept. This is not the stuff out of which great prime ministers are made! Melbourne lacked both the driving force of ambition and that of any deeply held convictions. Not for him was Chatham's 'I know that I can save this country and that no one else can'. Throughout his career Melbourne preferred to temporise and postpone. Nevertheless in the political circumstances of the day William IV's choice was not a bad one. It was true that Melbourne was the last man to deal constructively with the needs of a society in flux, when growing towns were posing ever greater problems of sanitation and power-driven factories were absorbing more and more of the labour force, while in rural areas the harshness of the new Poor Law was biting deep into agrarian society. Like Galileo Melbourne 'cared for none of these things'. It was only the disorder that they brought in their train that caused him concern. Nevertheless, because he was the kind of person he was, placed in the situation in which he found himself, he was able to do what a man of more drive and ambition could not have done, namely hold the Government together. This was no easy task. Parties were only beginning to develop much more than a rudimentary organisation; as a cohesive factor men were still more important than programmes in holding an administration together. It is still less misleading for modern readers to speak of Whigs and Tories than of a Whig or a Tory party, though there was probably more cohesion among the latter than the former.

This lack of common ground among the Whigs, many of whom called themselves Whigs not from any belief in a common policy or shared outlook but merely because they belonged to families traditionally Whig, was at once the great cause of Melbourne's troubles as Prime Minister and the reason why he was able to retain that office for so long. The Cabinet, which he inherited from Grey, contained too many divergent personalities, each with his own political programme, for his task to be an easy one. Lord John Russell was a man of doctrinaire outlook wedded to a limited conception of personal liberty. Lord Durham was wealthy, difficult to handle and Radical in his views. Lord Brougham, the Lord Chancellor, was wildly ambitious, a man of ideas and energy, a brilliant exhibitionist with considerable capacity for intrigue. Lord Palmerston, the Foreign Secretary, saw himself as the champion of constitutional liberty and was prepared to hector and bully autocratic rulers in a way that certainly did not make for smooth diplomatic relations. In contrast Lord Stanley, the future Lord Derby, leant to the extreme right and had more in common with Wellington than with Palmerston. To add to Melbourne's troubles this diverse bunch of Whigs did not by themselves command a majority in the Commons but were forced into an uneasy co-operation with the Radicals and the Irish under Daniel O'Connell. The Radicals can be described as a 'ginger group' ever pressing for further instalments of reform. They were critical of the Church, anxious to remodel the municipal corporations, anxious to cut out the dead wood of tradition from every part of the national administration and to reform it along the lines associated with the Benthamites. To please them was to antagonise the bulk of the true Whigs; to ignore their demands totally was to risk losing their support. The Irish were another headache. In spite of Roman Catholic emancipation Ireland had not settled down and O'Connell was now campaigning for a repeal of the Union. There was also the difficult question of the Protestant Church in Ireland. Should the Irish Catholic majority be forced to pay tithes for its upkeep? Should some of its revenues be diverted to secular ends, such as education? Whatever was decided was bound to displease one section of the uneasy triangle that between them supported the Government.

In circumstances where little could be done without everything collapsing Lord Melbourne's capacity to do absolutely nothing unless driven and then to do as little as possible was a definite asset. So too were his good looks, persuasive charm and his flair for personal relations. It was very difficult to pin him down and equally difficult to resent a failure that was masked by such good-humoured tact. Moreover behind his aversion to change for change's sake, and his conviction that to meddle with established practices would be productive of more harm than good, was a hard-headed realisation that he could not, any more than King Canute, hold back the tide, and that by conceding a little here and a little there, now conciliating the Radicals, now the Irish, and by keeping his colleagues from each other's throats, the Government could be carried on, even though its weakness was patent and it limped from crisis to crisis. This was possible, at least in part, because neither the Radicals nor the Irish genuinely wanted to pull the Government down if Melbourne were to be replaced by Wellington, from whom they expected even less than they were getting from the unsatisfactory, temporising Melbourne. Nor was Peel, now the effective leader of the

Tories, anxious to move prematurely; he was prepared to wait his time until his prey grew still weaker. The person who precipitated the crisis was William IV himself. Though Melbourne handled him with skill and the King had no personal animosity towards him, the royal preference was for Wellington and Peel, and when an opportunity occurred to get rid of the Whigs William IV seized it.

Lord Althrop, whose resignation over the Irish Coercion Bill had given Grey his excuse to resign also, had been persuaded to withdraw his resignation and serve in Melbourne's administration in his old capacity as Leader of the House. Unfortunately for the stability of the ministry his father, Lord Spencer, died, which meant that Althrop went to the Lords. This created a vacancy which Melbourne found difficult to fill. The King disliked the suggestion that Lord John might lead the House and, exercising for the last time the royal prerogative of dismissing a prime minister who still had the confidence of the Commons, asked for Lord Melbourne's resignation. William IV then sent for Wellington to hold the Government together until Peel, who was on a visit to Italy, could return and take over. In the few months that followed Melbourne played a passive part. He had found being Prime Minister a troublesome business and he hated trouble. It is interesting to speculate whether, in addition, he was influenced by the older tradition that the ministers were the King's servants and as such ought to be supported unless to do so were obviously against the national interest. On the score of national interest he would have had no qualms, having in many ways much more sympathy with the Tory outlook than with that of his own troublesome team. His period of release proved short. In January 1835 Peel went to the country and though in the general election the Tories increased their majority they remained a minority government, the Irish, despite their threats, having decided to support the Whigs as the lesser of two evils. Even so Melbourne did not force the issue and it was not not until Peel was defeated on the contentious question of the revenues of the Irish Church that the King was forced to ask Melbourne to form a new government. This he was reluctant to do; never possibly was there a more reluctant premier than he. Unfortunately for his peace of mind there seemed no alternative. Grey refused to come back and the moderate Tories, when approached, refused to form a coalition government. Because of his conviction that the King's government must be carried on Melbourne came back, though he was able to secure a slightly less troublesome Cabinet by refusing to include the difficult Lord Brougham in the new administration. Melbourne was to remain in office until 1841.

The results of his premiership were meagre if measured in the concrete terms of legislation. After difficulties and opposition in the Lords the Radicals succeeded in carrying the Municipal Government Act which effectively put the middle classes in control of urban local government in the boroughs. Something was also done to relieve the dissenters from the worst of their disabilities with regard to tithe. The registration of births, marriages and deaths was made official, so that for the first time reliable vital statistics were available. But the Irish problem continued to bedevil politics, and tinkering with it by introducing a new Poor Law, not well adapted to Irish conditions, did little to improve the situation. Melbourne was however lucky in his Undersecretary, Thomas Drummond, who was able, until he died of overwork, to blunt the edge of Irish discontent by providing that country with a competent administration. But for the most part, like the Abbé Sieyès who, when asked what he had done during the French Revolution replied that he had survived, Melbourne could only claim the same feat for his Government. This, until the accession of Victoria, was his major contribution to English political life. To Melbourne and his contemporaries this record would not seem as meagre as it may to his twentieth-century critics. In their eyes the responsibilities of government were confined to keeping order, raising taxes, dealing with foreign policy and, if war should break out, directing it. Men of the eighteenth century who dominated government circles saw no need for social change or for legislation to ease the process. Holding such views in an age in which both the economy and the society based on it were changing with a hitherto unknown rapidity Melbourne's contribution could not fail to be negative. His role was that of a caretaker until men of the stamp of Peel, heirs to the new industrial Britain, were able to take over the controls and leave the eighteenth century behind.

With the accession of Queen Victoria in 1837 a new chapter in both the history of the monarchy and in Melbourne's premiership opened. It was one in which all his talents and abilities, all the rich warmth of his charm and the depth of his maturity could be called into play. As a mentor to the young Queen he was able to assume a responsibility for which he was wonderfully fitted. Tiresome colleagues still remained; his parliamentary majority was small; Palmerston was still troublesome, forcing on Melbourne a foreign policy in the Middle East far too adventurous for his taste, but the burden that had seemed so heavy became bearable because Victoria depended on him. This was not surprising. The Duchess of Kent's strained relations with William IV and the ambitions of Conroy had isolated Victoria from the political world so that, with the exception of Baroness Lehzen, there was no one in her past on whom she could rely. She promptly therefore fell a willing victim to Melbourne's good looks, urbane charm and sympathetic manner. Almost immediately she was writing in her diary that she had had 'a comfortable talk' with him, while he found in her company something that had been lacking all his life. Melbourne was a man who needed female company; his mother, with whom his ties had been extremely close, died in 1818; his marriage had been disastrous; his long association with Mrs Norton had led to the scandal of the divorce court, even though his name had been cleared of adultery; Emily Eden and Lady Holland were not women who could fill his emotional needs. Now, at last, Fate had thrown him into the closest relationship with a girl of eighteen, full of vitality and a zest for life, yet in many ways naive and surprisingly innocent, whom it was his official duty to serve and his pleasure to train to fit herself for her role as Queen. His success in so doing must be the measure of his right to be considered among the more important of Britain's prime ministers.

To assess Melbourne's influence over Victoria is more difficult than at first sight might appear in view of the amount of time they spent together and her obvious admiration and affection for him. Contemporaries commented on the way in which her eyes would follow him, while she in turn could easily move him to tears of tender affection. To him fell the task of initiating her into the inner mysteries of political life, which the role of the monarchy in a changing world made it essential for her to develop if co-operation between the Crown and the Cabinet were to be smooth. Melbourne's own difficulties with William IV had made him all too conscious of this need. In 1837 the Crown was still far from being the mouthpiece of its ministers, though the balance of power was rapidly tilting in favour of the latter. Every morning Victoria and Melbourne discussed political business. As he informed Peel later, the Queen insisted on being kept in the picture but disliked having to listen to long involved expositions of a theoretical nature for which her mind was too concrete. His method was to explain in simple terms the basic problems and practical issues on which action had been taken from day to day as the need arose. It was an *ad hoc* way of educating the Queen in her political duty which was both painless and effective. It had however its dangers and its limitations. With a prime minister of Melbourne's tact and charm it worked well, but it left her ill prepared to deal with men like Gladstone or Palmerston who refused to play the game under the rules which Melbourne's initiation had conditioned her to expect. Moreover in order to lighten the burden of her official duties he told her that it was unnecessary for her to study in detail the mass of routine papers submitted to her. Baron Stockmar was later of the opinion that her failure to discuss political business with Albert in the early days of their marriage arose not so much from her reluctance to do so as from her inability because her mastery of detail was inadequate. In the years to come this pre-digestion of her official correspondence was a task that the Prince took over himself. Meanwhile it was natural that the young Queen should rely so heavily on her ever-helpful Prime Minister. But this reliance had its disadvantages in that it bred, or perhaps it would be more accurate to say confirmed, in Victoria a spirit of partisanship that was increasingly to come into conflict with the growing political convention that the Crown must be neutral and stand above party conflict, though it is true that neither of her royal predecessors had done so. This partisan quality, which Victoria was never to lose, set the pattern of her relationships with her prime ministers throughout her reign; the nearer they conformed to that which existed between her and Melbourne the more successful they were.

Even in the early years of her reign Melbourne had less influence over his royal mistress than might at first sight be supposed; nor was he always capable of applying the brake to her impulsive actions. This was demonstrated first in the unfortunate affair of Lady Flora Hastings and secondly in the so-called 'Bedchamber Crisis'. In her early years as Queen the deeply buried resentment that she had felt against the domination of her mother, the Duchess of Kent, and the Comptroller of her household, Sir John Conroy, showed itself in a cold dislike of anybody associated with them. When therefore Victoria and Baroness Lehren observed a change in the figure of Lady Flora Hastings, her mother's Lady-in-Waiting, after she returned from Scotland in company with Sir John, they immediately assumed that she was with child by him. The rumours grew and the Court buzzed with gossip, a gossip that should have been stilled but was not when an examination carried out by two doctors pronounced Lady Flora to be a virgin. As the

perhaps manipulated her.
changing face of Parl →

Hastings were an important Tory family the affair got considerable publicity, and when later it was proved that Lady Flora had died of a malignant tumour Victoria's own popularity was much damaged. How much blame for the mishandling of this affair accrued to Melbourne it is difficult to establish. In its early stages he had followed a policy of drift and almost seems to have shared Victoria's suspicions, though whether this was due to his desire not to cross her or to the laxer moral code of his youth can only be surmised. He was not likely to be shocked if Lady Flora was indeed pregnant. Though his mother was a woman who managed her domestic life with the utmost discretion Melbourne himself was quite well aware that gossip had it that the first Viscount had not been in fact his father. What is surprising is not that he believed the rumours about Lady Flora but that, used as he was to irregularities in the best families, he handled this particular scandal with so little discretion and with so little finesse. He was certainly aware of the dangers of publicity yet he failed to impress on Victoria the need to behave in such a way as to scotch them, which argues that it was never he but always she who was in command of the situation.

This is true also of the Bedchamber Crisis, though here Lord Melbourne's conduct was constitutionally correct. In spite of Victoria's unflinching support his control of the Commons was slipping. His majority had been still further reduced in the general election of 1837, obligatory on the accession of a new monarch, the Cabinet was neither strong nor united while the difficulties of being forced to rely on the co-operation of the Radicals and the Irish remained. In addition there was unrest in Canada and in Jamaica. The former, too complicated to be dealt with here, had arisen from the antagonism between Upper and Lower Canada and between the French and British settlers. It was not an issue about which Melbourne cared deeply, and it did appear to present him with an opportunity to get rid of that difficult colleague the Earl of Durham by sending him to deal with the aftermath of rebellion. This he did effectively but in so high-handed a manner as to provoke criticism in Parliament which, because of Melbourne's lukewarm defence, led to the Earl's resignation and further criticism of the Government. The trouble in Jamaica, which had arisen out of the difficulties inherent in the freeing of the slaves, had more immediate repercussions. Melbourne's majority on a motion to suspend the Constitution of the island sank to four, so that he felt it necessary to resign. In spite of his personal grief – both he and Victoria were near to tears –

Melbourn didn't sufficiently prepare V. for this!

Melbourne did everything he could to make the change easy for the Queen, perhaps too easy, because in the hope of softening the blow he had left her with the belief that her Ladies, all of them Whigs, would not be changed. Apart from that he did everything in his power to reconcile the Queen to accepting Peel as her new minister with a good grace, and while negotiations for a new government were in progress he refrained from dining with her. What followed provides an interesting barometer of the extent of his influence over her political conduct when this went against the grain. Victoria did not like Tories and she did not like Peel; when therefore a misunderstanding arose as to whether Peel had insisted on replacing some or all of her Whig Ladies by Tories the indignant young woman manoeuvred Peel into declining to form a ministry and the whole Cabinet into supporting her, though Melbourne was somewhat disconcerted to discover that in fact Peel had only asked for some replacements. As a consequence Victoria gained her point and retained Melbourne as her prop and stay until his defeat in the Commons by one vote on a motion of no confidence in June 1841. Though by this time she was becoming more and more dependent on Albert, the Queen made a last effort to save Melbourne, insisting against his better judgement in appealing to the country. The verdict went against him and he resigned. By then her apprenticeship was over.

Melbourne's influence over Victoria was not confined to training her to become a constitutional monarch. Her education had been limited and her knowledge of the world around her bounded by her mother's rigid determination to keep her daughter from all doubtful contacts. Nowhere could she have found a better mentor to broaden her interests beyond those of the schoolroom and to mature her outlook than Lord Melbourne. The mornings were devoted to public business but he usually dined with the Queen three or four times a week; he was a frequent visitor at Windsor when the Queen was there and often they rode together. In these early years her diary is full of his conversations on these occasions, which Victoria found highly entertaining and amusing, and which ranged widely over personalities past and present, over literature and painting and the world as he had known it, so that inevitably she began to see through his eyes. Contemporaries were agreed as to the stimulating flood of paradox, irony and observation that poured forth with a richness that even Victoria found too abundant to record in her journal. Yet even here it is difficult to estimate the permanence of Melbourne's influence because later it was to be over-laid by that of her 'dear Angel' Albert. Melbourne's own sense of values was that of an eighteenth-century nobleman, tempered in his conversations with her by the moral and religious restraints that he felt necessary when communicating with a young woman of impeccable moral standards. To his credit he strove to imbue his pupil with some of his own tolerance towards human frailties and some realisation that as Queen she must learn to show at least some measure of social complaisance towards persons whom she neither liked nor respected, trying to tone down with a little grey the black and white of her moral palette. But though he endeavoured to soften her judgement of people he did little to waken in her any understanding of the social problems that confronted the new industrial urban Britain. In so far as Victoria ever developed a social conscience, it was due to Albert. Nor did Melbourne contribute anything towards her later emotional response to the idea of empire.

Victoria was sad when Melbourne took his final leave of her as Prime Minister and for some months continued to keep up a regular correspondence with him, in itself an act of some constitutional impropriety which Baron Stockmar was terrified might reach the ears of her new Prime Minister, Sir Robert Peel. In this, as in the Bedchamber Crisis, the Queen went her own way; in both cases Melbourne allowed his heart to rule his head. Nevertheless any significant part that he had played both in the life of Britain and in that of her Queen was over by 1841. Life can be dull for prime ministers who have outlived their usefulness: this was to be Lord Melbourne's fate. When he died in 1848 his death brought to Victoria only the gentle grief of nostalgia: the era of her hero worship was long past. Even today it is as a man, as the husband of Lady Caroline Lamb and as the guide, philosopher and friend of the young Queen Victoria, and not as a prime minister *per se*, that Lord Melbourne is best remembered. How then is one to sum up his place in the gallery of Britain's prime ministers? He was responsible for no innovations in constitutional practice, no important legislation. He remained either unaware or disapproving of the changes that were taking place at home and in the colonies. His views on the role of government remained those of the eighteenth century. Even the extent of his long-term influence over Victoria is easy to overestimate. Though between her accession and her marriage he was the best-loved figure in her life, 'dear Lord M.', later she adopted Albert's values rather than his. Nevertheless during his term of office Lord Melbourne performed two valuable services for Britain. He held government together and maintained law and order until the country was ready to move forward under Peel. Above all he gave Victoria a breathing-space in which to prepare herself under his understanding and loving guidance for the tasks that lay ahead. She was the niece of George IV and William IV and a passionate, self-willed young woman when she came to the throne. Without the apprenticeship to constitutional monarchy that she served under Melbourne she might well have been a less successful queen.

BIOGRAPHICAL NOTES ON PERSONS MENTIONED IN THE TEXT, OTHER THAN PAST OR FUTURE PRIME MINISTERS, WHO WILL BE FOUND UNDER THE APPROPRIATE ESSAYS IN THE VOLUME

Lord Althrop, John Charles Spencer (1782–1845), later Earl Spencer. Leader of the House of Commons under Lord Grey. He was not a brilliant speaker, and preferred the life of a country landowner to that of a politician, but was completely trusted by friends and opponents alike because of his truthfulness and integrity.

The Benthamites. Followers of Jeremy Bentham (1748–1832), writer on ethics, jurisprudence, logic and political economy. Preached Utilitarianism based on the greatest good of the greatest number.

Lord Brougham, Henry Peter (1778–1868). Prominent lawyer. Defended Queen Caroline at her trial (1820). Active in promoting popular education, was instrumental in the founding of London University, the Society for the Diffusion of Useful Knowledge, etc. Became Lord Chancellor in 1830 and was created Baron Brougham and Vaux.

Conroy, Sir John, 1st baronet (1786–1854). Equerry to the Duke of Kent and after his death Comptroller of the Duchess's household. Intrigued to have the Duchess made Regent for Victoria if she succeeded to the throne before reaching the age of 21 in the hope of being the power behind the Duchess. Victoria detested him.

Lord Durham, John George Lambton (1791–1840). Created baron in 1830 and earl in 1832. Played an active part in the fight for the Reform Bill and headed the radical wing of the Whigs. Was sent as ambassador extraodinary to St Petersburg 1835–7 and sent to Canada to deal with the aftermath of the rebellion there in 1839. His subsequent report on British North America had considerable influence on subsequent British policy there.

[368]

Eden, Emily (1797–1869) daughter of William Eden 1st Baron Auckland. Traveller and novelist. Her 'The Semi-Attached Couple' and 'The Semi-Detached House' give very authentic pictures of the society in which she moved.

Fox, Elizabeth Vassall, Lady Holland (1770–1845). Born in Jamaica, married Sir Geofrey Webster, eloped with Lord Holland and married him 1797. A great Whig hostess who made Holland House a centre for politicians and men of letters.

O'Connell, Daniel (1775–1847). Called 'The Liberator'. A prominent Irish political leader. He led the successful fight for Catholic Emancipation (1829) and subsequently led the fight in the House of Commons for the repeal of the Union.

Baron von Stockmar, Christian Fredrich (1787–1863). Entered the service of Prince Leopold of Saxe-Coburg, afterwards King Leopold of the Belgians, as private physician in 1816 and remained the close friend and confidential advisor to the Coburgs.

24

SIR ROBERT PEEL

BY

ASA BRIGGS

Robert Peel, 2nd Bart., born 5 February 1788, son of Robert Peel, wealthy manufacturer. Educated at Harrow and Christ Church, Oxford. In 1809, aged 21, MP for Cashel, Tipperary; afterwards for Chippenham; University of Oxford 1817–29; Tamworth 1830–50; Under-secretary for War and the Colonies 1810; Chief Secretary for Ireland 1812–8; Home Secretary 1822–1827 and 1828–1830; Prime Minister, First Lord of the Treasury and Chancellor of the Exchequer 1834–5; Prime Minister 1841–5 (resigned) and 1845–6 (resigned). Died 2 July 1850. Married 1820 Julia Floyd; five sons and two daughters.

SIR ROBERT PEEL

When an obscure journalist, W. T. Haly 'of the Parliamentary Galleries', published a book in 1843 called *The Opinions of Sir Robert Peel*, he told his readers in the preface that the book was designed to be 'a sort of dictionary of general political knowledge'.

Peel was then fifty-five years old and had been Prime Minister for two years, a strong Prime Minister, concerned personally and directly with the management of all the affairs of the country, economic and political, domestic and foreign. During the course of his long political life, which had begun in 1809 when his father bought him a seat in the House of Commons, he had expressed opinions on all aspects of national policy in a changing society. Just before he became Prime Minister in 1841 he had made a speech in Parliament attacking the Whig ministers in which he very characteristically posed two rhetorical questions which Haly could take as the motto of his book and print on his title page. 'Where is the man who has more explicitly declared than I have, his opinions upon all the great constitutional questions that have of late years been raised? . . . Have I not, when any question has been brought forward of important public interest, invariably expressed my opinions in plain and explicit terms?'

Yet the 'political knowledge' which Peel acquired and expressed and which Haly accumulated was essentially practical rather than theoretical. It could be and even recently has been set out in the form of maxims, almost as succinct as those of Mao Tse-tung. 'There seem to me very few facts, at least ascertainable facts, in politics.' 'The great art of government is to work by such instruments as the world supplies.' 'No government can exist which does not control and restrain the popular sentiments.' 'I am not sure that those who clamour most suffer most.' 'There are many things which I know to be morally wrong, with which neither I nor you can interfere in the way of legislation.' 'The longer I live, the more clearly do I see the folly of yielding a rash and precipitate assent to any political measure.'

Peel had great intellectual power – he had been outstandingly successful in his examinations at Oxford in 1808 only one year before he entered Parliament – but it was the kind of intellectual power that drove him with unremitting industry from logical analysis first to determined advocacy and second to executive action. Harriet Martineau, who admired the way in which he brought about the repeal of the Corn Laws in 1846, his greatest and most controversial act, called him 'a great doer of the impossible'. Necessarily this meant that he frequently changed his mind on major issues, as he did in the case of the Corn Laws, whilst maintaining great consistency in the way in which he confronted every issue when it arose. In describing how he had selected extracts from Peel's writings and speeches Haly observed that scrupulous care had been taken 'never to injure a context' and that the extracts had been assembled irrespective of their specific content. Peel would have strongly approved of this approach. Knowledge for him was always related to context: the content of what he said at particular times, he argued, had to be interpreted and re-interpreted in the light of his unceasing endeavour to discover the necessary operational truth for the particular occasion. His contemporary and admirer, Guizot, who as Premier of France in 1847 and 1848 had to cope with revolutionary 'political knowledge' of a very different variety, wrote a book about Peel in 1856 in which he called him 'a man of essentially practical mind, consulting facts at every step, just as the mariner consults the face of heaven'. His close political colleague and equally fervent admirer, the Duke of Wellington, testified in the House of Lords after Peel's death that his oustanding quality was veracity: 'I never had in the whole course of my life, the slightest reason for suspecting that he stated any thing which he did not firmly believe to be the fact.'

Yet not everyone was unduly impressed by these qualities. Walter Bagehot wrote an essay on 'the character of Sir Robert Peel' in the same year as Guizot published his book. He acknowledged the veracity and the fact that Peel did not get 'into scrapes', like Lord John Russell, and he admitted that he got nearer than anyone else to 'our definition of a constitutional statesman'. Bagehot's half cynical definition of such a statesman, however, was that he combined 'the powers of a first-rate man and the creed of a second-rate man'. And so the brilliant essayist went on, comparing Peel unfavourably with his Harrow schoolfellow, Byron, whilst recognising that Byron could never have been a statesman. Byron's mind was volcanic: the lava flowed. 'The mind of Peel was the exact opposite of this. His opinions far more resembled the daily accumulating, insensible deposits of a rich alluvial soil. The great stream of time flows on with all things on its surface; and slowly, grain by grain, a mould of wise experience is unconsciously left on the still, extended intellect. You scarcely think of such a mind as acting; it always seems acted upon.'

From his mid-Victorian vantage point Bagehot looked back to Peel's early career as a member of Lord Liverpool's Government – Chief Secretary for Ireland from 1812 to 1818 and Home Secretary from 1822 to 1827 – commenting *en passant* that he had once defended the attitude of the authorities at Peterloo in 1819, the passing of the Six Acts, the Imposition of Tests and the rule of Orangemen. He had been once known, indeed, as 'Orange Peel'. He had started office as Under-secretary for War and the Colonies from 1810 to 1812, 'the chosen representative of a gentry untrained to great affairs, absorbed in a great war, only just recovering from the horror of a great revolution.' That was the original substratum.

'From a certain peculiarity of intellect and fortune, he was never in advance of his time. Of almost all the great measures with which his name is associated, he attained great eminence as an opponent before he attained even greater eminence as their advocate. On the Corn Laws, on the currency, on the amelioration of the criminal code, on Catholic emancipation . . . he was not one of the earliest labourers, or quickest converts. He did not bear the burden and heat of the day; other men laboured, and he entered into their labours. As long as these questions remained the property of first-class intellects, as long as they were confined to philanthropists or speculators, as long as they were only advocated by austere intangible Whigs, Sir Robert Peel was against them. So soon as these same measures, by the progress of time, the striving of understanding, the conversion of receptive minds, be-came the property of second-class intellects, Sir Robert Peel became possessed of them also. He was converted at the conversion of the average man.'

This alternative verdict is interesting but inadequate. It leaves out Peel's courage and it underestimates the power of prejudice not only inside Peel's own party – the wartime party of Pitt, which Peel more than any other man transformed into a viable Conservative party – but inside 'the average man'. Nor does it place in European perspective, as Guizot was able to do, Peel's character and achievements as a

Conservative statesman. The time perspective was wrong also, for we can now see clearly, far more clearly than in 1856, that without Peel's reforms there would have been no golden age of Victorian Britain. Bagehot was right, however, to add to his verdict that Peel was 'a great administrator':

'Civilisation requires this. In a simple age work may be difficult but it is scarce. There are fewer people and everybody wants fewer things. . . . Anybody can understand a rough despotic community – a small buying class of nobles, a small selling class of traders, a large producing class of serfs, are much the same in all quarters of the globe; but a free intellectual community is a complicated network of ramified relations interlacing and passing hither and thither, old and new – some of fine city weaving, some of gross agricultural construction. You are never sure what effect any force or any change may produce on a framework so exquisite and so involved. Govern as you may, it will be a work of great difficulty, labour and responsibility.'

Whatever our twentieth-century verdict on Peel, we must continue to take account of the relevant components to which Bagehot directed attention – not just intellect, fortune and character, but 'the progress of time' and the increasing complexity of society. We must note that Peel was not only able but rich, that the country in which he lived was only partially industrialised but that it was becoming more and more industrialised each year, that between the world of the Six Acts and the year of Peel's death in 1850 Luddites had given way to Chartists, broadsheets to newspapers and stage-coaches to railways. Given the flux, government depended not only on making wise choices but on making them at the right time. Moreover, because government was increasingly difficult, it had both a political and a moral dimension. The former was altered but not transformed after the passing of the Great Reform Bill of 1832, which gave the vote to large numbers of middle-class people: the latter was to be transformed mainly after Peel's death under the influence of Gladstone who started life as a High Tory – higher than Peel had ever been – and after the splits of 1846 became a 'Peelite'.

As for the added sense of responsibility, there was no one in the country who was more clear about this than Peel. Dedicated to an ideal of public service and as willing as Wellington to respond to the call, he felt many of the strains. As Prime Minister, he was general manager rather than co-ordinator, and there is no more systematic evidence of the strains of difficult management in any age than we can find in the voluminous private papers of Peel. Others could play with issues: he had to settle them. And he knew the cost. One of the most revealing letters he wrote was in 1845, when his party was already bitterly divided, particularly on the Corn Laws, and he himself was being subjected to unparalleled pressures:

'The fact is that the state of public business while Parliament sits is becoming in many ways a matter of most serious concern. I defy the [Prime] Minister of this country to perform properly the duties of his office – to read all he ought to read, including the whole of the foreign correspondence; to keep up the constant communication with the Queen *and the Prince*; to see all whom he ought to see; to superintend the grant of honours and the disposal of civil and ecclesiastical patronage; to write with his own hand to every person of note who chooses to write to him; to be prepared for every debate, including the most trumpery concerns; to do all these indispensable things, and also sit in the House of Commons eight hours a day for 118 days. It is impossible for me not to feel that the duties are incompatible, and above all human strength – at least above mine.'

Peel had great human strength. He needed every ounce of it. But he had to work unbelievably hard. In an age when exploited working men were pressing for a Ten Hours Bill to shorten the length of the working day, Peel never applied the limitations of a Ten Hours Bill to himself.

Peel was profoundly interested in the fortunes of working men in the changing society. 'What struck me above all in conversation with him,' wrote Guizot, 'was his constant and passionate preoccupation with the state of the working classes in England.' He described them as 'a disgrace as well as a danger to our civilisation'. His own fortune and background were directly relevant both in this connection and in the broader context of the development of his opinions. He was born in Lancashire, the son of one of England's greatest and richest industrialists, who had made a fortune out of the cotton industry, and the grandson of a man who had started life as a small Lancashire yeoman farmer. He never tried to hide this background, and he was often taunted for it by members of his own party who were willing to nickname him 'the Spinning Jenny'.

When during his great ministry of 1841 to 1846 he was forced to grapple with economic issues which fundamentally affected the interests of landlords, farmers, industrialists, traders and working men alike, he was fully aware of what was at stake in each case. He was an enlightened landlord, an improving farmer who was proud of his model farm at Drayton, and leader of a party which was still dominated by the agricultural interest. Yet his own origins lay in industry, and his father had risen by self-help not by privilege to a position of influence, whereby he could buy his son a seat in the House of Commons where he already sat himself. If any man was fitted by social upbringing to reconcile conflicting interests in an industrialising society, it was Peel. Significantly Richard Cobden, leader of the Anti-Corn Law League (whose love-hate relationship with Peel is one of the fascinating themes of the 1840s), said in a speech long before Peel decided to repeal the Corn Laws, 'I do not altogether like to give up Peel. You see he is a Lancashire man'. Likewise, Ebenezer Elliott, the Anti-Corn Law rhymer, commented in 1842, 'Peel, I have long thought, understands our position, and will do his best to prevent the coming catastrophe'.

Neither Elliott nor Cobden completely understood Peel's own position. After he had repealed the Corn Laws Cobden wrote to him privately urging him to dissolve Parliament and go to the country on the cry of 'Peel and Free Trade'. 'You represent the *idea* of the age,' he said, 'and it has no other representative among statesmen.' Peel could never have contemplated himself playing such a role. He did not want repeal of the Corn Laws to ruin agriculture or to destroy the power of the landlords; he disliked the thought of 'a dull succession of enormous manufacturing towns, connected by railways, intersecting abandoned tracks which it was no longer profitable to cultivate'; he tried to give guarantees to agriculture, maintaining that 'the land is subject to particular burdens' and that compensation was necessary in some form or other to replace the unconditional loss of duty; and he refused to consider seriously anything like a new middle-class system of government which would have meant revision of the tax system and further assaults, of the kind the Anti-Corn Law League had specialised in, on the social position of the landlord. Repeal, in his view, had become necessary by 1845 in the national interest – and because of what was happening in Ireland – and not in the interests of one class: its object was 'to terminate a conflict which . . . would soon place in hostile collision great and powerful classes in this country'. His reply to Cobden, therefore was reserved and dignified, tempered, perhaps, with mild contempt.

'If you say that I individually at this moment embody or personify an idea be it so. Then I must be very careful that, being the organ and representative of a prevailing conception of the public mind, I do not sully that which I represent by warranting the suspicion even, that I am using the power it confers for any personal object. . . . I must also ask you to consider this. After the passing of the Corn and Customs Bill, considering how much trade has suffered of late from delays, debates and uncertainty as to the final result, does not this country stand in need of *repose*? Would not a desperate political conflict throughout the length and breadth of the land impair or defer the beneficial effect of the passing of those measures?'

It was because Peel had an instinctive feeling for 'repose' and a deep-rooted fear of disorder (strongly influenced by his early experiences in Ireland) that he was Conservative. He did not wish to see ancient institutions lose their hold or crucial decisions about national policy be determined by 'agitation'. 'This country has been governed better than any other country on earth,' he argued in 1831 in the middle of the debates on the Great Reform Bill to which he was opposed. A few months later, when it was clear that the Reform Bill would be passed, he told a colleague that it was the task of their party

'to teach young inexperienced men . . . charged with the trust of the Government that, though they may be backed by popular clamour, they shall not override on the first spring tide of excitement every barrier and breakwater raised against popular impulses. . . . [and] that the carrying of extensive changes in the Constitution without previous deliberation shall not be a holiday task.'

Two years after that, when the Reform Act was a *fait accompli*, the Tamworth Manifesto, an address to his own constituents, urged the necessity of preserving limited constitutional monarchy and the rights of each branch of the legislature, of maintaining the establishment, property and privileges of the Church, and of resisting a series of specious reforms which would together convert Britain into a democratic republic. In 1848, when revolution was sweeping Europe and he had been out of office for more than two years, Peel reaffirmed the same convictions. 'I hope the people of this country has sense enough to comprehend the lesson which is written for their instruction and will cling the more strongly to their own institutions. Democracy on the continent is teaching us what it can do for the security of Life, Liberty and Property, as compared with Monarchy.'

Peel's intellectual and administrative ability as Prime Minister between 1841 and 1846 was one of the factors that saved Britain from revolution. He made necessary economic adjustments to the fiscal and banking system which ensured long-term economic prosperity just as he had made necessary religious adjustments in 1829 when he and Wellington (against their previous opinions and inclinations) carried Catholic emancipation. He was never reactionary. In his very first speech to the House of Commons after the general election which followed the passing of the Great Reform Bill he had looked to the future, not to the past, and had accepted what had happened without approving of it: he had added for good measure that 'he was for reforming every institution that really required reform; but he was for doing it gradually, dispassionately, and deliberately in order that reform might be lasting'. Thereafter he deliberately set out to win the support of middle-class manufacturers, traders and shopkeepers as well as aristocrats and country gentlemen. 'We deny that we are separated by any line of interest or any other line of demarcation, from the middling classes', he exclaimed in 1834 when for a hundred days he was Prime Minister for the first time with a majority of Members of the House of Commons against him. His predecessor, the languid Whig Lord Melbourne, who had been dismissed by William IV, belonged to the aristocracy: did not he, Peel, by contrast proclaim the possibilities of something more than continuingly exclusive aristocratic government?

'What was the grand charge against myself – that the King had sent for the son of a cotton-spinner . . . in order to make him Prime Minister of England. Did I feel that by any means a reflection on me? . . . No; but does it not make me, and ought it not make you, gentlemen, do all you can to reserve to other sons of other cotton-spinners the same opportunities, by the same system of laws under which this country has so long flourished, of arriving by the same honourable means at the like destination?'

When during the ministry of 1841 to 1846 he prepared the great budgets which involved drastic reductions in protective duties and in the range of articles subject to tariff protection, the re-imposition as a fiscal imperative of the Income Tax, and the balancing of the Government's accounts not by expedients but by deliberately planned policies, he was not making concessions either to vested interests or to ideological groups, but acting in conformity with his own convictions. And when he was converted to belief in free trade in corn, the biggest fiscal reform he could make, he was willing to provoke the interests without accepting any free trade ideology. He was influenced by industrial depression in England before he was forced, along with his colleagues, to make up his mind about the emergency situation in Ireland. 'Can we vote public money for the sustenance of any considerable portion of the people, on account of actual or apprehended scarcity,' he asked his colleagues in November 1845, 'and maintain in full operation the existing restrictions on the free import of grain?'

Once he had been converted, Peel felt that he could win working-class support on social grounds as well as middle-class support on economic grounds. It was not theory that had made him change his mind but experience: 'You may talk of improving the habits of the working classes, introducing education amongst them, purifying their dwellings, improving their cottages; but, believe me, the first step towards improvement of their social condition is an abundance of food.'

The change could be defended, he argued, on Conservative rather than on Radical grounds. 'I have thought it consistent with true Conservative policy, to promote so much of happiness and contentment among the people that the voice of disaffection should no longer be heard, and thoughts of the dissolution of our institutions should be forgotten in the midst of physical enjoyment.'

When the Corn Laws were in the last stages of being repealed, Peel dealt with what was basically the same point in his peroration to his last speech in the Commons on the subject, a speech which is too impregnated with self-praise to appeal without qualification to posterity:

'I shall leave a name execrated by every monopolist who . . . clamours for protection because it accrues to his individual benefit; but it may be that I shall leave a name sometimes remembered with expressions of goodwill in the abodes of those whose lot it is to labour, and to earn their daily bread by the sweat of their brow, when they shall recruit their exhausted strength with abundant and untaxed food, the sweeter because it is no longer leavened by a sense of injustice.'

In dwelling on this theme Peel was to win short-term dividends. He was cheered in the streets as he left the House of Commons, he was praised in the provincial newspapers and in *Punch*, and when he died in 1850 after a riding accident in the heart of London, popular funds were raised throughout the country to perpetuate his memory in statues and parks. The pennies of the poor were collected without difficulty. 'I thought he had a great hold on the country,' wrote Sir James Graham, who had been his Home Secretary and *alter ego* in the ministry of 1841 to 1846, 'but had no idea it was so deep and strong and general as now appears.'

The short-term dividends acquired long-term value as the country moved into quieter and more comfortable times during the middle years of the nineteenth century, what W. L. Burn called 'the age of equipoise'. We can see in retrospect how important Peel's conception of politics was in a political system where the majority still did not have the vote. 'I have a strong belief,' he had declared during the debates on repeal, 'that the greatest object which we or any other government can contemplate should be to elevate the social condition of that class of the people with whom we are brought into no direct relationship by their elective franchise.' Peel recognised that if these people were to remain disaffected and opposed to government, there would be such tensions and upheavals that demands for large-scale parliamentary and social reform might prove impossible to resist.

None the less, through the act of repealing the Corn Laws Peel broke up the party which he had laboriously built and faced an angry Opposition in Parliament which not only pushed him from power but made the process painful and at times humiliating for him. The fact that he had been such a powerful parliamentarian, in many respects the most powerful of his times, made the fall more dramatic. In 1836, when he was in opposition, a parliamentary commentator, John Grant, described in detail how Peel was especially effective 'in the serious mode of address'.

'No man in the House can appeal with a tittle of the effect with which he can to the fears of his audience. . . . The deepest stillness pervades the House while he is speaking. Even in the gallery, where there is generally a great deal of noise from the exits and entrances of strangers, the falling of a pin might be heard. All eyes are fixed on Sir Robert.'

Grant went on to note how Peel, who loved applause in Parliament, would often turn his face round to his own party and his back on the Speaker when he was

'urging any argument which appears to him particularly forcible, and which he thinks likely to be received by them with particular applause . . . which is scarcely ever refused him. . . . Never had the leader of a party a more complete ascendancy over that party than has this Tory Coryphaeus over the Conservatives in the House of Commons.'

All the same, Grant recognised that Peel had his 'sore points'. He could be too 'suspicious' and hold things back from his own followers. He was vulnerable in debate when anyone contrasted his professions and performance. Above all he was sensitive to one particular line of attack.

'There is not a man in the House more sensitive on the subject of honour than Sir Robert. You may apply to him epithets which are synonymous with fool, blockhead, &c, if you please, and he utters not a word of complaint; you may brand him with the name of bigot, either in politics or religion if you are so inclined, and he murmurs not a word of resentment; but charge him with anything, either in his private or public capacity, inconsistent with the character of a man of honour, and that moment he demands an explanation.'

There had always been some Conservatives who disliked Peel both on private and public grounds. Lord Ashley, for example, the Evangelical sponsor of the Ten Hours Bill, said that Peel reminded him of 'an iceberg with a slight thaw on the surface': all Peel's 'affinities', he maintained, were 'towards wealth and capital'. There was also a loosely organised cluster of Tory country gentlemen, each priding himself on his independence and distrusting everything that Peel had ever done – from his currency measures of 1819 ('the return to gold'), down through his creation of the Metropolitan Police and his emancipation of the Roman Catholics ten years later, his support of the New Poor Law of 1834 and the Municipal Reform Act of 1835, down to his fiscal policies of the 1840s. These Tories not only thought differently from Peel: they felt differently too. At heart they were critical of industry, cities, international trade and most foreigners. Their protectionism in 1846 was only one facet of their philosophy, and their philosophy was grounded in a way of life.

Peel was only half right when he wrote to a friend in 1845 that 'people like a certain degree of obstinacy and presumption in a Minister. They abuse him for dictation and arrogance, but they all like being governed'. There may have been reason behind such a claim so long as 'the country party' could not find alternative sources of leadership, but by 1845 Tory critics of Peel were listening intently to the gibes of the young Disraeli, whose background and personality were even more different from theirs than Peel's, and by early 1846 to the savage onslaughts of Sir George Bentinck, who possessed impeccable social qualifications, including membership of the Jockey Club. When the break finally came, Peel remarked that he was more surprised that the union had lasted so long inside his party than that it had been 'ultimately severed'. Graham had remarked earlier that 'the country gentlemen cannot be more ready to give us the death-blow than we are prepared to receive it'.

Disraeli, in particular, revelled in the opportunity of exploiting old memories of treachery and charges of misappropriation. He accused Peel of lacking any ideas of his own and of betraying every interest that had looked to him; and he well deserved Ponsonby's handsome tribute: 'I doubt if any classic orator of Rome or England ever did anything so well as you crucified Peel. Had I been him, I would have rushed at and murdered you, or run home and hanged myself.' Yet Disraeli was not content with a crucifixion scene. He profited from the divisions of 1845 and 1846 to enunciate far-reaching ideas of party which went much further than Peel himself or current usage accepted. While Peel looked to posterity to justify him, Disraeli pointed out that posterity was a limited assembly, 'not much more numerous than the planets', and that in the last resort free politics were more dangerous than free trade. He had a word of constitutional advice which could be set alongside Peel's maxims: 'Maintain the line of demarcation between parties, for it is only by maintaining the independence of parties that you maintain the integrity of public-men, and the power and influence of public men.' Disraeli in later life was to hold to this doctrine no more than he was to hold to the doctrine of free trade. Yet the fact that it was advanced so brilliantly at the time was an important by-product of the fiscal debate.

Peel himself stuck to his own doctrines of public service when pressed, very similar to the doctrines of Wellington. 'I am as proud of the confidence as any man can be, which a great party has placed in me; still I never can admit that he owes any personal obligation to those Members who have placed him in a certain position.' He made this statement not in relation to the Corn Laws but to the Maynooth grant, a grant to a Catholic college in Ireland which angered many members of his party and produced some strange temporary alliances. 'I claim for myself the right to give to my sovereign at any time,' he concluded, 'that advice which I believe the interests of the country require.' Taking the evidence of his career as a whole, it seems likely that he would have been willing to repeat this claim with equal force on the last day of judgement.

BIBLIOGRAPHY

Norman Gash, *Mr Secretary Peel* (Longmans, 1961); *Sir Robert Peel*, (Longmans, 1971); C. S. Parker, *Sir Robert Peel from his Private Papers* (3 vols, 1891–9); G. Kitson Clark, *Peel and the Conservative Party* (1929)

NOTES ON THE AUTHORS

———

AYLING, Stanley. Born 1909 and educated at Strand School, London, and Emmanuel College, Cambridge (Goldsmiths' Company exhibitioner). Married; two sons. Worked for many years as a schoolmaster. Author of *Portraits of Power*, *Nineteenth Century Gallery*, *George the Third*. Currently working on a biography of the elder Pitt.

BREWER, John. Born 1947 and educated at Liverpool College and Sidney Sussex College, Cambridge, BA (History, Class I with distinction) 1965–68, MA (1972), PhD (1973). Henry Fellow, Harvard University; Fulbright Travelling Fellow (1968–69); Research Fellow, Sidney Sussex College, Cambridge (1969–73); Visiting Professor, Washington University, St Louis (1972–73); Visiting Fellow, Huntington Library, San Marino, California (1973); Fellow, Corpus Christi College, Cambridge (1973–); Assistant Lecturer in History, Cambridge University (1973). Author of *Perspectives in American History* (1972); *Political Argument and propaganda in England 1760–1770* (forthcoming), and contributor to *The Historical Journal*.

BRIGGS, Asa. Born 1921. Married; two sons, two daughters. Fellow of Worcester College, Oxford, 1944–55; Reader in Recent Social and Economic History, Oxford, 1950–55; Professor of Modern History, Leeds University, 1955–61; Professor of History, Sussex University, since 1961 and Vice-Chancellor since 1967; Visiting Professor, Australian National University, 1960; University of Chicago, 1966 and 1972; D.Litt (Hon) East Anglia 1966 and Strathclyde 1972; LLD (Hon) York (Canada) 1968; Hon. Fellow of Sidney Sussex College, Cambridge, 1968 and of Worcester College, Oxford, 1969. Author of *Victorian People*, 1954; *Friends of the People*, 1956; *The Age of Improvement*, 1959; 3 volumes of the *History of Broadcasting in the United Kingdom*, 1961–70; *William Cobbett*, 1967; *How They Lived, 1700–1815*, 1969; etc.

BROWN, Peter Douglas, MA. Born 1925 and educated at Harrow and Balliol College, Oxford. Author of *The Chathamites*, 1967; and presently working on a life of *William Pitt, Earl of Chatham*.

CANNON, John. Educated at Peterhouse, Cambridge, and did research at the University of Bristol into eighteenth century electoral history. Served in the History of Parliament Trust with Sir Lewis Namier. Presently Reader in History, University of Bristol. Author of *The Fox-North Coalition*, and *Parliamentary Reform, 1640–1832*.

CLARKE, John. Born in Oxford 1947 and educated at Magdalen School, Brackley (Northants), and Wadham College, Oxford. Fellow of All Souls College, Oxford, 1967. Contributor to various journals. At present working on the Russia Company in the eighteenth century.

DERRY, J. W. Born 1933 and educated at Gateshead Grammar School and Emmanuel College, Cambridge. Lecturer, London School of Economics, 1961–65; Fellow and Director of Studies in History at Downing College, Cambridge, 1965–70; Lecturer in History, University of Newcastle-on-Tyne, 1970–73, and Senior Lecturer since 1973. Author of *William Pitt*, 1962; *The Regency Crisis and the Whigs*, 1963; *Reaction and Reform*, 1963; *The Radical Tradition*, 1967; *Charles James Fox*, 1972.

DICKINSON, Harry Thomas. Born 1939 and educated at Durham University (BA 1960, DipEd 1961, MA 1963). PhD (Newcastle) 1968. Earl Grey Fellow, Newcastle University, 1964–66. Lecturer in History, University of Edinburgh, 1966–73. Promoted to Reader in History, 1973. Married; one son, one daughter. Author of *Bolingbroke*, 1970; *Walpole and the Whig Supremacy*, 1973; editor of *The Correspondence of Sir James Clavering, 1708–40*, 1967; *Politics and Literature in the Eighteenth Century*, 1974; contributor to historical journals.

DURRANT, Peter. Born 1948 and educated at The Grammar School, Haywards Heath, Sussex, and Manchester University. At present working on a full-length political biography of the Third Duke of Grafton.

GASH, Norman. Born 1912 and educated at Oxford University (BA 1933, MA 1938, BLitt 1934). FRHistS, FBA, FRSL. Temporary Lecturer, Edinburgh University, 1935–36; Assistant Lecturer, University College, London, 1936–40; Lecturer, St Salvator's College, St Andrews, 1946–53; Professor of Modern History, Leeds University, 1953–55; Visiting Professor, John Hopkins University, Baltimore, 1962; Ford Lecturer, Oxford, 1964; Vice-Principal, St Andrew's University, 1967–71; Professor of History, St Salvator's College, St Andrews, since 1955; President of St Andrews British Historical Association 1955–70; Member of the Council of the Royal Historical Society, 1961–64. Married: two daughters. Author of *Politics in the Age of Peel*, 1953; *Mr Secretary Peel*, 1961; *Reaction and Reconstruction in English Politics, 1832–52*, 1965; *The Age of Peel*, 1968; *Sir Robert Peel*, 1972. Contributor to historical journals.

HOLMES, Geoffrey, born in Sheffield 1928 and educated at Woodhouse Grammar School, Sheffield, 1938–45, and Pembroke College, Oxford, 1945–8, 1950–51. On the staff of the Military Adviser to the UK High Commissioner in India, 1949–50; Assistant Lecturer, Lecturer and Senior Lecturer in History, University of Glasgow, 1952–69; Reader in History, University of Lancaster, 1969–72; Professor of History at Lancaster (Personal Chair) since January 1973. FRHistS. Married; two children. Author of *British Politics in the Age of Anne*, 1967; (with W. A. Speck) *The Divided Society*, 1967; (editor and contributor) *Britain after the Glorious Revolution*, 1969; *The Trial of Doctor Sacheverell*, 1973, and contributor to historical journals.

HOWAT, Gerald M. D., BLitt, MA, FRHistS, DipEd. Born 1928. Educated at Trinity College, Glenalmond; Exeter College, Oxford, Edinburgh and London Universities. Head of the Department of History, Culham College, Nuneham Park, Oxford, until 1973. Presently Head of the History Department, Radley College, Oxford. Author of *From Chatham to Churchill* (1966); (with Anne Howat) *The Story of Health* (1967); *Documents in European History, 1789–1970* (1973); *Stuart and Cromwellian Foreign Policy* (1974); *Learie Constantine* (in preparation). Editor of *Dictionary of World History* (1973); Consultant Editor, *Who did What* (1974). Author of an Historical Association pamphlet on Commonwealth History, and of articles on history, the teaching of history, and education.

JONES, George William. Born 1938 and educated at Jesus College, Oxford (BA 1960, MA 1965); doctorate for research at Nuffield College, Oxford, 1965. Assistant Lecturer in Government, Leeds University, 1963–65 and Lecturer 1965–66; Lecturer in Political Science, London School of Economics, 1966–71, and Senior Lecturer since 1971. Married; one son, one daughter. Author of *Borough Politics*, 1969; co-author of *Herbert Morrison: Portrait of a Politician*, 1973. Contributor to journals on Central and Local government.

JUPP, Peter. Educated at Owens School, Islington, and the University of Reading. Lecturer in Modern History, Queen's University, Belfast since 1964; Visiting Fellow, Huntington Library, San Marino, California, 1972; Visiting Fellow, Wolfson College, Cambridge, 1973–74. Author of a thesis on *Irish Parliamentary Representation, 1801–20*, a contribution to the official History of Parliament, 1790–1820; also a number of articles on aspects of British and Irish politics in the late eighteenth and early nineteenth centuries and *British and Irish Elections 1784–1831*, 1973.

LANGFORD, Paul. Born at Bridgend (Glamorgan) 1945 and educated at Monmouth School and Hertford College, Oxford. Elected to a Junior Research Fellowship at Lincoln College, Oxford in 1969, and to a Tutorial Fellowship in 1970. MA, DPhil. Has specialised in British domestic and imperial politics in the eighteenth century. Author of a book on Rockingham and articles on the Elder Pitt and the American Revolution.

LONGFORD, Countess of, Elizabeth Pakenham, born 30 August 1906, daughter of N. B. Harman, FRCS. Married 1931 the Hon. F. A. Pakenham, now 7th Earl of Longford; four sons, three daughters. Educated Headington School and Lady Margaret Hall, Oxford. WEA and University Extension lecturer 1929-35; contested (Lab.) Cheltenham 1935, Oxford 1950; Trustee, National Portrait Gallery since 1968; Member of the Advisory Council of the V & A Museum since 1969. Hon.DLitt (Sussex) 1970. FRSL. Author of *Victoria R.I.*, 1964; *Wellington, Years of the Sword*, 1969; *Wellington, Pillar of State*, 1972.

MARLOW, Joyce. Born in Manchester 1929 and educated at local State schools, which she left at the age of seventeen to train for the theatre. Worked for seventeen years as a professional actress in repertory, West End, films and television. Married; two sons. While acting she had her first book, a children's adventure story, published in 1964, followed by two more children's books and a novel (*Time to Die*). Author also of *The Peterloo Massacre*, 1969; *The Tolpuddle Martyrs*, 1971; *Captain Boycott and the Irish*, 1973; *The Life and Times of George I*, 1973.

MARSHALL, Dorothy. Born 26 March 1900 at Morecambe, Lancashire and educated at Park School, Preston, and Girton College, Cambridge, BA 1921, PhD 1925. Temporary Instructor, Vassar College, USA 1924-5; Senior History Mistress, Reigate County School, 1925-7; Temporary Lecturer, University of the Witwatersrand, 1927-8; Assistant Lecturer, Bedford College, London, 1930-34; Senior Tutor, St Mary's College, and Lecturer, Durham University 1934-6; Lecturer, Senior Lecturer and in 1965 Reader in History in the University of Wales at University College of Cardiff and Monmouthshire 1936-67; Visiting Lecturer at Wellesley College, USA, 1960-61. Author of *The English Poor in the 18th Century*, 1926; *The Rise of George Canning*, 1939; *English People in the 18th Century*, 1956; *Eighteenth Century England*, 1962; *John Wesley*, 1965; *Dr Johnson's London*, 1968; *Life and Times of Queen Victoria*, 1972; *Industrial England 1776-1850*, 1973.

NEWMAN, Aubrey Norris. Born 1927 and educated at Glasgow (MA 1949) and Oxford University (BA 1953, MA 1957, DPhil 1957). FRHistS 1964. Research Fellow, Bedford College (London), 1954-55, 1957-58; part-time temporary lecturer Nottingham University, 1958-59; Assistant Lecturer, Leicester University, 1959-61; Lecturer 1961-69, Senior Lecturer 1969-72, Reader in History since 1972; Research Assistant, History of Parliament, 1955-59. Married: one son, three daughters. Author of *The Stanhopes of Chevening*, 1969; *Leicester House Politics, 1750-60*, 1969; (with H. Miller) *A Bibliography of British History, 1485-1760*, 1970; etc.

O'GORMAN, Frank. Born 1940 and educated at the University of Leeds. BA (Leeds) 1962; PhD (Cambridge) 1965. Lecturer in Modern History at the University of Manchester since 1965. Author of *The Whig Party and the French Revolution*, 1967;

Edmund Burke: His Political Philosophy, 1973; *The Rise of Party in Britain* (in preparation); and contributions to historical journals.

SMITH, Ernest Anthony. Born 1924 and educated at Cambridge University (BA 1949, MA 1955); DipEd (Reading) 1950; FRHistS 1957. Assistant Lecturer in History, Reading University, 1951–54; Lecturer 1954–64; Senior Lecturer since 1964. Married; one son, one daughter. Author of *History of the Press*, 1968; Editor of *The Letters of Princess Lieven to Lady Holland, 1847–57*, 1955; (ed. with A. Aspinall) *English Historical Documents*, (Vol. XI, 1783–1832), 1959. Contributor to historical journals.

THOMAS, Peter David Garner. Born 1930 and educated at the University College of North Wales (BA 1951, MA 1953), and University College, London (PhD 1958); FRHistS; Assistant Lecturer, Glasgow University, 1956–59; Lecturer 1959–65; Lecturer, University College of Wales, 1965–68; Senior Lecturer 1968–71; Reader in History since 1971. Married, two sons, one daughter. Author of *The House of Commons in the Eighteenth Century*, 1971. Contributor to historical journals.

VAN THAL, Herbert. Born 1904 in Hampstead and educated at St Paul's School, London. Entered the book trade by way of bookselling and later migrated to publishing. Author of *Ernest Augustus, Duke of Cumberland*; *The Tops of the Mulberry Trees*, and a biography of Mrs Lynn Linton (in preparation); editor of biographical anthologies of Belloc and Landor, Thomas Adolphus Trollope's autobiography; etc.

WOODBRIDGE, George. Professor Emeritus, Barnard College, Columbia University. Born 1908 and educated at Columbia University (AB 1927 and MA 1934) and the University of Wisconsin (PhD 1937). Taught at Columbia University, 1937–42, and Barnard College, 1960–73. Visiting Professor at Queen Mary College, University of London 1968–69. Author of *UNRRA: The History of the United Nations Relief and Rehabilitation Administration*, New York, 1949; *The Reform Bill of 1832*, New York, 1971.

ZIEGLER, Philip Sanderman. Born 1929 and educated at Eton and New College, Oxford (1st Class Honours Jurisprudence; Chancellor's Essay Prize). HM Diplomatic Service 1952–65, serving in Vientiane, Paris, Pretoria and Bogotá. Editor, William Collins and Sons, 1966–73. FRSL 1972. Married (1) Sarah Collins (deceased), one son, one daughter; (2) Clare Charrington, one son. Author of *The Duchess of Dino*, 1962; *Addington*, 1965; *The Black Death*, 1968; *William IV*, 1972; *Omdurman*, 1973. Currently at work on a biography of Melbourne.